TRAINING

TRAINING IN SPORT

Applying Sport Science

Edited by

Bruce Elliott
Professor, Department of Human Movement,
The University of Western Australia,
Australia

Consulting Editor

J. Mester
Professor, German Sport University,
Cologne, Germany

JOHN WILEY & SONS
Chichester · New York · Weinheim · Brisbane · Singapore · Toronto

Copyright © 1998 John Wiley & Sons Ltd,
            Baffins Lane, Chichester,
            West Sussex PO19 1UD, England

            National   01243 779777
            International (+44) 1243 779777

            e-mail (for orders and customer service enquiries):
            cs-books@wiley.co.uk
            Visit our Home Page on http://www.wiley.co.uk
                          or http://www.wiley.com

Published in paperback November 1999

Other Wiley Editorial Offices

John Wiley & Sons, Inc., 605 Third Avenue,
New York, NY 10158-0012, USA

WILEY-VCH Verlag GmbH, Pappelallee 3,
D-69469, Weinheim, Germany

Jacaranda Wiley Ltd, 33 Park Road, Milton,
Queensland 4064, Australia

John Wiley & Sons (Asia) Pte Ltd, 2 Clementi Loop #02-01,
Jin Xing Distripark, Singapore 129809

John Wiley & Sons (Canada) Ltd, 22 Worcester Road,
Rexdale, Ontario M9W 1L1, Canada

Library of Congress in Cataloging-in-Publication Data

Training in sport: applying sport science/editor, Bruce Elliott.
        p.   cm.
    Includes bibliographical references and index.
    ISBN 0-471-97870-1 (cased : alk. paper)
    1. Physical education and training. 2. Sports sciences.
  1. Elliott, Bruce, Ph.D.
  GV341.T65 1998
  613.7' 1—dc21   97-34184
                                                             CIP

British Library Cataloguing in Publication Data

A catalogue record for this book is available from the British Library

ISBN 0-471-97870-1 (hbk); 0-471-98314-4 (pbk)

Typeset in 10/12pt Palatino by Dorwyn Ltd, Rowlands Castle, Hants
Printed and bound in Great Britain by Bookcraft (Bath) Ltd, Midsomer Norton, Somerset
This book is printed on acid-free paper responsibly manufactured from sustainable forestation,
in which at least two trees are planted for each one used for paper production.

CONTENTS

About the editors   xi
List of authors   xiii
About the authors   xv
Introduction   xix

1. **TRAINING PERCEPTUAL–MOTOR SKILLS FOR SPORT**
    B. Abernethy, J. Wann and S. Parks
    Introduction   1
    Defining skilled performance   1
    Purpose and structure of this chapter   4
    Perceptual skills and their training   6
    The process of perception   6
    Generalised visual skills   7
    Sport-specific visual skills   19
    Generalised kinesthetic skills   29
    Sport-specific kinesthetic skills   32
    Decision-making skills and their training   35
    The process of decision-making   35
    Selecting the correct option rapidly and accurately   36
    Making decisions in rapid succession   40
    Movement execution and control skills and their training   43
    The processes of movement execution and control   43
    Gross motor performance and behavioural tests of movement
        outcome   44
    The kinematics of movement patterns   45
    The kinetics of movement patterns   48
    The electrophysiology of movement patterns   49
    The attentional demands of movement execution and control   52
    Some concluding remarks   55

2. **MENTAL SKILLS TRAINING IN SPORT**
    D. Gould and N. Damarjian
    The nature of mental skills training   70
    What is mental skills training?   70

Common myths surrounding mental skills training 71
The importance and utility of mental skills training 72
The importance of mental skills 73
The utility of mental skills training 74
Topics to be included in mental skills training 75
Achieving excellence: the pyramid model of athletic excellence 75
Core areas of mental skills training 77
Self-confidence 80
Goal setting 81
Stress management and coping 85
Imagery and visualization 90
Concentration and attention 93
Motivation 97
How to implement a mental skills training programme 99
Who should implement a mental skills training programme? 99
At what time during the season is it best to implement a mental
skills training programme? 100
How long should a mental skills training programme last? 100
What are some specific steps to consider when designing a
mental skills training programme? 100
**An example mental skills training programme: The US freestyle
mogul ski team** 101
Programme purposes and content 102
Mental skills training staff 102
Delivery methods 103
Programme content and delivery schedule 103
Programme evaluation 105
Conclusion 108
Problems and pitfalls in mental training 108
Barriers to entry 108
Coach support and follow-up 110
Unrealistic expectations 110
Trying to do too much too soon 110
Conclusion 111

3. **THE ANALYSIS AND DEVELOPMENT OF TECHNIQUE IN SPORT**
R.N. Marshall and B.C. Elliott
Subjective analysis methods 118
**Objective Analysis: The Role of Data Collection and Processing
in Sport Performance Analysis** 121
Image analysis techniques 122
Dynamometry 128
Electromyography 134
Predictive Analysis Methods 138

Simulation   139
Optimisation   140
Biomechanical feedback   140
Summary   142

4. POSTURE AND PROPORTIONALITY IN SPORT
    J. Bloomfield
    Introduction   145
    Postural considerations in sport performance   146
    The evolution and development of human posture   146
    Postural changes during growth   147
    Maintenance of posture   147
    Advantages of good posture   147
    Postural diversity within individuals   148
    Posture and its relationship to somatotype   149
    Postural defects   150
    Static and dynamic posture   153
    Posture assessment   154
    Desirable postures for high-level sport performance   155
    Modifying posture and technique to improve performance   164
    Body proportions and their effect on sport performance 166
    Significance of proportionality modification in sport   166
    Effect of growth on proportionality   166
    Kinathropometric assessment   168
    Individual comparisons of athletes   168
    Proportionality applied to sport performance   169
    Proportionality characteristics of athletes   170
    Racial characteristics   181
    Body modification   183
    Technique modification   184
    Conclusion   186

5. STRENGTH AND POWER TRAINING IN SPORT
    W. Ritzdorf
    Introduction   189
    Sports with long-lasting applications of force   190
    Classification   190
    General structure   191
    General adaptations   194
    Specific structure and demands   196
    General training methods and planning of training   198
    Sports with short-duration, high concentric applications of force 201
    Classification   201
    General structure   202

General adaptations   204
Specific structure and demands   206
General training methods and planning of training   212
Sports with applications of force in a stretch–shortening cycle   **215**
Classification   215
General structure   216
General adaptations   221
Specific structure and demands   226
General training methods and planning of training   230
Diagnostics of strength and power   **233**
Diagnostics of strength   234
Diagnostics of power   236

6. **FLEXIBILITY IN SPORT**
    J. Bloomfield and G. Wilson
    The value of stretching   **239**
    General benefits   240
    Specific benefits   240
    Range of flexibility   **243**
    Hypermobility   243
    Hypomobility   244
    Specificity in flexibility   **244**
    Factors affecting flexibility   **247**
    Age   247
    Gender   248
    Environmental conditions   248
    Psychological effect   248
    Limitations to the range of movement   **249**
    Anatomical limitations   249
    Physiological limitations   250
    Elastic properties of muscles and tendons   **252**
    Flexibility and injury   **253**
    Injury prevention   253
    Injury rehabilitation   255
    The effect of growth on flexibility   **256**
    Childhood and adolescence   256
    Middle and old age   257
    Flexibility measurement   **258**
    Static testing   258
    Functional testing   259
    Methods used to increase flexibility   **259**
    Ballistic stretching   261
    Static stretching   262
    Proprioceptive neuromuscular facilitation (PNF)   263

Other techniques   265
Stretching guidelines   267
Preparation for stretching   268
Concentration during the exercises   268
Intensity of the stretch   269
Dangers involved in stretching   269
Specific Stretching Exercises   269
Specific guidelines for static stretching   270
General guidelines for PNF stretching (3S)   271
Specific exercises   271
Flexibility and sport performance   272
Racquet sports   272
Aquatic sports   273
Gymnastic and power sports   274
Track, field and cycling   277
Field sports (jumps)   278
Field sports (throwing events)   279
Mobile field sports   279
Contact field sports   280
Set field sports   281
Court sports   281
Martial arts   282
Additional specialized exercises   283
Conclusions   **283**

7. **SPEED TRAINING IN SPORT**
   N. Stein
   Introduction   287
   Speed as a motor phenomenon   288
   Structural approaches to speed   288
   Speed training—general orientations   301
   The relevance and execution of the warm-up in speed training   301
   The training of elementary movement programmes   301
   Reactive speed training   303
   Active speed training   305
   Frequency speed training   306
   Complex speed capability training   307
   Complex action speed training   310
   Foundations of planning and steering speed training   311
   General methodological foundations   312
   Long-term steering of speed training   314
   Short-term steering of speed training   317
   Conclusion   319
   Performance diagnostic procedures in speed training   320

General and sport-specific motor test systems   321
Biomechanical measuring and control systems   324
Physiological measurements of performance   325
Speed training in selected sports   325
The development of speed in selected individual sports   326
The improvement of speed in ball games   338
Synopsis of speed training theory and practice   343

8. ANAEROBIC AND AEROBIC TRAINING
    T. Reilly and J. Bangsbo
Introduction   351
Energy production during sport   352
Anaerobic energy production   353
Aerobic energy production   356
Energy production during continuous exercise   356
Energy production during intermittent exercise   358
Oxygen transport   360
Anaerobic performance   364
Anaerobic power   364
Anaerobic capacity   365
Fatigue during intense exercise   366
Effect of creatine on metabolism and performance during intense
    intermittent exercise   368
Anaerobic training   370
Anaerobic training and performance   370
Muscle cellular effects of anaerobic training   371
Principles of anaerobic training   376
Aerobic performance   378
Specificity of aerobic fitness assessment   382
Indirect assessment of aerobic performance   383
Aerobic training   385
Endurance training   385
Interval training   386
Circuit weight training   387
Aerobics   388
Combined and cross-training   390
Environmental factors   391
Training and time of day   391
Training and competing in the heat   392
Training and competing in the cold   396
Attitude training   398
Overview   402

Index   411

ABOUT THE EDITORS

Professor Bruce Elliott is a biomechanist and is the head of the Department of Human Movement and Exercise Science at the University of Western Australia, Australia. He was the chairman of the Western Australian Institute of Sport for 11 years, was the vice-president [sport science] of the Australian Association of Exercise and Sport Science and was the physical science program chair for the Third IOC World Congress on Sport Sciences [Atlanta, 1995] and is the conference co-chair of the Fifth IOC World Congress on Sport Sciences (Sydney, 1999). He was also on the inaugural selection committee for the International Olympic Committee, Olympic Prize. He is the author of seven books, written chapters in a further thirteen books and had over 100 papers published in refereed journals.

THE CONSULTING EDITOR

Professor Joachim Mester has the chair for science in training at the German Sport University Cologne and was the president of the university for 8 years. He is the president of the European College of Sport Science and member of various national and international scientific committees. In the field of elite sport he is scientific adviser for national teams in alpine skiing and tennis and consultant for numerous individual athletes. He is author and editor of 11 books and published about 100 papers in national and international journals.

LIST OF AUTHORS

B. ABERNETHY, PhD, BHMS (Hons), Int. Fellow, American Academy of Kinesiology and Physical Education. Professor and Head of Department of Human Movement Studies, The University of Queensland, Australia.

J. BANGSBO, PhD, DSc, Associate Professor.
August Krogh Institute, University of Copenhagen, Denmark.

J. BLOOMFIELD, AM, PhD, MSc, DipPE, FACHPER, FASMF, CBiol, FIBiol, FAIBiol, Emeritus Professor.
Department of Human Movement and Exercise Science, The University of Western Australia, Australia.

N. DAMARJIAN, PhD, MSc, BSc, Ladies Professional Golf Association Professional. Tallwood Country Club, Hebron, CT, USA.

B. ELLIOTT, PhD, MEd, BEd, DipPE, FACHPER, FASMF, FAIBiol, Professor and Head of Department of Human Movement and Exercise Science, The University of Western Australia, Australia.

D. GOULD, PhD, MSc, BSc, Professor.
Department of Exercise and Sport Science, The University of North Carolina, Greensboro, NC, USA.

R. MARSHALL, PhD, MSc, BPE, Associate Professor and Head of Department.
Department of Sport and Exercise Science, The University of Auckland, New Zealand.

S. PARKS, MSc, BSc, Doctoral student.
Department of Human Movement Studies, The University of Queensland.

T. REILLY, DSc, PhD, MSc, MIBiol, BA, DipPE, FErgS, Professor.
Research Institute for Sport and Exercise Sciences, Liverpool John Moores University, England.

W. RITZDORF, PhD, Dip German Sport University, Lecturer.
German Sport University, Germany.

N. STEIN, PhD, Dip. German Sport University, Lecturer, Coach of the German Athletic Association.
German Sport University, Germany.

J. WANN, PhD, MPEd, BA(Hons), Associate Professor.
Department of Human Movement Studies, The University of Queensland, Australia.

G. WILSON, PhD, BPE(Hons), Lecturer.
Centre for Human Movement Science and Sport Management, Southern Cross University, Australia.

ABOUT THE AUTHORS

Bruce Abernethy is currently Professor and Head of the Department of Human Movement Studies at the University of Queensland, Australia. He holds an Honours degree in human movement studies from the University of Queensland and a PhD from the University of Otago, where he completed a doctoral thesis on the visual search strategies of expert racquet sport players. An international fellow of the American Academy of Kinesiology and Physical Education and a fellow of Sports Medicine Australia, Prof. Abernethy's main research interests are in the nature of expert performance in perceptual–motor skills, with particular emphasis on the coupling of perception and action in movement tasks.

Jens Bangsbo is currently associate professor at the August Krogh Institute, University of Copenhagen, where he achieved his doctoral degree with the thesis 'Physiology of Soccer — with a special reference to high intensity intermittent exercise'. He has written more than one hundred original papers and reviews. He is, furthermore, the author of several books published in a number of different languages. He is a member of the International Steering Group on Science and Football (since 1991). He is a former professional soccer player and has played more than four hundred matches in the Danish top league as well as several matches in the Danish National team.

Professor **John Bloomfield** is a former national champion sportsman, a former high-level coach and currently an academic at the University of Western Australia. He has been Chairman of the Australian Institute of Sport, the Australian Sports Science Council and the Australian Sports Medicine Federation, and has written two government reports and numerous papers in the field of sport and sport science. Professor Bloomfield is also the author of one book and co-author of three others.

Nicole Damarjian is an LPGA (Ladies Professional Golf Association) professional at the Tallwood Country Club in Hebron, Connecticut. She completed her doctorate in exercise and sport science at the University of North Carolina at Greensboro. Her research interests included identifying what characterizes mental toughness in golf as well as how best to develop these psychological skills from a coaching perspective. She also researches factors affecting the quality of practice, specifically how variable practice affects golf performance. Dr Damarjian has consulted with a variety of amateur and professional athletes, including golfers, basketball players, track and field athletes and mountain bike racers.

Daniel Gould is a Professor in the Department of Exercise and Sport Science at the University of North Carolina at Greensboro where he focuses his efforts on research, teaching, and service activities in applied sport psychology. He has consulted extensively with numerous elite athletes and teams. Daniel has studied the relationship between stress and athletic performance, sources of athletic stress, athlete motivation, youth sport issues, and sport psychological skills training use and effectiveness. He has over 90 scholarly publications and over 50 applied sport psychology research dissemination-service publications. Daniel has co-authored three books, including *Foundations of Sport and Exercise Psychology* with Robert Weinberg and *Understanding Psychological Preparation for Sport* with Lew Hardy and Graham Jones. At present, he co-chairs the US Olympic Committee Science and Technology Committee.

Robert N. Marshall earned his PhD at The University of Western Australia. He is currently an Associate Professor and Head of the Department of Sport and Exercise Science at The University of Auckland, New Zealand. His current research interests centre on paediatric gait analysis and biomechanical analysis of elite cyclists.

Sheri Parks is a native Canadian currently completing her PhD studies within the Department of Human Movement Studies at the University of Queensland, Australia. She is completing research toward a thesis examining perceptual and cognitive differences between expert, intermediate, and novice squash players. Prior to commencing her doctoral studies Ms Parks completed BSc and MSc degrees from Dalhousie University, Canada.

Thomas Reilly has a first degree from University College Dublin and postgraduate qualifications in physical education (Diploma) and ergonomics (MSc) from the University of London. He completed his doctorates (both PhD and DSc) at Liverpool and is currently Professor of Sports Science and Head of the Graduate School at Liverpool John Moores University. He was editor of the *Journal of Sports Sciences* from 1983 to 1995 and is Chair of the International Steering Group on Science and Football (since 1987). He is also Chair of the Exercise Physiology Steering Group of the British Olympic Association.

Wolfgang Ritzdorf received his doctor's degree in sport sciences at the German Sport University, Cologne, Germany. He works there as a senior lecturer in the Department of Athletics. Much of his research focuses on the biomechanics of athletics and on strength training, especially on reactive strength. He was member of the IAAF Biomechanical Research Team at the WC's Rome 1987 and Athens 1997. For several years he was national coach for the women's high jump and now acts as an IAAF lecturer.

Norbert Stein was born in Germany in 1953, and is a Lecturer at the German Sport University, Cologne. He graduated in training sciences and sports medicine and is responsible for education in training sciences and track and field sports at the Institute of Athletics and Gymnastics. He is also a lecturer at the Academy for Coaches, Cologne and was formerly active in sprint and decathlon. He is National Coach of the German Athletic Association in the short hurdles, Head Coach of the 'Athletic-Team German Sports University Cologne', and a member of the IAAF lecture team.

John Wann holds a BA degree from the University of Leeds, an MPEd degree from the University of Western Australia and a PhD in psychology from Cambridge University, undertaken at the MRC Applied Psychology Unit. He is currently Reader in Psychology at the University of Reading, UK, having previously held positions in psychology at the University of Edinburgh and in human movement studies at the University of Queensland, Australia. Dr Wann has been researching aspects of human perceptual–motor control for the past 12 years, a particular recent focus being upon the use of virtual reality displays in both experimental and training contexts.

Greg Wilson is currently a senior lecturer in the School of Exercise Science at Southern Cross University. He has published over 50 refereed papers in scientific journals and is frequently an invited presenter for various scientific and professional conferences. His current area of speciality is applied performance enhancement where he combines both theoretical and practical knowledge in the pursuit of performance enhancement.

INTRODUCTION

B. Elliott

The University of Western Australia

Sport and exercise science is a recent development which has emerged from new research directions in the physical, biological, behavioural, social and medical sciences. The knowledge base within the field of sport science has increased dramatically over the past 20 years to cater for the specific needs of the total spectrum of athletic endeavour including: children and adolescents, disabled, the social participant and the elite performer. Scientific knowledge that will allow every prospective athlete to perform to their desired optimum in an injury free and emotionally safe environment has been a motivating theme for the major research thrusts in sport science.

This volume on 'Training in Sport: Applying Sport Science' adapts and applies sport science knowledge so that it can be used by the sport scientist, coach and athlete. While 'raw athletic talent' is the most important factor in the attainment of high levels of sport performance, coaching based on sound sport science principles is also an essential ingredient if this talent is to be fully developed. Athletes at all levels will only reach their desired potential if attention is paid to the following factors which collectively, to a large extent, determine the level of performance achieved.

- *The training of perceptual–motor skills.* Aiding the athlete in the acquisition of motor skills is at the very heart of sport coaching. An understanding of the applied science involved in this process which is discussed in Chapter 1 provides coaches and teachers with the best opportunity to facilitate an athlete's transition through the levels of performance.

  The ability of the teacher/coach to develop a clear vision of what constitutes elite performance in a specific sport and, in turn, what characteristics of an athlete need to be improved in order to attain, or at best approach, the expert state with reference to perceptual–motor skills, are fully discussed. An evaluation is included on the role of perception and decision-making and their training in sport. Control skills and their training with reference to movement execution are also explored from a research and an applied perspective. Underlying the relevant simplicity and apparent ease of elite sports performance is a level of complexity that sport scientists are only beginning to evaluate. This volume reviews the current research literature and proposed applied solutions as to how perceptual–motor skills can be trained to enhance performance.

- *The psychological factors which enable the athlete to compete successfully and enjoy participating need to be developed and maintained.* Skilled performance does not, however, ensure success in sport as an athlete's mental approach to varying levels of competition has been shown to dramatically influence the final outcome. Chapter 2 of this volume presents applied behavioural research that deals with mental skills training in sport in a way that is of practical benefit to all coaches and athletes.

- *Appropriate techniques for the sport need to be developed.* Life is characterised by movement and a growth of the understanding of movement is essential for progress in sport and exercise science. Such progress is closely tied to the ability to capture and measure relevant motion parameters in a wide range of skills. Chapter 3 provides coaches and teachers with a subjective and objective analysis structure that will enable movements of their choice to be better understood. A number of ways that technique can be developed in sport are also discussed.

- *The physical characteristics of the athlete which are important in a particular sport must be present.* Applied research in the areas of posture and proportionality as they in part self-select athletes for given sports and flexibility training for specified sports are both included. These chapters will assist athletes to select an appropriate sport with due consideration to their body structure, while also presenting means by which selected physical capacities can be enhanced to improve performance.

- *The level of fitness which is specific to the particular activity must be attained.* Fitness for a specific sport is an extremely important aspect of athlete development and requires consideration of exercise physiological and physical capacity research. Chapters on anaerobic/aerobic training, strength and power training and speed training in sport have been included to provide the coach, sport scientist and athlete with the appropriate research background to prepare training programmes for athletes at all levels of participation. Sections on the influences of environmental conditions (heat, cold, altitude) and circadian rhythms on performance are also discussed.

This volume therefore concentrates on the presentation of applied science in a way that will enhance the understanding and be of great interest to those interested in the development of sport skills.

$\boxed{1}$

TRAINING PERCEPTUAL–MOTOR SKILLS FOR SPORT

Bruce Abernethy
The University of Queensland, Australia

John Wann
The University of Reading, England

Sheri Parks
The University of Queensland, Australia

INTRODUCTION

Defining skilled performance

Any systematic attempt to design training methods and programmes to improve the perceptual–motor skills of athletes must start with a clear goal as to what it is that the coach or athlete is ultimately trying to achieve or produce through training. In the case of perceptual–motor skill this translates to developing a clear vision of what constitutes highly skilled (expert) performance in the specific sport of interest and, in turn, what characteristics of the particular athlete need to be improved in order to attain, or at least approach, the expert state.

A common exercise in sessions on skill acquisition in coach education courses is to ask participants to describe the essential characteristics of skilled performance in their particular sport. This is frequently done in the context of having coaches attempt to define the characteristics which distinguish the expert performer from the lesser skilled, as an intermediate step toward defining the major areas in which training might be most effectively directed in order to enhance skill acquisition and ultimately athletic performance. Characteristics which emerge from such exercises describe the skilled performer in a variety of ways. The skilled performer is frequently described as the one who:

Training in Sport: Applying Sport Science. Edited by B. Elliott
© 1998 John Wiley & Sons Ltd

- 'picks the right options' (i.e., consistently selects the course(s) of action most appropriate to the match or event situation);
- 'has all the time in the world' (i.e., reacts rapidly but in an apparently unhurried manner);
- 'reads the game well' (i.e., recognises game situations and patterns of play rapidly and responds accordingly);
- 'adapts his/her play to the conditions' (i.e., is able to adapt to meet novel task demands while, paradoxically, remaining highly consistent);
- 'is smooth and effortless' (i.e., produces movements which are both effective and efficient and require an apparent minimum of attention and effort);
- 'gets the job done' (i.e., responds in a way which (best) fulfils the objectives of the task).

The comment is also frequently made of the skilled performer's great capability to master a number of, what appear to be, paradoxical states e.g., to be rapid but accurate, consistent yet adaptable, effective though apparently applying a minimum of attention and/or effort.

Many of these characteristics articulated by sports practitioners as the cornerstones to skilled performance are also encapsulated in the numerous long standing scholarly attempts to define skilled performance. Guthrie, for example, suggested that skilled performance is:

> . . . the ability to bring about some end result with maximum certainty and minimum outlay of energy, or of time and energy. (Guthrie, 1952, p. 136)

John Whiting, in similar vein, has defined skilled performance as:

> . . . A complex, intentional action involving a whole chain of sensory, central and motor mechanisms which through the process of learning have come to be organised and coordinated in such a way as to achieve predetermined objectives with maximum certainty. (Whiting, 1975, p. 6)

In perhaps the most celebrated exposition on skilled performance Sir Frederick Bartlett emphasised the unhurried nature of expert performance as a fundamental behavioural phenomenon.

Bartlett (1947, p. 836) wrote:

> There is one characteristic which crops up over and over again in descriptions of expert skilled performance. The operator is said to have 'all the time in the world to do what he wants'. This has nothing to do with the absolute speed of the constituent movement, bodily or mental. These may be almost incredibly quick, or they may be leisurely and slow. What is impressive is

the absence of any appearance of hurrying in the whole operation. There is not jerkiness or snatching, no obvious racing to catch up on one part and forced sauntering to make up in another.

When one conducts an exercise of defining skilled performance with coaches or athletes or reads the scholarly literature on skilled (and expert) performance one thing that becomes readily apparent is that there is not, and likely cannot be, a single, generically useful and accepted definition of skilled performance. The characteristics which appear to set aside the highly skilled performer from the lesser skilled (or the ever more extreme case of the expert from the novice) differ substantially from sport to sport and markedly from sports performed in contexts of high time-stress and uncertainty (i.e., the so-called 'open' skill sports such as the ball sports) and sports performed in contexts where the performance conditions are highly predictable, the time constraints are less, and actions can be planned in advance (i.e., the so-called 'closed' skill sports such as gymnastics, pistol shooting and shot putting). As is the case with cognitive skill (Voss and Post, 1988), perceptual–motor skill is very context-specific. There is essentially zero transfer from one sport to the next (e.g., Lotter, 1960) such that the expert in one sport (or even sub-component of a sport) is frequently a novice or near-novice in the performance of other sport (or sub-component) skills. In some sports perceptual and decision-making aspects of performance are generally seen as the most critical to expert performance whereas in the others the execution and control elements of movement are seen as more important. Whilst such observations about specificity are perhaps obvious and amount to little more than a statement of common sense, the point is nevertheless an important one to make as many approaches to perceptual–motor training which are generic in nature frequently fail to appreciate the ubiquitous nature of skill specificity.

A less obvious but equally important point, and one which reveals itself if coaches are probed with respect to the amount of time they spend on different elements of skill training for their sport, is that the emphases placed in training on skills such as perception, decision-making and movement execution and control frequently do not match the perceived importance of each of these elements for the attainment of expert performance. In training for 'open' skill sport, in particular, practice of movement execution elements of skill (especially rote practice of basic technical skills) often occupies a disproportionately large amount of practice time even though perceptual and decision-making skills are frequently seen as being more important in determining success, especially at the elite level.

There appear to be two root causes of this discrepancy. The first relates to the perception by coaches and other practitioners that there is a lack of relevant research literature to guide them in the training of perceptual and decision-making skills in particular. In part this is true, and reflects the historical bias in the motor learning and control field to laboratory-based studies in which both perception and action have been typically studied in contexts bearing little resemblance, and arguably relevance, to the complex demands of sport tasks (Whiting, 1980; Singer, 1990; Glencross, Whiting and Abernethy, 1994). In this respect knowledge about skill acquisition from the motor learning and control field has certainly been less applied and more inaccessible to the sports coach than knowledge of relevance to sports training from the fields of sports physiology, sports biomechanics and sport psychology. It is nevertheless also true that there does exist a core of studies on skill acquisition which are directly relevant to sports coaches and do provide guidance for a principled approach to the training of perceptual–motor skills. Many of these studies have been conducted in the past decade as a direct result of renewed concern for ecological validity (Neisser, 1976) within the motor control and learning field, the emergence of ecological psychology as an influential branch of psychology explicitly concerned with perception and action in natural tasks (Gibson, 1979; Turvey and Carello, 1986) and burgeoning interest in the study of expertise from cognitive (e.g., Chi, Glaser and Farr, 1988), motor (e.g., Starkes and Allard, 1993) and computational science (e.g., Duda and Shortliffe, 1983) perspectives. It is clear therefore that a second major cause of continued training emphases on technical as opposed to perceptual and decision-making aspects of sport is that, at least in the sport science and coach education delivery systems of many countries, new information on perceptual–motor skills training has not been effectively disseminated to coaches in a form that they can readily incorporate into their training programmes. In this regard it is worth noting that, certainly in most Western countries, knowledge about skill acquisition (based on research from the field of motor learning and control) is a frequently neglected and under-valued element of many coach education programmes and, in turn, seasonal training programmes and schedules for athletes. Experts in the training of perceptual–motor skills are not routinely sought as sport science support staff for elite performers as are, for example, physiologists, psychologists and biomechanists.

Purpose and structure of this chapter

Our purpose in writing this chapter is to provide evidence of the applicability of a significant body of knowledge from the motor control and learning field to the training of the perceptual–motor skills and, in so doing, to alert both sport scientists and practitioners to some of the many systematic training options available for improving the perceptual–motor skill of sports performers. Some of the knowledge to be discussed derives from recent, applied studies of sport (and especially sport expertise); much, perhaps surprisingly, is derived from older, laboratory-based studies of movement control which have provided insight into ubiquitous human performance phenomena applicable as much to sport as to other elements of human performance.

This chapter is divided into three main sections which treat the training of perceptual, decision-making, and movement execution and control skills independently. This division, while based loosely on traditional information processing stage models of human performance (e.g., Stelmach, 1982), is primarily for heuristic purposes as it is now well recognised that stage models are overly simplistic (e.g., Miller, 1982, 1983), perception and action are tightly and reciprocally coupled (e.g., Gibson, 1979; Hofsten, 1987; Turvey, Carello and Kim, 1990) and viable ecological/dynamical alternatives exist to traditional information-processing models and theories of skill acquisition, movement control and expertise (e.g., see Abernethy, Burgess-Limerick and Parks, 1994 for a recent review). Readers should therefore recognise that the assignment of discussion of relevant literature and training implications to each of the areas of perception, decision-making and movement execution and control is necessarily somewhat arbitrary and that considerable overlap in training strategies in particular will occur across these respective components of skilled performance.

The organisation of each of the major sections of this chapter are fairly consistent. First, a brief description of the fundamental underlying processes and limiting factors (to perception, decision-making or movement execution and control) is provided and then this is followed by a review of the nature of expert performance (specifically the nature of any documented expert-novice differences) within each of these component skills. The rationale for reviewing the sport expertise literature at each process level is that such literature is important theoretically, in providing insight into the limiting factors to performance and practically, in providing a principled basis for the design of practice routines for performance enhancement (Abernethy, 1994). In each section the expertise literature is used as a foundation and reference point for the examination of training studies (where such studies exist) or (where empirical evidence is lacking) to make predictions about those training approaches which are likely to be effective and, equally importantly, those which are not likely to be effective. An attempt is made in all cases to provide guidelines, implications or at least educated inferences for best practice on the basis of the available evidence. The fundamental premise that is adopted throughout is that approaches which train factors known to be sources of expert–novice differences in performance are more likely to favour the continued enhancement of skills and the acquisition of expertise than approaches focusing training on non-discriminant factors.

PERCEPTUAL SKILLS AND THEIR TRAINING

The processes of perception

Perception is the collective process through which the performer determines what is occurring in their surrounding (external) environment (e.g., where are teammates located?), what is occurring within their own bodies (the internal environment) (e.g., how fatigued are they?), what configuration have their body and limbs adopted (e.g., what position is their leg in?), and what is the current and ongoing relationship between their body and the external environment (e.g., where is the hand positioned in relation to the oncoming ball?). All four of these sources of perceptual information (what Lee and Lishman, 1975 and others have termed respectively exteroceptive, interoceptive, proprioceptive and exproprioceptive information) are of critical importance to the sports performer. Perception is an active process which goes well beyond the simple reception of information by our various sensory systems (and the transduction of physical signals in the external and internal environments into a common neural code or 'language') to the detailed analysis and interpretation of the 'meaning' of the sensory information received. It is at this level that the performer's history of experience and life-time learning along with their perceptual biases, beliefs and expectations is actively imposed upon the physical stimulation picked up by the body's many elegant sensory receptors. Perception has been traditionally considered to consist of a number of sub-processes, including detection (the process of determining whether a particular signal/stimulus is present or absent), comparison (the process of determining whether two stimuli are the same or different), recognition (the process of identifying stimuli, objects and patterns which have been previously experienced) and selective attention (the process of selectively allocating processing resources to events of interest and ignoring distracting, irrelevant or less pertinent information). Any one or combination of these sub-processes of perception can act to limit sports performance.

In humans the major sensory system through which perceptual information is derived is vision, with visual information dominating information provided through any of the other sensory systems (Colavita, 1974; Posner, Nissen and Klein, 1976). In the case where there is a discrepancy between the information provided through vision and that arising from any other sensory system the brain and nervous system resolve the discrepancy by treating the visual information as correct. This occurs even in cases where the visual information is non-veridical (Lee and Lishman, 1975). Visual information appears to provide the criteria upon which the other sensory systems are calibrated (Smyth and Marriott, 1982). For movement control, kinesthesis (the 'movement sense' provided through receptors such as the muscle spindles, golgi tendon organs, joint and cutaneous receptors), along with balance information provided by the vestibular apparatus in the inner ear, provides the most important non-visual source of perceptual information. A hierarchy of sensory dominances therefore appears to exist in which perceptual priority is afforded, in order, to vision, kinesthesis, audition and then all other sensory sources.

In considering how perceptual skills impact on sport performance we will focus here only on vision and kinesthesis, these being without doubt the major sources of information available to support skilled performance. Within each of these perceptual systems distinction will be drawn between skills which are tested and treated as generalised ones and skills which are tested and treated as sport-specific ones. Generalised visual and kinesthetic skills are typically assessed using generic (usually alphanumeric) stimuli as compared to ones derived from or simulating the specific sport setting. Generalised tests frequently assess only the physical reception of sensory information whereas sport-specific tests are needed to assess an individual athlete's capability to actively process, interpret and use the information characteristic and unique to their particular sport. A common distinction, with clear roots in information processing or computational models of human performance, is to refer to generalised tests as tests of perceptual 'hardware' and sport-specific tests as tests of perceptual 'software' (Starkes and Deakin, 1984; Abernethy, 1987).

Generalised visual skills

Tests and assessment

Vision is a complex, multi-dimensional perceptual system. Consequently no single test or unitary measurement parameter can begin to comprehensively describe the functional capabilities and properties of the vision of any individual athlete. The tests of generalised visual skills which have been used in sport are primarily tests of the physical capabilities of the visual system and are essentially the same tests routinely employed by optometrists and some medical practitioners in assessing the vision of the general population. These tests have been used in two main ways with sports performers. The first, non-controversial, use is as clinical screening for the detection of possible performance-limiting visual defects. The second, more contentious, usage is to derive measures of vision which are then purportedly directly related to, and predictive of, the level of sports performance. Some of the more common visual parameters routinely measured by optometrists and others are briefly described below.

Visual acuity.   Visual acuity refers to the ability of an individual to discriminate and resolve fine detail in an object. Visual acuity is typically measured statically using standard eye charts, such as the Snellen eye charts, located in the surgeries of most medical practitioners and in the offices of authorities responsible for the issuing of automobile driving licences. In the static context there is no relative movement between the observer and the target and tests are often conducted both binocularly and monocularly over distances somewhat arbitrarily defined as optically near (typically around 30–35 cm (12–14 in)) and far (typically 5–6 m (16–20 ft)). Acuity scores are expressed either absolutely (e.g., in terms of minimum angles of resolution) or relative to population norms. The traditional notion of 20/20 (6/6) vision, for instance, indicates an ability to discriminate the same degree of visual detail from a viewing distance of 6 m (20 ft) as the 'average' person can see from that distance. In contrast a relative measure such as 20/15 would indicate acuity levels beyond the population norm with the person being able to distinguish detail from 6 m (20 ft) that the 'average' person could only resolve at 4.5 m (15 ft).

The importance of static acuity to sports performance might be expected to vary with the nature of the sport task being examined. Static acuity might be expected to be quite important in sports such as rifle and pistol shooting where both the athlete and target are essentially stationary but less likely to be significantly related to performance in sports where either the athlete, target or both are moving. In such circumstances dynamic visual acuity might be expected to be more important. Dynamic acuity refers to the capability to resolve detail in a target when there is relative motion between the observer and the target and is generally measured by having subjects view standard eye charts as they are rotated on a turntable (such as with the Kirschner Rotator; Coffey and Reichow, 1987) or projected in an arc around the subject using a rotating projector. Level of resolution is expressed in these tests with respect to the angular velocity of the target. While individuals with poor static acuity inevitably perform poorly on dynamic acuity tasks, good static acuity is no guarantee of good dynamic acuity. In other words good static acuity is a necessary but not sufficient condition for good dynamic acuity.

Ocular dominance.   Ocular dominance refers to the dominance of one eye over the other in the performance of sighting and visual alignment tasks in particular and can be readily ascertained by comparing binocular and monocular sighting alignments. In the sport context interest in ocular dominance has generally been directly linked to its relationship with manual dominance. In some aiming sports (such as archery) it has been hypothesised that it may be advantageous to have ipsilateral eye–hand dominance to facilitate precise alignment of the implement (arrow, gun, cue etc.) with the target whereas in some batting sports (such as baseball, softball and table tennis) possible advantages with respect to contralateral eye–hand dominance have been hypothesised on the grounds of the dominant eye being placed closer to the line of flight of the incoming ball with this configuration (e.g., Adams, 1965).

Ocular muscle balance.   Ocular muscle balance (or phoria) refers to the extent to which the axes of both eyes are in symmetry in viewing objects at different distances. The extent of this symmetry is directly dependent on the balance of the co-acting pairs of extra-ocular muscles respectively controlling the side-to-side and up–down movement of the eyes. Phorias are typically measured in both the horizontal and vertical planes over near and far test distances using apparatus such as the Maddox Wing and Rod. In perfect vision, the state referred to as orthophoria, the muscles are in symmetry and contribute equally to ocular alignment on a target. Deviations from this state (heterophoria) result in less than optimal binocular vision and this may be detrimental in sports requiring precise aiming and visual judgements of lateral position and depth. Measures of phoria are often combined with clinical measures of fixational disparity to derive composite measures of binocular visual performance and stability.

Accommodation.   A number of sports, especially the ball sports, require the performer to rapidly adjust depth of focus as objects, such as balls, rapidly approach toward or depart from the athlete's viewing position. Whenever focal distance has to be altered (the process of accommodation) the curvature of the crystalline lens of the eye must be adjusted by the action of the ciliary muscle to maintain maximum resolution. The lens must be made more spherical for the viewing of near objects and flatter for the viewing of distant objects. Accommodative effectiveness can be assessed by determining the speed with which an individual can repeatedly adjust resolution for different viewing distances. This is typically achieved in practice by counting the number of cycles per minute to which a subject can accommodate when the virtual distance of a target display is altered by alternating presentation of prism flippers (typically of +/−1 prism dioptre magnitude).

Vergence.   The vergence eye-movement system acts in concert with the accommodative system of the eyes to assist the athlete in maintaining sharp visual clarity on objects and events in surrounds that move rapidly toward and away from their point of observation. The axes of the two eyes converge in viewing a close object and diverge in viewing a more distant one. Vergence may be measured using devices such as the Risley rotating prism in which fusional reserves are calculated from the subject's self-reports of the blurring, breaking and recovery of images of letter targets.

Depth perception and stereopsis.   Depth perception refers to an individual's capability to accurately judge the distance between themselves and another object in the environment and make relative judgements with respect to the comparative distances and depths of two or more objects in the visual field. As such judgements are clearly important in many sport tasks it is not surprising that links between depth perception capability and sports performance have frequently been hypothesised (e.g., Banister and Black-burn, 1931; Miller, 1960). A particularly rich source of depth information for humans is stereopsis, which arises as a consequence of the partial overlap of our left and right visual fields. Stereopsis is the capability to discriminate relative differences in target object depth through the use of binocular disparity information and again, perhaps not surprisingly, strong predictions have frequently been made about the possibility of a relationship between stereopsis scores and sports performance (e.g., Zimmerman and Lane, 1976). Stereopsis is generally measured by having subjects view standardised random dot stereograms through red and green filtered goggles and determining (in minutes of arc) the finest stereoscopic depth discriminations subjects are able to make.

Given typical interocular distances in humans, stereopsis is only an effective method for depth discrimination for objects which are relatively close (approximately 1 m (3 ft) from the subject). Many, perhaps most, sport tasks require depth judgements to be made over much greater distances, ranging from a few metres in the case of most racquet sport players to hundreds of metres in the case of golfers or baseball outfielders. For judgements of depth over these larger distances the Howard–Dolman test procedure is typically used. In this test subjects are seated at a distance from an illuminated box containing two movable vertical uprights, highlighted against a white background. The subject's task, without using head movements, is to align the two uprights (using hand-held strings attached to each upright) so that both the uprights are judged to be equidistant from their point of observation. Measurement of the actual differences in depth between the two uprights therefore provides one possible measure of depth perception precision.

Colour vision.   An athlete's ability to discriminate differences in colour may, in some circumstances, act as a limiting factor to sports performance (Gavriysky, 1969, 1970). For example, advantages may exist in team sports like football and basketball for the athlete who is able to rapidly discriminate, often in peripheral vision, teammates from opponents on the basis of their jersey colour. Likewise colour vision defects, particularly the classic red–green defects may, under some circumstances, impede performance (e.g., the case of a golfer with such a defect attempting to locate a red flag against a green background). Standard colour defects are detected clinically using the standard Ishihara (1977) test which embeds red or green figures against opposing backgrounds.

Visual reaction time.   Visual reaction time is the time elapsed between the presentation of an unanticipated visual stimulus (usually a light) and the initiation of a response to that stimulus. Reaction time, along with movement time (which is the time from response initiation to completion), collectively constitute response time. Reaction time and movement time are independent, uncorrelated measures (Henry, 1961). Visual reaction time is the most used (and mis-used) measure in the perceptual–motor skills literature and has been frequently predicted to be a critical visual parameter for performance in sports which are time stressed. The obvious rationale for this prediction, especially in fast ball sports, is that

> . . . the player with the faster reaction time may, if he wishes, wait for later deviations in the flight of the ball and thus react more adaptively. (Whiting, 1969, p. 42).

While visual reaction time can be measured in a number of ways, the usual approach is to have the subjects make a simple finger-press response to the time of onset of a visual stimulus. The visual stimulus is typically illuminated at a variable period after a warning light in order to prevent the onset of the stimulus light being anticipated. Visual reaction times to a single stimulus (the so-called simple reaction time) are generally in the order of 200 ms and these laboratory-derived figures appear to also provide an accurate estimate of the kind of delays that are encountered in the actual performance of sports skills (McLeod, 1987).

Rate of visual information processing.   Adam and Wilberg (1992), among others, have suggested that because many 'open' skill sports clearly require athletes to process a great deal of information in a short period of time in order to be successful, individual differences in the rate (and/or quantity) of information processing may be directly linked to superior sports performance. Perceptually quick athletes may be advantaged in terms of either having more detailed information upon which to base their decision-making or earlier information for movement preparation, execution and control (Deary and Mitchell, 1989). To examine this notion tests have been developed, based on long-established paradigms for examining the sensory registration of visual stimuli (e.g., Sperling, 1960; Neisser, 1967), in which alphanumeric displays are presented for very short durations (25–300 ms), typically by a tachistoscope, and subjects are required to either verbally report or manually record as many stimulus items as possible that they can remember. A different stimulus pattern (a masking stimulus) is typically presented immediately following stimulus offset.

Peripheral vision.   The majority of the visual tests described thus far examine aspects of the athlete's use of central (foveal) vision yet many of the critical sources of visual information in sport occur in the periphery of the visual field. Central and peripheral vision have quite different functions and design characteristics, as articulated in two-mode theories of visual perception (e.g., Ingle, Schneider, Trevarthen and Held, 1967; Schneider, 1969; Leibowitz and Post, 1982). Central vision is ideally suited for performing recognition judgements which require high acuity and fine resolution of detail whereas peripheral vision is optimally designed for providing information about where objects are located and how quickly either the objects are moving or the observer is moving through the environment.

The peripheral vision of an athlete can be measured in a number of ways. Static measures of peripheral visual range can be made using perimeters (e.g., see Williams and Thirer, 1975) but these tend to over-estimate the athlete's functional visual field size. The difficulty with such measurements is that the functional visual field size of athletes is not fixed but rather varies according to a range of factors including the concurrent demands of any tasks being performed in central vision, and the level of stress, fatigue or arousal the athlete is experiencing. As a simple rule, the more complicated and demanding the task being performed centrally, or the more stressed the athlete, the narrower will be the functional visual field size, giving rise to the errors athletes and coaches typically describe phenomenologically as 'tunnel vision'. More elaborate measures of visual fields are now available than simple perimetry (e.g., devices such as the Humphrey Field Analyser which are capable of determining the detection threshold for stationary (static) and moving (kinetic) stimuli presented at various eccentricities) although comparison of visual field sizes across athletes remains problematic for the reasons outlined above.

In sport tasks the concern with peripheral vision is typically not just with the detection of events occurring in the periphery but more so with the rate of responding to such peripheral stimuli. Devices such as the Wayne Saccadic Fixator which require subjects to respond rapidly and successively to peripherally presented stimuli have therefore become popular diagnostic (and training) tools amongst sports optometrists.

Coincidence-timing skills.   Many sports skills require that actions not necessarily be initiated as rapidly as possible but that rather they be initiated at a precise time so as to coincide exactly with some external event, such as the arrival of an opponent or a ball. Tennis players, for example, must precisely time the initiation of their racquet downswing so that the racquet is travelling at maximal speed and with the correct racquet head angle exactly at the time when the ball arrives at the correct position to be struck. Likewise Judo players must initiate their offensive moves at precisely the correct instance so that the manoeuvre coincides exactly with a transient period of imbalance or weakness in the opponent's defence. The most common test of coincidence timing (or coincidence anticipation, as it is often called) involves variations on a standard piece of laboratory apparatus, the Bassin timer. With this apparatus, subjects are presented with the apparent motion of a light moving down a runway towards them, just in the same way as a ball might approach a player in a game situation. The velocity of the approaching object can be varied to provide time-stresses comparable to those experienced in actual playing situations, and the subject's task is to make a simple finger-press response of a button to precisely coincide with the light's arrival at the end of the runway. Coincidence-timing performance can then be expressed in terms of the magnitude of the error (in milliseconds) and in terms of the response bias (that is, early or late responding). With some reasonably simple modification, the task complexity can be altered to more closely resemble the sport setting, by having the subjects swing bats or racquets rather than making very simple manual responses. (While the Bassin timer may be modified for improved sport-specificity it is typically used as a generic test of coincidence timing ability, hence its consideration here as a generalised rather than sport-specific perceptual measure.)

Field dependence–independence. Field dependence–independence (or perceptual style) refers to an individual's ability to discriminate a target object from its surrounds and has attracted some research interest from sport scientists on the premise that the capability to avoid distraction and rapidly locate key objects (e.g., the ball or target) from within complex backgrounds (e.g, variegated backgrounds such as those presented in crowded playing stadia) may be an important element of successful sports performance. Perceptual style has typically been assessed using standardized, non-sport-specific stimuli such as the pencil-and-paper embedded figures test (Witkin, Dyk, Faterson, Goodenough and Karp, 1962) and the rod and frame test (see Jones, 1973 for descriptions). The expectation frequently advanced (e.g., MacGillivary, 1979, 1981) is that expert performers may be expected to be more field-independent than less successful performers given that

> *field independent persons are greatly affected by distraction, whereas field independent persons are able to ignore irrelevant stimuli and direct their attention to the important information.* (Jones, 1972, p. 107).

Relationship of generalised visual skills to sports performance

There exists a significant body of research literature, dating back to the early work of Banister and Blackburn (1931) on the interocular distance of superior Cambridge University athletes, which has attempted to demonstrate a relationship between performance on some generalised visual skills and sports performance. Such relationships are typically sought through comparison of the visual test scores of successful and less successful or expert and novice athletes. The balance of this evidence now suggests that expert–novice differences do not, as a rule, exist on generalised tests of visual function and that elite sportsmen and women are *not* characterised by supra-normal levels of vision, at least when vision is assessed using generalised optometric tests. The view that expert sports performers have 'super' vision is still held by many, especially sports optometrists (e.g. Sherman,

1980; Stine, Arterbrun and Stern, 1982; Reichow and Stern, 1986) but this is not substantiated by detailed reviews and critiques of the empirical evidence (e.g., Starkes and Deakin, 1984; Rothstein, 1986; Abernethy, 1987). A fairly consistent pattern of findings emerges on most of the generalised visual measures; namely, one or more initial positive findings from typically small group studies, often without appropriate control groups, which have not been able to be replicated in experiments with greater power. In cases where expertise effects are seen to exist, these generally account for only very small portions of the total performance variance. It should be clearly noted, however, before discarding completely the notion of a possible link between sports performance and generalised visual skills, that the incidence of un-corrected visual defects is generally lower in sports performers than the general population, although defects are nevertheless not uncommon even among elite athletes (Garner, 1977; Sherman, 1980). This suggests that there is probably a certain minimal level of visual performance necessary, but not sufficient, to support top level sports performance and that beyond this base level sports performance is determined by factors other than general visual skills.

Static visual acuity scores, for example, appear as poor correlates of sports performance (e.g., Tussing, 1940; Winograd, 1942). Dynamic visual acuity, while accounting for slightly more variance in sports performance than static acuity (Sanderson and Whiting, 1974, 1978), is incapable of discrimi-nating the expert performer from the novice with any kind of acceptable level of consistency (Beals, Mayyasi, Templeton and Johnston, 1971; Morris and Kreighbaum, 1977; Sanderson, 1981). Likewise studies of ocular domi-nance (e.g., Adams, 1965; Baughman, 1968; Whiting and Hendry, 1968) have failed to reveal any systematic link between hand–eye dominance configura-tions and sports performance. In the case of depth perception, while some early evidence exists arguing for better depth perception (e.g., Graybiel, Jokl and Trapp, 1955; Miller, 1960) and stereopsis (e.g., Zimmerman and Lane, 1976) for superior players, an equally impressive body of null findings also exists (e.g., Zimmerman, 1970; Cockerill, 1981a; Isaacs, 1981). Similarly stud-ies of visual reaction time (cf. Burke, 1972 and Bahnot and Sidhu, 1979 and Rasch and Pierson, 1963 and Parker, 1981), colour vision (cf. Gavriysky, 1970; Mizusawa, Sweeting and Knouse, 1983), visual fields (cf. Williams & Thirer, 1975; Cockerill 1981b), information processing rates (cf. Deary and Mitchell, 1989; Adam and Wilberg, 1992; and Starkes, Allard, Lindley & O'Reilly, 1994), coincidence-timing (e.g. Del Rey, Whitehurst, Wughalter and Barnwell, 1983; Blundell, 1984) and perceptual style (cf. Pargman, Schreiber and Stein, 1974; Petrakis, 1979 and Goulet, Talbot, Drouin and Trudel, 1988) have all failed to reveal anything in the way of consistently superior generalized visual performance by expert sports performers.

There are a number of possible reasons as to why these generalised tests of visual 'hardware' seem to be, at best, only poorly related to sports performance (Abernethy, 1986). One possibility is that single isolated measures of vision will not appear as good correlates of sports performance because of the multi-dimensional character of vision and the possibility that relatively poor performance in one aspect of vision may be offset by above average performance on other facets of vision. This possibility seems to be offset somewhat by the observation that even when multivariate approaches are taken no systematic profile of superior generalised visual skills emerges for the expert performer (e.g., Summers, 1974; Beitel, 1980; Mizusawa et al., 1983). A second possibility, an extension of the first, is that while vision may be important it is but one element of an athlete's total make-up and poor visual skills may be able to be compensated by exceptional performance in other components of performance, such as agility, mental toughness, or physical advantage. A final possibility is that the tests used are inappropriate and that the static and non sport-specific nature of the tests precludes the demonstration by the experts of any visual–perceptual advantage they may possess. This possibility will be explored in the section on sport-specific perceptual skills.

Methods and implications for training

The past decade has seen a proliferation of generalised visual training programmes arising from sports optometry in North America which claim to be able to improve sports performance through enhancing visual performance. These commercially available generalised visual training programmes (such as Harrison and Reilly's 1975 *Visiondynamics*; Revien and Gabor's 1981 *Sports Vision*; Revien's 1987 *Eyerobics*; Seiderman and Schneider's 1983 *The Athletic Eye*; and more recently the *Sports Vision Manuals* of the American Optometrical Association) are direct adaptations of programmes used previously in clinical and behavioural optometry in an attempt to enhance the vision of children, particularly those experiencing reading difficulties. The programmes involve the use of simple, repetitive eye exercises (e.g., attempting to read an eye chart while bouncing on a trampoline) and in some instances relatively simple training apparatus (such as the Wayne Saccadic Fixator and the Brock string—a length of string of some 3–6 m (10–20 ft) upon which are attached a number of beads which act as fixation points). In all cases the training stimuli are simple and non-sport-specific and the training approach is based on simple repetition and progression of a type reminiscent of physical training regimes.

The authors and clinical users of these programmes typically make very strong claims about the overall effectiveness of generalised visual training and the relatively limited training time which is needed in order to reap benefits. For example, Revien (1987) claims *Eyerobics*, a video-based home training package '. . . improves physical and mental performance and reduces visual fatigue'. Similarly Revien and Gabor's (1981) *Sports Vision* text includes such claims as:

visual training . . . may well make the difference between winning and losing, between revelling in keen competition or shrinking from it.

. . . fixated objects actually appear larger than they are, speeding objects seen to move more slowly, and things once unseen in the corner of the eye suddenly appear in sharp focus.

It is obviously tempting, given the claims made by these programmes and the historical absence of any alternative perceptual training guidelines from sports science, for coaches and athletes to use such approaches. However, despite their increasing popularity, the evidence to support the effectiveness of these programmes is almost exclusively anecdotal and consequently subject to all kinds of biases and expectancy effects. There is virtually no empirical evidence to demonstrate the effectiveness of these generalised visual training programmes nor, on the grounds of the evidence reviewed in the previous section, any principled *a priori* grounds to expect such non-specific training to indeed be useful. A number of recent reviews of the sports vision literature both by optometrists (e.g., Stine et al., 1982; Reichow and Stern, 1986) and sport scientists (e.g., Abernethy, 1986; Landers, 1988; Leibowitz, Vinger and Landers, 1989) have highlighted this dearth of controlled studies on the effectiveness of generalised visual training programmes for sport.

If generalised visual training is to be effective three basic assumptions must be fulfilled, namely:

(1) Generalised visual skills must play a major role in superior sports performance.
(2) Such generalised visual skills must be able to be trained.
(3) Improved generalised visual skills must translate directly to improved sports performance (Stine et al., 1982).

A significant body of knowledge exists with respect to the first assumption, but this evidence (as revealed in the earlier section) argues against a major role for generalised visual skills in expert performance. The evidence indicates that generalised visual skills do not constitute an important factor discriminating the performance of the expert from the novice. With respect to the second assumption, a substantial body of evidence exists within the clinical optometry literature to suggest that most commonly measured visual functions such as foveal acuity (Wittenberg, Brock and Folsom, 1969; McKee and Westheimer, 1978; Fendick and Westheimer, 1983), peripheral acuity (Low, 1946; Saugstad and Lie, 1964; Fendick and Westheimer, 1983), peripheral motion thresholds (Johnson and Leibowitz, 1974) and visual field expanses (Sailor, 1973; Wood, Wild, Hussey and Crews, 1987) can indeed be improved with practice. The only cautionary notes with respect to this literature are that many of the demonstrations of improvement are in patient groups and that in many cases the training exercises used precisely mimic the test instrument used to assess pre-post training improvement. The relevance of the former observation is that the possible existence of ceiling effects with respect to improvements in generalised visual skills cannot be ruled out. The relevance of the latter observation is that, in many cases, it cannot be determined definitively if the improvements observed are a function of genuine improvement in the subject's visual skills or simply familiarity effects on the test instrument.

The empirical evidence with respect to the third assumption (that improved generalised visual skills translate into improved sports performance), while limited, is far from supportive of the effectiveness of visual training. Harper, Landers and Wang (1985) found no significant differences in either visual parameters (dynamic visual acuity, depth perception and peripheral awareness) or motor performance between groups of Olympic level rifle and pistol shooters given two weeks of intensive visual training and a matched cohort given only relaxation training. The length of the training period in this case may well have been too short to provide a fair assessment of the potential benefits of visual training (although interestingly a number of the commercial visual training packages claim improvements will be noticed within this short time-frame). Some support for the effectiveness of Revien's (1987) *Eyerobics* in improving hand–eye coordination (McLeod and Hansen, 1989a) performance on soccer skills tested (McLeod, 1991) and static balance (McLeod and Hansen, 1989b) has been reported from one laboratory but these studies are sufficiently weak in both experimental power and experimental design (as pointed out by Cohn and Chaplik, 1991) to cast little useful light on the issue.

In a recent series of studies from our laboratory (Abernethy and Wood, 1992) 50 subjects with an absence of any detectable visual defects were randomly assigned to five equal groups—three visual training groups and two different control groups. All groups were pre-tested on a sport skill (hitting tennis forehand drives for accuracy) and an extensive range of general and tennis-specific visual–perceptual tests and then re-tested after four weeks of visual training (4×20 min sessions per week) and physical practice (1×20 min sessions per week). The three visual training groups differed only in the type of visual training programme they received. One group was given exercises as prescribed in Revien and Gabor's (1981) text; a second group was trained using the video-based Eyerobics package (Revien, 1987); and the third group was given visual training exercises of the type advocated in the AOA's Sports Vision Manual and prescribed most frequently on an individual basis by sports optometrists. The latter group's visual training included exercises using the Brock string, alternating and prism flippers, as well as exercises conducted on the tachistoscope, Wayne Saccadic Fixator and Peripheral Awareness Trainer. A fourth (placebo) group attended the same number of supervised training sessions as the visual training groups but were given reading about tennis rather than visual training and were given the same expectancies as the visual training group with respect to the likely benefits of the intervention they experienced on their sports performance. The final (control) group simply undertook physical practice in the absence of any other forms of training.

Post-training motor performance for all five groups in the Abernethy and Wood (1992) study were not significantly different indicating that no beneficial effects had arisen from any of the generalised visual training regimes examined. This is a finding consistent with that which would be predicted from the literature indicating generalised visual skills are typically not the limiting factor to sports performance; hence improving them is not likely to translate to improved sports performance. There were pre-post training improvements in some of the general visual parameters although in most cases these improvements were simply a consequence of test familiarity (see Figure 1.1), being equally evident for the groups experiencing no visual training as for the group(s) experiencing the visual training. In the absence of control groups (which is typical of the clinical context) these pre- to post-training improvements could be (incorrectly) interpreted as positive effects of generalised visual training. These studies clearly suggest that generalised visual training programmes should be used with caution by coaches and athletes as these programmes appear unlikely, either on the basis of logical inference or empirical data, to be able to provide the improvements in either visual or motor skill for sport that are claimed by their proponents. Effective perceptual training will necessitate a training focus on factors known to serve as important limiting factors to expert performance. Generalised visual training programmes are unlikely to be effective in improving the

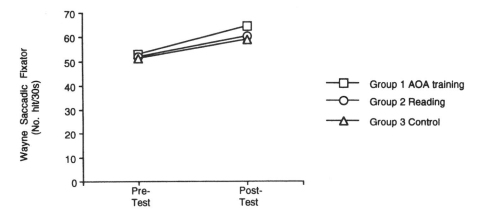

Figure 1.1: Pre- to post-training improvements on the Wayne Saccadic fixator for subjects given visual training (Group 1), a placebo training programme (Group 2) and no training (Group 3). Improvements are observed for all three groups and must be therefore attributed to familiarity effects on the test apparatus.

perceptual skills of athletes as generalised visual skills are not key characteristics that set the expert performer apart from the lesser skilled.

Sport-specific visual skills

Tests and assessment

Unlike tests of generalised visual skills, assessment of an athlete's sport-
specific visual skills must rely on the accurate reproduction, or at least
effective simulation, of the perceptual conditions of the actual sport task.
Such tests must reproduce the actual performance environment sufficiently
faithfully as to retain the essential perceptual information for the task which
may form the cornerstone of any expert perceptual advantage. Clearly with
this kind of requirement an endless range of visual skills tests could potentially be generated, although most will have a generic form consistent with
tapping into pre-supposed characteristics of expert performance such as
'reading the play' or 'having all the time in the world'. In this section we
examine briefly four such common forms of sport-specific visual tests—tests
of rapid information pick-up, of pattern recognition, of anticipation and of
visual search.

Tests of rapid information pick-up.   A number of researchers (e.g., Allard and
Starkes, 1980; Starkes, 1987; Millslagle, 1988; Abernethy and Neal, 1990)
have developed sport-specific tests to investigate the speed and accuracy
with which athletes are able to detect sport-relevant objects within the visual
field. The general approach taken here is similar to that described for rapid
rate of information processing in the generalised visual skills section (cf.
Adam and Wilberg, 1992) except that sport-specific stimuli are used in an
attempt to retain perceptual context and therefore a degree of ecological
validity. Subjects are typically presented slides of sport-specific information
(e.g., slides of scenes from ball sports filmed from a player's perspective)
with the exposure duration(s) controlled tachistoscopically. The subject's
task is to search the visual field rapidly in order to either locate a target
object, such as the ball (the location of which has to be verbally reported) or
to make categorical judgements on the presence or absence of the target
object. Exposure durations are typically very short (usually < 100 ms), effectively restricting information pick-up to one ocular fixation.

Tests of pattern recognition.   In many sports, especially team ball sports, one
of the key characteristics that coaches inevitably report about expert players,
is their apparent capability to predict what is about to occur by 'reading the
play'. This capability seems to reflect the skilled performer's acquired ability
to recognise the structures or patterns inherent within their particular sport.
Skilled athletes in pivotal positions in team ball sports (such as the

'playmaking' point guards in basketball, the quarterback in American football, or the mid-fielder in soccer) appear capable of recognising offensive and defensive patterns of play as they develop and from this knowledge are then able to locate weak (and strong) points in the opposing team's organisation.

Tests of pattern recognition which have been developed for sport (e.g., Allard, Graham and Paarsalu, 1980; Starkes, 1987) have been based on pre-existing tests developed for examining perceptual skill and expertise in chess (de Groot, 1966; Chase and Simon, 1973). These tests typically involve presenting subjects with brief views (usually of about 5–8 s duration) of slides depicting typical game situations, e.g., slides of a developing offensive pattern in basketball photographed from the point guard's perspective. The subject's task is then to recall the positions of each of the offensive and defensive players, usually reported by having the subject mark locations on a scaled representation of the court or playing field. Recall accuracy for items within these structured slides is then usually compared with recall accuracy for slides containing a similar number of target items (players in this example) but lacking the usual game structure (e.g., slides depicting player positions during a time-out). This comparison is an important one allowing the discrimination of any expert advantage due to specific pattern recognition from any possible advantage due to generically superior memory skills. Altering the time course of stimulus presentation allows the rate of pattern recognition to be systematically assessed.

Tests of anticipation. Just as the ability to 'read the play' through recognising patterns is frequently reported anecdotally as a key attribute of skilled performers, so too is the ability to anticipate an opponent's action. In 'open' skill sports in particular the ability to pick up early information (e.g., information in advance of ball flight) might provide the principled basis for Bartlett's observation about skilled performers having 'all the time in the world'. Given the speed at which many top-level athletic competitions are performed and the limitations imposed on human performance by in-built delays such as reaction time, anticipation of forthcoming events in sport may be a necessity for expert performance (Whiting, 1969; Abernethy and Russell, 1983). Sport-specific tests of anticipation which have been developed to date (e.g., Jones and Miles, 1978) involve simulating the visual display normally available to athletes in their specific sport by using film or video photographed from a position corresponding to the athlete's usual viewing position. This film is then selectively edited to either vary the time course of information available (a procedure known as temporal occlusion) or the location from which information may be extracted (a procedure known as spatial or event occlusion; Abernethy, 1985). The subject's task is typically to predict, from the information available, either what the opposing player or team is about to do or the result of the opponent's action (e.g., where will the ball land?). In temporal occlusion paradigms the use of a number of different cut-off positions both before and after ball flight, for example, allows the determination of the time in the opponent's actions at which useful advance information first becomes available. In spatial occlusion paradigms the use of masks over different regions of the opponent's body, for instance, allows the determination of those parts of the opponent's action which provide the best advance information for predicting the intention of their action. The advent of liquid crystal glasses (Milgram, 1987), which permit shuttered occlusion of vision during the actual performance of natural actions, offers a valuable technological advance which has the potential to support the development of more ecologically valid forms of temporal occlusion tests (e.g., see Elliott, Zuberec, and Milgram, 1994).

Assessment of visual search patterns.   An attractive and seemingly more direct method of assessing the sport-specific perceptual skills of athletes may be to record the athlete's eye movements as they either perform actual sport tasks or undertake more controlled perceptual tasks of the kind outlined above for the assessment of sport-specific pattern recognition and anticipation (Bard and Fleury, 1981). The measurement of an athlete's visual search patterns and especially the athlete's preferential distribution of information seeking ocular fixations may provide a good indication of both the individual athlete's perceptual strategy and the location of the most informative features within the visual display. While the monitoring of eye movement behaviour holds obvious attraction as a means of assessing expert-novice differences in perceptual strategy it needs to be recognised that eye movement recording does not equate directly with perception. Orientation of the eyes (as revealed through eye movement recording) may differ from perception because, *inter alia*, visual orientation does not guarantee information pick-up (one can 'look' without 'seeing') and attention can be moved around the visual field, including into the periphery, without eye movements being made (Shulman, Remington and McLean, 1979). Eye movement recording is therefore probably best used as an adjunct to other measures of sport-specific perceptual skill rather than as a stand alone measure (Abernethy, 1985).

Relationship of sport-specific visual skills to sports performance

Reviews of the expertise literature (e.g., Starkes and Deakin, 1984; Abernethy, 1987; Garland and Barry, 1990) are consistent in the conclusion that performance on sport-specific visual skills tests, of the type outlined in the previous section, are far better predictors of sports performance than the generalised visual skills tests described earlier. In a number of well-controlled and comprehensive studies, such as Starkes' (1987) study of field hockey players and Helsen and Pauwels' (1993a) study of soccer players, clear differences have emerged on visual tests requiring the processing of sport-specific information ('software' tests) in the absence of any differences on generalised visual skills ('hardware') tests. The extent to which systematic expert–novice differences are found on sport-specific visual skills tests does, however, differ somewhat between the different types of test tasks.

Tasks requiring rapid object detection, such as the ball detection tasks of Allard and Starkes (1980), Starkes (1987) and Millslagle (1988), are generally able to be performed with greater speed, but not necessarily greater accuracy, by experts. What is less clear in the available literature is the extent to which the context in which the ball or target is presented is critical to the expert's advantage (see Chamberlain and Coelho, 1993 for a discussion).

In studies of pattern recognition the evidence is consistent in indicating that context is critical with expert sports performers reliably outperforming novices on recognition tasks which contain patterns from their domain of expertise but with this advantage disappearing when unstructured displays are presented. This finding holds not only for expert athletes in team ball sports (e.g., Allard et al., 1980; Allard and Burnett, 1985; Borgeaud and Abernethy, 1987; Starkes, 1987) but also in 'closed' sports such as snooker (Abernethy, Neal and Koning, 1994) and is consistent with evidence from a diverse range of cognitive skills tasks (e.g., Chase and Simon, 1973; Sloboda, 1976; Egan and Schwartz, 1979; Howard and Kerst, 1981). The only major source of contention with this consistent finding of expert–novice differences in pattern recognition relates to whether the observed expert advantage is a direct cause or merely a by-product of the expert's experience (Holding, 1985).

Like the evidence accumulated on pattern-recognition a now extensive body of evidence from sport-specific anticipation tasks is consistent in its demonstration of superior performance by expert players. Studies of the racquet sports of tennis (Jones and Miles, 1978; Isaacs and Finch, 1983; Goulet, Bard and Fleury, 1989) badminton (Abernethy and Russell, 1987a) and squash (Abernethy, 1990a), of ice hockey (Salmela and Fiorito, 1979), volleyball (Wright, Pleasants and Gomez-Meza, 1990), soccer (Williams and Burwitz, 1993), and cricket (Abernethy and Russell, 1984) have all indicated earlier pick-up of information about the opponent's action by expert performers. Studies using spatial occlusion techniques and display presentations consisting simply of moving points of light representing the motion of the opponent's joints suggest that expert athletes are attuned to the essential kinematic detail in their opponent's actions with their information pick-up matching the typical proximal-to-distal biomechanical evolution of their opponent's actions (Abernethy, 1991, 1993). In essence, experts appear to conduct superior biomechanical analyses of their opponent's actions extracting useful information from earlier features of their opponent's action(s).

The evidence with respect to visual search patterns is much less clear cut. While there exist a number of studies (e.g., Bard and Fleury, 1976, 1981;

Ripoll and Fleurance, 1988; Goulet et al., 1988; Vickers, 1992; Helsen and Pauwels, 1993a, 1993b; Williams, Davids, Burwitz and Williams, 1994) that have indicated the presence of some systematic expert–novice differences in visual search pattern, be it either in the distribution rate or sequence of fixations, these differences are often relatively minor (see Abernethy, 1988a; Chamberlain and Coelho, 1993; and Williams, Davids, Burwitz and Williams, 1993; for reviews). Importantly the visual search patterns of experts and novices can be quite similar in situations where their information pick-up is markedly different (e.g., Abernethy and Russell, 1987b; Abernethy, 1990b; Handford and Williams, 1992), supporting the conclusion that the limiting factor in expert vision may be not so much the way in which the visual display is searched but the athlete's capability to interpret, use and 'understand' the visual information which is acquired.

Methods and implications for training

As with our earlier approach to the assessment of generalised visual training programmes, a useful starting point for examining sport-specific perceptual training is to make the assumption that methods which do not train factors associated with expertise are unlikely to result in performance enhancement. Following this line it would therefore appear improbable that training approaches which aim to teach athletes a particular visual search strategy (using the search patterns of the expert as a model or template) are likely to be effective. This is based theoretically on the equivocal evidence regarding any systematic relationship between visual search patterns and level of sports performance and on the range of individual differences in search pattern which are observed even amongst a homogeneous group of expert performers. While specific sport studies are lacking, the empirical evidence from aviation psychology supports the theoretical prediction that visual search pattern matching is not likely to be an effective approach to perceptual training. Attempts to improve the perceptual skills of trainee pilots by having them model their visual search patterns on those of expert pilots have generally proved fruitless (Papin, 1984).

The logical corollary to the arguments developed in the preceding paragraph is that approaches to perceptual training which *are* directed at known sources of expert advantage in perception are more likely to be fruitful in enhancing athletic performance. Given that experts have been shown, in some sports at least, to be clearly superior to lesser skilled athletes in their rapid detection of relevant objects in the visual field, in their recognition of sport-specific patterns, and in their anticipation of forthcoming events and actions by their opponent, the obvious follow-on questions are: can these sport-specific skills be improved with training and, if so, does this enhancement of visual–perception translate into improved sports performance? The evidence on these questions, especially the second one, is scant.

Just as it is possible to test an athlete's ability to rapidly detect or locate relevant stimuli in briefly presented slides it would appear feasible to be able to train this ability through the use of sets of training slides presented, over time, with progressively shorter exposure durations or with progressively greater display complexity or information extraction requirements. Some evidence is available, for example, from Thiffault's (1974, 1980) studies of ice hockey players, to indicate that speed of visual detection and even tactical decision-making on these rapid detection tasks can be improved substantially with slide-based practice. What is not yet conclusively demonstrated, however, is that these improvements go beyond performance on the slide-based detection tests to translate into actual improvements in sports performance. The lingering concern is that training on slides may improve one's ability to perform a test based on slides but that none of this improvement is actually beneficial to on-field (or in this case, on-ice) sports performance.

Essentially the same arguments also hold true for the training of pattern recognition skills using slides or even videotapes of a similar type to that used to assess pattern recognition skills. Again studies on this topic are scarce although Londerlee (1967), using film clips to train defensive players in American football to recognise offensive patterns, reported improvements in speed of play recognition as a consequence of this training. Wilkinson (1992) reported long-term retention of pattern-recognition skills in volleyball resulting from visual training, with a group given training outperforming an untrained group on pattern recognition 12 months after initial training. Again, however, there is a dearth of evidence (either positive or negative) to assess whether these reported improvements in sport-specific perceptual skill transfer to improvements in actual sports performance. Perception and action would assumedly need to be re-coupled to accommodate any improvements in perception achieved in isolation of experience in action.

While the research work is again far from extensive and comprehensive, there is more evidence to assess the enhancement of anticipatory skills by sport-specific visual training methods than there is for other aspects of perception known to be linked with expert performance. In keeping with Ericsson, Krampe and Tesch-Ramer's (1993) notions about the quantity of deliberate practice being the best predictor of the attainment of expertise, it is apparent from evidence on developmental trends in sport-specific anticipation skills (Abernethy, 1988b) that anticipatory skills are highly amenable to practice. Children experiencing substantial playing and training experience in racquet sports develop a capability, as they become older, to pick up useful advance information from earlier and earlier time windows in their opponent's action. In contrast, novice subjects who are maturing at the same rate as these players, but not experiencing regular sport-specific match play and practice, show no systematic shift toward earlier information pick-up with age. Anticipatory skills, therefore, appear to be able to be improved with usual practice and playing experience but is there any focused way of accelerating this improvement?

A number of researchers have attempted to train sport-specific anticipation skills directly by having subjects repetitively view film or video clips of opponent's actions. Haskins (1965), Jones (1974) and Day (1980) with tennis players and Burroughs (1984) with baseball batters have all reported improved anticipatory performance as a consequence of repeated exposure to film-presented display information and accompanying performance feedback. Unfortunately these studies, in the main, only demonstrate improved film task performance as a consequence of the film training. Improvements in actual sports performance are frequently not monitored or reported and where they have been (Day, 1980) performance improvements have not parallelled the perceptual improvements. Rather than relying simply on essentially passive and incidental forms of learning from film tasks (or 'live models' if players chose to train and observe 'live action' from as close to normal viewing positions as possible; Abernethy 1990b) it may be possible to have more profound influences on the rate of acquisition of anticipatory skills if the training environment can be made both more progressive and more directed.

One simple means of making training more progressive is to impose systematically shorter viewing periods on the videoclips of the opponent's action which are used for training (see Abernethy and Wollstein, 1989 for details). Selective use of the 'pause' facility on domestic video players can ensure only limited viewing of an opponent's preparatory actions (in a manner directly equivalent to the temporal occlusion conditions within the typical anticipation test protocol); the advantage of this approach being that release of the 'pause' button allows immediate feedback on the accuracy of anticipatory predictions made early in an event sequence. Any knowledge, derived from procedures such as spatial occlusion, about the specific location of the key sources of advance information for a particular sport skill may be invaluable in making training more directed. In a study in our laboratory (Abernethy and Wood, 1992) a group of subjects were given anticipation training for tennis over a four week period using a combination of video-based training (with progressively reduced viewing of the preparatory and contact actions of opposing players) and knowledge-based training. The knowledge-based training consisted of instruction about the location of key advance sources of information for racquet sports (based on the results of Abernethy and Russell, 1987a) and instruction about the biomechanics of tennis shots (given the links between perceptual skill and the kinematics of the action being viewed; Abernethy, 1991). The group trained in this way outperformed, on a standard anticipation test for tennis, a control group (given no perceptual training) and a placebo group (given comparable amounts of instruction viewing of tennis matches but without a specific focus on the development of anticipatory skills). Again however the extent to which this training translates to improved on-court performance remained indeterminate and this is clearly an essential focus for future studies in this area. The recent advent of occluding glasses (Milgram, 1987) that can be worn on-court offers some interesting and new possibilities for stimulating the acquisition of early information pick-up although the efficacy of training methods based around this technology has yet to be reported. An even larger and potentially wider avenue for improvements in sport-specific perceptual skills may well be through the technology of virtual reality environments. The possibilities in this area are briefly considered in the next section.

Future prospects: the promise and potential of training through virtual reality

A major impediment to both the analysis and training of perceptual skill has been our ability to control the information that arises as a consequence of the performer's actions. Hence it is difficult to confirm, for example, what information is actually used by a cricket fielder running to catch a ball. We are limited to the presentation of a range of balls in flight, and the demonstration that the fielder's behaviour is consistent with a particular model (McLeod and Deines, 1993). Similarly, if you wished to train a junior cricket squad to attend to specific cues, how, in a natural setting, could you make that source of information more salient, or other sources unreliable? What is needed is a means of controlling the visual and/or haptic environment that is presented to the performer. Furthermore, such control ideally needs to go beyond simple visual occlusion or the use of video displays that are not responsive to the performer's action.

The recent escalation in computing power and speed has radically changed the availability of real-time interactive computer graphics and the potential to apply such graphics to situations like perceptual training for sport. There are now a number of relatively low-cost interactive computer graphics systems available that can present the user with a stereoscopic visual display with photo-realistic texture mapping. The popular label used for such displays is *virtual reality* (VR). Stereoscopic VR displays provide binocular information that presents an illusion of the computer-generated objects at different depths. This depth information is reinforced by the perspective cues and texture gradients that are present in any depiction or photograph of a three-dimensional (3-D) scene and, like in a video display, objects loom as they move towards the observer, providing additional depth and timing information. Photo-realistic texture mapping means that the rather crude displays of early video games and VR displays are now superseded by systems where the designer can photograph the texture of a clay tennis court or the buildings surrounding the Monaco Grand Prix and paste these photographs onto the horizontal or vertical surfaces that the performer sees. Hence, when the virtual tennis player moves forward the visual detail of court moves under them appropriately, or the virtual driver sees the blur of detail as he passes the Monaco casino at 210 (virtual) km/h (130 mi/h).

Two critical differences between VR and a video display are that VR is user-responsive and the designer can manipulate the display in ways which do not adhere to the usual physical laws of nature. The user-responsive feature of VR means that the performer can turn their head to see what is happening to the side of them or explore the perceptual consequences of moving in a different way, at a different time, or at different speeds. A good example of such an application is the bob-sleigh simulator developed for training the US Olympic squad (Hubbard, 1994). This placed the driver in an enclosed capsule where a large screen visual display presented a realistic computer simulation of an actual bob-sleigh course. The motion of the display and the physical motion of the capsule changes in response to the actions of the driver. This presents the potential for the driver to experiment with different control strategies without the high risk and high cost of practice on a real bob-sleigh course. The problem with such a training device is that it is difficult to assess the degree of transfer from the simulated to the real setting or to be certain that skills learned in the simulator will not result in disaster on the real run, due to minor changes in the surface conditions. Despite these concerns, simulators have had a major impact on training in other high-risk activities and many commercial airline pilots are now transferred to new aircraft with zero flight time, all the training being undertaken on a flight simulator.

What has yet to be established with sports simulators is whether they can enhance either the rate of acquisition, or the information that is acquired, beyond that which would result from practice in a natural setting. This is where the untapped potential of VR to change the visual environment is important. In the case of the bob-sleigh simulator it would be possible to change the spatial detail or temporal characteristics of the texture that flows past the driver and monitor its effect upon the driver's control. Hence it is possible to posit questions as to whether the driver is controlling the heading of the sled using information from the visible edges of the run, or the optical flow resulting from the texture detail of the snow. If it is the latter, what effect does a change in spatial frequency have (coarse vs fine detail) or can a change in lighting alter the salience of the information available. It is then possible to examine whether drivers trained on a real run are sensitive to the same manipulations as those trained on the simulator. The attraction of a VR setting is that it opens up a new avenue to ask 'what perceptual information appears to be crucial to this task . . . and is there variance in the use of such information between performers or training techniques?'

There are limits to the potential of VR to simulate a number of sports settings. Where performance is determined primarily by interaction with an inanimate object, such as a ski-run or a golf ball, then a simulation can be close to veridical, particularly if the equipment that the observer controls can be easily interfaced to a computer (e.g. a bod-sled, ski or golf club). Hence driving simulators, VR ski simulators and golf simulators are commercially available. If the sport involves other participants that need to be observed, then VR systems run into difficulties. A person presents a complex geometric shape and storing and rendering a 3-D human image in real time is beyond the capabilities of all current systems. (There have been a number of media programmes that have displayed Virtual Reality systems that appear to be rendering moving human figures in real time, but these are either superimposed video images or pre-computed images that have been stored and then are replayed.) It is a relatively simple procedure to 'paste' a video image of a tennis opponent into a VR simulation and have a virtual ball fly from the opponent's racquet. When the receiving player moves forward or sideways, however, the video image will not change in the way that a true 3-D model would and the impression given is that of the opponent being a cardboard cut-out. It would also be difficult to anticipate where the return stroke would land and have pre-recorded the virtual opponent playing a spatially appropriate stroke. (It is of course possible to have two players, each playing in a virtual world, against a video image or each other, but one might ask why not just put them both on a real court? The ability to control/change/slow-down ball trajectory is an advantage of the virtual setting, but the errors in the computer prediction of flight resulting from a stroke may negate this advantage.) These technical difficulties do not completely undermine the use of VR in a tennis context as it would nevertheless be still feasible to expose junior players to a range of tennis serves struck by (a video image of) one of the world's leading players. To reiterate: the advantage of VR over existing perceptual training displays is that the ball can be made to fly along any chosen trajectory; the coach may increase the spin; introduce a sudden swerve; or slow down its flight over the net to emphasize some particular characteristics. It is also possible for the VR system to estimate the trajectory that would result from the player's racquet response and hence give the junior player some (approximate) feedback about the return of serve.

The issue of transfer of training from sports simulators to the natural context, however, remains unresolved. The potential of VR to selectively perturb particular cues and hence examine their importance to the performer presents an exciting avenue for future investigation. Preliminary studies of ball catching (Wann and Rushton, 1995) have provided insight into the use of looming and binocular information, but there a clear potential for VR displays to extend previous investigations of perception in sports tasks such as judging ball flight (Bahill and Karnavas, 1993; McLeod and Dienes, 1993); anticipating an opponent's action (Abernethy and Russell, 1987a); and recognising patterns (Allard et al., 1980). There is also potential in the provision of a remedial environment where information can be tailored to allow the guided acquisition of skills in motor delayed or motor impaired populations (Wann and Turnbull, 1993).

Generalised kinesthetic skills

For the sighted individual the information provided through the visual system provides the primary means of controlling many skilled actions. It has been demonstrated that in the early stages of development vision may dominate over other forms of body-referenced information. Lee and Aronson (1974) demonstrated that if a young child was placed in a suspended room where the walls, but not the floor, could be moved, then the sight of the moving walls caused the child to lose balance, despite a wealth of information from the child's internal, kinesthetic systems to specify that they were standing on a stable, unmoving floor. Adult participants placed in the 'swinging room' may sway, but do not fall over. The latter finding seems to suggest that during development other information about movement of the body serves to mediate (or is integrated with) vision. In the context of the swinging room, vestibular information from the inner ear specifies that the body is not moving to the same extent as is specified by vision of the moving walls, and kinesthetic receptors in the joints and muscles of the lower limbs also provide information that the body is stable. In the context of training for sport, the essential issues are what are the critical sources of non-visual information and how do they interact with vision; how might individual differences in kinesthetic skills be measured; do differences in generalized kinesthetic skills relate directly to level of sports performance and, if so, what are the implications for training?

Several models for the integration of visual and vestibular information have been posited (e.g. Wertheim, 1994). In a natural setting the vestibular system provides coherence and cooperation with the visual system. It is clear, however, that the visual system can provide veridical information, without concurrent vestibular information (e.g. simulated flight), whereas the information from the vestibular system, in the absence of vision, is ambiguous and may be grossly misinterpreted. (Some traditional fairground illusions and modern theme parks exploit this weakness by putting participants in motion, to provide some stimulation to the vestibular system, then rotating the visual scene to give participants the impression that they have somersaulted.) The primary shortcoming of the vestibular system in providing a performer with precise information about their extent and speed of travel is that the system senses acceleration, thereby conflating accelerative motion with orientation with respect to gravitational acceleration. It has been proposed that vestibular information may be integrated over time to provide speed and distance information (Potegal, 1982), but this hypothesis has not received general acceptance. A problem with the use of vestibular information without a visual reference is that the system that detects translational motion (the otoliths) cannot discern the instantaneous direction of travel; if the performer is moving forward but decelerating at 1 g, this produces the same vestibular stimulation as accelerating backwards at 1 g. The vestibular system has essential links with the oculo-motor system (to stabilise gaze) and with righting reflexes (to maintain an upright posture). Beyond this the main role of vestibular perception appears to be to complement vision. The reason the vestibular system cannot operate effectively in isolation of vision is not with the acuity of the system, which is very sensitive to body motion, but rather with the type of information it provides, which make it difficult to discern direction and extent of travel, as well as the respective role of gravity, without information from other perceptual systems.

Considerable attention has been directed to other sensations of body motion arising from musculo-skeletal sensors, which are encompassed within the general term 'kinesthesis'. In the example of the swinging room, considered previously, participants had cutaneous sensations about their weight distribution from the soles of their feet; information from the receptors in the ankle, knee and hip joints; information about muscle stretch from the receptors in the lower limb muscles; and related information from tendon receptors. There has been considerable debate over the respective roles of joint receptors (Gandevia and McCloskey, 1976), cutaneous receptors (Moberg, 1983), muscle spindles and central neural commands (Matthews, 1982) in the control of skilled movement. Applied and developmental research has not addressed the respective roles of each sub-system, but rather has focused on kinesthesis as a general sense of limb orientation and motion.

Tests and assessment

Due to technical constraints, measurement of kinesthesis has tended to use static limb position tasks, rather than tasks representative of everyday skills. A typical paradigm is to place a participant's limb at a specific orientation and then ask the subject to either match the position with their other limb, or for the experimenter to passively move the subject's other limb and then ask if the limb is higher/lower (e.g. Laszlo and Bairstow, 1980). A confounding effect running through almost all of the previous research is that skilled performance may require the use of kinesthesis in different and distinct ways. Some skills, particularly in a sports setting, require that the performer places their limb in a particular orientation, or matches the shape and orientation of the two limbs. Tasks that require this could be called kinesthetic matching. Equally common, however, is the requirement that both hands are brought to the same place, even though the limb orientations are very different (e.g. reaching under a sink or engine to place a nut and bolt together). In this case kinesthesis may specify the location of either hand relative to the performer's ego-centre, but the task can not be achieved by matching kinesthesis; such tasks require egocentric matching. These two tasks are radically different; one may be achieved through the comparison of musculo-skeletal sensations, the other requires transformation of such sensations, with regard to gravitational torques, to arrive at a body-referenced location. The lack of specificity as to which task participants were attempting severely devalues a number of the studies of kinesthetic perception (Wann, 1991). Studies that have restricted motion to a single degree of freedom around a joint avoid this problem, but equally reduce the task to one that is removed from dynamic bimanual skill. There is a paucity of research on the use of kinesthetic information in dynamic multi-joint tasks. The cricketer directs gaze towards the ball, yet moves the bat and his/her hands in unison through a smooth trajectory, while each arm moves through a different set of orientations. The information supporting such skill is not at all well addressed in existing studies of kinesthetic perception.

There is strong evidence that simple kinesthetic skills develop during early childhood. Laszlo and Bairstow (1980) used a kinesthetic matching task to demonstrate an increase in kinesthetic 'acuity' up to the age of 12 years, and subsequently suggested that a primary cause of movement coordination problems in children is poor kinesthetic acuity. There are methodological problems (Doyle, Elliott and Connolly, 1986) and problems of non-replicability (Lord and Hulme, 1988; Sugden and Wann, 1988; Hoare and Larkin, 1991) with the major findings of the Laszlo and Bairstow study. There are also conceptual concerns with the use of this kind of task with young children. Declarative judgements of high/low, near/far can be unreliable in young children, and it is not surprising that Laszlo and Bairstow (1980) reported that almost 25% of 5–6 year olds responded randomly in their judgements. The age-related performance on this task may in part reflect the cognitive demands of the empirical setting as well as the child's perceptual abilities. Observation of a 3–4 year old in play suggests that kinesthetic skills may be quite well developed, but we lack suitable paradigms to test this skill without requiring the child to make an explicit judgement. In this respect the swinging room of Lee and Aronson (1974) has an admirable simplicity in that one merely observes the infant's natural response to a perturbed visual environment. Providing equivalent controlled perturbations to a child's kinesthetic perception is difficult to contemplate, not least because of our limited knowledge of the respective roles of different sensory systems. It is clear that kinesthetic perception improves during the early developmental period, but the rate at which it develops, and how soon the child reaches the mean adult level, is difficult to determine from the existing research base.

Studies of kinesthetic perception in adults have produced some anomalies. On one level the stability of kinesthetic perception has been questioned, while equally it has been demonstrated that kinesthesis has a powerful effect on the perception of body scale. Paillard and Brouchon (1968) and Wann and Ibrahim (1992), demonstrated that if a limb was left inactive for as little as 15 seconds, then the kinesthetically perceived position of the limb would drift by several centimetres. Furthermore, Wann and Ibrahim found that brief glimpses of the limb or brief muscular activation could halt the drift, but did not reset perception to its original location. These studies suggest that kinesthesis may be unreliable and require frequent calibration by vision. This suggestion was supported by the studies of Prablanc, Echallier and Jeannerod (1979) who controlled vision of the hand prior to reaching for a target. In contrast Lackner (1988) reported that participants whose biceps/ triceps tendon was vibrated, thereby producing an illusion of lower limb motion, experienced some remarkable sensations. If participants placed the finger of the vibrated arm on their nose, they perceived their nose to be growing, or conversely their hand going into their head. Lackner's participants also reported 'growing in height' or whole-body rotation, depending on where they rested the vibrated arm. Hence it would seem that kinesthetic sensation can have a powerful effect on perceptions of the body and its motion, but evaluation of kinesthetic judgements suggest that they can be imprecise and prone to error if not calibrated through vision. Once again there are considerable shortcomings in experimental method that makes generalisation to natural contexts difficult. Does a cricket batsman really lose sense of where his/her hands are if the bowler takes more than 15 seconds to start his run up? Are the seemingly random twitches of the bat and glances down at the batsman's feet an unconscious strategy to maintain limb position sense (e.g. Wann and Ibrahim, 1992)? The void between the kinesthetic skills explored in the laboratory and those used in daily activities undermines useful extrapolation from the specific findings to the general context. There is strong evidence that, similar to the vestibular system, kinesthetic signals are used in controlling movement (e.g. Gandevia and Burke, 1992), but the broader role of kinesthetic perception and general kinesthetic skill is difficult to determine outside the constraints of the laboratory task. Given these enormous constraints within our existing knowledge it is impossible at this point in time to advocate generalised kinesthetic training as a means of enhancing sports performance.

Sport-specific kinesthetic skills

Given the parallel observation that the training of sport-specific visual skills offers potential for the improvement of perceptual skill for sport yet the benefits of generalised visual training appear very limited, there would also appear to be more value in pursuing the potential for sport-specific than generalised kinesthetic training. The potential of sport-specific kinesthetic training is assessed in this section through the established path of examining existing examples of sport-specific kinesthetic tests, their relationship to sports performance and their implications for training.

Tests and assessment

There is potentially an extremely large range of sport-specific kinesthetic tests which could be generated, yet to date very few have been. The reliance instead has been almost exclusively on generic tests of various elements of kinesthesis, typically developed for purposes other than the enhancement of sports performance. Two types of sport-specific kinesthetic skills tests are presented here as illustrations of the kind of innovations in testing that are possible—the first example is of an athlete's ability to judge limb position (in the absence of visual feedback); the second of an athlete's ability to judge self-effort. Both examples, unlike the majority of the examples provided from vision, are likely to be more important factors in the performance of 'closed' skill sports than 'open' skill sports.

Tests of limb positioning.   In activities such as diving, gymnastics and synchronised swimming the ability to produce specified whole-body positions is a criterion for performance. As, in many instances, this requires particular limbs to be placed in specified positions on the basis of non-visual information, an ability to accurately produce and reproduce desired limb positions kinesthetically might be reasonably expected to be an important characteristic of skilled performance in these activities. Blindfolded limb-positioning tasks have a long history of use in studies of fundamental motor control and hence adaptations of these tasks to examine putative characteristics of expert sports performance is relatively straightforward. Régnier and Salmela (1980), for example, had gymnasts attempt to reproduce a criterion movement of 90° shoulder abduction and used accuracy in doing this as a kinesthetic sensitivity component of a talent identification battery for gymnastics.

Tests of sensitivity to effort.   Kinesthetic receptors along with receptors within the cardio-respiratory and related physiological systems provide athletes with valuable information about their own physiological states and degree of exertion. The more precisely athletes such as swimmers, cyclists, distance runners, triathletes, rowers and kayakers can monitor their own physiological state the more capable they may be to swim, cycle, run, row or paddle at pre-determined or desired lap times or paces. Tests which objectively measure the concordance or otherwise between athlete's perception of their physiological state and objective measures of it would therefore appear to be of value. A number of possibilities exist in this regard. One possibility is simply to examine correlations for individual athletes between their subjective ratings of effort, on scales such as Borg's (1962) Ratings of Perceived Exertion, and objective measures of workload, such as pulse rate (cf. Borg and Linderholm, 1967).

A second possibility is to have athletes attempt to estimate their actual workloads in performance units such as lap times or cycle velocity and compare these with the actual times and cadences. A third possibility is to create a situation where the internal information (provided kinesthetically and physiologically) and external information (provided through sources such as speedometers on bicycles), which are usually in unison, are made disparate and subjects are forced to make judgements as to which source is veridical. In an example of this approach used by Lynagh (1987), cyclists of different levels of expertise were each presented with 18 pairs of work-bouts on a cycle ergometer, with each workout pair consisting of a two minute criterion workout followed by a two minute comparison work-bout. On each workout subjects were instructed to cycle at a target ca-dence, with this target displayed in visual analogue form on a monitor directly in front of them. Half of the workout pairs involved a manip-ulation of the actual cadence but with the displayed cadence remaining constant while in the other half the displayed cadence was systematically varied even though the actual cadence remained constant. In each case the manipulations were ± 30 r.p.m. from the criterion workrates of 170, 200 or 230 r.p.m. Situations were thus created where the internal information (provided by actual cadence) was in conflict with the external information (provided by the displayed cadence). The subject's task was simply to judge for each workout pair whether the comparison workout was higher, equal or lower in intensity than the criterion workout. Reliance on actual or displayed cadence in this test provided a measure of individual subjects' relative reliance on external or internal sources of information pertaining to effort.

Relationship of sport-specific kinesthetic skills to sports performance

The limited data base of sport-specific kinesthetic studies makes generalisations potentially hazardous. The available studies using limb positioning tasks in a sport-specific manner (e.g., Régnier and Salmela, 1980) have not discriminated expert from novice performers using their test protocols. The static nature of these test protocols and their restriction of testing typically to one motion about one joint (when the sport requires many motions about many joints) makes these null findings not surprising. Some of the studies of self-monitoring of effort show greater promise for a meaningful link between a measurable, non-visual skill and sports performance. Lynagh's (1987) study, for example, was clear in revealing a preferential reliance on internal, self-generated information about effort by expert cyclists when the opposite (a dependence on external, displayed sources of information quantifying workload) was apparent for untrained cyclists. Clearly self-monitoring of effort is an important perceptual component (or at the very least, by-product) of expertise in cycling and may be something that can be actively enhanced through systematic training.

Methods and implications for training

Some authors have suggested that there may be value in using blindfolded training as a means of enhancing kinesthetic sensitivity on some sports tasks where the dominant visual information is not sufficient or may be distracting and disruptive to performance (e.g., trampolining; Graydon and Townsend, 1984). The generally very weak relationship between both generalised and sport-specific measures of kinesthetic sensitivity and sports performance (e.g., Roloff, 1953; Régnier and Salmela, 1980), and the known significance of inter-sensory integration, visual dominance and perception–action coupling to motor performance, argues against the likelihood of such approaches being beneficial to performance enhancement and suggests that such approaches may be, in fact, detrimental. While the evidence upon which to base the case is clearly limited, a potentially more fruitful line of training for that sub-set of sports tasks in which pacing of effort is important is to seek out and develop training methods which enhance an athlete's ability to accurately self-monitor his or her own states of effort and exertion. While at least some of this skill may develop in parallel with training experience, the regular and systematic provision of opportunities for athletes to calibrate their self perceptions of effort with objective physiological or performance measures of workload and effort would appear to be logical and desirable.

DECISION-MAKING SKILLS AND THEIR TRAINING

The process of decision-making

Perceptual processes provide the bases by which the athlete is able to ascertain in both a current and prospective sense what is occurring in the surrounding environment (e.g., with respect to the speed, location and direction of motion of teammates, the ball, or the wind) and in their own bodies (e.g., with respect to limb and whole body position or physiological states). Decision-making processes are concerned with using this information to determine what, if any, response is needed. In other words, the decision-making process is the one of selecting the correct course of action in light of current circumstances, context and past experience. The quality of the decisions which are made (in terms of both their speed and accuracy) will be obviously influenced by the quality of the perceptual information received but also by the performer's knowledge of context and expectations based on past experience.

Decision-making is clearly an integral part of successful performance in virtually all sports although the time-constraints under which decisions must be made are generally much more stringent for 'open' skill sports. French and Thomas (1987), for example, found in junior basketball that decision-making was the best correlate of performance improvements over the duration of a competitive season. Both the speed and accuracy of decision-making is influenced, and limited, by a range of factors including the number of response choices which exist, the total time available for decision-making and the time-cost associated with making incorrect decisions. Our considerations of decision-making in sport will be restricted to two major constraints on sports performance, specifically (i) constraints in performance arising from selecting between variable numbers of options and (ii) constraints in performance arising in situations where two or more decisions must be made in rapid succession. Understanding of the impact of these constraints on sports performance is based on an extensive body of literature on two fundamental human performance phenomena—choice reaction time (CRT) and psychological refractory period (PRP).

Selecting the correct option rapidly and accurately

Tests and assessment

In many sport tasks athletes are frequently faced with the need to both rapidly and accurately select the correct course of action from a range of possible options. On each play in basketball, for example, the point guard has to select the best course of action from between shooting, dribbling or four possible passing options (one to each teammate). As information about each option is derived through perception, the speed and accuracy of selecting a particular option contains both elements of perceptual discrimination and elements of response choice.

Laboratory CRT tasks provide a direct analogue to decision-making as required in sports tasks. In classical laboratory CRT tasks subjects are presented with a number of possible stimuli (usually lights) each of which has an associated response (usually a designated response button to be pushed by one of the fingers). The subject's task is then, after an appropriate warning signal, to respond to the appearance of one of the stimuli by making the required response as quickly as possible. CRT is then recorded as the elapsed time between the presentation of the stimulus (typically the illumination of a light) and the initiation of the appropriate response. Manipulation of the number of possible stimulus–response pairs, the probability of occurrence of different stimuli or the order in which the stimuli appear then allows understanding of key determinants of CRT. The basic laboratory paradigm for the measurement of CRT can be easily modified to examine sport-specific decision-making by replacing the simple visual stimuli of the lab task with perceptual stimuli which are sport-specific and by seeking responses (often verbal) which reflect the main tactical options available in the particular sport (e.g., shoot, pass etc.). A number of examples of sport-specific decision-making tasks of this type are available in the literature (e.g.,

Bard and Fleury, 1976; Carrière, 1978; Tyldesley, Bootsma and Bomhoff, 1982).

Studies of CRT are extremely consistent in their basic findings to the point of being able to be described by a formal mathematical law, the Hick-Hyman Law (after Hick, 1952; Hyman, 1953). The Hick–Hyman law, stated in the form of a regression equation, is: $CRT = a + bH$ where a is the value of RT when there is no uncertainty, b is the information processing rate and H is the amount of information. The Hick–Hyman law states that CRT is directly proportional to the amount of information (H) which has to be processed, where H can be formally quantified from task uncertainty. The amount of information (H) is equivalent to the log of the number of stimulus response alternatives, such that CRT is increased by a proportional amount each time the number of alternatives is doubled. In other words the increases in CRT when the number of possible options the subject has to choose between is increased from one to two is the same as the increase in CRT brought about by doubling the number of response options from two to four (Figure 1.2). The amount of information is also influenced in a predictable and quantifiable way by varying the amount of uncertainty or predictability by manipulating the probabilities of competing stimulus–response options or the predictability of stimulus–response sequences. In all cases the fundamental observation is that CRT is directly proportional to the amount of information that has to be processed, regardless of how that information is manipulated. Anything that eliminates stimulus–response options or makes stimuli more predictable (or probable) reduces CRT; anything that adds stimulus–

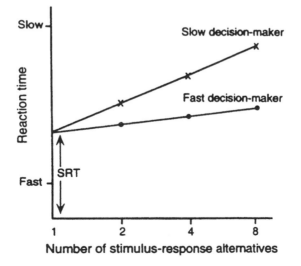

Figure 1.2: The relationship between choice reaction time and the amount of information to be processed. The amount of stimulus information is given by the log of the number of stimulus–response alternatives.

response options or makes stimulus prediction more difficult increases the time it takes for the subject to select a response for any particular stimulus. These basic phenomena provide a rich source of information which is actively and intuitively exploited by the expert sports performer.

Inspection of both the Hick–Hyman equation and Figure 1.2 shows that an individual subject's CRT for any particular task situation (and level of information) will be determined by two components. The first component, corresponding to variable a in the regression equation and the y-intercept on Figure 1.2, is the basal processing delay which occurs even when there is no choice to make and simply a single stimulus event to which a response must be made as rapidly as possible. This component equates with simple visual reaction time and, as we saw in an earlier section, is not influenced to any great extent by either practice or expertise. The second component is the slope of the regression line (b) and represents the average increase in CRT which occurs each time additional information is added to the task (such as the addition of an extra stimulus–response option or the removal of differential probabilities between two competing stimuli). This component, which is importantly independent of the first and varies considerably between individuals (Hyman, 1953), provides a direct measure of decision-making speed. If the individual is a slow decision-maker the slope of the regression line in Figure 1.2 will be steep. If the person is a fast decision-maker the slope will be small, approaching zero in the case where the subject is highly practised and the stimulus and response are linked in a very natural, compatible way (Mowbray and Rhoades, 1959).

Relationship to sports performance

Clearly, in many sports, a fast decision-making rate is advantageous. Practice may potentially act to reduce CRT by either facilitating overall decision-making rate and/or decreasing the absolute amount of information to be processed. Studies on CRT using both simple laboratory tasks (e.g., Olsen, 1956; Pierson, 1956; Burke, 1972; Blundell, 1984) and more sport-specific versions (e.g., Whiting and Hutt, 1972; Bard and Fleury, 1976; Carrière, 1978; Helsen and Pauwels, 1993a, 1993b) provide weak to moderate support for the view that expert sports performers may be faster decision-makers than less skilled performers. In other words, with reference to Figure 1.2, experts may have lower $RT:H$ slopes than novices.

A potentially more powerful means of expert sports performers decreasing their decision-making time, however, is to use sport-specific knowledge and strategies that allow the task situation to be made more predictable and hence decrease the total amount of information that must be processed. Any advance knowledge the athlete has, or play strategies the athlete can develop, that either decreases the total number of options available to their opponent or increases the probability of some specific options or sequences of play by their opponent, will act to reduce their own reaction time. Conversely the less predictable and more varied their own pattern of play becomes the larger will be the information processing load presented to their opponent and the slower will be their decision-making. Anecdotal evidence suggests that skilled players in many sports are able to dominate and dictate patterns of play in such a way as to eliminate many alternative options from their opponent's game, thus effectively reducing the amount of information they need to process in order to make decisions about their opponent's play. This, in turn, acts to reduce their own RT. Further, in sport tasks, the non-equiprobability of different events provides a potential basis for facilitating RT to more probable events (Alain and Girardin, 1978; Alain and Proteau, 1980) although, in laboratory tasks at least, large deviations from equiprobability for two events are needed before RT to the more probable stimulus is significantly decreased. Some limited evidence (Cohen and Dearnaley, 1962; Whiting, 1979) exists to suggest that the subjective estimates of event probabilities held by experts more closely match actual event probabilities than the estimates used by novices to guide their decision-making. The expert's knowledge of the probabilities and preferences in their opponent's play therefore acts also to reduce CRT, again through reducing the amount of information that has to be processed.

Methods and implications for training

The implications of the Hick–Hyman law for improvements in decision-making are straightforward but nevertheless profound. In order to reduce an athlete's decision-making time patterns of play should be actively developed which minimise the range of response options available to the opponent, thus reducing the amount of information that has to be processed (by reducing the number of stimulus and response options). Likewise, every attempt should be made to systematically study and become familiar with the patterns of play and preferred options of opponents as every piece of information acquired that either eliminates possible stimulus options or informs about one possible event being more probable than another reduces the amount of information to be processed and, through this, may speed up the rate of making decisions. Systematic video-based viewing of opponent's play may be beneficial in this regard (Christina, Barresi, and Shaffner, 1990). Computerised match statistics (e.g., Franks, Goodman & Miller, 1983) which provide objective data on the relative use, success rates and so on of different play options may also potentially assist in the learning of the strengths, weaknesses and probable patterns in an opponent's play. However, little empirical evidence is available, as yet, to demonstrate that the systematic use of these supplementary sources of information is actually beneficial (or otherwise) in the facilitation of both decision-making skills and, in turn, sports performance.

Just as the simple relationships between predictability and CRT described in the Hick–Hyman law can be exploited in order to reduce an athlete's own decision-making time, the same relationships can also be exploited, in theory at least, to slow the decision-making of an opponent. By remaining as unpredictable as possible in their own patterns of play and by developing the capability to execute a broad range of play options with proficiency, an experienced athlete can maximise the information-processing load facing their opponent and can, in turn, maximise their opponent's CRT delays. Video tape analyses of the athlete's own patterns of play and objective statistics on his/her own most frequently used options are also therefore equally important as analyses of opponents' and should be approached just as systematically. A clear case can be made for the systematic practice of deception as well as perception and decision-making skills. Whiting (1969, p. 39) noted that

> . . . the whole art of deception in games' skills consists in either masking the visual display in such a way that the opponent misinterprets the cues or in presenting distracting cues for response.

The use of some of the paradigms discussed previously for sport-specific perception may be of value in ascertaining the degree to which an athlete's deceptive skills are being effective and may also provide some additional clues to means of improving deception. Deception skills are clearly sport-specific and require careful consideration and practice of possible means of:

- disguising the critical cues;
- presenting false cues;
- increasing the number of 'possibly relevant' cues;
- varying all the possible dimensions of object flight (in ball games);
- presenting the critical cue as late as possible.

(Glencross and Cibich, 1977).

Making decisions in rapid succession

Tests and assessment

A number of situations in a range of sports require athletes to make two or more decisions and associated movement responses in rapid succession. It is well known in such situations, especially in manoeuvres such as 'fakes', 'dummies' or 'baulks' (as they are variously described), that response to a second stimulus or event is frequently significantly slowed if this second decision has to be made during the response time to the first stimulus.

Laboratory studies of how well subjects can react to two stimuli presented in rapid succession have a long history in experimental psychology. In the laboratory situation two stimulus–response pairs from different modalities are typically selected (e.g., a visual stimulus–manual response pairing with an auditory signal–vocal response pairing) and the time between the presentation of the two stimuli (the inter-stimulus interval; ISI) is varied systematically from about 10 to 500 ms. The subject's task is to respond to each stimulus as it appears as rapidly as possible and the interest experimentally is in ascertaining the extent to which the reaction time to the second stimulus is lengthened above the situation where it is handled in isolation of the first stimulus. The extent of the delays in responding to the second stimulus (known as the *psychological refractory period*; PRP) have been found to be directly dependent on the ISI (Welford, 1952; Davis, 1959), being greatest when the ISI is in the order of 50 ms and returning to normal values at some time after the response to the first stimulus has been completed (Karlin and Kestenbaum, 1968) (see Figure 1.3).

In using 'fake' movements in sport tasks athlete's attempt to catch their opponent's 'off guard' by making their definitive movement during the refractory period in which their opponent is responding to the first (false) stimulus. The laboratory data clearly indicate that if the opponent makes a response to the first (fake) stimulus then their response time to the critical second stimulus will be significantly delayed. In sport tasks, as compared to the laboratory analogue, this refractoriness will be compounded not only by the reaction time delays but also by movement delays associated with arresting the momentum of the first movement response in order to move back,

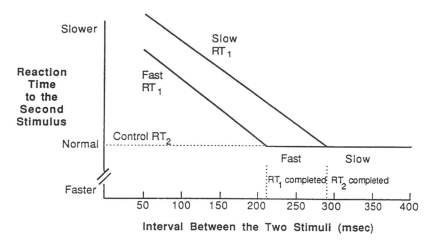

Figure 1.3: Psychological refractory period as a function of the inter-stimulus interval. [Reproduced with permission from Figure 6.10 of 'Attention' by B. Abernethy in R.N. Singer, M. Murphey and L.K. Tennant (Eds), *Handbook of Research on Sport Psychology*. New York: Macmillan, p. 147. Copyright International Society of Sport Psychology, 1993.]

usually in the opposite direction, to make the correct response to the second, critical stimulus.

Relationship to sports performance

Given the predominance of deceptive movements in many sports and the natural applicability of laboratory protocols for studying PRP to sport tasks, it is surprising that very few studies indeed have been conducted into PRP in sport. The evidence which is available is equivocal with respect to the presence or absence of PRP differences between expert and novice athletes. Smith (1973) reported no differences in PRP between athletes and non-athletes whereas Thorpe and Atha (1977) found faster reaction times for both the first and second stimuli in the series by athletes. What appears beyond contention is that the PRP phenomenon cannot be eliminated by practice (Gottsdanker and Stelmach, 1971) and that above-normal delays in responding to the second stimulus in a series are experienced as much by expert athletes as less skilled sportspeople. This suggests that the only useful means of overcoming the constraints imposed by the PRP phenomenon is to not respond to the first stimulus, if it is indeed a false one. From our earlier discussion of perceptual skill it would be reasonable to expect expert performers to have a superior capability to distinguish false from genuine cues presented by an opponent and, through so doing, to be less susceptible to PRP effects.

Methods and implications for training

It is apparent from the preceding discussion that knowledge of the opponent's normal strategies, preferred moves and frequently favoured deception manoeuvres is imperative to avoid unnecessary refractoriness. In this regard much of the video-based simulation training described in earlier sections for improving sport-specific anticipation and decision-making would again appear to be germane for avoiding unnecessary and costly PRP delays in sport. It needs to be recognised, however, that such recommendations must be based on extrapolation from theoretical principles and training regimes for other elements of skill as there is a complete dearth of research directed specifically at training methods to eliminate potential PRP delays in sport. Knowledge of the fundamental nature of PRP effects can, of course, be used by skilled athletes to slow the rate of responding by an opponent. Figure 1.3 suggests that 'fake' movements will be most effective if the second action occurs some 50–100 ms after the first and that any greater interval will minimise the effectiveness of such a movement. Systematic training to ensure both that the initial 'fake' move indeed appears sufficiently realistic to require a response and that the timing of the definitive move with respect to the fake is optimal would therefore appear worthwhile on the basis of the current evidence.

MOVEMENT EXECUTION AND CONTROL SKILLS AND THEIR TRAINING

The processes of movement execution and control

In order to produce and enact a selected course of action within their particular sport an athlete must be capable of precisely (and in many cases also rapidly) organising elements of the required movement in advance (by pre-planning, perhaps to the level of the desired efferent neural commands), initiating the required movement (by timing the release of the commands from the brain and central nervous system to the muscles) and then controlling the movement through to its completion (by monitoring sensory feedback concerning the movement's progress). These underlying movement execution and control processes are constrained in their speed and accuracy by a number of factors including the complexity of the movement, the number of joints, muscles and motor units involved, the acceptable error margins and the difficulties created with respect to the maintenance of normal posture and balance. In practical terms, and as a stage within perceptual–motor skills, movement execution and control equates most closely with notions of 'basic skill' or 'technique' training. Fast and accurate movement execution and control is important in the performance of all sports but its relative importance is especially pronounced in 'closed' skill sports such as gymnastics and diving, where the quality of the movement pattern produced is *the* criterion upon which performance is determined. As was noted earlier regarding the influence of the quality of perception upon decision-making, errors in either perception or decision-making inevitably translate into poor movement execution and control; the athlete in such circumstances is generally forced to attempt to correct 'on-line' a movement response which may be completely in the wrong 'ballpark'.

There is considerable current theoretical debate as to how movement execution and control occurs and how it might be examined, described and understood (Abernethy and Sparrow, 1992; Meijer and Roth, 1988). One approach (the traditional one) is to view movement control as essentially hierarchical and prescriptive, arising out of centrally represented movement plans (Keele, 1968; Schmidt, 1975, 1980). An alternative dynamical systems view is of movement control as an emergent property of a self-organising complex system (e.g., Kelso, 1981; Schöner and Kelso, 1988; Turvey, 1990). These theoretical differences result, to some degree, although clearly not exclusively, from different levels of analyses being used to observe movement production (Wieringen, 1988) and this also becomes an issue at the practical level in attempting to design tests and training requirements to maximize the movement execution and control skills of athletes. Brief consideration is given in the sections that follow to tests and training strategies based at the levels of:

(1) movement outcome (or product);
(2) movement pattern (or process), in turn qualified at a number of different levels.

Much of the description of movement outcomes and especially the quantification of movement patterns moves squarely into the field of biomechanics, a much more detailed consideration of which is made in Chapter 3.

Gross motor performance and behavioural tests of movement outcome

Tests of assessment

Tests of gross motor performance, such as simple tests of fundamental motor skills such as running, jumping, throwing and the like or of generic physiological properties such as upper body strength, power, and cardiorespiratory endurance, have been used quite extensively over a long period of time to assess normative motor skill development in children (e.g., Roberton, 1982; Keogh and Sugden, 1985) and to ascertain population and comparative norms on physical performance (e.g., American Alliance for Health, Physical Education, Recreation and Dance, 1989). The links of such generic tests to specific sport skills are tenuous at best. In contrast behavioural tests have been developed for many sports with the specific intent of objectively quantifying an individual's capability to perform the component movement skills used in particular sports. Many standardised tests of specific sport skills now exist; compilations of these form the basis for many traditional texts on measurement and evaluation in physical education (e.g., Barrow and McGee, 1971; Safrit, 1981). The emphasis in these tests is primarily, and usually exclusively, on movement outcome (e.g., time taken, number of successful shots etc.) with only limited reference to the movement pattern produced. In those tests where movement pattern assessment is included the assessment is qualitative rather than quantitative. Existing behavioural tests of sports skills are arguably of limited utility because they focus primarily on the movement execution or 'technical' aspects of sports performance and give little or no consideration to the perceptual and decision-making antecedents of observable movement.

Relationship to sports performance

While gross motor performance tests are poorly predictive of sports performance (with the exception that individuals performing poorly on such tests are, as a rule, unlikely to perform to high levels on most sport tasks), the relationship of behavioural tests of sports skills to sports performance is a more or less direct one. The predictive validity of sports skills tests varies from test to test and from sport to sport, generally dependent on the extent to which the test is of a coherent and essential sub-component of the sport itself. If the test is not drawn specifically from the sport itself then the predictive validity of the test (as determined by correlation of test scores with sport performance rankings) is typically low. If the test is drawn specifically from a skills component of the sport itself, relationship between performance on the test and overall skill level is naturally high but the data provided by such a test will be of limited diagnostic value to the coach and/or sport scientist.

Methods and implications for training

While a battery of sport-specific skills tests may be of some value to a coach with respect to the assessment of an individual player's overall weaknesses and strengths in movement execution and control such test results are typically of limited instructive value unless concurrent information is available on the movement patterns giving rise to the measured level of test performance. Selective practice of some sport movement sub-skills (i.e., effectively practising on the skills test items) *may* be useful in improving an athlete's sport-specific movement execution and control skills but will be subject to the limits imposed by task-specific part–whole transfer. In many movement tasks, especially tasks with an essentially continuous structure, part–whole transfer is frequently disappointingly low (see Schmidt, 1988 for a review).

The kinematics of movement patterns

Kinematics are descriptions of the motion of the whole body or separate body parts and form the basis for description of movement patterns rather than simply movement outcomes. The major kinematic descriptors are linear and angular displacement and their derivatives of velocity and acceleration and these are often displayed as time-series histories to capture key elements of movement execution. These base descriptions of motor patterns can be cross-plotted in forms such as angle–angle diagrams or phase plots to quantify patterns of inter- and intra-limb coordination (e.g., Sparrow, 1992).

Tests and assessment

A number of decades ago researchers (e.g., Pierson, 1959; Youngen, 1959; Rasch & Pierson, 1963) became interested in general measures of movement time and velocity, in a way parallelling interest in general measures of reaction time. Either whole-body displacements or specific limb displacements (most frequently arm movements) were timed using either stop watches or response keys linked to chronometers in an attempt to seek out a possible movement speed ability which might be fundamental to skilled performance in a number of sports. With the advent of more accessible technology for the extraction of task-specific kinematic measures most sports now have available to them the necessary technology to measure not only the durations, displacements, velocities, and accelerations of the whole body or specific limb segments during the performance of the specific actions required of their sport staged in a laboratory setting but also in the natural environment of competition itself (see Chapter 3 for technical details). Clearly these settings provide an opportunity for data collection with a level of ecological validity not available to the earlier recorders of movement patterns. In many sports the interest is not so much in the peak displacements, velocities or accelerations achieved in any given execution of the skill but rather in the consistency with which movement patterns can be reproduced from one execution of the skill to the next. For this reason measures such as the coefficient of variation (the standard deviation of points in a scaled time history) are now frequently included with measures of the timing and magnitude of peak events in the displacement, velocity and acceleration time series to provide a more complete description of movement pattern characteristics and reproducibility.

Relationship to sports performance

Some evidence (e.g., Keller, 1942; Pierson, 1956; Youngen, 1959) exists to suggest that movement times (MT) are faster for athletes compared to non-athletes and for 'open' skill athletes compared to 'closed' skill athletes (e.g., Burke, 1972) even when MT is measured in a general rather than sport-specific manner. Such effects may, however, be an artifact of the test protocols used and the amount of familiarization provided. For example, Yandell and Spirduso (1981) found MT superiority for an athletic group only on the first of five successive days of testing. In contrast, Konzag (1983), using a large sample of soccer players, found a close relationship between MT and level of performance with individual differences in MT preserved upon re-testing after 1–2 years. Whilst expertise-related differences in MT are not always reported on sport-specific measures (Sinclair, 1980) the majority of existing evidence, for time-constrained sports at least, appears to indicate systematically faster MTs for more skilled performers (e.g., Blundell, 1984). The most celebrated example of a measured MT advantage for an expert performer is the laboratory data collected on the boxer Muhammed Ali in 1969 showing that while his visual reaction time was similar to that of the general population his arm movement time over a distance of just less than 0.5 m was markedly faster than that of the general population. This case is a valuable sport illustration of the task-specific nature of athletic speed and the essential independence of RT and MT.

While measurement of MT essentially involves the extraction of a single discrete measure from an array of kinematic measures, the more continuous kinematic information contained in time-series arrays provides a more extensive profile of movement patterns than can simple measures such as movement time. Sport-specific measures of the linear and angular kinematics of the movements of highly skilled snooker players and clay target shooters respectively, clearly demonstrate greater movement pattern consistency (lower coefficients of variation) compared to less skilled athletes (Abernethy and Neal, 1990). This is in agreement with earlier evidence (e.g., Higgins and Spaeth, 1972; Spaeth-Arnold, 1976) of increased movement duration consistency with practice. In a similar vein, consideration of the displacement–time characteristics of the hand and bat motions of table tennis players of different skill levels is invaluable in demonstrating the more consistent downswing initiation of top-level players compared to less skilled players (Tyldesley and Whiting, 1975).

Methods and implications for training

Given that there appear to be systematic changes in movement kinematics with the acquisition of skill, the potential obviously exists to increase the rate of skill acquisition through the provision of suitable feedback about key kinematic features of performance. Indeed this is what coaches or teachers do routinely in providing qualitative feedback about movement patterning (e.g., 'your left knee flexed too early'). The key issue for the advancement of training beyond existing approaches is to ascertain whether the provision of quantitative kinematic feedback (of the type not typically readily available to either coach or performer) can enhance the rate of skill acquisition beyond traditional means.

The difficulty in examining this issue empirically is that there are many different kinematic features of any given movement that one could select as a basis for feedback and there are many different potential comparative models for the kinematics on any given practice trial (e.g., a model of ideal performance generated mathematically through simulation; a model based on the current best performer; or the individual athlete's own best performance). The selection of the kinematic variable upon which feedback is based cannot be an arbitrary one and should ideally be one verified empirically, *a priori*, as providing the essential information for skilled performance in that particular sport (Abernethy, 1993). There is some limited empirical evidence to demonstrate the value of different kinds of kinematic feedback for the training and rapid acquisition of movement skills, but to date the majority of research effort has been directed towards determining what particular kinds of kinematic information are most valuable (e.g., Newell and Walter, 1981; Newell, Sparrow, and Quinn, 1985).

The kinetics of movement patterns

Tests and assessment

Kinetic measures are descriptors of the underlying forces and masses which give rise to the patterns of motion described by kinematic measures. With respect to the understanding, assessment and training of perceptual–motor skills the principal interest in using kinetic measures of movement execution is to determine the timing, magnitude, consistency and precision of control of the force pulse outputs produced by the motor system during the performance of specific sport skills. Kinetic measures can be obtained directly from devices such as force transducers and force plates or determined indirectly from the output of accelerometers or standard kinematic data arrays (again see Chapter 3 for technical details). With recent improvements in kinetic as well as kinematic measurement technology sport-specific measures of movement kinetics can be derived relatively easily, usually in concert with the derivation of kinematic data. Indeed the interpretation of kinetic data usually relies on the availability of concurrent kinematic information.

It is also possible, with some innovation, to create ecologically valid measures of force control sensitivity through the adaptation of classical psychophysical methods for the determination of perceptual sensitivity (the so-called *jnd* or just noticeable difference). In studies in our laboratory to examine force control sensitivity in snooker players, for example, subjects were given a series of pairs of trials in which their task was, with the second movement in the pair, to either match exactly or increment or decrease by the smallest amount possible the force applied to the cue ball during the first movement (Abernethy and Neal, 1990). Similar tasks could easily be created for other sports where the precise, graduated control of force is expected to be central to successful performance.

Relationship to sports performance

There are surprisingly few studies which directly examine the relationship between the kinetic properties and sports performance. Those studies which have examined this relationship, typically through the use of a training paradigm, have generally observed a trend, with practice, toward the use of more discrete, efficiently located force pulses (Newell, Kugler, Emmerik and McDonald, 1989). Unnecessary and ill-timed force production, especially tonic levels of force production throughout the duration of a movement, typically diminish as skill acquisition proceeds. Force-time profiles show greater consistency for expert performers (Abernethy and Neal, 1990). Experts also demonstrate superior skill in force control both in terms of producing, for the second movement in a movement pair as required, either movements of identical force or of minimally incremented force. The increments in force production that experts appear capable of controlling are smaller (and hence more sensitive) than those able to be reliably controlled by less skilled performers.

Methods and implications for training

The potential clearly exists, as it did with kinematic variables, for selective feedback on key kinetic variables to be a valuable adjunct to perceptual–motor skill learning. The difficulty, again shared with kinematic aspects of movement patterns, is in reliably ascertaining, *a priori*, the key kinetic control variables upon which to provide feedback. Continuous kinetic feedback is most likely to aid skill learning if the feedback provided is on a kinetic variable directly linked to movement control for the particular task and not one which is merely a by-product or consequence of the actions of a different control variable. Some early evidence (Howell, 1956), in which sprint runners were provided after each start practice with force–time curves derived from instrumented starting blocks, suggests that subjects are indeed able to optimise the form of the force–time curve (in order to generate maximum impulse) if appropriate kinetic feedback is provided. More recent evidence on motor tasks derived from a context other than sport (Newell and Walter, 1981; Newell et al., 1985) corroborates this conclusion, although clearly more evidence is needed in this area in order to provide good guidance to either the coach or biomechanist eager to use kinetic feedback in a sport training context. Given the observation made in the previous section with respect to superior force sensitivity or force control by skilled athletes, there may also be some grounds to advocate the routine use in practice of force sensitivity training skills similar in form to the method of assessment described earlier (Abernethy, Neal, Engstrom and Koning, 1993).

The electrophysiology of movement patterns

Electrophysiological recording of a number of the systems underlying movement execution and control is possible. The electrical recording of activity in skeletal muscle (electromyography or EMG), in the brain (electroencephalography or EEG) and in the heart (electrocardiography or ECG), all provide some information, albeit at different points and levels of observation, which may ultimately prove useful with respect to the training of movement execution and control skills for sport.

Tests and assessment

EMG.   As a technique EMG has the potential to provide a more direct insight into the neuromuscular control of the execution of sport skills than can kinematic and kinetic measures of a given limb or whole-body motion. While the inferences regarding movement control which can be made from EMG and kinematic/kinetic analyses may vary little when the body segment to be moved has low inertia or electromechanical delay is minimal, inferences about control based on kinematic/kinetic measures may be less accurate than those based on EMG in instances of high inertia and/or electromechanical resistance to movement. EMG analyses need to be done in conjunction with kinematic analyses in order to determine the changes (or lack thereof) in muscle length which accompany EMG activity. While some constraints still exist with respect to EMG recording technology, EMG analyses of most sport movements can now be performed in essentially non-restrictive ways using tasks very closely resembling those in the natural sport setting. Particular interest exists in EMG analyses in ascertaining the magnitude and timing of burst activity in individual muscles or muscle groups, the extent of co-contraction (and extraneous activity) and recruitment consistency from one repetition of the skill to the next.

EEG.   EEG essentially provides a measure of cortical activity (or literally brain waves) and a number of features within EEG are known to bear particular relevance to movement preparation and execution. Suppression of one particular brain wave frequency in spontaneous EEG (viz., the alpha wave; 8–12 Hz) is commonly used as an indicator of increased neural activation in a particular region of the brain. A number of studies of static sport tasks such as rifle shooting and golf putting (e.g., Hatfield, Landers and Ray, 1984; Salazar, Landers, Petruzzello, Crews & Kubitz, 1988; Salazar, Landers, Petruzzello, Cresw, Kubitz, & Han, 1990; Crews and Landers, 1993) have consistently revealed a pattern of decreasing left-hemisphere activation with unchanged levels of right-hemisphere activation as the moment of response execution is approached. This hemispheric asymmetry is maximal 1 s before movement commences and is not apparent either earlier in movement preparation or following the execution of the movement.

A number of smaller event-related potentials related to movement preparation also emerge when appropriate averaging of the spontaneous EEG is undertaken for the 1–2 s period immediately prior to EMG onset in movement tasks. The readiness or *Bereitschaftspotential* (N_1), the premotion positivity (P_1) and the negative motor potential (N_2) have all been linked to movement preparation although the functional significance of each of these potentials is yet far from clear (Kornhuber and Deecke, 1965; Gilden, Vaughan and Costa, 1966). Because the electrical currents which can be recorded from the scalp are necessarily small and the instrumentation requirements are substantial, EEG measures of movement preparation and execution are effectively restricted to those tasks (such as shooting and archery) where an essentially static position is held for the period leading up to movement execution.

ECG. As is the case with the EEG, the ECG may be used, in some sport tasks at least, to provide measures known to correlate with movement preparation. It has now been consistently demonstrated in a range of sport and related tasks (e.g., Hatfield, Landers, and Ray, 1987; Molander and Backman, 1989; Boutcher and Zinsser, 1990; Crews and Landers, 1993) that heart rate systematically slows by some 4–11 beats per minute in the last 3–7 s prior to movement initiation (Landers, 1994). This slowing has been shown to be unrelated to the respiratory patterns of the athletes (Lacey and Lacey, 1970) although its presence is only detectable in sports where the subject is in a static position prior to the commencement of the movement of interest. Unfortunately cardiac deceleration will be masked in any sports where the period immediately preceding the movement of interest contains any other body movement or cardio-respiratory demand.

Relationship to sports performance

EMG. Because of difficulties in faithfully reproducing exact electrode placements from one subject to another valid comparisons of the EMG characteristics of the movement patterns of expert and novice sports performers are limited; rather, reliance must be placed upon the findings from training studies in which individual subjects serve as their own controls. Studies of this type indicate that with practice and improved movement execution and control skills (a) bursts of neural activity became more discrete (b) periods of co-contraction, extraneous to the movement, are diminished and (c) there is an overall reduction in EMG activity as performers become better able to harness the reactive and gravitational forces available within the movement which provide motion essentially 'for free', without the necessity for active recruitment of muscular activity (e.g., Slater-Hammel, 1949; Kamon & Gormley, 1968; Fowler and Turvey, 1978; Newell et al., 1989).

EEG. While existing evidence on the relationship between hemispheric asymmetries in EEG activity and sports performance is very limited, the evidence which is available (Salazar et al., 1990) suggests, for the sport of archery, that best performance is associated with moderate increases in left-hemispheric alpha activity (or decreased left-hemispheric neural activation) at the time of movement initiation. There is an absence of sufficient evidence to address the possible linkage of any of the event-related potentials associated with movement preparation and subsequent sports performance.

ECG. Studies comparing the pre-shot ECG for best and worst trial performance by elite performers strongly suggest that the extent of cardiac deceleration in the period immediately preceding movement execution appears to be directly linked to performance in shooting and aiming sports

(Keast and Elliott, 1990; Landers, 1994). Best trials in performance on golf putting tasks were associated with greater pre-putt cardiac deceleration with poor trials regularly showing HR acceleration rather than deceleration (Molander and Backman, 1989; Boutcher and Zinsser, 1990; Crews and Landers, 1993). Furthermore consistent patterns of cardiac deceleration for trial to trial were also more likely to be linked to good performance than a series of trials in which pre-shot ECG activity was irregular.

Methods and implications for training

Ample demonstrations now exist to show that specific EMG (e.g., Basmajian, 1963), EEG (e.g., Landers, Han, Salazar, Petruzzello, Kubitz and Gannon, 1994) and ECG (e.g., Arps, 1994) patterns can be learnt providing suitable biofeedback information is displayed in each case (Richter-Heinrich and Miller, 1982). While as a general clinical tool biofeedback has been somewhat disappointing in its effectiveness the potential for effective biofeedback training for the learning of desired movement patterns for sport should not be under-estimated. Landers et al. (1994) have recently demonstrated that providing pre-elite archers with biofeedback training in order to learn a model of hemispheric EEG asymmetry known to be linked with superior performance can be not only effective in the sense of the pattern being acquired but can, more importantly, translate into improved sports performance. Biofeedback training of this type essentially brings to conscious control physiological units normally below the level of voluntary control. While this may be beneficial in some instances a possible concern is the potential for 'analysis causing paralysis', especially when superior performance in many sports tasks is known to be associated with attentional sets in which the performers do not consciously attend to the action to be produced or to what one is doing during the execution phase of movement (Singer and Lidor, 1993; Singer, Lidor and Cauraugh, 1993). One thing that the evidence from the preceding section would appear to be clear on in terms of its inferences for training is for the necessity for skilled athletes to develop a consistent preparatory routine. On all the electrophysiological measures examined superior performance, for self-paced motor skills at least, appears to be unambiguously linked to the development of consistent patterns of pre-movement preparations.

The attentional demands of movement execution and control

Tests and assessment

As we noted at the outset of this chapter, the ability to perform skills apparently automatically (or at least with an apparent minimum of attention and effort) is frequently identified as one of the principal hallmarks of the expert performer. The development of means of objectively assessing such a putative characteristic of movement execution and control therefore represents an important challenge for the sport scientist focused on assessing and training skilled performance. While physiological correlates of attentional demand such as pupil diameter (e.g., Beatty, 1982), heart-rate variability (e.g., Mulder and Mulder, 1981) and EEG event-related potential components like the P300 amplitude (e.g., Israel, Wickens, Chesney and Donchin, 1980) and subjective, self-report measures of cognitive workload such as the Subjective Workload Assessment technique (Eggemeier, Crabtree and LaPointe, 1983) have been used at various times to assess the automaticity of performance in various cognitive and motor skills, by far the best-established method for assessing attentional demand and workload is the dual-task method.

In the dual-task method subjects are required to perform two tasks simultaneously—a *primary* task (which is typically the movement skill of interest) and a *secondary* task, such as a probe reaction time task, the performance of which is used to make inferences about the attentional demands of the primary task. The basic logic of the dual task method is appealingly simple. In cases where subjects are instructed to give attentional priority to the primary task, poor performance on the secondary task indicates that the primary task is attentionally demanding with few attentional resources left 'free' to allocate to performance of the secondary task. Conversely, good performance on both tasks is indicative of a low attention demand for the primary task (as we might expect if the primary task is being performed in an automatic-like manner) with relatively large amounts of spare attentional resource(s) to allocate to the performance of the secondary task. While it is intuitively appealing in its simplicity the practical implementation of dual-task methods is often difficult, especially in respect to the selection of an appropriate secondary task and the control of time-sharing between the two tasks. Fuller considerations of some of the methodological assumptions and constraints with the use of dual-task methods are available elsewhere (see Ogden, Levine and Eisner, 1979; Abernethy, 1988c, 1993).

Relationship to sports performance

Training studies on cognitive skills (e.g., Spelke, Hirst and Neisser, 1976) clearly demonstrate remarkable improvements in dual task performance with practice, consistent with the notion that the control of skills becomes increasingly automatic with practice (cf. Shiffrin and Schneider, 1977). While parallel evidence from training studies with sports skills is lacking there is nevertheless a quite clear body of evidence from tasks drawn from the sports of ice hockey (Leavitt, 1979) and netball (Parker, 1981), among others, to demonstrate systematically superior secondary task performance by expert players. The study by Parker (1981) had netballers of three different skill levels performing passing and catching as the primary task (the task was comparable to a behavioural skills test which coaches might typically use to examine skill development in this sport) and a peripheral visual detection task as the secondary task. The better players significantly out-performed the less skilled players on the secondary task but not on the primary task (Figure 1.4). The superior secondary task performance of the better players suggests more automatic control of the primary passing and catching skills by them. The presence of secondary task performance differences in the absence of significant primary task differences between skill groups is noteworthy in that it demonstrates, *inter alia*, some of the potential limitations in simply using behavioural sports skill tests. Behavioural sport skill tests (comparable to the primary task alone condition) administered in isolation may not be sufficiently sensitive to tease out skill-related differences in the level of automaticity underpinning movement production. Furthermore, as a rejoinder to our earlier discussions on perceptual training, this finding demonstrates that peripheral visual awareness can be effectively increased, not by specific peripheral vision training, but simply as a consequence of improving the automaticity of control of the basic technical skills of a sport, thereby freeing attentional resources for allocation to other concurrent tasks.

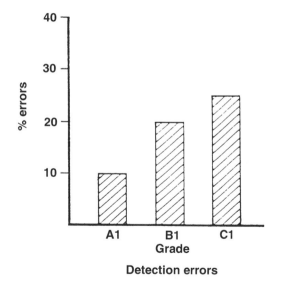

Detection errors

Figure 1.4: Secondary task performance of A, B & C grade netball players. The dependent measure is the number of errors in detecting visual stimuli presented in the subject's periphery. [Reproduced with permission from Figure 5.5 of 'Visual detection and perception in netball' by H.E. Parker in I.M. Cockerill and W.W. MacGillivary (Eds.), *Vision and Sport*. Cheltenham: Stanley Thornes, p. 49. Copyright Ian M. Cockerill and W.W. MacGillivary, 1981.]

Methods and implications for training

It is apparent from the preceding section that (a) increased automation of movement execution and control is indeed an important, distinguishing characteristic of highly skilled sports performance and that (b), extrapolating from the cognitive skills literature (especially Spelke et al., 1976), performance and long-term improvements in primary skill automatization are possible through extended periods of dual-task practice. These observations clearly suggest that there may be considerable value in employing progressively more demanding dual-task conditions in practice as a means of providing an ongoing stimulus for the automation of primary task movement control (Schneider, 1985). As skill development appears to be an ongoing process even for expert performers (Crossman, 1959; Ericsson, et al., 1993) continued attentional overload in practice may be a valuable means of facilitating continuous improvements in the movement execution and control skills of athletes. Such progressive overload could be achieved through either the addition of a more demanding secondary task or, if necessary, the addition of a third concurrent task. Examples of the application of such training methods (or empirical examinations of the effectiveness of such methods) are currently lacking from the motor skills literature.

SOME CONCLUDING REMARKS

The skilled perceptual–motor performances of elite athletes provide wonderful examples of the incredible movement capabilities of humans and of the extent to which intensive training can result in skill mastery. Underlying the elegant simplicity and apparent ease of expert sports performance is a level of complexity that sports scientists are only beginning to appreciate. Skilled sports performance results not simply from muscular effort but from a bewildering array of perceptual, decision-making and movement execution and control processes, each refined and coupled to others as a consequence of task-specific practice. Our purpose in writing this chapter has not only been to alert readers to the level of complexity and elaboration inherent in skilled sports performance but to also indicate areas of untapped or underexploited potential for the further enhancement of sports performance. In so doing we hope that we have not only provided clear evidence of the applicability of much of the current and older motor learning and control literature to sports training but also provided a sense of the limitations in knowledge that exist in many areas and the great prospects for improved practice that future skill acquisition research may provide.

REFERENCES

Abernethy, B. (1985) Cue usage in 'open' motor skills: a review of the available procedures, in *Motor Memory and Control: The Otago Symposium* (Eds. D.G. Russell and B. Abernethy), pp. 110–122, Human Performance Associates, Dunedin, New Zealand.

Abernethy, B. (1986) Enhancing sports performance through clinical and experimental optometry, *Clinical and Experimental Optometry*, **69**, 189–196.

Abernethy, B. (1987) Selective attention in fast ball sports. II: Expert–novice differences, *Australian Journal of Science and Medicine in Sport*, **19**(4), 7–16.

Abernethy, B. (1988a) Visual search in sport and ergonomics: its relationship to selective attention and performer expertise, *Human Performance*, **1**, 205–235.

Abernethy, B. (1988b) The effects of age and expertise upon perceptual skill development in a racquet sport, *Research Quarterly for Exercise and Sport*, **59**, 210–221.

Abernethy, B. (1988c) Dual-task methodology and motor skills research: some applications and methodological constraints, *Journal of Human Movement Studies*, **14**, 101–132.

Abernethy, B. (1990a) Anticipation in squash: differences in advance cue utilization between expert and novice players, *Journal of Sport Sciences*, **8**, 17–34.

Abernethy, B. (1990b) Expertise, visual search, and information pick-up in squash, *Perception*, **19**, 63–77.

Abernethy, B. (1991) Visual search strategies and decision-making in sport, *International Journal of Sport Psychology*, **22**, 189–210.

Abernethy, B. (1993) Searching for the minimal essential information for skilled perception and action, *Psychological Research*, **55**, 131–138.

Abernethy, B. (1994) The nature of expertise, in *International Perspectives on Sport and Exercise Psychology* (Eds. S. Serpa, J. Alves, and V. Pataco), pp. 57–68. FIT Press, Morgantown, VA.

Abernethy, B., Burgess-Limerick, R.J. and Parks, S. (1994) Contrasting approaches to the study of motor expertise, *Quest*, **46**, 186–198.

Abernethy, B. and Neal, R.J. (1990) *Perceptual–Motor Characteristics of Elite Performers in Aiming Sports*, Report to the Australian Sports Commission, 180pp.

Abernethy, B., Neal, R. J., Engstrom, C., and Koning, P. (1993) What makes the expert sports performer better than novice? *Sports Coach*, **16**(2), 31–37.

Abernethy, B., Neal, R.J. and Koning, P. (1994) Visual–perceptual and cognitive differences between expert, intermediate, and novice snooker players, *Applied Cognitive Psychology*, **8**, 185–211.

Abernethy, B. and Russell, D.G. (1983) Skill in tennis: considerations for talent identification and skill development, *Australian Journal of Sport Science*, **3**, 3–12.

Abernethy, B. and Russell, D.G. (1984) Advance cue utilisation by skilled cricket batsmen, *Australian Journal of Science and Medicine in Sport*, **16**(2), 2–10.

Abernethy, B. and Russell, D.G. (1987a) Expert–novice differences in an applied selective attention task, *Journal of Sport Psychology*, **9**, 326–345.

Abernethy, B. and Russell, D.G. (1987b) The relationship between expertise and visual search strategy in a racquet sport, *Human Movement Science*, **6**, 283–319.

Abernethy, B. and Sparrow, W.A. (1992) The rise and fall of dominant paradigms in motor behavior research, in *Approaches to the Study of Motor Control and Learning* (Ed. J.J. Summers), pp. 3–45, Elsevier, Amsterdam.

Abernethy, B. and Wollstein, J.R. (1989) Improving anticipation in racquet sports, *Sports Coach*, **12**, 15–18.

Abernethy, B. and Wood, J.M. (1992) *An Assessment of the Effectiveness of Selected Visual Training Programs in Enhancing Sports Performance*, Report to the Australian Sports Commission, 181pp.

Adam, J.J. and Wilberg, R.B. (1992) Individual differences in visual information processing rate and the prediction of performances in team sports: a preliminary investigation, *Journal of Sport Sciences*, **10**, 261–273.

Adams, G.L. (1965) Effect of eye dominance on baseball batting, *Research Quarterly*, **36**, 3–9.

Alain, C. and Girardin, Y. (1978) The use of uncertainty in racquet–ball competition, *Canadian Journal of Applied Sport Sciences*, **3**, 240–243.

Alain, C. and Proteau, L. (1980) Decision making in sport, in *Psychology of Motor Behavior and Sport, 1979* (Eds. C.H. Nadeau, W.R. Halliwell, K.M. Newell and G.C. Roberts), pp. 465–477, Human Kinetics, Champaign, IL.

Allard, F. and Burnett, N. (1985) Skill in sport, *Canadian Journal of Psychology*, **39**, 294–312.

Allard, F., Graham, S. and Paarsalu, M.E. (1980) Perception in sport: basketball, *Journal of Sport Psychology*, **2**, 14–21.

Allard, F. and Starkes, J.L. (1980) Perception in sport: volleyball, *Journal of Sport Psychology*, **2**, 22–33.

American Alliance for Health, Physical Education, Recreation and Dance (1989). AAHPERD Physical Test: The AAHPERD Guide to Physical Fitness Education and Assessment, Reston, VA.

Arps, K.P. (1994) The Effects of Phasic Heart Rate Control on Golf Putting Performance, Unpublished Master's thesis, Arizona State University.

Bahill, A.T. and Karnavas, W.J. (1983) The perceptual illusion of baseball's rising fastball and breaking curve ball, *Journal of Experimental Psychology: Human Perception and Performance*, **19**, 3–14.

Banister, H. and Blackburn, J.M. (1931) An eye factor affecting proficiency at ball games, *British Journal of Psychology*, **21**, 382–384.

Bard, C. and Fleury, M. (1976) Analysis of visual search activity in sport problem situations, *Journal of Human Movement Studies*, **3**, 214–222.

Bard, C. and Fleury, M. (1981) Considering eye movement as a predictor of attainment, in *Vision and Sport* (Eds. I.M. Cockerill and W.W. MacGillivary), pp. 28–41, Stanley Thornes, Cheltenham.

Barrow, H.M. and McGee, R. (1971) *A Practical Approach to Measurement in Physical Education* (2nd edn), Lea & Febiger, Philadelphia.

Bartlett, F.C. (1947) The measurement of human skill, *British Medical Journal,* June 14, 835–838, 877–880.

Basmajian, J.V. (1963) Control and training of individual motor units, *Science*, **141**, 440–441.

Baughman, L.G. (1968) Two methods of determining the effects of sighting dominance on baseball hitting, Unpublished MA Thesis, University of Maryland.

Beatty, J. (1982) Task-evoked pupillary responses, processing load, and the structure of processing resources, *Psychological Bulletin*, **91**, 276–292.

Beals, R.P., Mayyasi, A.M., Templeton, A.E. and Johnston, W.L. (1971) The relationship between basketball shooting performance and certain visual attributes, *American Journal of Optometry and Archives of the American Academy of Optometry*, **48**, 585–590.

Beitel, P. (1980) Multivariate relationships among visual-perceptual attributes and gross motor tasks with different environmental demands, *Journal of Motor Behavior*, **12**, 29–40.

Bhanot, J.L. and Sidhu, L.S. Reaction time of Indian hockey players with reference to three levels of participation, *Journal of Sports Medicine and Physical Fitness*, **19**, 199–204.

Blundell, N.L. (1984) Critical visual–perceptual attributes of championship level tennis players, in *Proceedings of the VII Commonwealth and International Conference on Sport, Physical Education, Recreation and Dance, Vol 7, Kinesiological Sciences* (Eds. M.L. Howell and B.D. Wilson), pp. 51–59, University of Queensland, Brisbane, Qld.

Borg, G.A.V. (1962) *Physical Performance and Perceived Exertion*, Gleerup, Lund.

Borg, G.A.V. and Linderholm, H. (1967) Perceived exertion and pulse rate during graded exercise in various age groups, *Acta Medicine Scandinavia*, **472**, 194–206.

Borgeaud, P. and Abernethy, B. (1987) Skilled perception in volleyball defence, *Journal of Sport Psychology*, **9**, 400–406.

Boutcher, S.H. and Zinsser, N.W. (1990) Cardiac deceleration of elite and beginning golfers during putting, *Journal of Sport and Exercise Psychology*, **12**, 37–47.

Burke, T.R. (1972) Athletes, athletic performance, and conditions in the environment, *Quest*, **17**, 56–60.

Burroughs, W.A. (1984) Visual simulation training of baseball batters, *International Journal of Sports Psychology*, **15**, 117–126.

Carrière, L. (1978) Les effets de la competition des réponses et du contexte sur la prise de décision dan des situations problèmes. [The effects of response competition and context on the speed of responding in problem situations], in *Motor Learning, Sport Psychology, Pedagogy and Didactics* (Eds. F. Landry, and W.A.R. Orban), pp. 77–84, Symposia Specialists, Quebec.

Chamberlain, D.J. and Coelho, A.J. (1993) The perceptual side of action: decision-making in sport, in *Cognitive Issues in Motor Expertise* (Eds. J.L. Starkes and F. Allard), pp. 135–157, North-Holland, Amsterdam.

Chase, W.G. and Simon, H.A. (1973) The mind's eye in chess, in *Visual Information Processing* (Ed. W.G. Chase), pp. 215–282, Academic Press, New York.

Chi, M.T.H., Glaser, R. and Farr, M.J. (Eds) (1988) *The Nature of Expertise*, Erlbaum, Hillsdale, NJ.

Christina, R.W., Barresi, J.V. and Shaffner, P. (1990) The development of response selection accuracy in a football linebacker using video training. *The Sport Psychologist*, **4**, 11–17.

Cockerill, I.M. (1981a) Distance estimation and sports performance, in *Vision and Sport* (Eds. I.M. Cockerill and W.W. MacGillivary), pp. 116–125, Stanley Thornes, Cheltenham.

Cockerill, I.M. (1981b) Peripheral vision and hockey, in *Vision and Sport* (Eds. I.M. Cockerill and W.W. MacGillivary), pp. 54–63, Stanley Thornes, Cheltenham.

Coffey, B. and Reichow, A.W. (1987) Guidelines for screening and testing the athlete's visual system—Part III, *Curriculum II (AOA)*, **59**(7), 355–368.

Cohen, J. and Dearnaley, E.J. (1962) Skill and judgement of footballers in attempting to score goals, *British Journal of Psychology*, **53**, 71–88.

Cohn, T.E. and Chaplik, D.D. (1991) Visual training in soccer, *Perceptual and Motor Skills*, **72**, 1238.

Colavita, F.B. (1974) Human sensory dominance, *Perception and Psychophysics*, **16**, 409–412.

Crews, D.J. and Landers, D.M. (1993) Electroencephalographic measures of attentional patterns prior to the golf putt, *Medicine and Science in Sports and Exercise*, **25**, 116–126.

Crossman, E.R.F.W. (1959) A theory of the acquisition of speed skill, *Ergonomics*, **2**, 153–166.

Davis, R. (1959) The role of 'attention' in the psychological refractory period, *Quarterly Journal of Experimental Psychology*, **11**, 211–220.

Day, L.J. (1980) Anticipation in junior tennis, in *Proceedings of the International Symposium on the Effective Teaching of Racquet Sports* (Eds. J. Groppel and R. Sears), pp. 107–116, University of Illinois, Champaign, IL.

Deary, I.J. and Mitchell, H. (1989) Inspection time and high-speed ball games, *Perception*, **18**, 789–792.

de Groot, A.D. (1966) Perception and memory versus thought, in *Problem solving research, methods and theory* (Ed. B. Kleinmuntz), pp. 19–50, Wiley, New York.

Del Rey, P., Whitehurst, M., Wughalter, E. and Barnwell, J. (1983) Contextual interference and experience in acquisition and transfer, *Perceptual and Motor Skills*, **57**, 241–242.

Doyle, A.J.R., Elliott, J.M. and Connolly, K.J. (1986) Measurement of kinaesthetic sensitivity, *Developmental Medicine and Child Neurology*, **28**, 188–193.

Duda, R.O. and Shortliffe, E.H. (1983) Expert systems research, *Science*, **220**, 261–268.

Egan, D.E. and Schwartz, E.J. (1979) Chunking in recall of symbolic drawings, *Memory and Cognition*, **7**, 149–158.

Eggemeier, F.T., Crabtree, M.S. and La Pointe, P.A. (1983) The effect of delayed effort on subjective ratings of mental workload, *Proceedings of the Human Factors Society*, **27**, 139–143.

Elliott, D., Zuberec, S., and Milgram, P. (1994) The effects of periodic visual occlusion on ball catching, *Journal of Motor Behavior*, **26**, 113–122.

Ericsson, K.A., Krampe, R.T. and Tesch-Ramer, C. (1993) The role of deliberate practice in acquisition of expert performance, *Psychological Review*, **100**, 363–406.

Fendick, M. and Westheimer, G. (1983) Effects of practise and the separation of test targets on foveal and peripheral stereoacuity, *Vision Research*, **23**, 145–159.

Fowler, C.A. and Turvey, M.T. (1978) Skill acquisition: an event approach with special reference to searching for the optimum of a function of several variables, in *Information processing in motor control and learning* (Ed. G.E. Stelmach), pp. 1–40, Academic Press, New York.

Franks, I.M., Goodman, D. and Miller, G. (1983) Analysis of performance: qualitative or quantitative? *Science Periodical of Research and Technology in Sport*, March.

French, K.E. and Thomas, J.R. (1987) The relation of knowledge development to children's basketball performance, *Journal of Sport Psychology*, **9**, 15–32.

Gandevia, S.C. and Burke, D. (1992) Does the nervous system depend on kinesthetic information to control natural limb movements? *Behavioral and Brain Sciences*, **15**, 614–632.

Gandevia, S.C. and McCloskey, D.I. (1976) Joint sense, muscle sense and their combination as position sense, measured at the digital interphalangeal joint of the middle finger, *Journal of Physiology*, **260**, 387–407.

Garland, D.J. and Barry, J.R. (1990) Sport expertise: the cognitive advantage, *Perceptual and Motor Skills*, **70**, 1299–1314.

Garner, A.I. (1977) An overlooked problem: athlete's visual needs, *Physician and Sports Medicine*, **5**, 74–82.

Gavriysky, V. St. (1969) The colours and colour vision in sport, *Journal of Sports Medicine and Physical Fitness*, **9**, 49–53.

Gavriysky, V. St. (1970) Vision and sporting results, *Journal of Sports Medicine and Physical Fitness*, **10**, 260–264.

Gibson, J.J. (1979) *The Ecological Approach to Visual Perception*, Houghton-Mifflin, Boston, MA.

Gilden, L., Vaughan, H.G., Jr. and Costa, L.D. (1966) Summated human EEG potentials with voluntary movement, *Electroencephalography and Clinical Neurophysiology*, **20**, 433–438.

Glencross, D.J. and Cibich, B.J. (1977) A decision analysis of games skills, *Australian Journal of Sports Medicine*, **9**, 72–75.

Glencross, D.J., Whiting, H.T.A. and Abernethy, B. (1994) Motor control, motor learning and the acquisition of skill: historical trends and future directions, *International Journal of Sport Psychology*, **25**, 32–52.

Gottsdanker, R. and Stelmach, G.E. (1971) The persistence of psychological refractoriness, *Journal of Motor Behavior*, **3**, 301–312.

Goulet, C., Bard, C. and Fleury, M. (1989) Expertise differences in preparing to return a tennis serve: a visual information processing approach, *Journal of Sport and Exercise Psychology*, **11**, 382–398.

Goulet, C., Talbot, S., Drouin, D., and Trudel, P. (1988) Effect of structured ice hockey training on scores on field-dependence/independence, *Perceptual and Motor Skills*, **66**, 175–181.

Graybiel, A., Jokl, E. and Trapp, C. (1955) Russian studies of vision in relation to physical activity and sports, *Research Quarterly*, **26**, 480–485.

Graydon, J.K. and Townsend, J. (1984) Proprioceptive and visual feedback in the learning of two gross motor skills, *International Journal of Sport Psychology*, **15**, 227–235.

Guthrie, E.R. (1952) *The Psychology of Learning*, Harper & Row, New York.

Handford, C. and Williams, M. (1992) Expert–novice differences in the use of advanced visual cues in volleyball blocking (abstract), *Canadian Journal of Sports Sciences*, **9**, 443–444.

Harper, W.S., Landers, D.M. and Wang, M.Q. (1985) The role of visual training exercises in visual abilities and shooting performance, *Paper presented at the Annual Conference of the North American Society for the Psychology of Sport and Physical Activity.*

Harrison, B. and Reilly, R.E. (1975) *Visiondynamics: Baseball Method*, Visiondynamics, California, Lacuna.

Haskins, M.J. (1965) Development of a response recognition training film in tennis, *Perceptual and Motor Skills*, 21, 207–211.

Hatfield, B.D., Landers, D.M. and Ray, W.J. (1984) Cognitive processes during self-paced motor performance: an electroencephalographic profile of skilled marksmen, *Journal of Sport Psychology*, **6**, 42–59.

Hatfield, B. D., Landers, D.M. and Ray, W.J. (1987) Cardiovascular CNS interactions during a self-paced, intentional state: elite marksmanship performance, *Psychophysiology*, **24**, 542–549.

Helsen, W. and Pauwels, J.M. (1993a) The relationship between expertise and visual information processing in sport, in *Cognitive Issues in Motor Expertise* (Eds. J.L. Starkes and F.A. Allard), pp. 109–134, North Holland, Amsterdam.

Helsen, W. and Pauwels, J. (1993b) A cognitive approach to skilled performance and perception in sport, in *Perception and Cognition* (Eds. G. d'Ydewalle and J. van Rensbergen), pp. 127–139, Elsevier, Amsterdam.

Henry, F. M. (1961) Reaction time–movement time correlations, *Perceptual and Motor Skills*, **12**, 63–66.

Hick, W.E. (1952) On the rate of gain of information, *Quarterly Journal of Experimental Psychology*, **4**, 11–26.

Higgins, J.R. and Spaeth, R. (1972) Relationship between consistency of movement and environmental condition, *Quest*, **XVII**, 61–69.

Hoare, D. and Larkin, D. (1991) Kinaesthetic abilities of clumsy children, *Developmental Medicine and Child Neurology*, **24**, 461–471.

Hofsten, C. von (1987) Catching, in *Perspectives on Perception and Action* (Eds. H. Heuer and A.F. Sanders), pp. 33–46, Erlbaum, Hillsdale, NJ.

Holding, D.H. (1985) *The Psychology of Chess Skill*, Erlbaum, Hillsdale, NJ.

Howard, J.H. and Kerst, S.M. (1981) Memory and Perception of Cartographic Information for Familiar and Unfamiliar Environments, *Human Factors*, **23**, 495–504.

Howell, M.L. (1956) Use of force–time graphs for performance analysis in facilitating motor learning, *Research Quarterly*, **27**, 12–22.

Hubbard, M. (1994) Simulating sensitive dynamic control of a bobsled, *Proceedings of the Mathematics and Computers in Sport Conference*, July, 1994, pp. 1–6, Bond University, Australia.

Hyman, R. (1953) Stimulus information as a determinant of reaction time, *Journal of Experimental Psychology*, **45**, 188–196.

Ingle, D., Schneider, G., Trevarthen, C. and Held, R. (1967) Locating and identifying: two modes of visual processing (a symposium), *Psychologische Forschung*, **31**, (1,4), 42–43.

Isaacs, L.D. (1981) Relationship between depth perception and basketball-shooting performance over a competitive season, *Perceptual and Motor Skills*, **53**, 554.

Isaacs, L.D. and Finch, A.E. (1983) Anticipatory timing of beginning and intermediate tennis players, *Perceptual and Motor Skills*, **57**, 451–454.

Ishihara, S. (1977) *Tests of Colour Blindness*, Kanehara Shuppan Company, Tokyo.

Israel, J.B., Wickens, C.D., Chesney, G.L. and Donchin, E. (1980) The event-related brain potential as an index of display monitoring workload, *Human Factors*, **22**, 211–224.

Johnson, C.A. and Leibowitz, H.W. (1974) Practise, refractive error and feedback as factors influencing peripheral motion thresholds, *Perception and Psychophysics*, **15**, 276–280.

Jones, C.M. (1974) Reaction timing and the need to 'read' tennis, *Sport and Recreation*, **15**(3), 23, 25–28.

Jones, C.M. and Miles, T.R. (1978) Use of advance cues in predicting the flight of a lawn tennis ball, *Journal of Human Movement Studies*, **4**, 231–235.

Jones, M.G. (1972) Perceptual characteristics and athletic performance, in *Readings in Sports Psychology* (Ed. H.T.A. Whiting), pp. 96–115, Henry Kimpton, London.

Jones, M.G. (1973) Personality and perceptual characteristics, in *Personality and Performance in Physical Education and Sport* (Eds. H.T.A. Whiting, K. Hardman, L.B. Hendry, and M.G. Jones), pp. 11–42, Henry Kimpton, London.

Kamon, E. and Gormley, J. (1968) Muscular activity pattern for skilled performance and during learning of a horizontal bar exercise, *Ergonomics*, **11**, 345–357.

Karlin, L. and Kestenbaum, R. (1968) Effects of number of alternatives on psychological refractory period, *Quarterly Journal of Experimental Psychology*, **20**, 167–178.

Keast, D. and Elliott, B. (1990) Fine body movements and the cardiac cycle in archery, *Journal of Sports Sciences*, **8**, 203–213.

Keele, S.W. (1968) Movement control in skilled motor performance, *Psychological Bulletin*, **70**, 387–403.

Keller, L.F. (1942) Relation of 'quickness of bodily movement' to success in athletics, *Research Quarterly*, **13**, 146–155.

Kelso, J.A.S. (1981) Contrasting perspectives on order and regulation in movement, in *Attention and Performance IX* (Eds. J. Long and A. Baddeley), pp. 437–458. Erlbaum, Hillsdale, NJ.

Keogh, J.F. and Sugden, D.A. (1985) *Movement Skill Development*, Macmillan, New York.

Konzag, G. (1983) Diagnosis of action time in connection with sports-relevant cognitive components of players in sport, *Theory and Practice of Physical Culture*, **32**(8), 592–597.

Kornhuber, H.H., and Deecke, L. (1965) Hirnpotentialänderungen bei Willkürbewegungen und passiven Bewegungen des Menschen: Bereitschaftspotential und Reafferente Potentiale, *Pflügers Archiv für die gesammte Physiologie*, **248**, 1–17.

Lacey, B.C. and Lacey, J.I. (1970) Some autonomic–central nervous system interrelationships, in *Physiological correlates of emotion* (Ed. P. Block), pp. 50–83), Academic Press, New York.

Lackner, J.R. (1988) Some proprioceptive influences on the perceptual representation of body shape and orientation, *Brain*, **111**, 281–297.

Landers, D.M. (1988) Improving motor skills, in *Enhancing Human Performance: Issues, Theories and Techniques* (Eds. D. Druckman and J.A. Swets), pp. 61–101, National Academy Press, Washington, DC.

Landers, D.M. (1994) Psychophysiology of sports performance, *Abstracts of the 1994 International Conference on Science and Medicine in Sport*, Sports Medicine Australia, Canberra.

Landers, D.M., Han, M.W., Salazar, W. Petruzzello S.J., Kubitz, K.A. and Gannon, T. (1994) Effects of learning on electroencephalographic and electrocardiographic patterns in novice archers, *International Journal of Sports Psychology*, **25**, 56–70.

Laszlo, J.I. and Bairstow, P.J. (1980) The measurement of kinaesthetic sensitivity in children and adults, *Developmental Medicine and Child Neurology*, **22**, 454–464.

Leavitt, J.L. (1979) Cognitive demands of skating and stick handling in ice hockey, *Canadian Journal of Applied Sport Sciences*, **4**, 46–55.

Lee, D.N. and Aronson, E. (1974) Visual proprioceptive control of standing in human infants, *Perception and Psychophysics*, **15**, 529–532.

Lee, D.N. and Lishman, J.R. (1975) Visual proprioceptive control of stance, *Journal of Human Movement Studies*, **1**, 87–95.

Leibowitz, H.W. and Post, R.B. (1982) The two modes of processing concept and some implications, in *Organization and Representation in Perception* (Ed. J. Beck), pp. 343–363, Erlbaum, Hillsdale, NJ.

Leibowitz, H.W., Vinger, P.F. and Landers, D.M. (1989) *Can Visual Training Improve Athletic Performance?* Report to the U.S. Olympic Committee.

Londerlee, B.R., Jr (1967) Effect of training with motion pictures versus flash cards upon football play recognition, *Research Quarterly*, **38**, 202–207.

Lord, R. and Hulme, C. (1988) Perceptual judgements of normal and clumsy children, *Developmental Medicine and Child Neurology*, **29**, 250–257.

Lotter, W.S. (1960) Interrelationships among reaction times and speeds of movement in different limbs, *Research Quarterly*, **31**, 147–155.

Low, F.N. (1946) Some characteristics of peripheral visual performance, *American Journal of Physiological Optics*, **146**, 573–584.

Lynagh, M. (1987) The role of internal and external sensory cues in the perception of effort, Unpublished Honours Thesis, The University of Queensland.

MacGillivary, W.W. (1979) Perceptual style and ball skill acquisition, *Research Quarterly*, **50**, 222–229.

MacGillivary, W.W. (1981) The contribution of perceptual style to human performance, in *Vision and Sport* (Eds. I.M. Cockerill & W.W. MacGillivary), pp. 8–16, Stanley Thornes, London.

McKee, S.P. and Westheimer, G. (1978) Improvement in Vernier acuity with practise, *Perception and Psychophysics*, **24**, 258–262.

McLeod, P.N. (1987) Visual reaction time and high-speed ball games, *Perception*, **16**, 49–59.

McLeod, P.N. and Dienes, Z. (1993) Running to catch the ball, *Nature*, **362**, 23.

McLeod, W. (1991) Effects of Eyerobics visual skills training on selected performance measures of female varsity soccer players, *Perceptual and Motor Skills*, **72**, 863–866.

McLeod, W. and Hansen, E. (1989a) The effects of Eyerobics visual skills training program on hand–eye coordination (abstract), *Canadian Journal of Sports Sciences*, **14**, 127.

McLeod, W. and Hansen, E. (1989b) Effects of the Eyerobics visual skills training program on static balance performance of male and female subjects, *Perceptual and Motor Skills*, **69**, 1123–1126.

Matthews, P.B.C. (1982) Where does Sherrington's muscular sense originate? Muscle, joints, corollary discharges? *Annual Review of Neuroscience*, **5**, 189–218.

Meijer, O.G. and Roth, K. (Eds.) (1988) *Complex Movement Behavior: 'The' Motor-Action Controversy*, North-Holland, Amsterdam.

Milgram, P. (1987) A spectacle-mounted liquid-crystal tachistoscope, *Behavior Research Methods, Instruments and Computers*, **19**, 449–456.

Miller, D.M. (1960) The relation between some visual perceptual factors and the degree of success realized by sport performers, *Dissertation Abstract International*, **21**, 1455–A.

Miller, J. (1982) Discrete versus continuous stage models of human information processing: in search of partial output, *Journal of Experimental Psychology: Human Perception and Performance*, **8**, 273–296.

Miller, J. (1983) Can response preparation begin before stimulus recognition finishes? *Journal of Experimental Psychology: Human Perception and Performance*, **9**, 161–182.

Millslagle, D.G. (1988) Visual perception, recognition, recall and mode of visual search control in basketball involving novice and inexperienced basketball players, *Journal of Sport Behavior*, **11**, 32–44.

Mizusawa, K., Sweeting, R.L., and Knouse, S.B. (1983) Comparative studies of color fields, visual acuity fields, and movement perception limits among varsity athletes and non-varsity groups, *Perceptual and Motor Skills*, **56**, 887–892.

Moberg, E. (1983) The role of cutaneous afferents in position sense, kinaesthesia and motor function of the hand, *Brain*, **106**, 1–19.

Molander, B. and Backman, L. (1989) Age differences in heart rate patterns during concentration in a precision sport: implications for attentional functioning, *Journal of Gerontology: Psychological Sciences*, **44**, 80–87.

Mowbray, G.H. and Rhoades, M.V. (1959) On the reduction of choice reaction times with practice, *Quarterly Journal of Experimental Psychology*, **11**, 16–23.

Morris, G.S.D. and Kreighbaum, E. (1977) Dynamic visual acuity of varsity women volleyball and basketball players, *Research Quarterly*, **48**, 480–483.

Mulder, G. and Mulder, L.J.M. (1981) Information processing and cardiovascular control, *Psychophysiology*, **118**, 392–401.

Neisser, U. (1967) *Cognitive Psychology*, Appleton-Century-Crofts, New York.

Neisser, U. (1976) *Cognition and Reality: Principles and Implications of Cognitive Psychology*, Freeman, San Francisco.

Newell, K.M., Kugler, P.N., Emmerik, R.E.A. van, and McDonald, P.V. (1989) Search strategies and the acquisition of coordination, in *Perspectives on the Coordination of Movement* (Ed. S.A. Wallace), pp. 85–122.

Newell, K.M., Sparrow, W.A., and Quinn, J.T. (1985) Kinetic information feedback for learning isometric tasks, *Journal of Human Movement Studies*, **11**, 113–123.

Newell, K.M. and Walter, C.B. (1981) Kinematic and kinetic parameters as information feedback in motor skill acquisition, *Journal of Human Movement Studies*, **7**, 235–254.

Ogden, G.D., Levine, J.M., and Eisner, E.J. (1979) Measurement of workload by secondary tasks, *Human Factors*, **21**, 529–548.

Olsen, E.A. (1956) Relationship between psychological capacities and success in college athletics, *Research Quarterly*, **27**, 79–89.

Paillard, J. and Brouchon, M. (1968) Active and passive movements in the calibration of position sense, in *The Neuropsychology of Spatially Oriented Behavior* (Ed. S.J. Freeman), pp. 37–55, Dorsey, Homewood, IL.

Papin, J-P. (1984) Use of the NAC eye mark recorder to study visual strategies of military aircraft pilots, in *Theoretical and Applied Aspects of Eye Movement Research* (Eds. A.G. Gale and F. Johnson), North-Holland, Amsterdam.

Pargman, D., Schreiber, L.E. and Stein, F. (1974) Field dependence of selected athletic sub-groups, *Medicine and Science in Sports*, **6**, 283–286.

Parker, H. (1981) Visual detection and perception in netball, in *Vision and Sport* (Eds. I.M. Cockerill and W.W. MacGillivary), pp. 42–53, Stanley Thornes, Cheltenham.

Petrakis, E. (1979) Perceptual style of varsity tennis players, *Perceptual and Motor Skills*, **48**, 266.

Pierson, W.R. (1956) Comparison of fencers and nonfencers by psychomotor, space perception and anthropometric measures, *Research Quarterly*, **27**(1), 90–96.

Pierson, W.R. (1959) The relationship of movement time and reaction time for childhood to senility, *Research Quarterly*, **30**, 227–231.

Posner, M.I., Nissen, M.J., and Klein, R.M. (1976) Visual dominance: an information-processing account of its origins and significance, *Psychological Review*, **83**, 157–170.

Potegal, M. (1982) Vestibular and neostriatal contributions to spatial orientation, in *Spatial Abilities: Development and Physiological Foundations* (Ed. M. Potegal), pp. 361–388, Academic, New York.

Prablanc, C., Echallier, J.F. and Jeannerod, M. (1979) Optimal response of eye and hand motor systems in pointing at a visual target, in spatio-temporal characteristics of arm and hand movements and their relationships when varying the amount of information, *Biological Cybernetics*, **35**, 113–124.

Rasch, P.J. and Pierson, W.R. (1963) Reaction and movement time of experienced Karateka, *Research Quarterly*, **34**, 242–243.

Régnier, G. and Salmela, J.H. (1980) Perceptual variables and gymnastic performance: developmental considerations, in *Motor Learning and Biomechanical Factors in Sport* (Eds. P. Klavora, and J. Flowers), pp. 218–238, University of Toronto, Toronto, Ontario.

Reichow, A.W. and Stern, N.S. (1986) Sports vision: a review of the literature, *Curriculum II (AOA)*, **59**(2), 83–91.

Revien, L. (1987) *Eyerobics* (Videotape), Visual Skills, Great Neck, NY.

Revien, L. and Gabor, M. (1981) *Sports Vision. Dr. Revien's Eye Exercises for Athletes*, Workman Publishing, New York.

Richter-Heinrich, E. and Miller, N. (Eds.) (1982) *Biofeedback: Basic Problems and Clinical Applications*, North-Holland, Amsterdam.

Ripoll, H. and Fleurance, P. (1988) What does keeping one's eye on the ball mean? *Ergonomics*, **31**, 647–654.

Roberton, M.A. (1982) Describing 'stages' within and across motor tasks, in *The Development of Movement Control and Co-ordination* (Eds. J.A.S. Kelso and J.E. Clark), pp. 293–307, Wiley, Chichester, UK.

Roloff, L.L. (1953) Kinesthesis in relation to the learning of selected motor skills, *Research Quarterly*, **24**, 210–217.

Rothstein, A.L. (1986) The perceptual process, vision and motor skills, in *The Psychology of Motor Behavior: Development, Control, Learning and Performance* (Eds. L.D. Zaichkowsky and C.Z. Fuchs), pp. 191–214, Mouvement, Ithaca, NY.

Safrit, M.J. (1981) *Evaluation in Physical Education* (2nd edn), Prentice-Hall, Englewood Cliffs, NJ.

Sailor, A.L. (1973) Effect of practice on expansion of peripheral vision, *Perception and Motor Skills*, **37**, 720–722.

Salazar, W., Landers, D.M., Petruzzello, S.J., Crews, D.J. and Kubitz, K. (1988) The effects of physical/cognitive load on electrocortical patterns preceding response execution in archery, *Psychophysiology*, **25**, 478–479.

Salazar, W., Landers, D.M., Petruzzello, S.J., Crews, D.J., Kubitz, K. and Han, M.W. (1990) Hemispheric asymmetry, cardiac response, and performance in elite archers, *Research Quarterly for Exercise and Sport*, **61**, 351–359.

Salmela, J.H. and Fiorito, P. (1979) Visual cues in ice hockey goaltending, *Canadian Journal of Applied Sport Sciences*, **4**, 56–59.

Sanderson, F.H. (1981) Visual acuity and sports performance, in *Vision and Sport* (Eds. I.M. Cockerill and W.W. MacGillivary), pp. 64–79, Stanley Thornes, Cheltenham.

Sanderson, F.H. and Whiting, H.T.A. (1974) Dynamic visual acuity and performance in a catching task, *Journal of Motor Behavior*, **6**, 87–94.

Sanderson, F.H. and Whiting, H.T.A. (1978) Dynamic visual acuity: a possible factor in catching performance, *Journal of Motor Behavior*, **10**, 7–14.

Saugstad, P. and Lie, I. (1964) Training of peripheral visual acuity, *Scandinavian Journal of Physiology*, **5**, 218–224.

Schmidt, R.A. (1975) A schema theory of discrete motor skill learning, *Psychological Review*, **82**, 225–260.

Schmidt, R.A. (1980) Past and future issues in motor programming, *Research Quarterly for Exercise and Sport*, **51**, 122–140.

Schmidt, R.A. (1988) *Motor Control and Learning: A Behavioral Emphasis* (2nd edn). Human Kinetics, Champaign, IL.

Schneider, G.E. (1969) Two visual systems, *Science*, **163**, 895–902.

Schneider, W. (1985) Towards a model of attention and the development of automatic processing, in *Attention and Performance XI* (Eds. M.I. Posner, and O. Marin), pp. 475–492, Erlbaum, Hillsdale, NJ.

Schöner, G. and Kelso, J.A.S. (1988) A synergetic theory of environmentally specified and learned patterns of movement coordination. 1. Relative phase dynamics. *Biological Cybernetics*, **58**, 71–80.

Seiderman, A. and Schneider, S. (1983) *The Athletic Eye: Improved Sports Performance Through Visual Training*, Hearst Books, New York.

Sherman, A. (1980) Overview of research information regarding vision and sports, *Journal of the American Optometric Association*, **51**, 661–666.

Shiffrin, R.M. and Schneider, W. (1977) Controlled and automatic human information processing: II. Perceptual learning, automatic attending, and a general theory, *Psychological Review*, **84**, 127–190.

Shulman, G.L., Remington, R.W. and McLean, J.P. (1979) Moving attention through visual space, *Journal of Experimental Psychology: Human Perception and Performance*, **5**, 522–526.

Sinclair, G.D. (1980) Speed of response characteristics of goalkeepers from Pee Wee through national hockey leagues, in *Psychology of Motor Behavior and Sport–1979* (Eds. C.H. Nadeau, W.R. Halliwell, K.M. Newell, and G.C. Roberts), pp. 702–713. Human Kinetics, Champaign, Illinois.

Singer, R.N. (1990) Motor learning research; meaningful for physical educators or a waste of time? *Quest*, **42**, 114–125.

Singer, R.N. and Lidor, R. (1993) Learning sports skills: the 'just do it' approach, *International Journal of Physical Education*, **30**, 10–14.

Singer, R.N., Lidor, R. and Cauraugh, J.H. (1993) To be aware or not aware? What to think about while learning and performing a motor skill, *The Sport Psychologist*, **7**, 19–30.

Slater-Hammel, A.T. (1949) An action current study of contraction-movement relationships in the tennis stroke, *Research Quarterly*, **20**, 424–431.

Sloboda, J.A. (1976) Visual perception of musical notation: registering pitch symbols in memory. *Quarterly Journal of Experimental Psychology*, **28**, 1–16.

Smith, C.B. (1973) An investigation of the psychological refractory period of athletes and non-athletes (Doctoral dissertation, Indiana University, 1972), *Dissertation Abstracts International*, **33**, 4160–A.

Smyth, M.M. and Marriott, A.M. (1982) Vision and proprioception in simple catching, *Journal of Motor Behavior*, **14**, 143–152.

Spaeth-Arnold, R.K. (1976) Skill acquisition under variable temporal constraint: cinematographical analysis of movement organisation, *Journal of Human Movement Studies*, **2**, 98–113.

Sparrow, W.A. (1992) Measuring changes in coordination and control, in *Approaches to the Study of Motor Control and Learning* (Ed. J.J. Summers), pp. 147–162, North-Holland, Amsterdam.

Spelke, E., Hirst, W. and Neisser, U. (1976) Skills of divided attention, *Cognition*, **4**, 215–230.

Sperling, G. (1960) The information available in brief visual presentations, *Psychological Monographs*, **74**, No. 498.

Starkes, J.L. (1987) Skill in field hockey: the nature of the cognitive advantage, *Journal of Sport Psychology*, **9**, 146–160.

Starkes, J.L. and Allard, F. (Eds) (1993) *Cognitive Issues in Motor Expertise*, Elsevier, Amsterdam.

Starkes, J.L., Allard, F., Lindley, S. and O'Reilly, K. (1994) Abilities and skill in basketball, *International Journal of Sport Psychology*, **25**, 249–265.

Starkes, J.L. and Deakin, J. (1984) Perception in sport: a cognitive approach to skilled performance, in *Cognitive Sport Psychology* (Eds. W.F. Straub and J.M. Williams), pp. 115–128, Sport Science Associates, Lansing, NY.

Stelmach, G.E. (1982) Information-processing framework for understanding motor behavior, in *Human Motor Behavior: An Introduction* (Ed. J.A.S. Kelso), pp. 63–91, Erlbaum, Hillsdale, NJ.

Stine, C.D., Arterbrun, M.R. and Stern, N.S. (1982) Vision and sports: a review of the literature, *Journal of the American Optometric Association*, **53**, 627–633.

Sugden, D.A. and Wann, C. (1988) Kinaesthesis and motor impairment in children with moderate learning difficulties, *British Journal of Educational Psychology*, **57**, 225–236.

Summers, E.F. (1974) Tennis ability and its relationship to seven performance tasks, *Dissertation Abstracts International*, **34**, 5697–A.

Thiffault, C. (1974) Tachistoscopic training and its effect upon visual perceptual speed of ice hockey players, in *Proceedings of the Canadian Association of Sport Sciences*, Edmonton, Alberta.

Thiffault, C. (1980) Construction et validation d'une mesure de la rapidité de la pansée tactique des joueurs sur glace. (Construction and validation of a test of the speed of tactical judgment in ice hockey players), in *Psychology of Motor Behavior and Sport 1979* (Eds. C.H. Nadeau, W.R. Halliwell, K.M. Newell, and G.C. Roberts), pp. 643–649. Human Kinetics, Champaign, Illinois.

Thorpe, R.D. and Atha, J. (1977) Serial response speed in game players, *British Journal of Sports Medicine*, **11**(4), 187.

Turvey, M.T. (1990) The challenge of a physical account of action: a personal view, in *The Natural–Physical Approach to Movement Control* (Eds. H.T.A. Whiting, O.G. Meijer, and P.C.W. van Wieringen), pp. 57–93, Free University, Amsterdam.

Turvey, M.T. and Carello, C. (1986) The ecological approach to perceiving–acting: a pictorial essay, *Acta Psychologica*, **63**, 133–155.

Turvey, M.T., Carello, C. and Kim, N-G. (1990) Links between active perception and the control of action, in *Synergetics of Cognition* (Eds. H. Haken and M. Stadler), pp. 269–295, Springer-Verlag, Berlin.

Tussing, L. (1940) The effects of football and basketball on vision, *Research Quarterly*, **11**, 16–18.

Tyldesley, D.A., Bootsma, R.J. and Bomhoff, G.T. (1982) Skill level and eye-movement patterns in a sport-oriented reaction time task, in *Proceedings of an International Symposium on Motor Learning and Movement Behavior: Contribution to Learning in Sport*, pp. 290–296. Hofmann, Cologne.

Tyldesley, D.A. and Whiting, H.T.A. (1975) Operational timing, *Journal of Human Movement Studies*, **1**(4), 172–177.

Vickers, J.N. (1992) Gaze control in putting, *Perception*, **21**, 117–132.

Voss, J.F. and Post, T.A. (1988) On the solving of ill-structured problems, in *The Nature of Expertise* (Eds. M.T.H. Chi, R. Glaser, and M.J. Farr), pp. 261–285, Erlbaum, Hillsdale, NJ.

Wann, J.P. (1991) The integrity of visual-proprioceptive mapping in cerebral palsy, *Neuropsychologia*, **29**, 1095–1106.

Wann, J.P. and Ibrahim, S. (1992) Does proprioception drift? *Experimental Brain Research*, **91**, 162–166.

Wann, J.P. and Rushton, S.K. (1995) The use of virtual environments in perception–action research: grasping the impossible and controlling the improbable, in *Motor Control and Sensory-Motor Integration* (Eds. D.J. Glencross and J. Piek), pp. 341–360, North-Holland, Amsterdam.

Wann, J.P. and Turnbull, J. (1993) Motor skill learning in cerebral palsy: movement, action and computer-assisted therapy, *Baillière's Clinical Neurology*, **2**, 15–28.

Welford, A.T. (1952) The psychological refractory period and the timing of high-speed performance: a review and a theory, *British Journal of Psychology*, **43**, 2–19.

Wertheim, A.H. (1994) Motion perception during self-motion: the direct versus inferential controversy revisited, *Behavioral and Brain Sciences*, **17**, 213–311.

Whiting, H.T.A. (1969) *Acquiring Ball Skill: A Psychological Interpretation*, Bell, London.

Whiting, H.T.A. (1975) *Concepts in Skill Learning*, Lepus Books, London.

Whiting, H.T.A. (1979) Subjective probability in sport, in *Psychology of Motor Behavior and Sport, 1978* (Eds G.C. Roberts and K.M. Newell), pp. 3–25, Human Kinetics, Champaign, IL.

Whiting, H.T.A. (1980) Dimensions of control in learning, in *Tutorials in Motor Behavior* (Eds G.E. Stelmach and J. Requin), pp. 537–550. North-Holland, Amsterdam.

Whiting, H.T.A. and Hendry, L.B. (1968) A Study of International Table Tennis Players, Unpublished memorandum cited by Whiting (1969).

Whiting, H.T.A. and Hutt, J.W.R. (1972) The effects of personality and ability on speed of decisions regarding the directional aspects of ball flight, *Journal of Motor Behavior*, **4**(2), 89–97.

Wieringen, P.C.W., van (1988) Discussion: self-organization or representation? Let's have both! in *Cognition and Action in Skilled Behavior* (Eds. A.M. Colley and J.R. Beech), pp. 247–253. North-Holland, Amsterdam.

Wilkinson, S. (1992) Effects of training in visual discrimination after one year: visual analyses of volleyball skills, *Perceptual and Motor Skills*, **75**, 19–24.

Williams, A.M. and Burwitz, L. (1993) Advance cue utilization in soccer, in *Science and Football II* (Eds. T. Reilly, J. Clarys and A. Stibbe), pp. 239–244. E. & F.N. Spon, London.

Williams, A.M., Davids, K., Burwitz, L. and Williams, J.G. (1993) Visual search and sports performance, *Australian Journal of Science and Medicine in Sport*, **25**, 55–65.

Williams, A.M., Davids, K., Burwitz, L. and Williams, J.G. (1994) Visual search strategies in experienced and inexperienced soccer players, *Research Quarterly for Exercise and Sport*, **65**, 127–135.

Williams, J.M. and Thirer, J. (1975) Vertical and horizontal peripheral vision in male and female athletes and non-athletes, *Research Quarterly*, **46**, 200–205.

Winograd, S. (1942) The relationship of timing and vision to baseball performance, *Research Quarterly*, **13**, 481–493.

Witkin, H.A., Dyk, R., Faterson, H.F., Goodenough, D.R. and Karp, S.A. (1962) *Psychological Differentiation*, Wiley, New York.

Wittenberg, S., Brock, F. and Folsom, W. (1969) Effect of training on stereroscopic acuity, *American Journal of Optometry and Archives of the American Academy of Optometry*, **46**, 645–653.

Wood, J.M., Wild, J.M., Hussey, M.K. and Crews, S.J. (1987) Serial examination of the normal visual field using octopus automated projection perimetry evidence for a learning effect, *Acta Opthalmologica*, **65**, 326–333.

Wright, D.L., Pleasants, F. and Gomez-Meza, M. (1990) Use of advanced visual cue sources in volleyball, *Journal of Sport and Exercise Psychology*, **12**, 406–414.

Yandell, K.M. and Spirduso, W.W. (1981) Sex and athletic status as factors in reaction latency and movement time, *Research Quarterly for Exercise and Sport*, **52**(4), 495–504.

Youngen, L. (1959) A comparison of reaction and movement times of women athletes and non-athletes, *Research Quarterly*, **30**, 349–355.

Zimmerman, M.N. (1970) The influence of stereoscopic depth perception training and level of stereopsis upon accuracy in anticipating the landing point of moving objects in three-dimensional space, *Dissertation Abstracts International*, **31**, 1062–A.

Zimmerman, M.N. and Lane, E.C. (1976) Comparison of total body reaction/movement time and stereopsis of female athletes, in *Motor Learning in Physical Education and Sport* (Ed. U Simri), pp. 161–167, Wingate Institute for Physical Education and Sport, Netanya, Israel.

$\boxed{2}$

MENTAL SKILLS TRAINING IN SPORT

Daniel Gould

University of North Carolina at Greensboro, North Carolina, USA

Nicole Damarjian

Tallwood Country Club, Hebron, Connecticut

American speed skater Dan Jansen turns in a world record gold medal performance in the 1000 metre event at the 1994 Winter Olympics. Jansen becomes the hero of the games because in winning the 1000 metres, he overcame numerous disappointing performances in two previous Olympiads and in the 500 metres at the Lillehammer Games.

After a disastrous World Championships in 1993, figure skater Nancy Kerigan skates the performance of her life at the Lillehammer Games, earning the silver medal. This feat is made even more noteworthy because of the extraordinary pressure placed on Ms Kerigan in conjunction with the media attention surrounding her Olympic effort as a result of a physical attack made on her by supporters of one of her rivals.

Going into the 1994 Winter Olympics, the US ski team is described as 'pathetic' by the popular press. However, led by the medal winning efforts of Tommy Moe, Diann Roffe-Steinrotter, Picabo Street and Liz McIntyre the team is one of the most successful in US Olympic history.

What was it that allowed these athletes to perform so well in one of the biggest competitions of their lives, despite the fact that leading up to the Lillehammer Olympic Games they had not achieved levels of success that would have made them favourites? Or in the case of Dan Jensen what allowed him to finally live-up to expectations and perform well in Olympic competition? One answer might be mental training. All of these athletes participated in systematic mental training programmes in the years

Training in Sport: Applying Sport Science. Edited by B. Elliott
© 1998 John Wiley & Sons Ltd

immediately prior to the Lillehammer Olympic Games. And in their cases mental training appeared to be highly successful.

While mental training appears to have been a benefit to these elite athletes does it always lead to improved performance? What exactly does mental training involve? Which mental skills should be emphasized in such a program and how should it be best organized and implemented? These are just some of the important questions being asked as sport psychology and specifically mental training becomes increasingly more popular with coaches, athletes and sport administrators.

This chapter is designed to address the above questions by examining research findings, theoretical constructs, and professional practice literature on mental skills training and the role it plays in enhancing athletic performance. In particular, six specific issues will be addressed:

(1) the nature of mental skills training and who it is appropriate for;
(2) evidence examining the importance and utility of mental skills training programs;
(3) the identification of the most critical topics to be included in a mental skills training program;
(4) recommendations on how to implement a mental skills training program;
(5) a description and critical evaluation of a recently conducted mental training program;
(6) the identification of problems and pitfalls often made in mental skills training programs and how they can be avoided.

THE NATURE OF MENTAL SKILLS TRAINING

What is mental skills training?

Mental skills training refers to procedures that enhance an athlete's ability to use his or her mind effectively and readily in the execution of sport-related goals. Mental skills training is part of the larger field of sport psychology. As a whole, sport psychology is the study of how physiological factors (e.g., confidence, concentration, anxiety) influence performance and how participation in sport influences the psychological make-up of the athlete (Gould and Eklund, 1991). Mental skills training involves developing those psychological factors that are found to enhance athletic performance. It can also be used to help develop important personal characteristics in athletes such as self-esteem and moral values (Danish, Petitpas and Hale, 1993). However, in this review the focus will be placed solely on using mental skills training to enhance athletic performance.

Common myths surrounding mental skills training

Given the recent media attention surrounding the use of mental training by elite athletes, many misconceptions have developed regarding the use of this form of training and the extent to which it can enhance performance. Before designing a mental skills training program, it is important to recognize and refute these myths. The following is a brief description of five common myths surrounding sport psychology and the use of mental training (Gould and Eklund, 1991).

Myth 1: Sport psychology consultants only work with mentally sick athletes

One of the most common misconceptions a sport psychology consultant implementing a mental skills training program must overcome is the 'shrink' image they are often associated with. Many athletes assume for example, that if you work with a sport psychologist, you must be 'sick'. This is not true. It is important to understand that some sport psychologists are specifically trained in clinical psychology. For example, they may help an athlete suffering from an eating disorder or severe depression. Other sport psychologists, however, are not trained to deal with such clinical disorders and instead focus on helping athletes learn how they can best develop the mental skills needed to achieve their goals. These individuals are better thought of as mental coaches than as clinicians. For example, they may help an athlete develop relaxation skills to better handle the pressures of competition. Both clinical and educational sport psychologists have an important role. Both are able to assist athletes reach their potential; however, only a clinically trained sport psychologist is able to deal with athletes with clinically based problems.

Myth 2: Sport psychology is only for elite athletes

Because the media attention surrounding sport psychology is often associated with elite performers, many falsely assume sport psychology is only for top-ranked amateur or professional athletes. In reality sport psychology and mental training are for athletes of all ability levels. For example, the work of Tara Scanlan and her colleagues (Scanlan, Carpenter, Schmidt, Simons and Keeler, 1993; Scanlan, Simons, Carpenter, Schmidt and Keeler, 1993) has focused on the construct of sport enjoyment and the implications this may have on sport commitment, while Smoll and Smith (1993) have examined how coaching behaviours influence self-esteem and motivation in young athletes. How can we better structure sport to make it a more positive experience for children? What can we do to make sport more enjoyable for adults and thus help them to maintain the level of physical activity associated with good health? These are only a few examples of how sport psychology can enhance the sport experience for all people with differing abilities and aspirations.

Myth 3: Sport psychology will cause revolutionary changes in athletics

There have been many successful coaches in the past who have had an excellent understanding of applied sport psychology and there will continue to be many more in the future. Sport psychology is not going to rock the athletic community with such revolutionary ideas that it will change sport as we know it. Coleman Griffith, the founding father of North American sport psychology, stated 'it is supposed that [the sport psychologist] is merely waiting until he can jump into an athletic field, tell the old-time successful coach that he is all wrong and begin, then, to expound his own magical and fanciful theories as to proper method of coaching . . . this of course is far from the truth' (Griffith, 1925, p. 193). One of the goals of sport psychology is to better understand the actions of great coaches and athletes in order to convey this understanding to less experienced coaches and athletes. It is unrealistic to think that sport psychologists have all the answers to achieving athletic success.

Myth 4: Mental skills training is a quick fix for performance woes

Many coaches and athletes approach sport psychologists in search of an easy and quick solution to complex problems. For example, an athlete may suffer from a lack of self-confidence with his or her putting and want to be 'fixed' by next week's golf championship. This thinking is consistent with the desire for instant gratification so prevalent in Western society today. In reality, developing mental skills requires the same systematic practice that developing physical skills do. As Martens (1987) pointed out, mental skills are only acquired and maintained through consistent effort.

Myth 5: Sport psychology is not useful

It is evident both from the claims of athletes in the popular press as well as from a growing body of research that sport psychology can have a positive influence in assisting athletes to achieve their potential. As previously stated, sport psychology is not revolutionizing sport, but as a key component of sport science it is helping many athletes to reach a higher level of performance.

THE IMPORTANCE AND UTILITY OF MENTAL SKILLS TRAINING

Having established a better understanding of what mental skills training is and is not, we will turn our attention to why mental skills training is important and whether mental skills training can be used to facilitate athletic performance.

The importance of mental skills

How important are psychological skills in determining athletic performance? Are there distinctions between more and less successful athletes with regard to psychological skills and attributes? What are the psychological characteristics of peak performance? These are just some of the questions sport psychologists have studied in their quest to better understand the role that mental factors play in athletic performance. While space limitations prohibit a detailed review of this literature, a brief summary is included below.

In a recent review of the psychology of superior performance literature, Williams and Krane (1993) have concluded that certain mental skills and psychological attributes have been repeatedly found to be associated with superior performance in athletes. These include: goal setting; higher self-confidence; heightened concentration; the use of visualization and imagery; self-regulation of arousal; well-developed coping skills for dealing with unforeseen events and distractions; mental preparation plans; well-developed competitive routines and plans; and high levels of motivation and commitment. They also indicated that while the research that these conclusions are derived is not without some limitations (e.g., the inability to show causation in most cases), it's consistency and intuitive appeal have led many researchers and practitioners to conclude that some optimal emotional climate (combination of mental states) is associated with superior performance and that effective performers have developed mental skills which help them attain these states.

An excellent example of how this may happen is provided in an investigation conducted by Gould, Eklund and Jackson (1992a,b). All 20 members of the 1988 United States Olympic wrestling team were interviewed regarding their performance in the Seoul games. They were specifically asked to describe their mental preparation and precompetitive thoughts and feelings prior to their best international performance, worst Olympic performance, and most crucial Olympic match. Before their all-time best performance the athletes tended to report prematch mental states characterized by positive expectancies, optimal arousal states, and a sensation of heightened effort and commitment. The achievement of these optimal thought and emotional patterns were also found to be associated with the systematic use of mental preparation strategies that included preparation routines, a tactical strategy focus, and some mention of motivational strategies. In contrast, the athletes characterized their all-time worst Olympic performance as having negative feeling states, negative, irrelevant, or irregular patterns of thought, and a non-adherence to preparation routines.

Finally, as part of a major investigation of the mental readiness of Canadian Olympians, Orlick and Partington (1988) asked these athletes to rate their physical, mental and technical readiness. Only mental readiness significantly predicted performance success, verifying numerous anecdotal reports of athletes and coaches regarding the extremely important role that mental factors play in performance success.

From this research, then, the importance of mental skills in producing superior athletic performance has been clearly established. The question remains, however, whether athletes can be taught to control their mental states and in so doing facilitate performance.

The utility of mental skills training

The previous research and the anecdotal examples discussed at the outset of this chapter suggest that mental training can effectively help athletes perform up to their capabilities. However, a number of leaders (Smith, 1989; Weinberg, 1989) in the field of applied sport psychology have voiced concern that for the field to truly advance, an empirical data base supporting its utility must be developed. While the data base in this area is still relatively scant, researchers have begun to heed this call and examine the question of whether mental training works.

No one single research paradigm has been derived for studying the mental skills training area. However, most studies examine whether single athletes or groups of athletes differ in their performance, self-evaluation of program effectiveness, and/or thoughts after participation in a mental skills training program, regardless of whether that program involves imagery training, goal setting, arousal regulation, mental preparation procedures or some combination of these techniques.

For example, Kendall, Hrycaiko, Martin, and Kendall (1990) used a multiple baseline design to examine the effects of a relaxation, imagery and self-talk mental training package on the performance of defensive basketball skills in game situations. Subjects took part in an initial intervention program (consisting of lectures, viewing of an imagery video, exercises and actual practice of the self-talk, imagery and relaxation skills stressed) lasting approximately 3.5 hours and spread over five days. In addition, after this initial training they used the mental training package 15 minutes a day for the remainder of their season. Performance measures taken across the season clearly showed that the intervention enhanced player performance above baseline levels, although a potential Hawthorne effect could not be completely ruled out.

In a group study, Crocker, Alderman, and Smith (1988) assessed the effectiveness of Smith's (1980) Cognitive–Affective Stress Management Training intervention on performance, cognitions and affect in high-performance youth volleyball players. The intervention consisted of an integrated coping response made up of both physical and cognitive relaxation strategies presented in eight modules to the intervention subjects over an eight week period. Control group subjects were similar calibre players taken from a waiting list of athletes planning to take part in the intervention. Results revealed that intervention group players significantly differed from control group in that they emitted fewer negative thoughts when faced with a videotaped stressor and had superior service reception. The authors concluded that convergent support (between the cognitive and performance measures) was found for Smith's stress coping program.

Recent comprehensive reviews (Greenspan and Feltz, 1989; Burton, 1990; Mace, 1990; Murphy, 1994; Weinberg, 1994; Vealey, 1994) and a meta analysis (Whelan, Meyers and Berman, 1989) have shown that mental training can be effective in enhancing athlete performance and positively influencing cognitive and affective states. However, the effects on performance are not nearly as consistent as would be desired considering not all programs have been found to be effective, and a host of methodological concerns inhibit conclusive interpretations of the literature. All reviewers agree that future research employing single subject and more-traditional group designs is badly needed if the area is to continue to advance. Vealey (1992) proposed the following improvements in future investigations:

- the need to incorporate more placebo controls in the designs;
- the incorporation of manipulation checks to insure that the training programmes were used as designed;
- the importance of examining the efficacy of these programmes over extended lengths of time;
- the need for more specific descriptions of interventions used;
- the importance of accounting for individual and situational moderators.

In summary, then, this initial evaluation research shows that mental training can work to enhance athlete performance. However, more, better designed and controlled investigations are needed. Moreover, since mental training programmes have not been found to always be effective those involved in the development and use of such programmes must constantly evaluate their utility. Automatically assuming they will be effective is a grave mistake, as is being afraid to utilize mental training because a complete data base is not developed.

TOPICS TO BE INCLUDED IN MENTAL SKILLS TRAINING

Achieving excellence: the pyramid model of athletic excellence

Before considering the most important topics to include in a mental skills training program it is useful to consider a general framework for conceptualizing the role that mental skills play in achieving athletic excellence. One such framework appears in Figure 2.1. This framework considers three important sets of psychological factors that interact to produce peak performance in an athlete. These include: the psychological make-up/personality of the individual involved; psychology of peak performance strategies; and coping with adversity strategies.

At the base of our pyramid of success is the psychological make-up/personality of the individual. While our understanding of the role of personality in sport is far from complete and the identification of the personality profile of the superior athlete has not been identified (Vealey, 1992), a number of personal characteristics have been shown to influence the quest for athletic excellence. For example, an individual's achievement goal motivational orientations, trait self-confidence and trait anxiety are examples of important factors to consider.

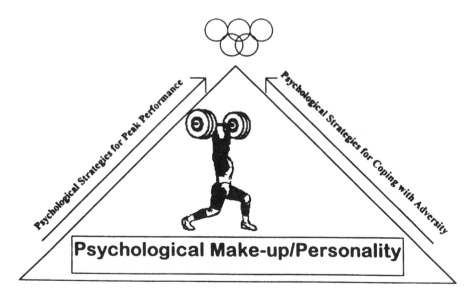

Figure 2.1:

The left side of the pyramid consists of peak performance strategies and the literature contained in this review showed that sport psychologists have spent considerable time identifying psychological states and strategies needed for peak performance. Examples include such things as concentration, a focus on performance goals, and the use of specific mental preparation routines and strategies. While the use of such skills will not ensure success, their use 'sets the table for success' by creating a psychological climate that increases the probability of success. Hence, when designing mental skills training programmes, decisions should be made to teach and develop specific peak performance strategies most relevant to the sport and athletes involved.

A common mistake made in mental skills training is to focus sole attention on peak performance strategies. This is problematic because athletes must also learn to deal with adversity. For example, Gould, Jackson and Finch (1993) found that National Champion figure skaters experienced more stress after winning their national titles than when initially trying to achieve this goal. Stress resulted from such factors as their own and others' performance expectations, time demands, the media, injuries and general life concerns. Therefore, to achieve and maintain athletic excellence, athletes not only need psychology of peak performance skills, but also psychological coping strategies which can be used to effectively help them cope with adversity. Such psychological skills might involve stress management techniques, thought stopping, or social support mechanisms.

It is highly recommended that this psychological pyramid model of peak performance be considered when selecting content for a mental training programme. Consider the personality and psychological make-up of the clientele the programme is aimed at and if components of the programme should be focused on developing or enhancing specific personal characteristics or orientations deemed important. In addition, identify the most important psychology of peak performance skills to be taught and what strategies will be most useful in coping with adversity. Mental skills training programmes which address psychological factors at the base and on the two sides of this pyramid have the greatest probability of helping athletes consistently enhance performance and achieve success.

Core areas of mental skills training

Given the research that suggests that mental skills training is an important factor in athletic success, which particular psychological skills are most important? In 1991, Gould and his colleagues surveyed elite athletes and coaches representing a wide variety of Olympic sports to determine which psychological factors they felt were most important. They were asked to rate a list of psychological skills, both performance (e.g., arousal regulation, visualization-imagery) and non-performance (e.g., communication skills) related, on a scale from one to 10, one being 'not important' and 10 being 'very important'. The results from the elite athletes showed performance-related skills to be ranked the highest with visualization-imagery (9.13) and concentration-attention (8.96) rated as the two most important skills. Similar results were found from the elite coaches. Visualization-imagery (8.72) and concentration-attention (8.68) were again ranked 1 and 2 respectively. A list of some of the top mental skills as rated by the elite athletes and coaches can be found in Table 2.1.

When sport psychology specialists were surveyed (Gould, Tammen, Murphy and May, 1989) as to what topics they used most often in their consulting practices, performance topics were rated as more frequently used than non-performance topics. Arousal regulation and visualization-imagery were ranked the two most used topics for both individual and group consultations. Personal self-esteem ranked the highest for non-performance topics, but it was still less used than most of the lower ranking performance enhancement topics. Table 2.2 summarizes the performance and non-performance topics frequency of use by sport psychology specialists.

In contrast to the surveys completed by elite athletes and coaches as well as the sport psychology consultants that work with this elite population, Gould (1982) found quite different results when he surveyed youth sport coaches and administrators. When asked what sport psychological topics were most important with regard to youth sports, non-performance issues

Table 2.1: Sport psychology topic ratings (Adapted from Gould, Murphy, Tammen, and May, 1991)

Elite Athletes

Rank Topic Rating

(1 = not important; 10 = very important)

1	visualization-imagery	9.13
2	concentration-attention	8.96
3	relaxation training	8.55
4	self-talk strategies	8.51
5	arousal regulation	8.27
6	stress management	8.25

Elite Coaches

Rank Topic Rating

(1 = not important; 10 = very important)

1	visualization-imagery	8.72
2	concentration-attention	8.68
3	stress management	8.45
4	relaxation training	8.41
5	athlete-coach communication	8.40

Table 2.2: Current Practices used by Applied Sport Psychology Specialists (Adapted from Gould, Tammen, Murphy, and May, 1989)

Performance enhancement topic importance ratings

(1 = not important; 10 = very important)

Individual consultations		*Group consultations*	
1. arousal regulation	8.44	visualization-imagery	8.21
2. visualization-imagery	8.35	arousal regulation	8.09
3. relaxation training	7.65	goal setting	7.92
4. other stress management techniques	7.57	relaxation training	7.64
5. goal setting	7.51	self-talk	7.39

Non-performance topic importance ratings

(1 = not important; 10 = very important)

Individual consultations		*Group consultations*	
1. personal self-esteem	7.50	personal self-esteem	7.28
2. crisis management	5.85	interpersonal conflicts	6.28

were rated much higher than they were with the elite athletes and coaches. The six topics most important to youth sport coaches and administrators were:

(1) the causes of discontinuing involvement or dropout in youth athletes;
(2) the effect of competitive stress placed on young athletes;
(3) strategies to help young athletes cope with stress;
(4) the effects of competition on the psychological health and development of children;
(5) skills for communicating with young athletes;
(6) strategies for developing self-confidence.

Taken together these studies suggest that performance topics are rated as more important and used more often than non-performance topics in mental skills training. Stress management, visualization, and confidence are the three mental skills consistently rated as most important for inclusion in a training pro-gramme. However, it is important to understand that these findings may be age and skill level dependent. Gould's study (1982) with youth sport coaches and administrators found non-performance topics to be more important than per-formance topics. Perhaps young children or athletes with less skill have dif-ferent mental training needs or the programmes in which they are involved have differing goals. Regardless, until more research is conducted with various ages and skill levels, it is important to consider the individual needs of the athlete or group when designing mental skills training programmes.

The remainder of this section will examine in more detail specific areas of mental training as they relate to performance enhancement. These areas will include:

(1) self-confidence;
(2) goal setting;
(3) stress management and coping;
(4) imagery and visualization;
(5) concentration and attention;
(6) motivation

Self-confidence

Few will dispute the value of self-confidence in achieving success. However, there are many misconceptions about self-confidence. Some athletes and coaches mistakenly equate self-confidence with arrogance or cockiness. Others falsely assume that self-confidence means you never doubt yourself. You believe you can do anything and you usually do. In reality, self-confidence is none of these things. Martens defined true self-confidence as 'an athlete's realistic expectation about achieving success' (Martens, 1987, p. 151). Self-confidence is not what athletes hope to accomplish, but rather what they realistically expect to accomplish.

Given the importance of self-confidence to performance success, how can athletes develop this attribute? Most of the research examining self-confidence and sport is based on Bandura's (1977) theory of self-efficacy. Bandura contended that self-efficacy was a situation specific form of self-confidence (e.g., one expects to run the 100 metre dash in 10.8 seconds), as compared to traditional views of self-confidence which have been thought of much more globally (e.g., one is a good athlete). Moreover, numerous studies (see Feltz, 1988 for a review) have shown that self-efficacy is a strong predictor of athletic performance.

Most relevant to this chapter are the theory's contentions relative to sources of efficacy information. In particular, Bandura contends that there are four sources of efficacy information:

(1) performance or mastery experiences;
(2) vicarious experiences;
(3) verbal persuasion;
(4) physiological information states.

The strongest source of efficacy information involves a performance or mastery experience. It is therefore critical that athletes develop the necessary skills to enable them to experience some level of success. This will require appropriate skill instruction, guided participation, simulated experiences, or appropriate goal setting. Although typically not as strong as a mastery experience, vicarious experiences (e.g., watching others succeed) can also influence self-confidence. Coaches may find it helpful to use 'similar others' for athletes to model. The final two sources of efficacy information, verbal persuasion (e.g., a coach trying to verbally convince an athlete that he or she can execute a skill) and physiological information states (e.g., an athlete tries to increase her or his confidence by interpreting increased heart rate as excitement not nervousness), are the weakest of the four sources. However, they may be an important component within the overall strategy to enhancing an athlete's self-confidence. In addition to providing mastery experiences, coaches can directly reassure athletes of their ability. They can help athletes to better interpret their arousal levels as something positive and actually important for peak performance. If arousal levels become too high, an athlete can learn to reduce these levels through appropriate relaxation techniques.

In an exploratory study to assess the strategies elite coaches use to enhance self-confidence, Gould, Hodge, Peterson and Giannini (1989) surveyed 101 NCAA wrestling coaches and 124 national Olympic team coaches. The coaches were asked to rate 13 self-efficacy enhancement strategies on a five-point Likert scale with regard to frequency of use as well as effectiveness. Both sets of coaches reported instruction drilling as the most often used and the most effective strategy, supporting the importance placed on mastery experiences in Bandura's self-efficacy theory (1977). Other strategies found to be effective included modelling confidence oneself, liberally using rewarding statements, using positive self-talk, and emphasizing technique improvements while downplaying performance outcome. In an interesting follow-up investigation, Weinberg, Grove and Jackson (1992) replicated most of these findings with both American and Australian tennis coaches. Hence, these findings were found to generalize across two different cultures.

The sources of self-efficacy outlined in Bandura's (1977) theory serve as a helpful framework from which to design studies and implement interventions. However, more research is needed to focus on the systematic use of various strategies. For example, how might a coach or sport psychology consultant best incorporate all four sources of efficacy information in an effort to enhance self-confidence? Do sources of efficacy information differ depending on an athlete's age and skill level? More field studies with athletes are needed to better understand these questions and the effectiveness of various strategies already in existence.

Goal setting

Goal setting is another core skill within mental training. Simply defined, goals are what an individual consciously tries to do (Weinberg, 1994). Goal setting has been shown to enhance performance as well as create positive changes in anxiety, confidence, and motivation (Gould, 1993). However, when goal setting is used improperly, it can also become a major source of anxiety, diffidence, and performance impairment. To avoid potential problems associated with the misuse of goals, it is important to understand how and why goal setting influences performance.

Much of the contemporary research on goal setting comes from industrial and organizational psychology. The majority of research in this area has primarily revolved around a mechanistic cognitive framework where goals are viewed as motivational tools to enhance performance (Locke, Shaw, Saari, and Latham, 1981; Locke and Latham, 1990). Specifically, goals are considered to influence performance by:

(1) directing the performer's attention and action to important aspects of a given task;
(2) mobilizing effort;
(3) increasing persistence;
(4) increasing the likelihood that the performer will develop new learning strategies through the process of setting goals.

The impact goals have on performance will depend on a number of mediating factors including ability, commitment, feedback, task complexity, as well as situational factors.

Research in areas outside of industrial and organizational psychology have developed various other conceptual approaches to understanding the goal–performance relationship. For example, in clinical psychology, researchers have employed a cognitive behaviour modification model to assess the impact of goals on behavioural change (Bandura and Cervone, 1983). Furthermore, motivation theorists contend that goal orientations explain motivation and behaviour in educational and business settings. For example, Nicholls (1984) suggested that children who have a 'task goal orientation' (e.g., improve one's time in swimming) were motivated by the desire to continually learn and improve their skill regardless of whether they win or lose. On the other hand, children who have an 'ego goal orientation' (e.g., beat a particular competitor) were motivated to demonstrate competence relative to others. Thus performance outcome (winning or losing) is very important to people with this goal orientation.

Within the field of sport and exercise psychology, Burton (1992) suggested that researchers integrate the various conceptual approaches into a comprehensive framework that can be applied to sport. Rather than advance a new theory of goal setting, Burton has developed the Competition-Goal-Setting (CGS) model which incorporates elements of existing theories. Briefly, the CGS model suggests that goal orientations interact with perceived ability in the development of three distinct goal-setting styles (performance-oriented, success-oriented and failure-oriented). The influence of these goal-setting styles, along with situation type and performance expectancies, help to determine the specific goal set. These discrete goals interact with perceived goal commitment to prompt specific goal responses that will determine how an athlete performs.

Although the overall CGS model has not been tested, research has found support for selected components of the model. However, the majority of this support comes from non-sport achievement domains. For example, in general psychology the motivational orientation literature has shown support for the existence of performance-, success- and failure-oriented goal setting styles and the impact these are likely to have on perceptions and attributions of success and failure (Nicholls, 1984; Dweck, 1986; Elliot and Dweck, 1988). This research also supports the CGS model's prediction that performance-, success-, and failure-oriented athletes will demonstrate differential goal responses for task choice, effort/intensity, strategy development, and persistence. The limited research conducted within a sport context has found support for the CGS model with collegiate swimmers (Burton, 1989) and junior high school gymnasts (Pierce and Burton, 1995). (See Burton, 1992 for a more comprehensive review of the empirical support for the CGS model, its components, and its specific predictions.)

Future research is greatly needed to specifically examine the impact goal setting has on sport and exercise performance. Of the 13 studies identified in sport (Burton, 1993), only two-thirds have demonstrated that athletes setting specific difficult goals performed significantly better than performers setting general goals, do-your-best goals, or no goals. These results are surprising when you consider the magnitude and consistency of goal-setting effects in settings outside of sport such as business and industry. Burton (1993) suggested three plausible explanations as to why research has found such mixed results in sport. First, athletes in previous research may have been operating close to their performance potential. This is consistent with Locke and Latham's (1990) prediction that the goal effectiveness curve flattens out as individuals approach the limits of their ability. Second, when athletes are asked to perform highly complex skills, greater time may be necessary to demonstrate positive effects from goal setting. This is consistent with Locke and Latham's prediction that a greater lag time is required to show enhanced performance with a new and complex task because strategies often have to be developed in order to perform the skill more effectively. Finally, individual difference variables, particularly self-efficacy, may significantly influence how individuals respond to goal setting.

Despite the limited number and equivocal findings of goal setting studies in sport, both researchers and experienced consultants have found various types of goals to be more effective than others in enhancing athletic performance (Gould, 1993; Weinberg, 1994). Table 2.3 summarizes some of the more important guidelines to consider when developing a goal-setting programme.

Table 2.3: Basic goal setting guidelines

- *Set specific and measurable goals.* Goals such as doing one's best or improving one's free-throw shootings are vague and ineffective. Specific and measurable goals, on the other hand, allow athletes to determine objectively whether or not they have actually achieved their goal. For example, if an athlete sets a goal to improve his or her free-throw shooting percentage from 60 to 75 percent, he or she will be able to evaluate any performance improvements from game statistics.
- *Set difficult but realistic goals.* Difficult goals elicit greater performance improvements than easier goals (Locke et al., 1981). However, it is important that goals be realistic and not exceed the performer's ability. Unrealistic goals will only lead to failure and frustration. Ideally, goals should be challenging yet attainable.
- *Set short-range as well as long-range goals.* Many athletes focus on long-range goals such as qualifying for a national championship. However, it is important also to establish short-range and daily practice goals. Short-range goals help to better focus one's efforts during practice, thus improving the quality and efficiency of practice. Also, short-range goals allow athletes to experience success while they are progressing toward their ultimate long-range-goal.
- *Set performance goals as opposed to outcome goals.* Outcome goals such as winning the conference title can be useful motivators in the off-season. Overall, however, outcome goals have been shown to be less effective than performance goals for two reasons. First, an athlete has only partial control over the outcome of an event. For example, a golfer may shoot his or her lowest career round and still lose because another golfer happened to play exceptionally well that day. A second reason why outcome goals are less effective than performance goals is that athletes usually become less flexible with the goals they set. With outcome goals you either achieve your goal or you do not. Outcome goals fail to recognize success in a desired direction. By emphasizing performance goals, athletes at a variety of skill levels will be able to experience success.
- *Set positive goals as opposed to negative goals.* Whenever possible, it is important to state goals in the positive rather than the negative. For example, rather than stating that one wants to eliminate the number of times he or she three-putted a green, a better goal is to state that one wants to lower his or her number of putts per round from 38 to 34. Positive goal setting will help athletes focus on what they want to achieve rather than what they hope to avoid.
- *Identify a target date for attaining each goal.* Establishing target dates help to motivate athletes by reminding them of the need to accomplish their objectives within a realistic length of time.
- *Identify goal achievement strategies.* The best set goals will never be realized without an appropriate plan of action. Therefore, it is important that athletes work with their coaches and instructors to determine how best to achieve their performance objectives.
- *Record goals in writing.* Unfortunately, many athletes fail to record the goals they set for themselves and consequently they are often soon forgotten. Having athletes record their goals in writing will help to keep them focused on their performance objectives as well as their goal achievement strategies.
- *Continually evaluate progress.* Simply setting appropriate goals and strategies is not enough. Evaluative feedback is essential if goal setting is to enhance performance. It provides athletes with a picture of where they are currently compared to where they hope to be in the future. Without evaluating performance, athletes often fail to realize the improvements they have made. Consequently, their efforts go unrewarded. Evaluative feedback also helps athletes realize when they are not improving despite effort and persistence. In these cases, feedback may indicate the need to lower certain goals or perhaps to employ an alternative achievement strategy.

In summary, goal setting can be an important tool for helping athletes increase self-confidence, satisfaction, motivation, and persistence, decrease anxiety, focus attention, mobilize effort, and aid in the development of achievement strategies. However, more research is needed to examine the goal–performance relationship in sport-specific settings. In addition, rather than focus attention only on whether or not goal setting is effective, researchers also need to examine which goals are most appropriate for people with different personalities and motivational styles.

Stress management and coping

After a poor performance athletes often report having experienced feelings of self-doubt and/or physical tension, while after good performances they often report feelings of confidence-enhanced physical and mental energy. Numerous theories have been proposed to explain the relationship between such feelings and athletic performance. These include the inverted-U hypothesis (Yerkes and Dodson, 1908); Hanin's (1980) zones of optimal functioning model; Hardy's (1990) catastrophe model; and Kerr's (1993) application of reversal theory. Although it is beyond the scope of this chapter to discuss each of these views, some of their common implications for mental training must be understood because stress management and coping strategies do little good in enhancing performance unless an athlete knows which optimal arousal-related state leads to peak performance.

For years sport psychologists have almost unconditionally endorsed the inverted-U hypothesis. This hypothesis holds that an optimal or medium level of athlete arousal results in best performance with low and high levels of arousal being associated with inferior performance. In recent years, however, the inverted-U hypothesis has come under increased criticism and has been deemed as an inadequate explanation of the arousal-performance relationship (Neiss, 1988; Hardy, 1990; Gould and Krane, 1992; Raglin, 1992). Specifically, these reviewers contended that the inverted-U was inadequate because of a lack of convincing evidence supporting it and the possibility that it may even be untestable. In addition, no explanation is offered for explaining why arousal influences performance and the hypothesis fails to view arousal as a multidimensional construct made up of a variety of physiological and affective states such as confidence, cognitive state anxiety and somatic state anxiety (all of which have been found to differentially influence performance). In place of the inverted-U, a number of new theories and hypotheses such as optimal zones of functioning, reversal theory and catastrophe theory have been proposed.

Although these more recent models are very different, they suggest a number of important implications for mental training (Gould and Udry, 1994). These include:

(1) Arousal is a multidimensional construct which comprises both physiological (e.g., increased heart rate) and cognitive interpretation–appraisal components (e.g., confidence, state anxiety).
(2) The interaction between these physiological and cognitive-related arousal components may be more important than absolute levels of each.
(3) Some optimal recipe of these arousal-related emotional states is associated with peak performance.
(4) Optimal arousal-related states will differ across individual athletes. This suggests then that athletes must become cognizant of their individual-specific optimal recipe of arousal-related emotions needed for peak performance.

Helping athletes recognize their optimal recipe of arousal-related emotions needed for peak performance is a primary function of mental skills training. This can be accomplished by having individuals retrospectively rate and compare arousal-related emotions such as heart rate, butterflies in the stomach, cognitive anxiety or worry, and confidence levels between previous best versus worst performances (Orlick, 1986a; Udry and Gould, 1992). The result is the identification of the optimal recipe of arousal-related emotions associated with peak performance. Considering that athletes must reach their optimal levels and mixtures of arousal-related emotions for peak performance to occur, regulation of these states becomes extremely important. At times they will need to be elevated (i.e., the athlete will need to psyche up), at other times lowered (i.e., the athlete will need to manage stress and cope), and at still other times simply maintained. Stress management and coping is perhaps the biggest need in this area as most athletes report more problems in managing stress than in the inability of psyching up (Percival, 1971). However, it is a grave mistake to simply cognitively and physiologically relax athletes without considering the optimal mixture and amounts of arousal-related emotions needed for best performance.

Considering that athletes perform well when they are at an optimal cognitive and affective arousal level, what can be done to help athletes who have difficulty achieving this zone? Martens (1987) has identified three categories of stress management techniques. These include:

(1) environmental engineering techniques;
(2) physical stress management techniques;
(3) cognitive stress management techniques.

Environmental engineering techniques deal with the aspects of the environment that increase the likelihood that an athlete will experience stress. Stress occurs when athletes are uncertain whether or not they will be able to meet the demands of an event that is important to them. Therefore, coaches can minimize stress by reducing uncertainty and perceived importance

(Martens, Vealey, and Burton, 1990). Martens (1987) suggested that coaches could reduce uncertainty by better communicating with athletes. For example, rather than having athletes worry about their role on the team, coaches should keep athletes informed on a consistent basis. Parents must also learn to communicate consistently with their son or daughter. Uncertainty and stress can arise when a parent acts one way when a child wins and another way when a child loses. The unrealistic importance placed on a game or competition can be controlled by changing game rules to maximize the chances of success (e.g., T-ball), ensuring that opposing teams are equally skilled, eliminating bleachers in order to reduce crowd size, or perhaps participating without keeping score (Smoll and Smith, 1982). Although not all of the environmental engineering techniques are feasible with more established elite sport programmes, they are important to consider when dealing with stress and young developing athletes.

In addition to environmental engineering stress management techniques, Martens also identified physical stress management techniques. These techniques include imagery relaxation, progressive relaxation, self-directed relaxation, and biofeedback. Imagery relaxation involves an athlete learning how to imagine him or herself in a relaxing environment (e.g., sitting on a sunny beach listening to the waves). With practice, the athlete will be able to imagine this calming environment during a stressful situation and thus promote relaxation.

Progressive relaxation training was developed in the 1930s by Edmund Jacobson. It has been used in sport settings to help athletes identify and decrease excess muscle tension. Progressive relaxation training involves systematically tensing and relaxing muscle groups throughout the body. During training the athlete focuses on what tension and relaxation feel like. Through practice an athlete begins to develop an awareness of when and where tension develops. The athlete is then able to use the strategies learned in progressive relaxation training to quickly relax specific muscle groups during a stressful event (e.g., championship game).

Self-directed relaxation is an abbreviated form of progressive relaxation. This type of stress management involves an athlete relaxing various muscle groups throughout the body by focusing on breathing. For example, a softball player may experience tension in her shoulders before she steps up to bat. To decrease this tension, she focuses her thoughts on her shoulders as she inhales. As she exhales she imagines that all of the tension in her shoulders is leaving her body, so she is relaxed and ready to bat.

The final physical stress management technique discussed is biofeedback. Biofeedback has been defined as 'the use of instrumentation to detect and amplify internal physiological processes in order to make this ordinarily unavailable information available to the individual in a form that is meaningful, rapid, precise, and consistent' (Zaichkowsky and Fuchs, 1988, p. 381). The core of this concept is feedback from a biological system. Various equipment is used to obtain information about biological functions. Signals are transduced and amplified by a biofeedback instrument. Individuals then use the biological feedback to raise or lower the specific biological function. In the early stages, biofeedback is a continual process of adjustment. The subject attempts to control the specific function ('feed forward'). The biofeedback instrument indicates whether the appropriate biological changes have been made. The subject evaluates the feedback and makes whatever necessary adjustments are needed. Another attempt is made and the process begins again. The ultimate goal of biofeedback is for the athlete to learn to monitor and control internal physical states in the absence of the biofeedback apparatus.

Biofeedback can be used, for example, with a skier who wishes to develop his relaxation skills by learning how to control his heart rate. He would use biofeedback to determine what strategies best lower his heart rate. He would then use these strategies on the ski slopes to promote relaxation before competition. It is important to realize that biofeedback as well as the other relaxation strategies require considerable practice to be effectively used in a pressure situation.

Cognitive stress management is the final category of stress management techniques. These techniques are most appropriate for athletes troubled by negative, irrational, or unproductive thoughts. Two of the more popular intervention strategies are thought stopping and rational thinking. Thought stopping involves first helping athletes to identify negative thoughts which are so automatic that athletes are unaware of them. To increase awareness, athletes are instructed to pay greater attention to what they tell themselves as well as to keep a personal journal of their thoughts and feelings. When athletes notice themselves having negative thoughts, they are instructed to immediately stop these unproductive thoughts and replace them with more appropriate self-enhancing ones. For example, a tennis player may notice that on matches where she does not serve well, she is typically preoccupied with images of double-faulting. Realizing this, she decides to imagine a big red stop sign whenever these thoughts occur. She then substitutes the images of double-faulting with images of successful serves.

Ellis (1982) developed another cognitive stress management technique involving rational thinking. Ellis contended that performance was frequently hindered by four basic irrational beliefs. These include:

(1) perfectionism—'I must do well at the sports I participate in and if I fail to do as well as I must, it is awful and I am an incompetent, pretty worthless person';
(2) the need to please others—'I must excel at sports in order to please others such as my coach, my teammates, and my friends. If I lose or get rejected by any significant others that is horrible! I am an unestimable slob if such rejection occurs';

(3) the world must be fair—'You must do exactly what I want, treat me kindly in all respects and enable me to get out of sports a completely fair deal';

(4) what you want should come easily and quickly—'I should not have to train and discipline myself so heavily, but should be able to pursue all the enjoyments of life—such as eating, drinking, and carousing—that I want to pursue without being at all handicapped in my sporting abilities'.

(Ellis, 1982, p. 12).

Similar to thought stopping, rational thinking involves becoming aware of one's irrational beliefs so he or she can then question and replace these beliefs with more appropriate ones. For example, a cricket player is troubled by a recent batting slump. He notices that he has an irrational belief that good players are never out without getting off the mark. Rather than let this irrational belief continue to create unnecessary tension, the player questions and disputes this belief. All batters, including the best, have been out for a 'duck'. This is part of playing cricket and does not necessarily indicate a lack of ability. Eventually, after disputing the irrational belief enough times, the player will begin to develop new belief systems that are more appropriate and realistic.

Approaches to stress management are based on the athletic environment as well as the individual athlete. In many instances, however, it is not possible to alter the athletic environment to reduce stress. Therefore sport psychologists and coaches must help athletes find ways to effectively handle the stresses within their environments, so they are able to perform well under these conditions. Individual coping strategies include both physical and cognitive techniques.

To determine when an athlete is over-aroused, coaches should establish behaviour profiles for individual athletes. One athlete may, for example, withdraw before a big competition while another becomes more talkative. Either of these examples may indicate higher than normal arousal levels. What a coach must consider is if these behaviours deviate from how the athlete behaves normally. If a given behaviour is not typical for the athlete, one of the stress management techniques presented above could be employed.

Whether physical (progressive relaxation) or cognitive (thought-stopping) stress management strategies are used is not as important as the quality of the coping response. When Gould and his colleagues (Gould, Eklund and Jackson, 1993; Gould, Finch and Jackson, 1993) examined coping responses in Olympic wrestlers and figure skaters, they found a variety of successful coping strategies. What determined whether the strategy was effective was the extent to which the coping response was automatic. Therefore, it is important for coaches to realize that none of these coping strategies will be effective without systematic practice.

Imagery and visualization

After a record-setting victory in the 1994 Professional Golf Association (PGA) Players Championship, Greg Norman was quoted as saying 'I don't know if I'm getting better, but I'm getting smarter . . . Every time I'm over the ball, I visualize the shot twice. I like to see things happen.' In Norman's mind, it's as though he has already executed the shot successfully before he even takes the golf club back.

What is imagery and how does it help athletes like Greg Norman to perform better? Imagery can be defined as a process by which sensory experiences are stored in memory and internally recalled and performed in the absence of external stimuli (Murphy, 1994). Although imagery is often associated with visualization, it is important to note that imagery includes all of the senses. For example, some athletes' imagery may include a feeling or a sound.

Imagery strategies have been used for a variety of purposes in sport. These include technique enhancement, error analysis, error correction, preparation for competition conditions, and confidence enhancement (Suinn, 1993). Within the sport psychology literature, two main theories have been forwarded to explain how imagery influences performance: (1) the psychoneuromuscular theory, and (2) the symbolic learning theory (Murphy and Jowdy, 1992).

The psychoneuromuscular theory proposes that vivid, imagined behaviours will produce neuromuscular responses similar to those of an actual experience. For example, Suinn (1980) monitored muscle activity in the legs of skiers as they imagined a downhill run. He found that the electrical patterns in the muscles closely approximated those expected if the person had actually been skiing. Unfortunately, not all research supports Suinn's results and the psychoneuromuscular theory. In a meta-analysis of the literature, Feltz and Landers (1983) concluded that it is doubtful that imagery effects result in low gain innervations or activation of muscles. Furthermore, from the experimental psychology field, research suggests that the effects of imagery are more a function of operations within the central nervous system than muscular activity during imagery (Kohl and Roenker, 1983). These studies support the contention that muscular responses are an effect mechanism rather than a cause of performance changes.

An alternative to the psychoneuromuscular theory is the symbolic learning theory. This theory proposes that imagery functions help athletes cognitively prepare for and plan their performance. Support for the symbolic learning theory has come from two areas of research (Murphy and Jowdy, 1992). First, a number of studies have shown that imagery is more effective for tasks that have a high cognitive component as opposed to a high motor component. Second, motor learning theories contending that early stages of learning are primarily cognitive are compatible with the notion that imagery will have its greatest effects during the early stages of learning.

Although the research examining the relationship between imagery training and performance is substantial, much remains to be done with regard to theory development. Murphy and Jowdy (1992) suggested that sport psychology researchers look beyond the psychoneuromuscular and symbolic learning theories and investigate the relevance of imagery theories developed in other areas such as cognitive and clinical psychology. For example, Lang (1977, 1979) has developed a psychophysiological information-processing theory to better understand research in the area of phobia and anxiety disorders. The theory is based on the assumption that an image is a functionally organized, finite set of propositions stored by the brain. This image contains both stimulus propositions (statements that describe the content of the scenario to be imagined) and response propositions (statements that describe the imager's response to that scenario). In addition to these proposition statements, the theory proposes that an image also contains a motor programme of instructions for the imager on how to respond to the image.

Within Lang's theory (1977, 1979), it is important to highlight the existence of the response propositions as a fundamental part of the image structure. Rather than conceptualizing an image as merely a stimulus in the athlete's mind to which he or she responds, the information-processing theory suggests that images also contain 'response scenarios' enabling athletes to access the appropriate motor programme to effectively alter athletic performance.

Similar to Lang's information-processing theory, Ahsen's (1984) triple-code model of imagery also recognizes the primary importance of psychophysiological processes in the imagery process. However, Ahsen's theory goes one step further to incorporate the *meaning* the image has for an individual. According to the triple-code model, there are three essential parts of imagery that must be described by both theorists and clinicians. These include the image itself, the somatic response to the image, and the meaning of the image. Although other theories have included both the content of the image and associated psychophysiological changes, no other model has addressed the importance of the meaning an individual attaches to a particular image. (See Murphy and Jowdy, 1992 and Suinn, 1993 for a more detailed review of imagery theories.)

Despite the need to further develop theories regarding the effectiveness of imagery and sport performance, substantial research exists to support the notion that imagery does in fact enhance performance (Murphy and Jowdy, 1992; Suinn, 1993). However, not all studies have shown a consistent effect size due to imagery interventions. Murphy (1994) suggested that these mixed results were due to a number of factors mediating the effectiveness of imagery. These include:

(1) imagery ability;
(2) imagery perspective;

(3) imagery outcome;
(4) the role of relaxation.

A variety of studies have examined the effect of imagery ability on the imagery–performance relationship (Ryan and Simons, 1981; Housner, 1984). These studies suggest that imagery will have the greatest effect on performance for those individuals who are better imagers. Imagery ability is defined by the level of vividness and controllability a person has over their imagery. Vividness refers to the clarity and reality in an athletes' image. Controllability refers to the athlete's ability to influence the content of the image. Although logic would suggest that imagery ability influences performance effects, it has not received adequate attention from researchers. Without considering the effects of imagery ability when investigating performance effects, researchers are likely to find mixed results.

Another factor mediating the effectiveness of imagery is imagery perspective. Some athletes, for example, imagine themselves from the perspective that they are inside their body actually experiencing the imagined sensations. A number of researchers have suggested that an internal perspective may be more effective at enhancing performance than an external perspective (e.g., imagining oneself from a spectator's perspective). For example, Mahoney and Avener (1977) found that qualifiers for the United States Olympic gymnastic team reported using more internal imagery compared with external imagery than did non-qualifiers. It has been suggested that the influence of imagery perspective may be greater in athletic performance than in other areas because of the importance of kinesthetic awareness to sport performance. Internal imagery may serve to enhance skill learning through kinesthetic feedback. However, it is also possible that external imagery can enhance performance, but through a different process. For example, external imagery may help an athlete see him or herself performing successfully in an important competition and thus enhance self-confidence. It is important that future research examine what features each imagery perspective has to offer in an attempt to better understand its effectiveness, rather than simply trying to determine if one perspective is better than another (Murphy, 1994).

A third mediating factor influencing the effectiveness of imagery is image outcome. Studies examining the effect of negative imagery rehearsal suggest that performance is inhibited. However, theories have failed to explain how negative imagery might degrade performance. Does negative imagery affect performance by disturbing a motor programme or does it influence variables such as confidence, concentration, or motivation? More research is needed in this area to better understand how positive and negative images differently affect performance.

Finally, it is important to examine how relaxation influences the effectiveness of imagery training. Many writers suggest that relaxation prior to imagery instructions will facilitate imagery control. For example, Suinn's (1993) visuo-motor behaviour rehearsal (VMBR) requires that each imagery session begin with a relaxation exercise. However, many of the studies that have demonstrated a strong positive effect on performance have not used relaxation procedures in combination with imagery rehearsal (e.g., Woolfolk, Parrish and Murphy, 1985). Future research needs to assess how relaxation interacts with imagery effectiveness.

Overall, it is important that future research in this area begin to examine the various mediating variables in imagery interventions. By merely asking 'Does imagery work?' researchers will limit possible discoveries. Imagery rehearsal is not a homogeneous distinct intervention. Imagery for one athlete may be very different from the imagery of another athlete. Researchers need to examine the multitude of variables associated with imagery if they are to fully understand how and why imagery affects performance.

From the research conducted thus far, many practical implications have been suggested to help coaches and athletes. For example, in his mental training book for coaches, Martens (1987) described a three-part Sports Imagery Training (SIT) programme. The first phase involves increasing the athletes' awareness of their sport experience. Athletes often perform on 'automatic pilot', especially more skilled athletes. They fail to notice sensory experiences that will contribute to higher-quality imagery. The second phase involves vividness training. Athletes are instructed to imagine their sport experience in the greatest detail possible. Often athletes must first practice imagining more familiar daily settings (e.g., bedroom) before progressing to more sport specific settings. The final phase of the SIT programme involves controllability training. Here athletes are instructed to practice manipulating their images.

With an appropriate training programme, such as the one outlined above, imagery skills can increase self-awareness, facilitate skill acquisition and maintenance, build self-confidence, control emotions, relieve pain, regulate arousal, and enhance preparation strategies (Murphy and Jowdy, 1992).

Concentration and attention

Have you ever been to a little league game and heard the coach yell to one of the players, 'Get your head in the game, CONCENTRATE!' Often coaches are able to recognize when an athlete is not paying attention, but they are unable to determine the necessary strategies to remedy the situation. Many coaches eagerly tell their players what to do psychologically, but not how.

Before discussing strategies to help athletes to improve concentration, it is important first to have a general understanding of what attention is. Attention can be defined as the thought process that directs and maintains our awareness of our sensory experiences. Attention involves three basic skills:

(1) the selection of the right stimuli to focus on;
(2) the ability to shift attention as the environment changes;
(3) the ability to sustain attention or concentrate.

Each of these skills will be explained in more detail below.

The first basic skill involves the ability to select the right things from the environment to focus on. Different tasks require different types of attentional focus. For example, to be successful, a softball pitcher must have a 'broad' attentional focus. She must attend to the batter as well as the players on base. If her attention is narrowly focused on the batter only, she may inadvertently allow a player on base to steal home and score. In contrast to a softball pitcher, a marksman must focus attention narrowly on the target. Thus, it is important to understand that not all athletes require the same attentional focus. What athletes attend to is dependent on the nature of their task.

In an effort to better understand attention, Nideffer (1976, 1993) has identified two dimensions of attention: width and direction. Width refers to the degree to which attention has either a broad or a narrow focus. The comparison between the softball pitcher and the marksman illustrates the distinction between a broad and narrow focus. The other dimension of attention involves direction, either internal or external. Internal attentional focus refers to attention that is directed inward. For example, a runner monitoring her physiological responses (heart rate, temperature) during a marathon has an internal focus of attention. In contrast, a quarterback scanning the football field to determine where to pass the ball has an external focus of attention. It is important that athletes are able to select the attentional focus (broad vs. narrow, internal vs. external) that best fits the nature of their task.

The second basic skill involves the ability to shift attention as the task or situation changes. For example, a golfer may approach a shot with a broad–external focus to determine what type of shot is best for the given situation. This may require focusing on various things such as the lie of the ball, the direction of the wind, or the location of a troublesome hazard. After making a decision regarding what type of shot to hit, attention may shift from a broad–external to a narrow–external focus. The golfer now directs attention solely on the selected target. Nideffer (1976) suggested that under pressure our ability to shift attention is influenced by our dominant style of attention. The attentional styles Nideffer identified include broad–internal, broad–external, narrow–external, or narrow–internal. No one style is better than another. Each possesses various strengths and weaknesses. Therefore, it is important that athletes develop each type of attentional focus so they will be better able to shift to the style most appropriate for a given situation.

The final basic attentional skill involves the ability to concentrate. Concentration can be defined as 'the ability to sustain attention on a selected stimulus for a period of time' (Martens, 1987, p. 146). In other words, whether your focus is internal/external or broad/narrow, concentration refers to the intensity of your attentional focus. For example, some athletes become so absorbed in their performance that time seems to stand still and their actions feel almost effortless. This performance state is often referred to as flow (Jackson, 1993).

As with any mental skill, developing concentration and attention skills requires a systematic training programme. First, it is important to educate athletes about the influence that selecting and shifting attention and concentration skills may have on their performance. They need to understand the various attentional demands of their sport. If a weakness is identified or if they are interested in further enhancing already strong attentional skills, there are ways to help individuals develop these skills.

Boutcher (1992b), Burke (1992), and Hardy, Jones and Gould (1996) have all identified ways to enhance attention/concentration skills. These include the following:

- *Simulation training*. Competitive environments often contain attentional demands which are different from normal practice settings. For example, officials and a large audience may be present, as well as a host of differing psychological distracters. Simulation training simply involves creating a practice environment that contains as many of these potential distracters as possible and then having the athletes learn to perform in their presence. For example, a professional golfer may report being distracted by the camera shutter clicks of press photographers when putting in major tournaments. Simulation training would involve practising one's putting as shutters were clicking at unexpected times.

- *Mental preparation routines and concentration cues.* Considerable evidence has shown that having consistent mental preparation routines (physical and psychological procedures that one adheres to before or during performance) are associated with superior performance (Crews, 1993). For example, a baseball player may always visualize himself hitting while in the on-deck circle, assume his batting stance in a predetermined way, and take a centring breath before readying for the pitch. One explanation of why mental preparation routines are associated with superior performance is that they help athletes learn to focus attention on task-appropriate cues and off task-inappropriate and distracting cues (Boutcher, 1992a,b; Burke, 1992). Hence, helping athletes establish mental preparation routines is an excellent way to help focus attention.

- *Focus on process-oriented goals.* Similar to mental preparation routines, it has been suggested that focusing on process goals (e.g., a few task relevant cues) as opposed to outcome goals (e.g., winning, the score of the competition) facilitates attention and performance (Hardy et al., 1996). For example, when interviewed on television Tommy Moe, Olympic ski racing champion, indicated that he skis best in the downhill when he focuses his attention on his goals of 'keeping his hands forward and letting his outside ski run'. However, when he focuses on winning races he does not perform as well. Thus, a key component of mental training is to teach athletes to set process as opposed to outcome goals.

- *Mental imagery.* Burke (1992) has indicated that an excellent way to develop attention and concentration is to systematically rehearse athletic skills via imagery. This would seem especially appropriate in light of the previously discussed symbolic learning theory of imagery.

- *Relaxation.* Teaching athletes relaxation skills not only helps them regulate their physiological arousal, but also has the advantage of focusing their attention away from anxiety producing thoughts and worries. A relaxed state is also thought to be conducive to helping people to use imagery. For these reasons, most sport psychologists view relaxation training as a strategy that can be used to facilitate attention and concentration.

- *Concentration awareness and training exercises.* A number of sport psychologists (Gauron, 1984; Harris and Harris, 1984) have identified exercises which are thought to help develop one's general attentional capabilities. For example, an athlete may be asked to circle a series of numbers in consecutive order from a large matrix of random numbers with the goal of increasing the speed that this can be done. It is suggested that as one's ability to perform this task improves, a concomitant increase in concentration will be evident and can be transferred to the sport domain.

As with any mental skill, developing concentration or attention skills require a systematic training programme. First, it is important to educate athletes about the influence selecting, shifting, and concentration skills may have on their performance. They need to understand that the various attentional demands of each skill they are to perform is important. If a weakness is identified, there are ways to help individuals develop the necessary skills to improve attention.

Following the education phase of a training programme is the actual skill development phase. Here athletes identify where their skills are weak and determine which strategies they can implement to improve their current skill level. These strategies include developing performance routines, imagery skills, and stress management skills. It is important to realize that like any physical skill, developing attention and concentration skills will require systematic practice!

An excellent example of an attentional training programme for sport has been provided by Boutcher (1992a). Specifically, Boutcher has proposed a training programme focusing on an evaluation of an athlete's attentional skills via a variety of measures (questionnaire, observation, psychophysiological), basic attentional training strategies including such things as performance tests like those previously mentioned and psychophysiological (e.g., eye movement control) measures, and advanced sport-specific training where these skills are customized to the specific demands of one's sport.

Finally, it must be recognized that sport psychology attentional research is in its infancy, especially investigations examining the utility of attentional skills training. For this reason evaluation research is essential in this area.

Motivation

Coaches often regard motivation as a key component to performance success. What is motivation and how can coaches reach those seemingly unmotivated athletes? In general, motivation can be defined as the direction and intensity of effort (Sage, 1977). Direction involves whether or not an athlete is motivated to approach or avoid a particular situation. For example, some children are highly motivated to participate in a sport team, while others will do anything to avoid such activities. Intensity involves the magnitude of motivation. Different athletes exhibit different levels of motivation in different situations.

Motivation in sport is a multidimensional construct that can be approached from a variety of theoretical perspectives. For example, in the achievement motivation literature, Nicholls (1984) contended that motivation is dependent on an individual's goal orientation. People who are 'task-involved' are motivated by the desire to continually learn and improve their skill regardless of whether they win or lose. In contrast, people who are 'ego-involved' are motivated to demonstrate competence relative to others. Thus performance outcome (winning or losing) is very important to people with this goal orientation. Similar models have also been developed around the concept of goal orientations. For example, Dweck (1986) has examined learning versus performance goals and the influence perceived competence will have on motivation. Similarly, Ames (1992) has examined environmental influences on mastery and ability goal orientations.

Motivation has also been studied from the theoretical perspective of intrinsic versus extrinsic motivational orientations. For example, the Cognitive Evaluation Theory (Deci and Ryan, 1985, 1991) suggests that people behave on the basis of intrinsic motivation, extrinsic motivation, or amotivation. Intrinsically motivated behaviours are engaged in for the inherent pleasure and satisfaction within the activity itself. On the other hand, extrinsically motivated behaviours are engaged in for reasons outside the activity, such as social recognition or awards. Apart from intrinsic and extrinsic motivation, amotivation is also considered within the Cognitive Evaluation Theory. Amotivated behaviour occurs when an individual perceives a lack of contingency between his or her behaviour and the outcome. There are no intrinsic or extrinsic rewards and participation in the activity will eventually cease.

An important component of the Cognitive Evaluation Theory is the inter-action between intrinsic motivation and extrinsic rewards. Deci and Ryan (1985) suggested that extrinsic rewards often decrease intrinsic motivation because they undermine people's need to feel competent and self-determined. For example, negative feedback information that implies incompetence can result in a decrease of intrinsic motivation. Extrinsic rewards can also decrease intrinsic motivation by making the activity dependent on the extrinsic reward, leading to a shift in the perceived locus of causality from internal to external. Because extrinsic reward can lose its 'motivating value' more quickly and easily than intrinsic rewards, it is important that coaches enhance the intrinsic motivation within each of their athletes. This can be accomplished by creating an environment that provides athletes with a sense of competence and choice.

Goal-orientation theories and the Cognitive Evaluation Theory are only a few of the many approaches that have been used to examine motivation in sport. Weiss and Chaumeton (1992) proposed an integrated model of sport motivation that includes the various theoretical perspectives and provides a common language for similar constructs in different theories. Briefly, the model accounts for the influences of:

(1) an individual's motivational orientation (intrinsic/mastery or extrinsic/ outcome);
(2) mastery attempts and performance outcomes;
(3) responses by significant others;
(4) the reward system and standard of goals developed;
(5) perceptions of competence and control;
(6) affect.

Outside of these 'core' constructs, the theory also includes the influences of individual difference (e.g., cognitive and physical maturity, gender, salience of success in sport) and contextual factors (e.g., reward structure, coaching style, sport type, sociocultural factors) that help to explain motivational processes. The interested reader is encouraged to consult Weiss and Chaumeton (1992) for a more complete review of the sport motivation literature.

Considering the various motivational theories presented thus far, what are some practical implications for coaches? For one, it is important that coaches understand that individual athletes participate in sport for many different reasons. Sport participation is thought to fulfil various needs including fun, affiliation, and competence. Many children, for example, participate in sport because they consider the activity to be fun. If something within the sport environment prevents the athlete from having fun (excessive pressure to win), then the athlete's motivation is likely to decrease. In addition to fun, some athletes participate in sport because they have a need to be with others. To these athletes, winning or losing may be secondary to socializing with their

1friends. If performance outcomes overshadow affiliation needs, motivation for these athletes is also likely to decrease. Finally, some athletes participate in sport in order to demonstrate competence. If the sport environment fails to provide competency information (performance improvements), motivation for athletes with these needs is likely to drop. Coaches must determine the needs of individual athletes so they are better able to structure the athletic environment to meet these needs. Many athletes lose motivation when their coaches mistakenly assume that they all participate for the same reason.

HOW TO IMPLEMENT A MENTAL SKILLS TRAINING PROGRAMME

Having established that mental skills training is an important factor in athletic success and having briefly reviewed core topics of mental training, the next area to address is how best to implement a mental skills training programme. This section is designed to answer the following questions:

- Who should implement a mental skills training programme?
- At what time during the season is it best to implement a mental skills training programme?
- How long should a mental skills training programme last?
- What are some specific steps to consider when designing a mental skills training programme?

Who should implement a mental skills training programme?

Mental skills training programmes can be successfully implemented by either a sport psychologist or a coach (Martens, 1987; Weinberg and Williams, 1993). Sport psychologists are best in situations where the coach has limited time and knowledge to plan a mental training programme. Sport psychologists are also beneficial in helping athletes deal with issues that they feel uncomfortable discussing with their coach. Some athletes feel that if they disclose any self-doubt, their coach will be less likely to play them in a competitive situation. However, not all athletic programmes have the financial resources to employ a sport psychologist on a regular basis. In these instances, a sport psychologist can be consulted temporarily to help launch a mental skills programme as well as to provide the coach with the necessary tools to maintain the programme in the future. Even if sport psychologists are consulted on a regular basis, coaches are critical factors in determining whether a training programme will succeed or fail. Many athletes are more likely to be influenced by their coach than by a sport psychologist. Thus, it is critical that sport psychologists and coaches work together to ensure the success of any mental skills training programme.

At what time during the season is it best to implement a mental skills training programme?

Ideally, it is best to introduce a mental skills training programme during the off-season or early in pre-season (Martens, 1987; Weinberg and Williams, 1993). This is when coaches typically have fewer demands on their time and therefore are better able to help plan and deliver a training programme. Unfortunately, many coaches turn to mental training in a panic to revive a failing team just prior to the season-ending tournament. This is the worst time to implement a mental skills training programme, not only because of the extra demands on both coaches and athletes, but also because mental skills, like physical skills, require practice before they can be mastered.

How long should a mental skills training programme last?

Mental skills are like physical skills. To develop and maintain them requires a commitment throughout the season (Martens, 1987). Ideally, mental skills training should become an integral part of daily practice. This is not to suggest that mental skills take precedence over physical skills. Both are important components of performance success. However, it is not always necessary to isolate mental and physical skill training. It has been suggested that mental skills can be used to enhance physical skill acquisition (Sinclair and Sinclair, 1994).

What are some specific steps to consider when designing a mental skills training programme?

There are a number of steps to consider when designing a mental skills training programme. First, what objective does one hope to accomplish? Coaches often enthusiastically list a dozen or more mental skills they want their athletes to work on. Considerations should be given to when the programme is to be implemented and how much time athletes and coaches are willing to devote to mental skills training (Weinberg and Williams, 1993). Coaches and sport psychologists can meet together to determine which mental skills are most important for a particular team or athlete.

After determining several realistic objectives, the sport psychologist must then determine how best to achieve these objectives. Currently, a variety of strategies exists to help athletes develop specific mental skills. For example, stress management strategies include progressive relaxation, biofeedback, thought stopping, and imagery. Coaches and sport psychologists must carefully select those strategies that will be most efficient and effective given the individual team or athlete they are working with.

After deciding which strategies to use, it is important to determine a mental skills training schedule. Questions to consider include how many meetings will be necessary to introduce the selected topics, how long should these meetings last, and when and where should they occur? Generally, it is best to hold more frequent meetings of shorter duration than it is to hold one long meeting at the beginning of the season. It is also best not to hold these meetings when athletes are tired and hungry after a long day of practice. Athletes will begin to resent mental training as an 'extra' nuisance after practice.

Training schedules should include both an education and a practice phase (Martens, 1987). Many coaches want to jump immediately into practising specific skills. Unfortunately, these efforts are often undermined because of the lack of understanding many athletes have regarding what mental training is and is not. Coaches and sport psychologists need to address the myths and misconceptions addressed earlier in this chapter. They must convince athletes of the importance of mental skills for performance success. Once athletes appreciate the value of mental skills training, it should be incorporated into daily practice sessions. Mental skills require the same effort and commitment that physical skills require.

The final step in any successful mental training programme involves evaluating whether or not the programme is meeting the established objectives (Weinberg and Williams, 1993). If the programme is meeting the objectives, you can continue with the confidence that what you are doing is effective. However, if the programme is not meeting its objectives, one needs to examine the situation to determine what obstacles are preventing the programme from reaching its goals and how these obstacles can be overcome. One of the most common problems encountered is a lack of time. Coaches often enthusiastically start a mental skills training programme, but fail to follow the programme through as the season progresses. Coaches and athletes must make mental training one of their priorities if they are to develop the necessary mental skills to enhance performance.

The following section will provide a specific example of how the first author designed and implemented a mental skill training programme with the US freestyle ski team. It also includes an evaluation of the programme with specific suggestions for any future projects.

AN EXAMPLE MENTAL SKILLS TRAINING PROGRAMME: THE US FREESTYLE MOGUL SKI TEAM

In May of 1992 the first author was contacted by US Skiing and asked to provide input regarding the development of a mental skills training programme designed to enhance team performance. The ski team's goal was to develop a systematic mental skills training programme which would educate athletes about key psychological skills needed for enhanced performance and to help facilitate the development of these skills. Prior to this time the freestyle mogul ski team had not used a sport psychology specialist to help develop mental skills in their athletes. The team, however, had experienced considerable World Cup and Olympic success.

As is the case with many sport organizations, the consultant was not hired sight unseen. His work with other sport groups was investigated and his ability was field tested (unbeknownst to him at the time) by having him present on mental training topics at a US Ski Team National Ski Coaches school and at the meeting of all US Ski team coaches. After successfully passing these tests he was asked to present to the entire freestyle ski team. Following this presentation, athlete and team input was solicited and a decision was made to hire the first author as a sport psychology consultant for the next season (1992–93). The consultants services were also retained for the 1993–94 season.

Programme purposes and content

Unlike many sport organizations, US Skiing had very specific gaols in mind for their mental skills training programme. After considerable discussion, coaches, administrators and sport science staff elected to have the following topics emphasized:

- performance planning and goal setting;
- mental preparation focusing on the identification of optimal emotional states needed for peak performance and strategies for regulating arousal levels (e.g., centring, arousal regulation);
- visualization and imagery.

Mental skills training staff

The primary consultant for this programme, a male in his early 40s, is an educational (as opposed to counselling or clinical) sport psychology specialist with all of his degrees (B.S., M.S., PhD.) in physical education/sport science. The consultant was 'certified' by the Association for the Advancement of Applied Sport Psychology (under the grandparenting option) and had over 10 years of consulting experience working with athletes in a variety of sports and at all levels of competition (from novice to world champions). However, he was a non-skier and had little knowledge of the sport apart from watching videos and reading books in an effort to prepare for his position with the ski team. Over the two-year period he also took ski lessons in an effort to become more familiar with the sport.

In addition to the primary consultant, Laurie Beck, the full-time US Skiing academic and career counsellor, who was trained in psychology (MS) served as a co-consultant. Laurie who was in her early 40s, is an experienced skier and knew all the athletes from her academic and career counsulting duties.

In the initial year of the programme she observed all group presentations and sat in on all athlete–consultant individual meetings because of her inexperience in sport psychology. In the second year of the programme, however, she took a more active role in the individual consultations and made group presentations to development team members. Throughout the two-year consultation this individual's knowledge of freestyle skiing and the athletes was extremely helpful in formulating the mental skills training programme. It was also intended that over time she would move from a co-consulting to a primary consulting role.

Delivery methods

The mental skills training programme was delivered in several ways. First, a series of formal group (team) presentations were made to the athletes over the two years. These lasted between 60 and 90 minutes and consisted of lectures, exercises, group discussions, and observations of mental training video tapes. Handouts and worksheets were designed for each session and distributed to the athletes. Second, individual athlete consultations were held on a voluntary basis. These typically involved the athlete and the two consultants and in a small number of cases, the coach. Third, prior to the start of the programme, coaches attended a coaching seminar and received mental skills training in the areas which were to be featured in the programme. Mid-way through the programme a series of applied articles (Beck, 1992; Gould, 1992a,b; Udry and Gould, 1992) were written for *The American Ski Coach* on topics featured in the programme. Finally, meetings were held with the coaches to keep them fully informed of both individual and team mental skills training programmes (working within predetermined athlete confidentiality guidelines). At times, individual sessions were also held with the coaches to assist them in implementing mental training with their athletes, as well as to provide performance enhancement counselling to them individually (e.g., deal with coaching stress that may interfere with one's ability to assist athletes).

Programme content and delivery schedule

Table 2.4 summarizes the educational content conveyed to the athletes in this total programme. It can be seen that general sessions were held on:

- defining sport psychology and psychological skills training;
- performance planning and goal setting;
- mental preparation and emotional arousal regulation;
- visualization and imagery.

Major resources used to develop these materials included Orlick's (1986a,b; 1990) *Psyching for Sport, Coaches Training Manual for Psyching For*

Table 2.4: US freestyle ski team mental skills training programme

Major area specific content description

Introduction
- What is sport psychology and psychology skills training?
- Psychological skills training myths

Goal setting
- Goal setting exercise (long-term dream goal, dream goal this year, realistic current season performance goal, monthly goal, next practice goal) based on Orlick (1986a)
- Staircase goals
- Evaluating goals by using goal setting principles
- Factors to consider and areas in which to set goals
- Common problems in setting goals
- Individualized seasonal goals

Mental preparation and energy management
- Optimal zones of functioning: the relationship between emotional arousal and athletic performance
- Determining and controlling optimal emotional arousal levels
- Complete a more extensive skiing-specific competitive reflections form based on Orlick's (1986a) original form
- Formulate a race mental preparation plan for optimal performance
- Formulate emergency 'shrink or stretch' mental preparation plans for use when faced with less or more than normal time available for mental preparation
- Formulate refocusing plans for coping with unexpected events and distractions
- Arousal management: psyching-up or chilling-out strategies
- Nideffer's (1985) 'centring' breathing relaxation and focusing strategy
- Thought-stopping exercise (Bump, 1989)
- US Olympic Committee Sports Mental Training Relaxation and Energy Management For Athletes brochure distributed and discussed

Visualization-imagery
- Observe Orlick and Botterill Coaching Association of Canada 'What You See is What You Get' video and respond to worksheet questions examining uses of imagery, tips for using imagery, and ways they can use imagery
- Summary of key points of video
- Sports imagery training guidelines based on Martens (1987)— What is imagery? How does imagery work? Why use imagery? Developing imagery skills, and motor imagery guidelines

Staying focused at the Olympics
- Understanding and embracing the Olympic challenge
- Keys to Olympic success (staying focused by following mental preparation plans, challenge, having fun, keeping things in perspective, expecting and preparing for the unexpected, staying cool under pressure)
- Exercise identifying Olympic challenges (positive and negative distractions) and methods of coping with them

Sport, and *In Pursuit of Excellence* texts, Martens' (1987) *Coaches' Guide to Sport Psychology*, Nideffer's (1985) *Athlete's Guide to Mental Training*, review articles on goal setting (Gould, 1993), psychological skills training (Gould and Eklund, 1991), and arousal regulation (Gould and Udry, 1994), as well as numerous articles from *The Sport Psychologist*.

The schedule for delivering the mental skills training programme is contained in Table 2.5. Inspection of this table shows that nine group sessions were held in the two-year period. Because of scheduling conflicts, injuries, and changes made to the World Cup team roster, not all athletes attended all group sessions. Additionally, some sessions were repeated to 'catch-up' new team members or skiers who missed previous meetings.

During the two-year time period a number of individual sessions were held. These varied from 30 to 90 minutes in length and ranged from a low of one to a high of nine (mean of 3.6) for the 14 individual athletes involved. Much of the time in these meetings was focused on 'customizing' the general session content (e.g., devise mental preparation plans, set individual goals) to meet individual skier needs. Other salient issues not covered in the group sessions arose, however, and were enthusiastically addressed. These individual-specific topics are contained in Table 2.6.

Programme evaluation

Unfortunately, no formal evaluation process was planned as part of this programme. However, the programme was continually evaluated at an informal level during its first two years. This was accomplished in several ways. First, team and individual athlete performances were examined. Second, coach and athlete feedback was sought on a regular basis.

In terms of performance, the athletes performed well during the two-year period with 50 percent achieving top ten world cup finishes and five performers achieving top three finishes. More importantly, the vast majority of skiers and all the coaches felt the programme was helpful to the skiers. For example, of the three men and three women who competed in the 1994 Winter Olympic Games four of the six performed to potential, one performed below and one above potential in the estimation of the head coach. One Olympic silver medal was achieved. Given the team's previous success on the World Cup circuit and unavailability of stable performance statistics in skiing (e.g., 1500 metre times) it is not possible to tell if the programme enhanced skier performance. However, in terms of World rankings it certainly did not hurt performance and in the impression of most of the individual athletes and coaches involved, facilitated their performance.

The consultant involved felt that the programme was successful for a number of reasons. First and foremost was the head coach's receptive attitude toward sport psychology. He believed in the importance of mental skills training, had an intuitive 'feel' for the material taught, and became

Table 2.5: US freestyle mental skills training programme schedule

Date of contact	Place and type of contact
May 1992	*Off-season dryland camp*

- Group sessions (introduction to psych skills training; mental preparation; competitive-reflections)
- Meeting with coaching staff

November 1992	*Pre-season training camp*

- Group sessions (goal setting; competitive reflections; thought stopping; centring)
- Individual session with skiers
- Meeting with head coach

December 1992	*World Cup race check in*

- Individual sessions with skiers
- Meeting with coaching staff

May 1993	*Off-season dryland camp*

- Group sessions (repeat of previous sessions)
- Individual sessions with skiers (1992–1993 programme evaluation; off-season goal setting)
- Meeting with coaching staff (1992–1993 programme evaluation; Year 2 planning)

July 1993	*Summer on mountain training camp*

- Individual sessions with skiers
- Meeting with head coach

September 1993	*Pre-season training camp*

- Group session (imagery-visualization)
- Individual sessions with skiers

November 1994	*Pre-season training camp*

- Group Session (team goals for upcoming season; team communication; Introduction of US Olympic team Lillehammer games sport psychologist)
- Individual sessions with skiers

January 1994	*World Cup race check in*

- Individual sessions with skiers
- Meeting with head coach

January 1994	*Olympic Games preparation meeting*

- Group session (staying focused at the Olympics)
- Individual sessions with skiers
- Meeting with coaching staff

May 1994	*Review and evaluate programme*

- Athlete–coach programme evaluations
- Coach–consultant planning for future

involved in all aspects of the programme. For example, when the athletes set performance goals, so too did the coach. In fact he went as far as to share his personal coaching goals with the group. This not only allowed the coach to improve his coaching, but demonstrated to all involved his belief in and commitment to mental skills training. As the coach was very well organized,

Table 2.6: Other individual athletics meeting topics discussed

Time management
Insomnia
Coping with performance pressure
Adapting to World Cup ski circuit
Improving athlete–coach communication
Confidence enhancement
Dealing with time away from family
Motivation
Handling fear of injury
Psychology of injury rehabilitation
Dealing with distractions
Media interactions
Teammate relations
Sport retirement
Keeping winning in perspective
Failure to make Olympic team/demotion from World Cup team
National governing body/team politics

points discussed and information conveyed during consultant visits were always followed up and emphasized throughout the season. Hence, mental training was not limited to the brief time periods the consultants were able to have direct contact with the skiers.

A second strength of the programme was the positive rapport between the consultant and the mogul skiers. Throughout this time period the consultant also worked with the men's and women's alpine programmes, as well as other elements of freestyle skiing. However, the fit (e.g., personality, communication style) seemed to be best between the consultant and freestyle skiers (particularly the mogul skiers). This is not to say that personality or 'fit' problems arose with any of the other groups, only that the fit was best with this team. While this relationship can not be easily explained, it was an important reason for the programme's success and, in the authors' opinion, is a critical aspect of the mental skills training programme.

While the programme was mainly successful, several limitations were evident. Chief among these was the consultant's inability to ski. His inability to ski inhibited him from attending practices where critical observations could be made, or mountain instructions given (e.g., using imagery during training) while also eliminating the opportunity to conduct micro-consults (e.g., discuss athlete concerns in chair lift rides up the mountain). The inability to ski at times also hindered his ability to fully understand the experiences of the athletes (e.g. flat light or difficulty in seeing because of sunlight changes on course) although even taking basic ski lessons helped a good deal in this regard.

Finally, as with most consults, a major limitation of the programme was the lack of time available to spend with the team. More contacts during the year and travelling with the team for several weeks during the European portion of the World Cup season would have been highly desirable, but was not possible due to budgetary considerations.

Conclusion

Because of the personalities and orientations of the specific individuals involved, the particular needs of the athletes and coaches, as well as organized contexts, no two mental training programmes will be the same. However, this example has been included because while it was felt to be successful it was not without problems. Moreover, in the authors' opinions many of the issues involved are generic to all mental training programmes. For this reason it provides a model of how a particular programme might be formulated.

PROBLEMS AND PITFALLS IN MENTAL TRAINING

Although each situation presents its own unique set of challenges, a number of common problems have been identified by coaches, athletes, and consultants involving the actual implementation of a mental skills training programme. These obstacles include:

- barriers to entry;
- lack of coach support and follow-up;
- unrealistic expectations;
- trying to do too much too soon.

This section will address each of these consulting issues and will make specific suggestions as how to handle potential problems.

Barriers to entry

Sport psychology consultants often must prove themselves before being accepted to work for an extended time with an individual team or athlete (Ravizza, 1988; Weinberg and Williams, 1993). In the previous section, the first author recounted having to pass informal 'field tests' before being hired for the 1992–93 season. As this is not uncommon, it is important that sport psychology consultants become aware of the potential obstacles to gaining acceptance by a team and develop the necessary strategies to deal with these situations. After all, even the soundest mental training programme will not be of much use if it is never allowed to be implemented!

Ravizza (1988) has identified three significant barriers to entry. The first is overcoming the 'shrink' image. Many coaches and athletes still mistakenly associate mental training/sport psychology with a sole focus on clinical issues. Athletes are often apprehensive about working with a sport psychology consultant because they fear that others, especially their coach, will assume they are a 'head-case'. It is therefore critical that consultants explain what mental training is and is not. Consultants should emphasize that mental training can help even the most skilled athletes to perform up to their potential on a more consistent basis. And while clinical issues do arise with athletes (just as they do in the population at large) and need attention from trained clinicians, most of what is done in sport psychology is aimed at improving the skills of healthy, normal functioning athletes.

The second barrier to entry identified by Ravizza (1988) is a lack of sport specific knowledge. Coaches and athletes will respond more favourably to a consultant that speaks their 'language' and can relate mental skills to their specific individual needs, than to a consultant who comes in with a generic pre-packaged programme (Orlick and Partington, 1987; Partington and Orlick, 1987). To individualize a mental training programme to a specific team, a consultant needs to understand task-relevant demands of the sport. For example, there are significant differences between the psychological demands of an individual sport such as golf and a team sport such as netball. A consultant must demonstrate knowledge of a particular sport to establish respect and credibility of the coach. This includes understanding general terminology as well as basic strategies. This expertise can be developed through reading, taking physical education courses, or talking to people who participate in the sport. In the previous section, the first author described how he studied videos, read books, and took ski lessons in order to better understand certain aspects of the sport in which he was consulting.

The third barrier to entry is an inadequate knowledge of organizational politics. Coaches often make decisions regarding retaining or releasing a consultant on the basis of feedback from athletes and other staff members (Partington and Orlick, 1987). Consultants must quickly determine who the key figures are on a particular team. If just one influential person misunderstands the consultant's role or intentions, the entire mental skills training programme could be undermined. Therefore, it is important that consultants educate the whole staff as to what mental training is and how each individual can help to ensure the programmes success (Ravizza, 1988).

Gaining entry requires that a consultant establish respect, credibility, and trust with both coaches and athletes. Without this, it is unlikely that even the best mental skills training programme will be effective. It is important that sport psychology consultants address the barriers outlined by Ravizza (1988). The first few meetings with a new team are critical in establishing a good working relationship. At this time a consultant's objectives should include educating the entire staff as to what mental training is and is not, demonstrating sport specific knowledge, as well as acquiring adequate knowledge of organizational politics.

Coach support and follow-up

In addition to the challenges regarding gaining entry with a team, sport psychology consultants must also find ways to maintain coach support throughout the season (Ravizza, 1988; Weinberg and Williams, 1993). Unlike coaches, consultants are rarely able to meet with a team or athlete on a daily basis. It is therefore critical that coaches reinforce mental training in the consultant's absence. Consultants can help coaches by outlining ways to integrate mental skills training into practice. For example, a swim coach may stress that warm-up is not only a time to physically stretch, but also to visualize successfully executing various stroke mechanics to be practised that day. Consultants should emphasize that mental skills training will not take away from physical practice, but will instead enhance it.

During pre-season, many coaches are enthusiastic about implementing a mental skills training programme. Unfortunately, as the season progresses and coaches have greater time demands and pressures, mental training is often reduced to a handful of brief meetings added on to an already demanding practice schedule. Rather than viewing mental training as an integral part of practice, athletes begin to see it as an 'add on' that cuts into their limited free time. Coaches must be encouraged to make mental training as much a priority as physical training. Athletes will know mental training is valuable to the coach when practice time is given to it. Consultants must emphasize that a programme's success is dependent on the support and involvement of the coaches.

Unrealistic expectations

Some coaches and athletes turn to mental training for a quick performance fix. Sport psychology consultants need to explain what mental training is and is not. Mental skills will not make-up for poor physical skills or technique. Also, mental skills require the same time and patience to develop that physical skills do. Many well-meaning coaches panic before an important tournament when a player suddenly starts performing poorly. They look to mental training for a quick 'cure'. When mental training does not produce the results they had hoped for, they mistakenly assume mental training does not work. Consultants must be honest with these coaches about what they can realistically expect from mental training given the time and commitment they are willing to put forth. Consultants who promise dramatic performance improvements, only set themselves up for failure and undermine the credibility of mental training (Ravizza, 1988).

Trying to do too much too soon

Another common problem facing sport psychology consultants is determining what skills to include in a mental training programme. Many coaches are eager to try all that mental training has to offer. A consultant needs to help coaches select those skills that are most appropriate given the constraints of the individual situation. For example, Weinberg and Williams (1993) suggested determining what and how many skills to include based on when the programme is first being implemented and how much time athletes and coaches are willing to devote to mental skills training. If the season is almost over and the coach does not intend to take more than 30 minutes a week for mental training, it would be unrealistic to attempt to develop more than one or two psychological skills. On the other hand, if a coach is committed to implementing a mental training programme over the course of an entire season, more skills can be introduced and developed over time. Generally, it is best that consultants develop a few skills well to establish credibility with coaches and athletes. This will help create or maintain an interest in mental training in the future. If consultants try to do too much too soon, they risk accomplishing little as well as losing credibility and respect.

CONCLUSION

Given the benefits of mental skills training discussed throughout this chapter, it is important that coaches and athletes understand what mental skills training is and how it can be used to enhance athletic performance. Mental skills training is not meant to help athletes deal with serious clinical issues nor is it a quick fix for performance woes. Mental skills training involves developing skills such as self-confidence, goal setting, stress management, imagery, concentration, and motivation that have been found to enhance sport performance. Furthermore, mental skills training can benefit not only elite athletes, but also athletes of various ages and skill levels.

To help ensure the effectiveness of a mental skills training programme, sport psychology consultants and coaches must work together to carefully design a programme to meet the specific needs of a given team or athlete. Consideration should be given to questions such as what specific skills are most needed and how much practice time will be provided for mental skills training. With an organized plan of action, many of the potential problems associated with mental training can be overcome.

While much has been learned about mental skills training in recent years, there is a need for additional research. Intervention evaluations employing both single subject and more traditional group designs are needed and a variety of methodological improvements must take place. Moreover, this review has demonstrated the importance of using theory to guide this research.

Despite the need for continued research, both the research and professional practice evidence presented in this review clearly show that mental training has the potential to help athletes both perform better and enjoy sport participation more. It is our hope that, in forthcoming years, mental training will not only help elite athletes like the ones discussed at the onset of this review, but all athletes regardless of their ability who hope to achieve their own brand of personal excellence.

REFERENCES

Ahsen, A. (1984) ISM: The triple code model for imagery and psychophysiology, *Journal of Mental Imagery*, **8**, 15–42.

Ames, C. (1992) Achievement goals, motivational climate, and motivational processes. In *Motivation in Sport and Exercise* (Ed. G. Roberts), pp. 161–176, Human Kinetics, Champaign, IL.

Bandura, A. (1977) Self-efficacy: Toward a unifying theory of behavioral change, *Psychological Review*, **84**, 191–215.

Bandura, A. and Cervone, D. (1983) Self-evaluative and self-efficacy mechanisms governing the motivational effects of goal systems, *Journal of Personality and Social Psychology*, **45**, 1017–1028.

Beck, L. (1992) Designing a program: Establishing a structure for USST sport psychology, *The American Ski Coach*, **15**, 37–40.

Boutcher, S.H. (1992a) Attention and athletic performance: An integrated approach. In *Advances in Sport Psychology* (Ed. T. Horn), pp. 251–266, Human Kinetics, Champaign, IL.

Boutcher, S. (1992b) Developing consistency, *Sport Psychology Training Bulletin*, **3**, 1–8.

Bump, L.A. (1989) *Sport Psychology Study Guide*. Human Kinetics, Champaign, IL.

Burke, K.L. (1992) Concentration. *Sport Psychology Training Bulletin*, **4**, 1–8.

Burton, D. (1989) Winning isn't everything: Examining the impact of performance goals on collegiate swimmers' cognitions and performance, *The Sport Psychologist*, **3**, 105–132.

Burton, D. (1990) Multimodal stress management in sport: Current status and future directions. In *Stress and Performance in Sport* (Eds. J.G. Jones and L. Hardy), pp. 171–202, Wiley, Chichester.

Burton, D. (1992) The Jekyll/Hyde nature of goals: Reconceptualizing goal setting in sport. In *Advances in Sport Psychology* (Ed. T. Horn), pp. 267–297, Human Kinetics, Champaign, IL.

Burton, D. (1993) Goal setting in sport. In *Handbook of Research On Sports Psychology* (Eds. R.N. Singer, M. Murphey, and L.K. Tennant), pp. 467–491, Macmillan, New York.

Crews, D.J. (1993) Self regulation strategies in sport and exercise. In *Handbook of Research On Sports Psychology* (Eds. R.N. Singer, M. Murphey, and L.K. Tennant) pp. 557–568, Macmillan, New York.

Crocker, P.R.E., Alderman, R.B. and Smith, M.R. (1988) Cognitive-affective stress management training with high performance youth volleyball players: Effects on affect, cognition, and performance, *Journal of Sport and Exercise Psychology*, **10**, 448–460.

Danish, S.J., Petitpas, A.J., and Hale, B.D. (1993) Life development intervention for athletes: Life skills through sports, *The Counselling Psychologist*, **21**, 352–385.

Deci, E. and Ryan, R. (1985) *Intrinsic Motivation and Self-Determination in Human Behavior*. Plenum, NY.

Deci, E. and Ryan, R. (1991) A motivational approach to self: Integration in personality. In *Nebraska Symposium on Motivation, 1990: Perspectives on Motivation* (Ed. R.A. Dienstbier), pp. 237–288, University of Nebraska Press, Lincoln.

Dweck, C.S. (1986) Motivational processes affecting learning, *American Psychologist*, **41**, 1040–1048.

Elliot, E.S. and Dweck, C.S. (1988) Goals: An approach to motivation and achievement, *Journal of Personality and Social Psychology*, **54**, 5–12.

Ellis, A. (1982) Self-direction in sport and life/becoming self-directed. In *Coaching Association of Canada* (Eds. T. Orlick, J.T. Partington, and J.H. Salmela), pp. 10–15, 37–42, Ottawa, Canada.

Feltz, D.L. (1988) Self-confidence and sports performance, *Exercise and Sport Science Reviews*, **16**, 423–458.

Feltz, D.L. and Landers, D.M. (1983) The effects of mental practice on motor skill learning and performance: A meta-analysis, *Journal of Sport Psychology*, **5**, 25–57.

Gauron, E.F. (1984) *Mental Training for Peak Performance*. Sport Science Associates, Lancing, NY.

Gould, D. (1982) Sport psychology in the 1980s: Current status and future directions in youth sports research, *Journal of Sport Psychology*, **4**, 203–218.

Gould, D. (1992a) Exercising your ski racer's mental muscles, *The American Ski Coach*, **15**, 3–4.

Gould, D. (1992b) Why goal setting fails, *The American Ski Coach*, **15**, 8–11.

Gould, D. (1993) Goal setting for peak performance. In *Applied Sport Psychology: Personal Growth to Peak Performance* (Ed. J.M. Williams, 2nd edition), pp. 158–169, Mayfield, Mountain View, CA.

Gould, D. and Eklund, R.C. (1991) The application of sport psychology for performance of optimization, *Thai Journal of Sports Science*, **1**(1), 10–21.

Gould, D., Eklund, R. and Jackson, S. (1992a) 1988 U.S. Olympic wrestling excellence: I. mental precompetitive cognition, and affect, *The Sport Psychologist*, **6**, 358–382.

Gould, D., Eklund, R. and Jackson, S. (1992b) 1988 U.S. Olympic wrestling excellence: II. thoughts and affect occurring during competition, *The Sports Psychologist*, **6**, 383–402.

Gould, D., Eklund, R. and Jackson, S. (1993) Coping strategies used by U.S. Olympic wrestlers, *Research Quarterly for Exercise and Sport*, **64**, 83–93.

Gould, D., Finch, L.M., and Jackson, S. (1993) Coping strategies used by national champion figure skaters, *Research Quarterly for Exercise and Sport*, **64**, 453–468.

Gould, D., Hodge, K., Peterson, K. and Giannini, J. (1989) An exploratory examination of strategies used by elite coaches to enhance self-efficacy in athletes, *Journal of Sport and Exercise Psychology*, **11**, 128–140.

Gould, D., Jackson, S.A. and Finch, L.M. (1993) Sources of stress in national champion figure skaters, *The Journal of Sport and Exercise Psychology*, **14**, 134–159.

Gould, D. and Krane, V. (1992) The arousal-athletic performance relationship: Current status and future directions. In *Advances in Sport Psychology* (Ed. T. Horn), pp. 119–141, Human Kinetics, Champaign, IL.

Gould, D., Murphy, S., Tammen, V., and May, J. (1991) An evaluation of U.S. Olympic sport psychology consultant effectiveness, *The Sports Psychologist*, **5**, 111–127.

Gould, D., Tammen, V., Murphy, S. and May, J. (1989) An examination of U.S. Olympic sport psychology consultants and the services they provide, *The Sport Psychologist*, **3**, 300–312.

Gould, D. and Udry, E. (1994) Psychological skills for enhancing performance: Arousal regulation strategies, *Medicine and Science in Sports and Exercise*, **26**, 478–485.

Greenspan, M. and Feltz, D. (1989) Psychological interventions with athletes in competitive situations, *Journal of Sport Psychology*, **3**, 219–236.

Griffith, C.R. (1925) Psychology and its relations to athletic competition, *American Physical Education Review*, **30**, 193–199.

Hanin, Y. (1980) A study of anxiety in sports. In *Sport Psychology: An Analysis of Athlete Behavior* (Ed. W. Straub), pp. 236–249, Movement, Ithaca, NY.

Hardy, L. (1990) A catastrophe model of performance in sport. In *Stress and Performance in Sport* (Eds. G. Jones and L. Hardy), pp. 81–106, Wiley, Chichester.

Hardy, L., Jones, G. and Gould, D. (1996), *The Psychological Preparation of Elite Sport Performers: Theory and Practice*, Wiley, Chichester.

Harris, D.V. and Harris, B.L. (1984) *The Athlete's Guide to Sports Psychology: Mental Training for Physical People*, Leisure Press, New York.

Housner, L.D. (1984) The role of visual imagery in recall of modeled motoric stimuli, *Journal of Sport Psychology*, **6**, 148–158.

Jackson, S.A. (1993) Athletes in flow: A qualitative investigation of flow states in elite figure skaters, *Journal of Applied Sport Psychology*, **4**, 161–180.

Jacobson, E. (1932) Electrophysiology of mental activities, *American Journal of Psychology*, **44**, 677–694.

Kendall, G., Hrycaiko, G., Martin, L., and Kendall, T. (1990) The effects of an imagery rehearsal, relaxation, and self-talk package on basketball game performance, *Journal of Sport and Exercise Psychology*, **12**, 157–166.

Kerr, J.H. (1993) An eclectic approach to psychological interventions in sport: Reversal theory, *The Sport Psychologist*, **7**, 400–418.

Kohl, R.M. and Roenker, D. L. (1983) Mechanism involvement during skill imagery, *Journal of Motor Behavior*, **15**, 179–190.

Lang, P.J. (1977) Imagery in therapy: An information processing analysis of fear, *Behavior Therapy*, **8**, 862–886.

Lang, P. J. (1979) A bio-informational theory of emotional imagery, *Psychophysiology*, **16**, 495–512.

Locke, E.A. and Latham, G.P. (1990) *A Theory of Goal Setting and Task Performance*, Prentice-Hall, Englewood Cliffs, NJ.

Locke, E.A., Shaw, K.N., Saari, L.M. and Latham, G.P. (1981) Goal setting and task performance: 1969–1980, *Psychological Bulletin*, **90**, 125–152.

Mace, R. (1990) Cognitive behavioral interventions in sport. In *Stress and Performance in Sport* (Eds. G. Jones and L. Hardy), pp. 203–231, Wiley, Chichester.

Mahoney, M.J. and Avener, M. (1977) Psychology of the elite athlete: An exploratory study, *Cognitive Therapy and Research*, **3**, 361–366.

Martens, R. (1987) *Coaches' Guide to Sport Psychology*, Human Kinetics, Champaign, IL.

Martens, R., Vealey, R.S. and Burton, D. (1990) *Competitive Anxiety in Sports*, Human Kinetics, Champaign, IL.

Murphy, S.M. (1994) Imagery interventions in sport, *Medicine and Science in Sports and Exercise*, **26**, 486–494.

Murphy, S. and Jowdy, D. (1992) Imagery and mental rehearsal. In *Advances in Sport Psychology* (Ed. T. Horn), pp. 221–250, Human Kinetics, Champaign, IL.

Neiss, R. (1988) Reconceptualizing arousal: Psychological states in motor performance, *Psychological Bulletin*, **103**, 345–366.

Nicholls, J.G. (1984) Achievement motivation: Conceptions of ability, subjective experience, task choice, and performance, *Psychological Review*, **91**, 328–346.

Nideffer, R. (1976) *The Inner Athlete: Mind Plus Muscle for Winning*, Crowell, New York.

Nideffer, R.M. (1985) *Athletes' Guide to Mental Training*. Leisure Press, Champaign, IL.

Nideffer, R.M. (1993) Attentional control training. In *Handbook of Research On Sports Psychology* (Eds. R.N. Singer, M. Murphey, and L.K. Tennant), pp. 542–556, Macmillan, New York.

Orlick, T. (1986a) *Psyching for Sport: Mental Training for Athletes*. Leisure Press, Champaign, IL.

Orlick, T. (1986b) *Coaches Training Manual for Psyching for Sport*, Leisure Press, Champaign, IL.

Orlick, T. (1990) *In Pursuit of Excellence*, Human Kinetics, Champaign, IL.

Orlick, T. and Partingon, J. (1987) The sport psychology consultant: Analysis of critical components as viewed by Canadian athletes, *The Sport Psychologist*, **1**, 4–7.

Orlick, T. and Partington, J. (1988) Mental links to excellence, *The Sport Psychologist*, **2**, 105–130.

Partington, J. and Orlick, T. (1987) The sport psychology consultant: Olympic coaches' views, *The Sport Psychologist*, **1**, 95–102.

Percival, L. (1971) *Proceedings of the First International Symposium on the Art and Science of Coaching. Fitness Institute Proceedings*. Vol. 1, Ontario, Toronto, Canada, pp. 285–326.

Pierce, B.E. & Burton, D. (1995) Effects of goal setting styles of the competitive cognitions and performance of female junior high school gymnasts. Manuscript submitted for publication.

Raglin, J. (1992) Anxiety and sport performance. In *Exercise Sport Science Review*, **20**, (Ed. J.O. Holloszy), pp. 243–274, Williams & Wilkins, Baltimore.

Ravizza, K. (1988) Gaining entry with athletic personnel for season-long consulting, *The Sport Psychologist*, **2**, 243–254.

Ryan, E.D., and Simons, J. (1981) Cognitive demand imagery and frequency of mental practice as factors influencing the acquisition of mental skills, *Journal of Sport Psychology*, **4**, 35–45.

Sage, G.H. (1977) *Introduction to Motor-Behavior: A Neuropsychological Approach* (2nd Edition). Addison-Wesley, Reading, MA.

Scanlan, T.K., Carpenter, P.J., Schmidt, G.W., Simons, J.P. and Keeler, B. (1993) An introduction to the sport commitment model, *Journal of Sport and Exercise Psychology*, **15**, 1–15.

Scanlan, T.K., Simons, J.P., Carpenter, P.J., Schmidt, G.W. and Keeler, B. (1993) The sport commitment model: Measurement development for the youth-sport domain, *Journal of Sport and Exercise Psychology*, **15**, 16–38.

Sinclair, G.D. and Sinclair, D.A. (1994) Developing reflective performers by integrating mental management skills with the learning process, *The Sport Psychologist*, **8**, 13–27.

Smith, R.E. (1980) A cognitive–affective approach to stress management training for athletes. In *Psychology of Motor Behavior in Sport—1979* (Eds. C.H. Nadeau, W.R. Halliwell, K.M. Newell and G.C. Roberts), Human Kinetics, Champaign, IL.

Smith, R.E. (1989) Applied sport psychology in an age of accountability, *Journal of Applied Sport Psychology*, **1**, 166–180.

Smoll, F.L. and Smith, R.E. (1982) Reducing stress in youth sport: Theory and application. In *Children in Sport* (Eds. F.L. Smoll, R.A. Magill, and M.J. Ash) (3rd Edition), pp. 229–250, Human Kinetics, Champaign, IL.

Smoll, F.L. and Smith, R.E. (1993) Educating youth sport coaches: An applied sport psychology perspective. In *Applied Sport Psychology: Personal Growth to Peak Performance* (Ed. J.M. Williams), (2nd edition), pp. 36–57, Mountain View, California.

Suinn, R.M. (1980) Psychology and sports performance: Principles and applications. In *Psychology in Sports: Methods and Applications* (Ed. R. Suinn), pp. 26–36 Burgess, Minneapolis, MN.

Suinn, R. (1993) Imagery. In *Handbook of Research On Sports Psychology* (Eds. R.N. Singer, M. Murphey, and L.K. Tennant), pp. 492–510, Macmillan, New York.

Udry, E. and Gould, D. (1992) Mental preparation profiles, *The American Ski Coach*, **15**, 15–23.

Vealey, R.S. (1992) Personality and sport: A comprehensive review. In *Advances in Sport Psychology* (Ed. T.S. Horn), pp. 25–59, Human Kinetics, Champaign, IL.

Vealey, R.S. (1994) Current status and prominent issues in sport psychology interventions, *Medicine and Science in Sports and Exercise*, **26**, 495–502.

Weinberg, R.S. (1989) Applied sport psychology: Issues and challenges, *Journal of Applied Sport Psychology*, **1**, 181–195.

Weinberg, R.S. (1994) Goal setting and performance in sport and exercise settings: A synthesis and critique, *Medicine and Science in Sports and Exercise*, **26**, 469–477.

Weinberg, R.S., Grove, R., & Jackson, A. (1992) Strategies for building self-efficacy in tennis players: A comparative analysis of Australian and American coaches, *The Sport Psychologist*, **1**, 3–13.

Weinberg, R.S. & Williams, J.M. (1993) Integrating and implementing a psychological skills training programme. In *Applied Sport Psychology: Personal Growth to Peak Performance* (Ed. J.M. Williams), (2nd edition), pp. 274–298, Mayfield, Mountain View, CA.

Weiss, M. and Chaumeton, N. (1992) Motivational orientations in sport. In *Advances in Sport Psychology* (Ed. T.S. Horn), pp. 61–99, Human Kinetics, Champaign, IL.

Whelan, J., Meyers, A., and Berman, J. (1989) *Cognitive-behavioral interventions for athletic enhancement*. Paper presented at the American Psychological Association, New Orleans.

Williams, J.M. and Krane, V. (1993) Psychological characteristics of peak performance. In *Applied Sport Psychology: Personal Growth to Peak Performance* (Ed. J.M. Williams), (2nd edition), pp. 137–147, Mayfield, Mountain View, CA.

Woolfolk, R., Parrish, W., and Murphy, S.M. (1985) The effects of positive and negative imagery on motor skill performance, *Cognitive Therapy and Research*, **9**, 335–341.

Yerkes, R.M. and Dodson, J.D. (1908) The relation of strength of stimulus to rapidity of habit formation, *Journal of Comparative Neurology and Psychology*, **18**, 459–482.

Zaichkowsky, L.D. and Fuchs, C.Z. (1988) Biofeedback applications in exercise and athletic performance, *Exercise and Sports Science Review*, **16**, 381–422.

3

THE ANALYSIS AND DEVELOPMENT OF TECHNIQUE IN SPORT

R.N. Marshall

University of Auckland

B.C. Elliott

University of Western Australia

Methods of analysis used in the biomechanical assessment of sport activities vary from those requiring complex equipment to those that use little else than an acute eye and an understanding of the mechanics of the movement. Irrespective of what method is used, however, it is essential that a systematic approach to the analysis of sport movement is adopted if athletes are truly to be helped.

Barrett (1979, 1983) discussed the need for coaches to plan both what they were going to observe and how they were going to observe it. In particular she focused attention on the need to observe the 'critical features' of each movement. Allison (1987) noted that inexperienced observers did not give attention to movement details and attributed that omission to a difficulty in distinguishing relevant from irrelevant features. Bird and Hudson (1990) also reported that experienced coaches were able to report more observations as well as providing more specific information than less experienced coaches. If a coach is not able to perceive a part of a sport skill unless it is

Training in Sport: Applying Sport Science. Edited by B. Elliott
© 1998 John Wiley & Sons Ltd

believed to be relevant, it would seem logical to assume that experienced coaches report more variables because they are aware of more of the critical features of the movement.

The use of a systematic approach to the analysis of sport performance is therefore essential if athletes are to be helped to reach their goals. Lees (1992) stated that a systematic approach to the analysis of movement provided a framework which gave direction in the collection of biomechanical data and which led naturally to a consideration of the underlying mechanisms governing performance.

It is important for coaches to understand that the mechanical characteristics identified as critical variables may be selected for several reasons: the coach and or athlete think they are important; or sport science has demonstrated their importance. The fact that little information is often given to explain *why* these variables have been identified is an indication that there is little by way of a systematic approach to the analysis of sporting movements.

The early subjective attempts to systematically identify the basic mechanical factors integral to specific sporting movements, without apportioning importance, were popularised by Hay (Hay, 1985; Hay and Reid, 1988). In this approach the mechanical characteristics and their interrelationships were identified. Coaches, athletes or sport scientists could then individually decide on the relative importance of each of these factors. This approach was further developed by Lees (1992) who placed greater emphasis on cause–effect relationships of the mechanical factors identified within the previous model. In this model accepted causal relationships, such as in the long jump where an increase in velocity at take-off from the board is linked to an increased jump displacement, are therefore used as the basis of the structure for identifying the critical features of a skill. The structure of these models will be discussed later in this chapter.

A systematic approach to the analysis of a sporting skill may be classified under three general areas, namely: subjective (qualitative); objective (quantitative) and predictive techniques. Most coaches use a variety of subjective evaluation techniques during their normal interaction with athletes. They watch an athlete, for example, to assess the range of motion of the leg or point of impact between the ball and the foot in the soccer kick. Objective techniques refer to the collection, measurement and evaluation of data from the activity of interest. Here the coach may measure the range of motion of the leg using a camera to determine the influence of increased knee flexion on resulting ball velocity. Predictive techniques attempt to answer the 'what if?' questions. For example, what effect would increasing the range of motion of the leg or changing the weight of the boot have on the velocity of the foot on impact?

SUBJECTIVE ANALYSIS METHODS

This analysis method involves the non-numerical analysis of a skill. The importance of the development of the ability to 'see what is occurring' is often underrated by sport scientists, although it is the most common bio-mechanical analysis method used by coaches. Recent work to refine the structure used in subjective or qualitative analysis has produced methods which improve the *art of observation* through selective attention on the critical features of a skill (Hay and Reid, 1988; McPherson, 1988; Lees, 1992; Figure 3.1).

These authors proposed the employment of a pre-observation phase, where a 'model' of the skill to be analysed is developed, and the mechanical variables concerned and their relationships are described. Figure 3.2 is a mechanical model (ignoring air resistance) of the high jump, although with minor modification it could be used for all jumping events. High-jump coaches using such a model can then direct their attention to the critical

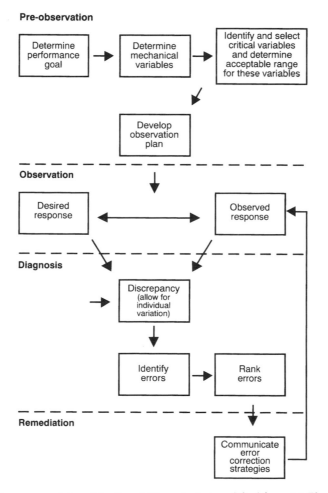

Figure 3.1: An approach to subjective skill analysis (modified from McPherson, 1988).

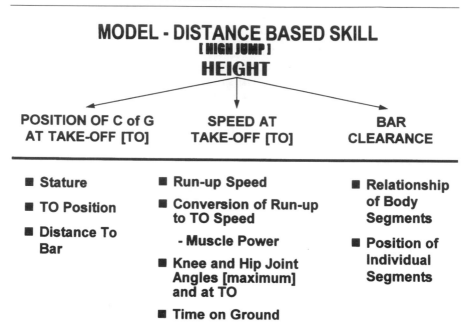

Figure 3.2: A mechanical model of the high jump.

mechanical variables associated with the skill rather than only viewing the entire movement (for further examples of these models and their construction see Hay and Reid, 1988). This method, which does not apportion the importance of the critical variables, works extremely well in the analysis of 'closed skills' such as a drive in golf, a shot in archery, a service in tennis or a gymnastics vault, where the skill is controlled by the performer. It is important to state that the importance placed by coaches on these critical variables may change with the level of the group. While the relationship of body segments when clearing the bar may be very important with beginners, the conversion of run-up to take-off speed (at the appropriate angle) would be more important with advanced level jumpers.

In 'open skills', however, such as a squash forehand, badminton smash, soccer pass or basketball jump shot, other factors must also be considered in the performance of the skill and minor modifications to this analysis method are required. In these skills the coach should not assume that an error in technique is necessarily a technical one. Before making this assumption it is necessary to check if the problem is psychological, physical or tactical.

The coach must first decide if the athlete or pupil, if in a school environment, is psychologically ready to perform the given skill. Stress from home or school, anxiety caused by a fear of failure or straight lack of interest on a given day may need to be addressed prior to any technical correction. The problem, however, may also be a physical one. The athlete may not have the required stature, muscle strength/power or flexibility to perform a particular skill with a given technique. The error in technique could equally be caused by a poor tactical choice. The athlete may not therefore be in the correct position to play a given shot in tennis or may not have the required strength to shoot over a large distance in basketball.

Only when all of these options have been considered can a coach assume that the error is a technical one and deal with it accordingly. The subjective skill analysis approach outlined in Figure 3.1 with some modification can then also be put into operation in the analysis of 'open skills'. This procedure usually involves repeated observations from different views and may utilise a videotape recorder to obtain a permanent copy of these trials. A comparison then occurs between the observed response and the previously determined desired response.

This observation phase of the analysis is followed by diagnosis of the skill. In this phase the errors in performance are identified and it is from a list of these errors that correction strategies are communicated to the athlete. The coach must rank the errors observed based on such factors as: the number and seriousness of the problems; the time needed for correction of each fault with reference to the occurrence of the next major event and the aspirations of the athlete.

The aim of this approach is to determine the causes of the problem, as opposed to the effects, and to determine the best way to correct those faults. The coach who tells a basketballer to reduce the excessive forward movement during a jump shot is attempting to modify an effect, and is not addressing the cause of this error. It is essential that attention is paid to various aspects of the shot prior to take-off and at take-off, so that the body moves vertically rather than horizontally during the jump. Similarly the gymnastic coach who pays too much attention to a poor landing in a vault by emphasising that the gymnast must 'stick the landing' may be addressing the effect of a poor push-off from the box or the incorrect timing of selected aspects of the vault rather than a poor landing.

Remember this skill analysis method will only allow the athlete to be provided with technical information. In teaching open skills it is also important to teach perception and decision-making skills. The athlete must be able to perceive the play correctly by identifying, for example, the spin on the ball and the tactical context of a situation in soccer and then decide what to do.

OBJECTIVE ANALYSIS: THE ROLE OF DATA COLLECTION AND PROCESSING IN SPORT PERFORMANCE ANALYSIS

At any level of technique analysis there is a need for interaction between the coach and biomechanist if maximum performance is to be achieved. Evaluation of a sporting performance in order to provide data on which to base decisions for performance enhancement requires a quantitative approach, necessitating a permanent record of the skill be collected for a number of trials so that each can be viewed and analysed.

A variety of aspects of the movement may be of interest. From the performance model, or from decisions in conjunction with the coach and/or athlete, one or more of the following might be of interest: movement characteristics (kinematics); causative factors in the motion (kinetics); or muscle activity (electromyography). Thus, recording of movement data may take a number of different forms, such as cinematography, videography, electromyography (EMG), accelerometry, dynamometry or electrogoniometry. While some of these techniques may not be available for general use, a more informed reading of the scientific biomechanics literature can only occur if the reader understands how objective data are derived. Such an understanding should assist the coaching professional to ask more pertinent questions on the causes of specific body movements.

An illustration of a biomechanical data acquisition system can be seen in Figure 3.3, which shows the general components of data collection and recording situations. Typically, a transducer is used to convert changes in a variable of interest into an analogue, or continuous, electrical signal. This signal is then amplified, passed through a signal conditioner which frequently converts it to a numerical (or digital) representation, and recorded. In Figure 3.3, the force platform is a transducer, converting forces exerted on the ground into an electrical signal. This signal is then amplified, passed to an analogue-to-digital (A–D) converter (a signal conditioner), and the digital information which represent the characteristics of the ground reaction forces is recorded by the computer. Other transducer–amplifier–signal conditioner–recorder systems may also be seen in Figure 3.3. The process of recording body movement characteristics on videotape, through to the production of segmented angular positions, velocities and accelerations, represents another system, while the attachment of electrodes to selected muscles, and the subsequent amplification, A–D conversion and recording of the EMG signals illustrates a third.

In the following sections, measurement procedures will be discussed primarily in isolation, although it is common, and often preferable, to use more than one technique during an analysis to gain additional information and thereby provide greater insight into the characteristics of a particular movement. A few textbooks also discuss analysis techniques or list suppliers or manufacturers of specialist equipment for biomechanics, and the reader may also wish to refer to them (e.g., Dainty and Norman, 1987; Whittle, 1991; Biewener, 1992) for further information.

Image analysis techniques

Image analysis techniques, including both movie photography and videography, provide the opportunity to capture complex movement sequences on film or videotape so that a detailed analysis can be performed. However, an understanding of sampling frequency relative to photography or videography is needed prior to discussing different image analysis

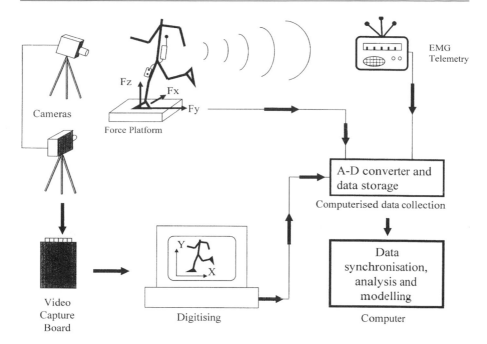

Figure 3.3: A general data acquisition system in biomechanics.

techniques, as both are sampling processes that record information at discrete points in time during a continuous motion.

The sampling rate needed for an accurate representation of movement must be at least twice the value of the highest frequency component contained in the movement (Shannon's sampling theorem), although many researchers believe sampling rates of 5 to 10 times the maximum frequency component are preferable. Under-sampling will cause vital movement characteristics such as the point of impact or release to be missed, or distortions to arise. Excessive sampling either increases the financial cost when using high-speed photography or limits the choice of cameras when using high-speed videography.

At the subjective level of analysis, film or video techniques may be used to record movement and allow general comments to be made on the observed characteristics. At an objective level it is not sufficient to just record and observe movement, as detailed measurements must be completed and inferences drawn with reference to the movement. Specific equipment and procedures must be used if accurate objective data are to be collected using image analysis techniques.

Movie photography

In high-speed cinematography a motor-driven camera capable of providing frame rates up to approximately 500 Hz (cycles per second) and exposure times up to approximately 1/10 000 s is needed to accommodate movement and sport skills of differing speeds. In a golf drive, for example, the ability to clearly record the impact of the ball and club head would require an exposure time of approximately 1/3600 s and a frame rate of 400 Hz. The 400 Hz frame rate ensures that the moment of impact is captured on film, while the exposure time guarantees that no blurring of the image occurs. For an analysis of jogging, an exposure time of 1/800 s would provide a clear image of the leg, while a frame rate of 100 Hz is sufficient to sample leg movement at the required frequency.

The collection of data from film for analytical purposes (digitising) is the most time consuming and tedious aspect of cinematographic research. A stop-action projector is required so that a single frame of film may be projected while an operator moves an X–Y coordinate system until a pointer, pen, light or cross-hairs lie(s) over the desired point to be digitised (see Figure 3.4). The coordinates of this point are then stored on a computer. In

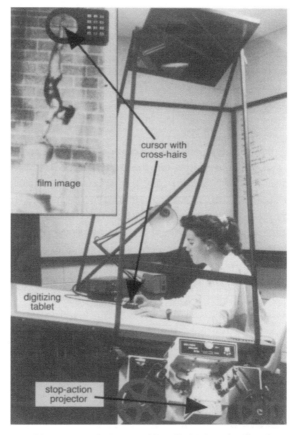

Figure 3.4: A 16 mm film digitising facility.

order for an anatomical landmark to be located, it must be clearly marked on the subject being filmed, so that an accurate identification of the segment end point or joint centre is possible. These coordinate data are then smoothed (this topic is not discussed in this chapter; however, the reader is directed to Winter (1990) or Woltring (1985) for a review of this area) prior to being mathematically manipulated in the calculation of kinematic and kinetic data (see Figure 3.5).

Usually the purpose of filming and digitising an athlete's performance is to permit the calculation of other variables of interest, such as the linear velocity of a segment endpoint, the angular velocity of the segment and the angular joint velocity. As can be seen from Figure 3.5, information additional to the coordinates of the selected landmarks is required to do this. Some means of determining the elapsed time between images is essential in order to develop the time scale necessary for calculating numerical derivatives. This may be done by filming a large sweep-hand clock located in the photographic field, or using internal camera lights which flash at a set rate, marking the film and allowing film-speed calculation. A spatial scale must also be filmed in a two-dimensional analysis, or a structure encompassing the volume of action in three-dimensional reconstructions is required to convert film-scale measures to real values.

Data from film may be collected in a number of formats and the following studies illustrate common practices.

Single camera planar analysis

Herzog and Read (1993) filmed World Cup downhill skiers to estimate cruciate ligament forces during a landing which had previously been associated with knee injury. Although the data were inconclusive they suggested

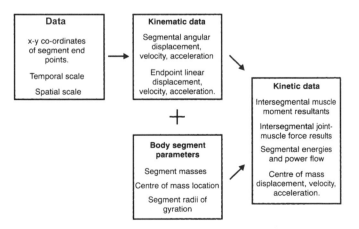

Figure 3.5: The information yield from a motion analysis system.

that one skier's poor technique created the potential for the anterior cruciate ligament to be damaged.

Multi-camera planar analysis

Fast bowlers in cricket were filmed both from the side and above while bowling, so that their front foot impacted a force platform during the delivery stride in a study by Foster et al. (1989). Data from these two planes of motion were used to identify biomechanical correlates of back injuries to fast bowlers.

Multi-camera three-dimensional analysis

A common practice in cinematographic analysis is to perform three-dimensional (3D) spatial reconstructions from two-dimensional (2D) film images, using a technique such as the direct linear transformation (DLT) method, which has been adapted from analytical close-range photogrammetry (Marzan and Karara 1975). In this method two or more cameras initially film a reference structure containing markers of known coordinates in space encompassing the field of movement. The reference structure is then removed and the subject filmed in the same area without altering the camera positions or settings. The 2D images of both the reference structure and subject are then digitized and the unknown 3D coordinates of each of the subject's landmarks are determined. Inaccuracies in 3D reconstruction are likely to occur if the digitized movement lies outside the reference structure distribution space (Wood and Marshall, 1986) and the use of control points distributed around the outside rather than within the space to be calibrated produces superior results (Challis and Kerwin, 1992). Subsequent development of 3D filming procedures has seen the refinement of computer software so that panning is possible (de Groot et al., 1989) and less reliance placed on large 3D reference structures (Woltring et al., 1989).

Elliott et al. (1989) provide an example of 3D cinematographic data collection where they described the mechanics of the multi-segment and single unit topspin forehand drives in tennis. A greater understanding of the mechanics, particularly of the multi-segment stroke, will assist coaches to teach this technique with correct body mechanics and thus reduce the potential for upper limb injury.

High-speed photography therefore permits a relatively flexible approach to data recording, with acceptable accuracy and minimal interference to the subject's movements from the attachment of external measuring devices. However, film costs and time delays caused by processing and digitising may make film less than a perfect medium to study motion. Advances in electronic image analysis technology now permit other techniques, which are frequently videotape based, to be used in preference to film as an accurate and cost-effective medium to collect objective data on movement.

Video photography

For videography to be used as an objective rather than subjective analysis tool, cameras had to be developed which provided a variety of frame rates and exposure times. In general, the addition of mechanical or electronic shutters reduced the exposure time and removed the problem of blurring in the recording of fast moving images, while an increase in frame rates from 25 frames s^{-1} up to 2000 frames s^{-1} or more illustrate other recent advances in video technology.

The collection of data from these approaches for analytical purposes may be far quicker than in film analysis. Three different types of systems currently being used in video analysis are described below; however, continuous technological developments will result in new systems and techniques appearing regularly. For example, in addition to videotape-based systems, Motion Analysis Corporation also produces a real-time analysis system based upon video cameras and high-speed computer pattern recognition techniques. In addition, relatively inexpensive commercial manual video digitising packages are appearing (i.e. Motion Plus, Calgary, Canada).

Opto-electronic measurement systems. In these systems light-emitting diodes are attached to the subject, and then video-like cameras, a marker detection module and a computer track the diodes in space almost instantaneously (examples—Selspot II, Selective Electronic Inc., Sweden; Optotrak, Northern Digital, Canada). They are geared primarily for laboratory analysis and provide accurate data that can be very quickly produced. However, they experience substantial performance reduction when used outdoors. If a recorded image of the performance is required, a video-based analysis system may be preferable.

Closed circuit TV image analysis. With this approach, processing of computer-stored TV images is carried out but these are not usually recorded on videotape (examples—Elite, BTS Bioengineering Technology and Systems, Italy; Vicon, Oxford Metrics Ltd, England). Again, these systems produce accurate data within a relatively short time frame, but are primarily geared for the laboratory setting and their performance may be degraded when used outdoors.

Video image analysis. Like the two previous groups, these systems enable the user to analyse 2D or 3D motion patterns, but record the images from the camera(s) on videotape (examples—ExpertVision, Motion Analysis Corp., USA; Peak Performance, Peak Performance Technologies, Inc., USA; Ariel Performance Analysis System, USA). This provides not only an image which can be viewed at a later date, but also the opportunity to modify and repeat the A–D processing and analysis of the recording of the motion, a feature not available with some of the opto-electronic systems discussed previously. By producing a video image this method provides a wider user base in the area of sport biomechanics.

Dynamometry

Dynamometry refers to the measurement of force. While it is possible to estimate both internal and external forces (i.e., bone-on-bone, and ground reaction forces respectively) from segment position, velocity and acceleration data obtained from cinematography/videography combined with anthropometric information, it is preferable to measure the actual force or forces directly where possible.

The explicit measurement of external forces, generally collected using a force platform, when combined with cinematographic/videographic and anthropometric data, permit more accurate estimates of internal forces to be calculated than with a purely cinematographic technique. An understanding of internal forces is essential in sport medicine, as they constitute one of the key factors in the cause of many sporting injuries, particularly those related to overuse. It is possible, although not always practical, to measure *in vivo* (internal) forces by attaching a transducer to selected parts of the body, such as the Achilles tendon, and have the subject perform various activities so that forces in this tendon can be measured.

Dynamometers consist of a transducer which transforms mechanical deformation (strain) into an electrical signal that is proportional to the applied force (stress). These transducers are frequently of a strain-gauge or piezo-electric type. In a strain gauge, very thin electrically resistive elements are bonded to a stiff yet elastic support material and then one or more of these are attached to the object where the force is to be applied. These gauges are then used to measure small deformations caused by an applied force in terms of a change in electrical resistance. Piezo-electric transducers, however, rely on the electrical properties of certain crystalline materials such as quartz, where the deformation caused by the applied force results in a change in electrical resistance. With this type of transducer the crystalline structure is enclosed in a 'load cell' which can be mounted between a fixed surface and the applied force. The small changes in resistance in both these types of transducers requires amplification prior to the recording of the signal.

Strain-gauge dynamometers have been used in a wide variety of bio-mechanical studies. For example, the *in vivo* measurement of force in the Achilles tendon was calculated during a number of stretch–shorten cycle activities. The loadings associated with walking, running and jumping, which in some cases reached values as high as 9000 N, corresponding to 12.5 times body weight, provide insight into the potential of a selected activity to cause injury (Komi, 1990). Similarly, maximum forces generated during actual-performances on the asymmetric bars in women's gymnastics were measured using strain gauges and this force information was then used in the mechanical design of this equipment (Hay et al., 1979). The forces generated by a rower were measured within a competitive environment by attaching strain gauges to the oarlock of a racing shell. These results were then used to assess the force profile of the subject during each stroke cycle so as to match rowers on opposite sides of a shell (Dal Monte and Komor, 1989).

Force platforms

The most common dynamometer used in biomechanics is the force platform, which is usually mounted on a concrete pad, mechanically isolated from its environment and positioned so that it is flush with the laboratory floor (Figure 3.6). The transducers may be either piezo-electric or strain gauge, and typically in these platforms a number of force transducers are positioned under each of the four corners of a rigid plate. From these force measures the three perpendicular components of the resultant ground reaction forces (upward (F_z); anterio-posterior (F_y) and lateral (F_x)) are calculated. Further, the point of resultant force application (CP_x CP_y) with reference to the centre of the platform, a position commonly referred to as the centre of pressure, and a moment (M'_z) about a perpendicular axis through the centre of pressure can also be derived.

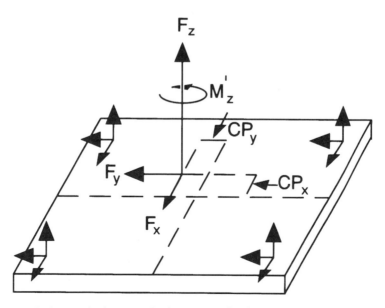

Figure 3.6: A force platform with the perpendicular components of the ground reaction force (F_z, F_y, F_x), the point of resultant force application (CP_x, CP_y) and the perpendicular moment (M'_z) included.

These measures are used to assist in the understanding of many human movements, and the following examples illustrate this. The external forces and centre of pressure data are often used to determine load on the body in conjunction with cinematographic/videographic data in a kinetic analysis. The measures may also be used to assist in the monitoring of technique changes in athletes as a result of training. The centre of pressure movement, although *not* a measure of the motion of the centre of gravity of the body, has been used as an index of postural sway in activities such as archery, rifle-shooting or balance tests.

The force platform measures in Figure 3.7(b) and (c) show that fast bowling in cricket is certainly an impact sport, where the bowler experiences a series of minor 'collisions' during the run-up, followed by two major collisions when the back foot and front foot impact with the ground (Figure 3.7(a)). Peak vertical (F_z) and horizontal (F_y) ground reaction forces of 3.0 BW and −0.7 BW respectively at back foot strike and 4.0 BW and −2.0 BW respectively at front foot impact certainly indicate that this is a potentially dangerous activity, as these impact forces must be absorbed by the body while the trunk is extending, laterally flexing and rotating in an endeavour to achieve maximum power in delivery. Further, the large twisting moments (M') under the back foot which occur initially away from the batsman (peak of 40 N m at back foot impact) and later toward the batsman (peak after front foot impact of 35 N m) are indicative of both the level and reversal in direction of trunk rotation during the delivery stride, a factor which researchers have found to be related to the incidence of stress fractures.

Figure 3.7a (above),b,c (opposite): Forces and moments under the feet of a fast bowler (a) in cricket at (b) back foot and (c) front foot impact during the delivery stride.

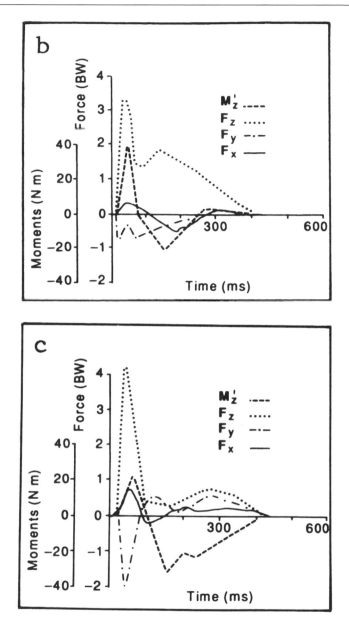

Pressure mats

The centre of pressure information derived from a force platform provides the coordinates of the location of the resultant force. In many situations it is more important to know how these forces are distributed under the foot, and for this reason pressure mats are used. These consist of a large matrix of miniature transducers (often < 5 mm diameter) recording pressure at discrete points on the contact surface. These have been constructed as innersoles which may be placed in shoes to monitor pressures under the foot, or as a mat which may be placed on the contact surface for more general applications. The pressures sensed by the transducers during a movement are captured on computer, and a graphical display is typically used to provide an indication of the time-history of the distribution of pressure over the contact surface. Figure 3.8 shows a single 'frame' of pressure mat data from under the foot of a cricket bowler during delivery, as well as the corresponding resultant force and the (misleading) centre of pressure information from a force platform. This figure shows how the force platform centre of pressure information is in reality an average of the pressure on the plantar surface, and may occur at a point where there is little or no actual pressure. A good example of the utility of pressure mats can be seen in the work of Cavanagh et al. (1985), who have used pressure distribution measurements obtained from the plantar surface of the foot as information on which to base prophylactic procedures in the management of diabetics' feet.

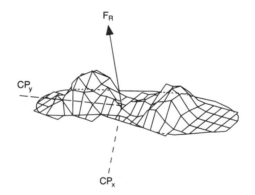

Figure 3.8: One 'frame' of pressure mat data recorded under the front foot of a bowler during delivery (the higher the 'hill' the greater the pressure). The location of the centre of pressure measure given by a force platform is also shown, and is seen in this instance to be quite meaningless as an index of plantar surface loading.

Strength-measuring devices

Strength is the ability of a muscle or muscle group to generate force, but it is often difficult to measure the actual forces produced. What is usually measured in humans is the torque or moment of force produced about a joint. Evaluation of the mechanics of an athlete's performance is often aided by a knowledge of his or her muscular strength characteristics. Force generation characteristics of muscles may be tested isometrically (with a fixed joint angle and virtually no muscle shortening) or dynamically, where dynamometers are used to measure force production during movement. Methods used to assess the dynamic characteristics of muscle have commonly taken two forms: controlled shortening velocity protocols where a limb segment moves at a constant angular velocity or where a muscle group is required to shorten at a constant rate; and controlled loading protocols where muscle is loaded with a constant mass and then required to produce its maximal shortening velocity. Most research has used the first protocol, and has assessed strength and power of a muscle group acting about an isolated joint at a variety of joint angular velocities using an 'isokinetic' dynamometer (more properly described as an isokinematic dynamometer). While most dynamometers developed specifically for muscle function testing use this mode, other types of dynamometers are available, and isokinetic machines are only one form of accommodating resistance devices. Isometric (fixed muscle length), concentric (muscle shortening), eccentric (forced muscle lengthening) and isotonic (constant load allowing variable speed) actions may be assessed with a number of the commercially available dynamometers. These latter approaches provide information on dynamic properties of muscle such as peak torque or power, which may be more appropriate to an athlete's performance than information on isometric strength at specific angles (Figure 3.9).

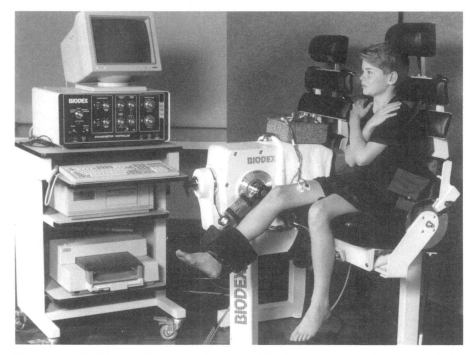

Figure 3.9: Isokinetic dynamometers provide data on strength characteristics throughout a range of movement. This is important for both the coach and the clinician interested in improving performance through strength development.

The mechanical characteristics of some dynamometers may cause arte-facts to be generated and recorded. These may arise, for example, as the result of impacts between the limb and the dynamometer as the limb reaches the pre-set speed and is decelerated abruptly (resulting in a 'torque over-shoot'); as interactions between the limb and the dynamometer's velocity-feedback system; or as a result of the dynamometer's acceleration or deceleration at the extremes of the range of movement. These all influence the recorded torque, and thus care is sometimes needed in the interpretation of the results.

Strength testing has often been used in conjunction with other bio-mechanical techniques in the evaluation of subjects, and this was the ap-proach taken by McNair et al. (1989). They examined the jogging gait of subjects with anterior cruciate ligament (ACL) deficiency, and used an iso-kinetic strength-testing dynamometer to assess concentric quadriceps and hamstring muscle group torque generation capabilities. The strength dif-ferences between the ACL-deficient and normal limbs were then integrated with EMG and movement information to evaluate the techniques used by subjects to compensate for their knee condition. The subjects demonstrated symmetric inter-limb kinematic patterns, but had significantly increased EMG activity in the quadriceps of the ACL-deficient limb immediately be-fore and after heel strike when compared to the normal limb. On the surface this would appear to be disadvantageous to these subjects, since excessive quadriceps activity in that phase of the gait cycle would exacerbate the ACL deficiency problems. However, when the strength results were included in the analysis and it was noted that the quadriceps were significantly weaker on the ACL-deficient limb, the authors suggested an alternative explanation. They proposed that the quadriceps on the ACL-deficient limb were not in fact producing excessive forces at an inappropriate time, but rather that they were working at a higher proportion of their maximum ability in order to enable inter-limb symmetry.

Electromyography

Muscle action is initiated by electrical activity, and the detection and record-ing of these signals is a technique known as electromyography. The record-ing is known as an electromyogram (EMG), and shows the changes in electrical potential which occur as electric currents are propagated along the muscle membranes. These fluctuations in current, or action potentials, are produced by the transfer of ions across the muscle cell wall following electri-cal stimulation. As such, they are only indirectly related to the overall ten-sion produced by a muscle, a point which must be kept in mind during the interpretation of an electromyogram. At a basic level of analysis, the EMG provides only an indication of activity or non-activity, and comparisons of levels of EMG activity either within or between muscles must be made with caution. The size of the EMG signal recorded from a muscle depends on a variety of factors. The electrode type, size, preparation and placement all affect the recording of the signal, as do factors such as muscle fibre length and arrangement, rate of fibre length change and type of muscle action. Only under carefully controlled conditions can the EMG recording be used as an indicator of the forces produced by a muscle. The factors which affect the force developed in a muscle, such as motor unit firing rates, are also important considerations in the interpretation of an EMG signal. Technical guidelines for EMG recording and research reporting have been compiled by the International Society of Electrophysiological Kinesiology (ISEK) and published in various places (e.g., Dainty and Norman, 1987), and the reader is directed to these for more specific information.

The complexity of the muscle contractile activity to output force relationship is illustrated schematically in Figure 3.10. The lower left portion of this figure shows a simple muscle model which includes the major elements which affect the overall tension produced. The spring-like character of the series and parallel elastic elements (muscle tendon and sheath, respectively, for example) affect the force or rate of force development, while the viscous

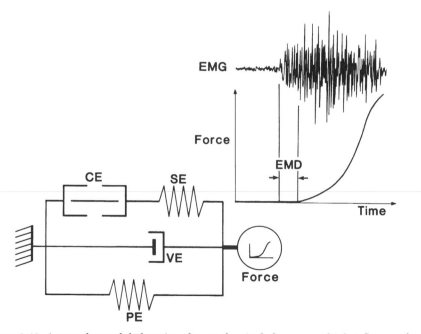

Figure 3.10: A muscle model showing the mechanical elements which influence force production [contractile element (CE), series elastic element (SE), viscous element (VE), parallel elastic element (PE)]. EMG is only associated with the contractile element, and because of the effects of the other components there is always some electromechanical delay (EMD) between the onset of EMG and the externally measured force.

element has an effect on the speed with which muscle forces change. All of these factors modify either the magnitude or the time course of the forces generated by the contractile element, which is the only component of the muscle associated with EMG activity.

Figure 3.11 depicts the surface EMG activity of selected muscles of the lower extremity during stationary cycling. The rectus femoris (RF), representative of the knee extensors, shows two bursts of activity. One begins just after the top of the pedal stroke and ends slightly before the knee is fully extended at the bottom of the stroke cycle. A second burst is seen starting at about the bottom of the stroke and finishing about half-way through the recovery (upward) movement. The knee flexors, represented by the muscle biceps femoris (BF), show slight to moderate activity during the propulsive (downward) stroke, and a major burst at the start of the recovery movement.

Initially, this might appear to be an inefficient muscle activation pattern, since both knee flexors and extensors are active simultaneously. This apparent conflict of the RF and BF muscles during cycling and walking as well as running is an example of Lombard's paradox. However, since both RF and BF are two-joint muscles, and have effects at the hip joint as well as at the knee, perhaps their activity is not so paradoxical. One explanation is that the

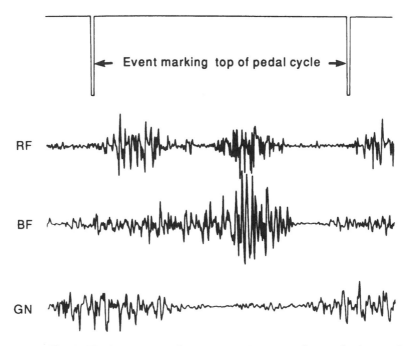

Figure 3.11: Phasic EMG activity in lower extremity musculature during stationary cycling. (RF = Rectus femoris, BF = Biceps femoris, GN = Gastrocnemium.)

moment arms of RF and BF at the hip- and knee-joints change throughout the cycle, giving precedence to one muscle at one stage, and then the other in a later phase. Other factors, such as the actual change of muscle length during the motion, are also involved, and interested readers are referred to Andrews (1987) for a more detailed discussion.

The gastrocnemius muscle (GN) assists with the final aspect of knee flexion prior to the top of the cycle, and is then active in the early part of the propulsive phase either in producing plantar flexion, or in ensuring good force transmission through to the pedal by holding the foot in a static position.

Changes in the magnitude of an EMG are usually indicative of an alteration in the tension produced, although the complexity of the EMG signal has hampered many researchers' efforts to determine useful relationships. A common method of quantifying an EMG signal is to perform an integration procedure (see Winter 1990 for a review of techniques). One integration approach involves converting all the negative voltages to positive ones (a process referred to as full-wave rectification), followed by an operation which smooths the EMG (low pass filtering) and accumulates this signal to provide an indication of the total activity (the 'linear envelope'). The typical relationship found between the load lifted and the integrated EMG (IEMG) is a non-linear one, with increasing levels of IEMG seen for constant increases in load. This relationship is shown in Figure 3.12, where the raw and integrated EMG data recorded from the rectus femoris during isometric knee extension are seen.

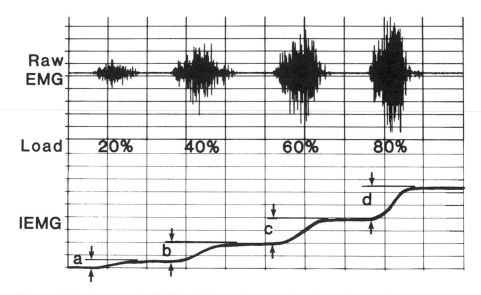

Figure 3.12: Changes in EMG activity with increasing load during knee-extension. Both raw and integrated EMG signals are shown. IEMG levels are seen to exhibit a non-linear increase for constant load increments.

The non-linear relationship is evident from the increases in magnitude of the IEMG (a-d) for constant load increases (from 20% to 80% of maximum).

Researchers are also developing and using other techniques to extract more information from the EMG signal. For example, during a sustained muscular effort an EMG will often exhibit consistent changes in the magnitude and frequency of its action potentials, and these changes can be used as an indication of underlying neuromuscular processes. In order to see these effects, the EMG signal is transformed from the time domain into the frequency domain using spectral analysis, which gives information on the amplitude and frequency content of the signal. A fast Fourier transform is typically used for this, and produces a power spectrum showing the strength of the signal over a frequency range.

PREDICTIVE ANALYSIS METHODS

The previous sections have outlined the major qualitative and quantitative data collection techniques used in biomechanics, and this section reviews some of the predictive approaches. Computer simulation and optimisation techniques have been applied widely in studies of sport and human movement. Since 'simulation' and 'optimisation' often have a variety of connotations, for the purposes of this discussion they will be defined as follows:

- Computer simulation is the use of a validated computer model (a set of mathematical equations describing the system of interest) to evaluate the response of the model to changes in the system parameters.
- Optimisation is the iterative use of a computer simulation to determine parameter values or control variables which optimise (minimise or maximise) a specified criterion (the performance objective).

The general aim of predictive analysis methods is to use a computer model of a person or piece of equipment (the 'system') to predict changes which would occur as a consequence of alterations to the input parameters. That is, one aims to answer the question, 'What would happen to the movement if this factor was changed to . . .?' The advantages of using computer simulation or optimisation include the complete safety of the subjects, an increased speed of assessing changes, the potential for prediction of optimal performance and reduced expense compared to building physical models (Vaughan, 1984). Limitations of this approach include the frequent need to simplify the 'real-world' system to make it amenable to modelling while attempting to maintain validity and the expertise and computer power necessary to develop and run the simulation/optimisation, and difficulties with translation of the results into practical terms.

Simulation

Computer simulation has been used to evaluate the biomechanics of a wide variety of equipment and body movements, from an equally wide variety of approaches. It is beyond the scope of this chapter to list and comment on the approaches used and the systems modelled, but they vary from the consideration of the human body as a point mass representing the centre of gravity, to a simulation of the 3D muscle mechanics and skeletal dynamics of the lower limb during walking. Most of these programs were written specifically for the system under consideration, although the use of generalised simulation packages, such as symbolic manipulation programs, is increasing (see, for example, van den Bogert et al., 1989).

Schneider and Zernicke (1988) used a validated head–neck–torso model to simulate head impacts in soccer heading in order to estimate the injury risk. Critical output variables were the linear and angular acceleration of the head, and these were compared to standard head-injury tolerance levels. They concluded that head-injury risk can be reduced most effectively in all subjects by increasing the mass ratio between the head and the ball. They stressed that children should therefore use only smaller and lighter soccer balls and that the increases in weight of a ball on a wet day was a potential danger.

Considerable controversy existed over the techniques used by divers and gymnasts to produce twists in somersaults. Yeadon (1988) simulated twisting somersaults to determine the contribution of asymmetrical arm, chest and hip movements to aerial twists. He demonstrated that sustained twists are most frequently produced by asymmetrical arm movements and further, that even in situations where twist was evident at take-off, the major contributions were still made by aerial techniques.

Computer simulation approaches are also being profitably applied to animals. Van den Bogert et al. (1989) have simulated locomotion in the horse, and examined the influence of a therapeutic horseshoe on the distribution of tendon forces in the hind leg. In order to reduce the load on the deep digital flexor (DDF) muscle, horse trainers frequently employ a shoe which raises the heel of the hoof. The simulation showed the forces in the DDF to be substantially reduced, but due to the polyarticular nature of this muscle, the movements of several joints were changed and therefore the loading patterns of other tendons were also altered. They suggested that while the heel rise effectively reduced loads in the DDF, its side-effects on other tendons may not be favourable.

One of the exciting developments in computer simulation in sport is in the area of 'virtual reality' (VR). For example, Hubbard (1994) discussed the development of a VR system representing bobsledding and its use with elite athletes to complement their 'on ice' training. In this simulation the bob driver sits in a sled holding the normal controls, which have been linked to movement transducers. The driver is faced with a large computer screen on which is drawn a 3D image of the bobsled track from the driver's viewpoint.

As the sled moves down the track (in the computer simulation) the view of the driver changes instantaneously. Position on the track and consequent view are also responsive to movement of the sled controls. In addition, two large computer screens placed laterally to the driver display accurate visual flow information to enhance the simulation. After a run it is possible to compare the performance with the driver's or track best records. Thus, for example, the drivers could immediately view their velocity down the track relative to the track record, and determine the corners in which they need to improve their performance. Programs such as this illustrate the exciting potential computers have in sports.

Optimisation

Optimisation research may be categorised into two general procedures. Parameter optimisation refers to those studies where parameters are successively modified to produce an optimal result, such as described in the javelin study below. Optimal control refers to the technique of altering variables which control or determine the output of the system, and an example of this is the cycling study discussed later in this chapter. Interpretation and appraisal of results from optimisation studies are guided by the same considerations as for simulation studies, with the added need to evaluate the appropriateness of the performance objective.

Changes made in 1986 by the International Amateur Athletics Federation to the rules for the construction of the men's javelin prompted Hubbard and Alaways (1987) to simulate the flight of the New Rules javelin and to determine optimum release characteristics. They discovered that the range of the new javelin was decreased, and that it was less sensitive to release conditions when compared to the old one. They also showed that the optimal release conditions were velocity-dependent, and concluded '. . . the javelin throw has been changed from an event in which finesse and skill were important . . . to one for which strength and power are once again pre-eminent'.

Hull et al. (1988), as part of an on-going project aimed at maximising cyclist performance, examined the relationships between pedalling rate and the forces in 12 lower limb muscles while pedalling with a constant power output. For steady state cycling, their results showed an optimum pedalling rate of 95–100 revolutions per minute (r.p.m.) which is in close agreement with rates normally observed in cyclists, but in contrast to the 65 r.p.m. optimum found by previous researches.

BIOMECHANICAL FEEDBACK

The performance of an athlete can only be permanently modified if in the first instance the person has an accurate perception of that performance

(Daly and Parkin, 1991). This perception will best be gained and therefore the re-learning process given the greatest potential for success, if feedback relies on the two major senses of sight and hearing (Malouf, 1988). Biomechanical feedback therefore has the potential to play a major role in this process as it is primarily a sport science capable of presenting data in a visual format. The visual presentation of an activity in its entirety (and qualitative assessment), or data on the critical features of the performance (quantitative assessment) enables the teacher or coach to support the suggested technique modifications with visual evidence of the need for change.

While the visual presentation of images on videotape or on high-speed film are common it is only recently that quantitative data have been visually presented to athletes in a form other than as a table or graph. Biomechanists working with National teams have over a number of years presented quantitative data to these elite athletes in an endeavour to improve their performance. Research, however, that attempts to assess improvements in performance following this form of feedback has only occurred recently.

Smith and Spinks (1989) visually presented force–angle profiles to their rowers in an endeavour to develop consistency in performance. These athletes, who were able to view these parameters on a screen positioned in front of a rowing ergometer, then attempted to match the profile of each stroke with a template of their best force–angle profile. Similarly Broker et al. (1993) attempted to improve cycling performance by removing the counterproductive forces that were evident in that section of the upstroke 90° before top-dead-centre. Computer feedback on the level of these forces while cycling then took place over a four-week training period. While no cyclist was able to attain the above goal, pedalling technique did improve in the phase of the stroke which involved pulling the pedal through the bottom section of the stroke.

Mendoza and Schöllhorn (1993) used visual biomechanical feedback to improve the starting techniques of high-performance junior sprinters. Results on time to 10 m, block spacing to the start line, front knee angle and proportion of body weight on the hands were displayed on a computer screen approximately 20 s following trials where the latter three of the above variables were modified. This study showed that start technique can be effectively modified using biomechanical feedback, if data on the critical features in the movement are immediately presented to the athlete.

Morriss and Bartlett (1993) used biomechanical feedback to alter the techniques used by elite British hammer throwers. The positive and negative acceleration profiles of the path of the hammer were presented to these athletes as different colours on a computer screen. The negative acceleration phases were then linked to specific techniques used by the throwers. Coaching then occurred to alter a throwing technique so that positive acceleration values were sought at key sections of the throwing action. The effectiveness of the coaching may then be reassessed, not only by measuring the distance thrown but also the new acceleration profile recorded using high-speed photography or videography.

Computer simulation has also been used by Best and associates (Best et al., 1990) as a form of biomechanical feedback to assist in performance enhancement of elite male and female javelin throwers. An interactive computer program was developed that simulated the flight of the men's and ladies' new rules javelins based on the release data from each individual thrower. This interactive procedure then allows input data to be modified so that optimum performance can be achieved. Such an approach permits small modifications in throwing technique to be evaluated.

Such visual presentations of biomechanical data permit a two-way communication process to occur between the coach and the athlete. The reason for the required technique modification along with a clear understanding of the steps needed to achieve this goal can then be discussed by the athlete and coach. Too often coaches transmit information *to*, but do *not* receive questions *from* the athlete on the required technique modifications. The use of biomechanical feedback, which most commonly will be in a visual form, can certainly assist in this interaction between the coach and athlete.

SUMMARY

Biomechanical evaluation of performance for the purpose of improving technique in sport or aiding in clinical diagnosis is still in its developmental stages. A great deal of progress has been made in the techniques available for data collection and analysis, but the application of biomechanics for the enhancement of sporting performances is not yet commonplace. The potential for profitable interaction between biomechanists, coaches, and athletes is enormous and future developments in this arena will be exciting.

REFERENCES

Allison, P. (1987) What and how preservice physical education teachers observe during an early field experience, *Research Quarterly for Exercise and Sport*, **58**, 242–249.

Andrews, J.G. (1987) The functional roles of the hamstrings and quadriceps during cycling: Lombard's Paradox revisited, *Journal of Biomechanics*, **20**, 565–576.

Barrett, K. (1979) Observation for teaching and coaching, *Journal of Physical Education and Recreation*, **50**, 23–25.

Barrett, K. (1983) A hypothetical model of observing as a teaching skill, *Journal of Teaching Physical Education*, **3**, 22–23.

Best, R.J., Bartlett, R.M. and Sawyer, R.A. (1990) Javelin flight simulation—interactive software for research and coaches, in *Biomechanics in Sports VIII* (Eds. M. Nosek, D. Sojka, W. Morrison and P. Susanka), 279–286, Conex, Prague.

Biewener, A.A. (1992) *Biomechanics: Structures and Systems*, IRL Press, Oxford.

Bird, M. and Hudson, J. (1990) Biomechanical observation: visually accessible variables, in *Biomechanics in Sport VIII* (Eds M. Nosek, O. Sojka, W. Morrison and P. Susanka), pp. 321–326, Conex, Prague.

Broker, J.P., Gregor, R.J. and Schmidt, R.A. (1993) Extrinsic feedback and the learning of kinetic patterns in cycling, *Journal of Applied Biomechanics*, **9**, 111–123.

Cavanagh, P.V., Hennig, E.M., Rodgers, M.M. and Sanderson, D.J. (1985) The measurement of pressure distribution on the plantar surface of diabetic feet, in *Biomechanical Measurement in Orthopaedic Practice* (Eds. M. Whittle, and D. Harris), pp. 159–168, Clarendon Press, Oxford.

Challis, J. and Kerwin, D. (1992) Accuracy assessment and control point configuration when using the DLT for photogrammetry, *Journal of Biomechanics*, **25**, 1053–1058.

Dainty, D.A. and Norman, R.W. (1987) *Standardising Biomechanical Testing in Sport*, Human Kinetics Publishers, Champaign, IL.

Dal Monte, A. and Komor, A. (1989) Rowing and sculling mechanics, in *Biomechanics of Sport* (Ed. C.L. Vaughan), pp. 53–119, CRC Press, Boca Raton, CA.

Daly, J. and Parkin, D. (1991) The role of the coach, in *Better Coaching* (Ed. F.S. Pyke), pp. 3–14, Australian Coaching Council, Canberra.

de Groot, G., de Koning, J. and van Ingen Schenau, G.J. (1989) A method to determine 3-D coordinates with panning cameras, in *Proceedings XII International Congress of Biomechanics* (Eds. R.J. Gregor, R.F. Zernicke and W.C. Whiting), Abstract 297, UCLA Press, Los Angeles, CA.

Elliott, B., Marsh, T. and Overheu, P. (1989) A biomechanical comparison of the multisegment and single unit topspin forehand drives in tennis, *International Journal of Sport Biomechanics*, **5**, 350–364.

Foster, D., John, D., Elliott, B., Ackland, T. and Fitch, K. (1989) Back injuries to fast bowlers in cricket: A prospective study, *British Journal of Sport Medicine*, **23**, 150–154.

Hay, J.G. (1985) *The Biomechanics of Sports Techniques*, 3rd edn, Prentice-Hall, Englewood Cliffs, NJ.

Hay, J.G. and Reid, J.G. (1988) *Anatomy, Mechanics and Human Motion*, 2nd edn, Prentice-Hall, Englewood Cliffs, NJ.

Hay, J.G., Putnam, C.A. and Wilson, B.D. (1979) Forces exerted during exercises on the uneven bars, *Medicine and Science in Sports*, **11**, 123–130.

Herzog, W. and Read, L. (1993) Anterior ligament forces in alpine skiing, *Journal of Applied Biomechanics*, **9**, 260–278.

Hubbard, M. (1994) Simulating sensitive dynamic control of a bobsled, Paper presented at the *2nd Conference on Mathematics and Computers in Sport*, Bond University, Australia.

Hubbard, M. and Alaways, L. (1987) Optimum release conditions for the new rules javelin, *International Journal of Sport Biomechanics*, **3**, 207–221.

Hull, M., Gonzalez, H. and Redfield, R. (1988) Optimization of pedalling rate in cycling using a muscle stress-based objective function, *International Journal of Sport Biomechanics*, **4**, 1–20.

Komi, P. (1990) Relevance of in-vivo force measurements to human biomechanics, *Journal of Biomechanics*, **23**, 23–34.

Lees, A. (1992) Biomechanics in teaching and coaching—systematic approaches to the identification of mechanisms in performance and injury, in *10th symposium of the International Society of Biomechanism in Sports* (Eds, R. Rodano, G. Ferrigno and G. Santambrogio), pp. 171–177, Edi. Ermes, Milano.

McNair, P.J., Marshall, R.N. and Matheson, J.A. (1989) Gait of subjects with anterior cruciate ligament deficiency, *Clinical Biomechanics*, **4**, 243–248.

McPherson, M.N. (1988) The development, implementation and evaluation of a program designed to promote competency in skill analysis. PhD Thesis, The University of Alberta, Edmonton, Canada.

Malouf, D. (1988) *How to Deliver a Dynamic Presentation*, Simon and Schuster, Brookvale, Australia.

Marzan, G.T. and Karara, H.M. (1975) A computer program for direct linear transformation solution of the collinearity condition and some applications of it, in *Symposium on Close Range Photogrammetric Systems*, pp. 420–476. American Society of Photogrammetry, Falls Church.

Mendoza, L. and Schöllhorn, W. (1993) Training of the sprint start technique with biomechanical feedback, *Journal of Sports Sciences*, **11**, 25–29.

Morriss, C.J. and Bartlett, R.M. (1993) Biomechanical analysis of the hammer throw, in *Report on the AAA/WAAA National Championships*, Volume 2 (Ed. R.M. Bartlett), British Athletic Federation, Alsager, U.K.

Schneider, K. and Zernicke, R. (1988) Computer simulation of head impact: estimation of head-injury risk during soccer heading, *International Journal of Sport Biomechanics*, **4**, 358–371.

Smith, R.M. and Spinks, W.L. (1989) A system for optimising feedback to rowers and their coaches. Paper presented at the *Olympic Solidarity Seminar*, Canberra.

Van den Bogert, A.J., Sauren, A. and Hartman, W. (1989) Simulation of locomotion in the horse: principles and applications, in *Proceedings of the Second International Symposium on Computer Simulation in Biomechanics* (Eds. M. Hubbard and A. Komor), pp. 22–23. Department of Mechanical Engineering, University of California, Davis, CA.

Vaughan, C.L. (1984) Computer simulation of human motion in sports biomechanics, in *Exercise and Sport Science Reviews*, Vol. 12 (Ed. R.L. Terjung), pp. 373–416. Collamore Press, Lexington, KY.

Whittle, M. (1991) *Gait Analysis—an Introduction*, Butterworth Heinemann, Oxford.

Winter, D.A. (1990) *Biomechanics and Motor Control of Human Movement*, 2nd edn, Wiley Interscience, Toronto.

Woltring, H.J. (1985) On optimal smoothing and derivative estimation from noisy displacement data in biomechanics, *Human Movement Science*, **4**, 229–245.

Woltring, H.J., McClay, I.S. and Cavanagh, P.R. (1989) 3-D Calibration without a calibration object, in *Proceedings XII International Congress of Biomechanics* (Eds. R.J. Gregor, R.F. Zernicke and W.C. Whiting), Abstract 197, UCLA Press, Los Angeles, CA.

Wood, G.A. and Marshall, R.N. (1986) The accuracy of DLT extrapolation in three-dimensional film analysis, *Journal of Biomechanics*, **19**, 781–785.

Yeadon, M. (1988) Techniques used in twisting somersaults, in *Biomechanics XI-B* (Eds. G. de Groot, A.P. Hollander, P.A. Huijing and G.J. van Ingen Schenau), pp. 740–741, Free University Press, Amsterdam.

$$\boxed{4}$$

POSTURE AND PROPORTIONALITY IN SPORT

J. Bloomfield

The University of Western Australia

INTRODUCTION

Although the areas of *posture* and *proportionality* play an important role in sport performance, they have not yet received as much in-depth objective investigation as the other physical capacities which appear in this volume, e.g. strength, power, flexibility and speed. This, however, should not detract from their value in this handbook because a knowledge of both posture and proportionality is fundamental for both the practising sport scientist and the coach.

This chapter therefore should be seen as *prospective* in its basic approach to both of these fields. It should be pointed out that although some of the research in both areas is somewhat dated, this is not a good reason to discount it. Anecdotal evidence for over a decade from highly trained coaches working with top athletes, has not only validated the earlier findings, but has established a considerable applied body of knowledge which supports the existing literature, particularly in North America. The application of this knowledge about posture and proportionality has led to excellent international performances in technique-oriented events, where body modification and/or technique modification is necessary to produce an athlete's ultimate performance. It has also been of great value in selecting athletes for

Training in Sport: Applying Sport Science. Edited by B. Elliott
© 1998 John Wiley & Sons Ltd

various sports and events within them. The combination of the existing literature, 'best practice' and anecdotal evidence has been very useful in the applied coaching field; however, much more research is needed to authenticate it further. This chapter should therefore act as a stimulus for more sophisticated research to be done in the future, as well as presenting the most recent applied information in the field to assist the coach.

POSTURAL CONSIDERATIONS IN SPORT PERFORMANCE

An individual's posture can provide definite advantages or disadvantages in many sports. In fact, after proportionality, posture is probably the most important self-selector for many sports and events.

No two people have identical postures, although some are very similar. The determinants of an individual's posture are linked to the structure and size of bones, the position of the bony landmarks, injury and disease, static and dynamic living habits and the person's psychological state.

Good posture, both *static* and *dynamic*, is important for an attractive appearance, but more importantly it is essential if the body is to function with an economy of effort. If posture is poor it can lead to fatigue, muscular strain and poor muscle tone, the sagging of some parts of the body and low self-esteem.

The evolution and development of human posture

The evolution of Homo sapiens from quadrupedal to bipedal hominid was accomplished through many adaptations of the musculoskeletal system over millions of years. The four-legged animal possesses a skeletal system similar to a bridge, with an arched backbone to support the internal structures and the legs acting as stanchions to support it. When primates slowly moved towards an upright posture, the advantages of such a system were lost, as the body was solely supported by the hind legs. The following structural changes and their ramifications occurred during this evolutionary period (Krogman, 1951; Napier, 1967):

- The vertebrae had to adapt to vertical weight-bearing stress and this was achieved by changing from a curved C shaped vertebral arch into an S shaped one.
- The erect posture places an extra burden on the pelvis which now has to support the entire weight of the upper body. By standing erect, the whole structure was tilted upward and additional weight was placed on the pelvic basin.
- The foot has changed shape to become less of a grasping appendage and more of a weight supporter. This has occurred by a shortening of the toes and a lengthening of the remainder of the foot; these changes place

considerable stress on the arches, sometimes causing problems such as pronated feet and functional flat feet.

- To permit the bending and twisting movements of the human spine, the vertebrae have changed shape to the point where they are now a partial wedge. This shape, although very good for mobility, has weakened the vertebral column, especially in the lumbar region where the discs may herniate with overstress.

Postural changes during growth

At birth the infant has two primary vertebral curves. The major curve is in the thoracic region, while the minor one is in the area of the sacrum. Around 6 months, a secondary curve develops in the cervical area and is the result of the infant holding its head up. When the child stands upright, the lumbar curve starts to develop, and by the time the individual reaches 6 years of age there are two definite primary and two secondary curves.

When the infant is born, the legs are flexed at the knee joints and the feet are inverted, but as the child stands and the legs develop, the feet become everted. An 18 month old child will have 'bow legs' when standing, but by 3 years of age will develop 'knock knees'. In most cases by 6–7 years of age the legs will have straightened.

Maintenance of posture

The maintenance of posture in an upright position depends upon a series of reflexes which are smoothly coordinated as part of the nervous system. The reflex which plays the major part in this development is known as the myotatic reflex, which basically responds to stretch.

The mechanism which enables humans to assume various postures, and maintain them, works in the following way. If a joint starts to flex, the muscle spindles of the major muscle group controlling the joint are stretched and an impulse is generated which goes to the spinal cord, where a synapse is made with a motorneuron. This then innervates the fibres of the controlling muscle group so that they contract and re-extend the joint, thus placing it into a normal position. The reflex only operates in the presence of facilitation by the vestibular nucleus in the medulla through the spinal cord, as well as through the extrapyramidal and autogenetic governor system. These mechanisms enable very smooth and coordinated contractions which maintain normal posture (Alter, 1988; de Vries, 1986).

Advantages of good posture

Posture can be defined as the relative arrangement of body parts or segments, but generally it is the term used to describe the way a person stands. *Good posture* (Figure 4.1) therefore, is a state of muscular and skeletal balance which protects the supporting structures of the body against progressive deformity or injury. *Poor posture* on the other hand is the faulty relationship of the various segments of the body, producing increased stress on supporting structures (Figure 4.2). This type of posture makes it more difficult to maintain efficient balance over the base of support and causes habitual sagging which can permanently stretch some muscle groups and shorten others. The advantage of having good posture is that the least use of energy occurs when the vertical line of gravity falls through the supporting column of bones, and the body does not have to continually adjust its position to counter the forces of gravity. Good posture therefore, is both mechanically functional and economical.

Postural diversity within individuals

Postural diversity can occur within individuals because they have disharmony between different regions of their body, and this phenomenon is known as *dysplasia*.

Figure 4.1: In 'good posture', a vertical line should pass through the anterior portion of the ear and then through the centre of each joint of the lower extremity.

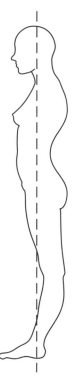

Figure 4.2: If any segment of the body deviates from its vertical alignment, its weight must be counterbalanced by the deviation of another segment in the opposite direction. Also note the severe genu recurvartum of the legs.

One sees dysplasic characteristics in many people, but this does not always mean that they have poor posture, because they have in some cases adjusted to it naturally, so that their general postural alignment is quite good. Figure 4.3 gives examples of individuals with dysplasic characteristics such as small hips and a large head, or heavy legs and buttocks, or large breasts. These subjects certainly have dysplasia but their posture is basically good.

Posture and its relationship to somatotype

There is a strong postural relationship with body type, especially among ectomorphs and endomorphs. The *ectomorph* has more postural deformities than the other groups, especially as these relate to the vertebral column. Such defects as a poked or forward head, abducted scapulae or round shoulders, kyphosis or round back, lordosis or hollow back and scoliosis or lateral curvature of the spine, are common with primary ectomorphs, and at times two of the above problems can be combined. *Endomorphs* suffer mainly

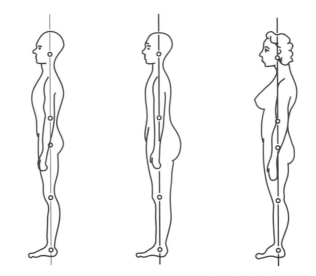

Figure 4.3: Examples of individuals with dysplasic characteristics.

from leg deformities, due to the added burden of additional weight and such problems as genu valgum (or knock knees), flat feet, and everted (or duck) feet are common. *Mesomorphs* are generally free from major postural defects but may develop minor problems as they grow older, especially if they increase their body weight.

Postural defects

Causes of postural defects

There are several factors causing postural defects, some of which are genetic while the others are environmental. They are as follows (Ackland and Bloomfield, 1995):

- *Injury.* When a bone, ligament or muscle injury occurs, it may weaken the support normally provided to the total framework.
- *Disease.* Diseases often weaken bones and muscles or cause joints to lose their stability, thus upsetting posture. Examples of such diseases include arthritis and osteoporosis.
- *Habit.* Postural habits are acquired by repeating the same body alignment on many occasions, such as when leaning over a desk or slouching in a chair. If body segments are held out of alignment for extended periods of time, the surrounding musculature rests in a lengthened or shortened position.
- *Skeletal imbalance.* The most familiar imbalance of skeletal lengths is seen in the lower limbs, and in extreme cases this causes a lateral pelvic tilt and

may result in the development of scoliosis. However, more subtle skeletal differences such as the location of the acetabulum (Figure 4.4) and length of the clavicle provide equal potential for defective posture.

Postural defects can also be caused by such variables as an individual's mental attitude over a prolonged period of time, or the wearing of high-heeled shoes, which shift the centre of gravity forward.

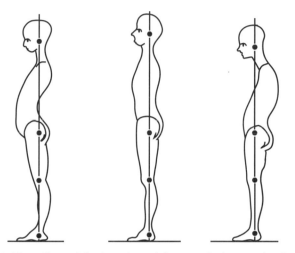

Figure 4.4: The effect of the location of the acetabulum on back posture.

Interrelationships of postural defects

Normally, postural defects are treated segmentally, but it must be stressed that these abnormalities are usually associated with other changes within the body. They mostly occur because the downward gravitational pull on any part of the body is borne by the segment below, and if any segment deviates from its vertical alignment, its weight must be counterbalanced by the deviation of another segment in the opposite direction. Therefore postural defects must be seen from a total body perspective and Figure 4.2 illustrates this phenomenon in the following way. The subject, by standing in a tense position, increases the pelvic tilt so that the pelvis rotates forward on the femur, carrying the lumbar spine forward and with it the body's centre of gravity. To compensate for this position two additional actions occur. First the lower limbs tend to adopt a hyperextended position (genu recurvartum), while the upper part of the body is thrust backwards, thus increasing the lumbar and dorsal curvatures.

Specific postural defects

The following defects range from those which are only just visible to the trained eye, to those which are very extreme. Individuals with minor defects may not need a corrective programme because their bodies have gradually adapted to them; however, those with moderate to severe postural deviations will need various levels of remediation and, in extreme cases, surgery.

Anterioposterior defects.

- *Poked or forward head.* This is a defect in which the neck is slightly flexed and the head is partially tilted forward. It is often associated with abducted scapulae (round shoulders).
- *Abducted scapulae* (round shoulders). This debilitating defect occurs when the scapulae assume an abducted position due to a weakened condition of the trapezius and rhomboid muscles and the medial borders protrude from the individual's back.
- *Kyphosis* (round back or Sheuermann's disease). This defect increases the convexity of the thoracic curve and is caused by wedging of the thoracic vertebrae.
- *Lordosis* (hollow back). Lordosis is characterized by an exaggerated lumbar curve, usually caused by the pelvis tilting too far forward.
- *Visceral ptosis* (protruding abdomen). This condition is characterized by the sagging of the abdominal organs and often accompanies lordosis. The downward drag upon the mesenteries occurs when there is not sufficient tension in the abdominal wall to hold them in place.
- *Kypholordosis.* This defect is a combination of kyphosis and lordosis and as a result places a great deal of stress on the trunk, because the anti-gravity muscles are forced to contract vigorously in order to balance the body segments. It is a condition where the individual is often in a state of chronic fatigue.
- *Genu recurvartum* (leg hyperextension). This defect is characterized by a backward curve of the legs which creates an unstable knee joint for agility sports (Figure 4.2).

Lateral defects.
- *Scoliosis.* This common defect manifests itself in a lateral curvature of the spine and in many severe cases is accompanied by a longitudinal rotation of the vertebrae (Rasch and Burke, 1978). Scoliosis usually begins with a C shaped curve (functional scoliosis) but over a period of time a righting reflex creates a reversal of the C at the upper spinal levels, producing an S shaped curve (structural scoliosis). This defect can be caused by uneven lower limb lengths, muscle imbalance and ligament lengthening.

- *Genu varum* (bow legs) and *genu valgum* (knock knees). These conditions are genetic and individuals may need medical attention early in their life if they appear to be serious. They are usually caused by knee joint irregularities or partial deformities of the femur or tibia bones.
- *Tibial torsion* ('pigeon toes'). Often referred to as *inverted feet*, this condition is characterized by internal rotation at the hip joints. This in turn causes the knees to inwardly rotate ('crossed knees or squinting patellae') so that the feet become inverted.
- *Pronated feet* ('duck feet'). This defect is also known as *everted feet* and is characterized by a protruding medial malleolus and pseudo flat feet caused by the rolling inward of the ankles.
- *Flat feet.* There are several classifications of flat feet and these are as follows:
  —*True flat feet* (pes planus). This is the most serious of the foot defects in which the longitudinal arch is flat. The condition may be accompanied by discomfort and interference with the foot's normal function.
  —*Functional flat feet.* This is a defect which is caused by weakened and stretched muscles, ligaments and fascia in the foot.
  —*Flexible flat feet.* This condition is characterized by a loss of the arches of the feet during weight bearing, but when there is no weight on the feet they appear normal.
  —*False flat feet.* This is not a true postural defect but a condition which results from the presence of a fat pad on the plantar surface of the feet.

Static and dynamic posture

Posture is *static* when a person is in equilibrium or motionless. In sport science we are much more interested in *dynamic* posture, i.e. when an individual is in motion. Generally there is a high positive correlation between static and dynamic posture, a phenomenon which has been observed by high-level coaches for many years. One further item of interest when one compares static and dynamic posture relates to injuries, which can be the result of postural defects. The following section briefly examines this:

Injuries resulting from static postural defects

Lorenzton (1988) reported, in a study of injured runners, that 40% of them had a variety of postural defects, muscle weakness and imbalance, or decreased flexibility. Malalignment problems of the following types were involved:

- Pronated feet or flat feet, which caused excessive pronation during running, resulting in injury.

- During the running cycle, it is necessary to have the correct alignment of the feet and the leg. Runners who did not possess this characteristic, or who had eversion of the heel, predisposed themselves to injury.
- Runners with flat feet (pes planus) were liable to develop a further depressed longitudinal arch without eversion, while those with high arches (pes cavas) suffered from injuries attributed to excessive motion of the subtalar joint.
- Individuals with a wide Q-angle, (i.e. a measure obtained by connecting the central point of the patella with the anterior superior iliac spine and the tibial tuberosity) or genu valgum (knock knees), experienced injuries to the patellofemoral joint and the patella itself. Athletes with genu varum (bow legs) also predisposed themselves to injuries in the patella region, as well as iliotibial band friction syndrome.
- Athletes with leg length discrepancies accompanied by a pelvic tilt developed trochanteric bursitis and iliotibial band friction syndrome, as well as intervertebral compression on the concave side of the lateral lumbar curve.

The above injuries can be partially eliminated if coaches and sports medicine specialists become more aware of the increased risk of injury among athletes with the above postural defects. Astute observation can often save an athlete from developing a chronic and debilitating injury which could have been avoided.

Prevention of postural defects

In order to prevent minor postural defects occurring, most athletes should, as part of their flexibility and strength training programmes, carry out a proactive exercise routine designed to assist in the maintenance of good posture. Many postural defects can develop from the overuse of one of several regions of the body and they can cause physical discomfort and injury in the more mature athlete. Figure 4.5 shows the overdevelopment of the left side of the upper body of a high-performance left-handed fast bowler in cricket and the accompanying minor scoliosis which developed over several years. This can occur with all unilateral athletes if it is not guarded against, while bilateral athletes such as swimmers, cyclists, wrestlers and boxers, may develop various anterioposterior curvatures, the most common of these being round shoulders resulting from their intensive sport-specific training programs. There are however some postural characteristics which, if not too extreme, are a definite advantage to the athlete and these are explained in the section on posture modification later in this chapter.

Posture assessment

Static posture is usually assessed subjectively in the standing position using a rating chart as a guide for the observer. The alignment of body segments

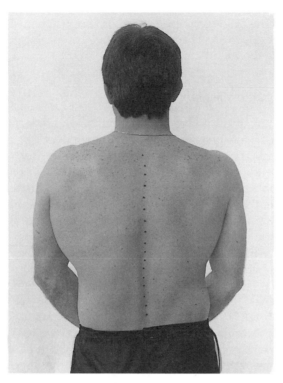

Figure 4.5: Overdevelopment of the left side of the upper body of a high-level fast bowler in cricket, with an accompanying scoliosis.

when viewed from the posterior and lateral perspective is thus examined. More objective tests which focus on a particular postural deformity rather than mass screening, include medical imaging techniques using radiography and computerized tomography. In addition, special photographic techniques such as Morié Topology have been developed for the accurate assessment of scoliosis and other spinal postural disorders. Instrumentation and methodologies for measuring dynamic posture are not generally available; however, these may eventually be developed in association with the biomechanical techniques of cinematography/videography and electrogoniometry (Marshall and Elliott, 1995).

Desirable postures for high-level sport performance

There are various minor postural deviations which are well suited to different sports and events, because the alignment of the bones and the muscles covering them produce a mechanical advantage, with either speed and/or power or balance (Bloomfield, 1979). Posture has a marked effect on performance, but little research has been carried out on its advantages or disadvantages. The following application of various postural phenomena to the major sports groups has been mainly done by coaches, who by trial and error have made the following observations.

Racquet sports (tennis, badminton, squash)

Competitors in this group have variable postures; however, those with inverted feet (pigeon toes) have a speed advantage over a short distance such as on small courts, because they automatically take short steps which are usually very rapid. There has been some debate as to why this postural characteristic enables them to move fast over a limited distance and the most quoted theory is that tibial torsion tends to shorten the hamstring muscle group, preventing the individual from 'striding out' and taking long steps. This characteristic is of little value to athletes who wish to move very fast over any distance more than 15–20 m, because to attain very high speeds one needs both a fast stride rate and a reasonably long stride. Furthermore it is also thought that by cutting down the player's stride length, the dynamic balance is improved, because there is more ground contact while moving.

It is also important to reinforce the point which was made earlier in this chapter relating to unilateral athletes, and many racquet sports players fit into this category, especially mesomorphic males. Such players should have compensatory strength and flexibility training on the opposite side of their body to their preferred side, in order to prevent muscle overdevelopment, and in some cases scoliosis, from occurring (Bloomfield et al., 1994).

Aquatic sports

Swimming and water polo. Swimmers with square shoulders and upright trunks, who possess long clavicles and large scapulae, appear to have lower levels of shoulder flexion–extension than those with sloping shoulders. If square-shouldered swimmers need high levels of flexibility, then they must undergo a particularly intensive programme to improve this physical capacity. Swimmers with inverted feet (pigeon toes) are admirably suited for back and front crawl or butterfly kicking, while those with everted feet (duck feet) are very well suited to breaststroke kicking. It is well known that leg hyperextension is very prevalent in swimmers and some sports medicine doctors have suggested that it occurs because the cruciate ligaments of the knee slowly stretch as a result of constant kicking, thus allowing more recurvartum to develop. High-level coaches and biomechanists, however, do not seem to have reached a consensus as to whether it is an advantage to the swimmer or not, some stating that it makes little difference in kicking, others suggesting that this posture gives a greater range of anterior and posterior motion at the knee joint.

Rowing and canoeing.   *Rowers and canoeists* do not appear to need any inherent postural characteristics in order to gain an advantage over other competitors in their sports. It is true that many of them have a slightly rounded back; however, this phenomenon is thought to be the result of intensive training with slightly hunched shoulders, rather than being a contributing factor to their self-selection for these two sports (Bloomfield et al., 1994).

Gymnastic and power sports

Gymnastics.   Female *gymnasts* with lordosis and an anterior pelvic tilt (APT) are able to hyperextend their spine more easily than those who are more flat backed. If they have protruding buttocks as well as the above characteristics, they will possess hip extension advantages over flat buttocked competitors and will also be able to spring very effectively in the floor exercise part of their programmes.

Weight-lifting.   These athletes do not appear to need any one major postural characteristic in order to gain a distinct advantage over their fellow competitors. From a postural perspective they are a very variable group of individuals.

Track, field and cycling

Sprinting.   Athletes with APT as well as protruding buttocks, (provided they have all the other necessary physical capacities) are usually excellent *sprinters* (Figure 4.6). This postural phenomenon is commonly found in Africans (currently in or originally from Africa) and is less common in Europeans, while Asian males very rarely possess it. It should be noted however, that this characteristic is more common among European females and is sometimes found in Asian women. Webster (1948) appears to be the first coach to comment on it when he stated that 'actual dissection of negroes has shown that they have a more forward pitch of the pelvic bones and consequently a more forward hang of the thigh'. Brodecker (1952) supported this observation and linked it to protruding buttocks. He further stated that many African American athletes possess APT and that it is also 'typical of the female'. He also suggested that the 'overhanging knee joint' (overhanging thigh), where the patella is well forward of the junction of the anterior part of the ankle joint when viewed laterally (the exact anatomical position is with the patella vertically above the tarsometatarsal joint), occurs in individuals with a tilted pelvis (Figure 4.7). This is a contrasting leg posture to that of swimmers, who generally have little pelvic tilt, relatively flat buttocks, and almost no overhanging thigh. Brodecker (1952) suggested that individuals with APT and protruding buttocks are able to exert more force in running as the thigh is extended back. This is in agreement with many sprint coaches, who believe that the above posture gives the sprinter an optimal driving angle in the extension phase of the running cycle. The high hurdler, although taller, has an almost identical posture to the sprinter and Figure 4.7 illustrates this phenomenon.

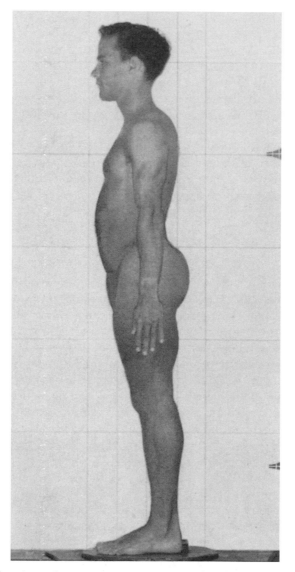

Figure 4.6: This sprinter demonstrates an anterior pelvic tilt and protruding buttocks (courtesy of Tanner 1964).

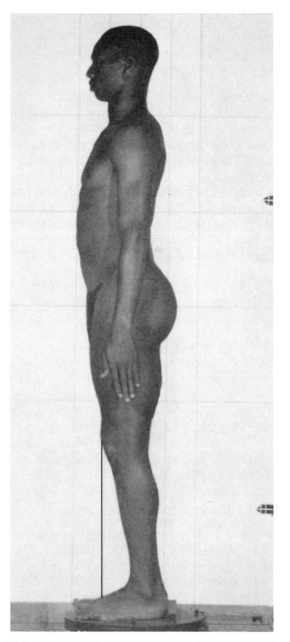

Figure 4.7: This high hurdler, although taller than the majority of sprinters, has an almost identical posture to them and as well displays an overhanging thigh (courtesy of Tanner 1964).

The above postural characteristics in very fast runners are accompanied by large and powerful buttocks (gluteus maximus muscle) and thighs, particularly the hamstring muscle group (biceps femoris—long head, semitendinosus, semimembranosus) which, with the gluteus maximus, extend the thigh with a powerful 'driving action'.

Middle distance running.   Athletes in these events, particularly those in the 400 m, and some in the 800 m events, have a similar buttocks posture, though usually not so extreme, as that of sprinters (Figure 4.8). As the races get longer, the protruding buttocks characteristic disappears, while long-distance runners have reasonably flat backs and buttocks (Figure 4.9).

Jumping.   This group of *field athletes*, although different to sprinters in their proportions, have almost identical postures to them. Figure 4.10 of an outstanding long jumper illustrates this and demonstrates the APT and particularly the protruding buttocks which are accompanied by the overhanging thigh of the vast majority of agility athletes.

Throwing.   Elite level *throwers*, like weight-lifters, have no single postural characteristic which is obvious. Their performances are related more to body bulk, proportionality and explosive power.

Cycling. Cyclists have definite postural characteristics but these are thought to relate more to their heavy training routines over prolonged periods of time than to their constitutional bone shape. They tend to have slightly rounded backs and possess the overhanging thigh phenomenon. It is thought that the latter posture is caused more by the heavy musculature in the thighs and buttocks, particularly in sprint cyclists, than by natural APT and protruding buttocks, which the majority of sprint and agility athletes display. In other words, it would appear that their very heavy power training has influenced their posture (Bloomfield et al., 1994).

Mobile field sports (field hockey, soccer, lacrosse)

These athletes are usually a varied group with no rigid postural requirements. Players in positions where they have limited territory to cover may have a specialized posture such as inverted feet. Where a high level of speed is needed for a reasonable distance, for example in wing positions in the above sports, APT and protruding buttocks can be of value, provided that the player has the necessary skill and other physical requirements to be a valuable team member. In these sports a non-rigid or non-upright spine is an advantage, because the player is in a slightly flexed position for a reasonable period of time during the game. It is an advantage therefore for these athletes to have at least moderate lumbar and dorsal curves. As for all agility sports, genu recurvartum (Figure 4.2) is an inferior leg posture in

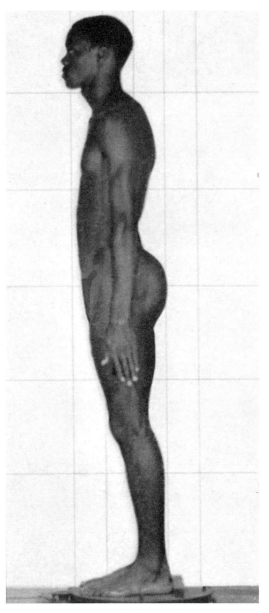

Figure 4.8: This 400 m runner has a similar buttock posture to sprinters (courtesy of Tanner 1964).

comparison to the overhanging thigh posture (Figure 4.7), not only because the knee joint is already hyperextended and takes a longer time to straighten than the slightly flexed knee joint, but also because the genu recurvartum posture creates an unstable knee joint for twisting and turning movements.

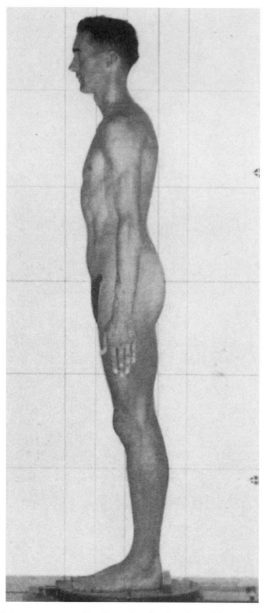

Figure 4.9: This distance runner displays the flat back and buttocks of the majority of the athletes in his group (courtesy of Tanner 1964).

Contact field sports (rugby codes, Australian football, American football)

Players in this group are posturally similar to the former group but generally have more body bulk. Postural characteristics which are advantageous

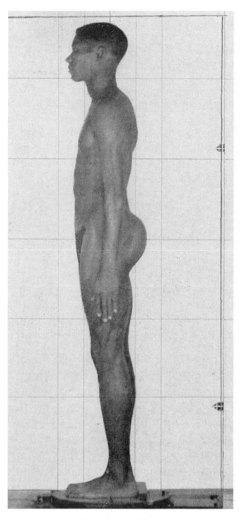

Figure 4.10: This jumper has a similar hip and buttock posture to sprinters (courtesy of Tanner 1964).

are those with a reasonable degree of spinal curvature rather than a rigid upright posture; inverted feet, where quick stepping and elusive running are needed for short distances; and APT, protruding buttocks and an over-hanging thigh for players who need bursts of speed. Genu recurvartum is a poor posture for contact sport, therefore any swimmers who have this char-acteristic and who also play contact sports should be advised against doing very much front or back crawl kicking, which accentuates the problem, making the knee joint more unstable and less functional for agile movement (Bloomfield et al., 1994).

Set field sports (baseball, cricket, golf)

One sees a wide variety of postures in these sports and no one posture seems to give any advantage to players in them.

Court sports (basketball, netball, volleyball)

Basketball, volleyball and *netball* are agility sports where superior height, re-flexive movement, and jumping ability are important. Inverted feet, which promote fast steps and good balance, are desirable, as are APT and protruding buttocks, accompanied by an overhanging thigh, along with reasonable spinal curvatures both in the lower and upper back.

Martial arts (judo, wrestling, boxing)

In the grappling sports good balance is important, therefore inverted feet could be advantageous. Reasonably accentuated spinal curves will also give the competitor more trunk mobility, which should be an advantage.

Modifying posture and technique to improve performance

It will be quite obvious to the reader by now that there are several postures which, if not too extreme, may be advantageous to top athletic performance and that posture is another way in which self-selection may occur for various sports or events. Therefore, there should be no attempt to modify these characteristics in any way, even though at first glance they may appear to be partially defective. Other postures, however, may be detrimental to performance, so that a strategy should be worked out to modify them.

A decision therefore must be made by the coach as to whether the athlete should undergo a modification programme or not. In many cases this will not be necessary, but should be considered if it is felt that a high-level athlete can benefit from it, particularly in sports where winning margins are very small. The following actions can be taken:

- The first approach should be to modify any *static* defects which may need correction, using a series of exercises which will stretch tight muscles and strengthen those which have become slack. This intervention programme should be undertaken if at all possible in pre- or early-adolescence. In post-adolescence it will take longer, but reasonable results can still be obtained at this time if the programme is intensive enough. It must always be kept in mind that static defects which are evident just prior to and in adolescence will become more extreme as the individual ages and that physical discomfort and the incidence of injury will probably increase as time goes on.

- The second action is one which only a few enlightened coaches have used thus far, but it will become more popular in the future. This is to accentuate those postures which are known to be advantageous for various sports. This is particularly important for individuals who appear to have almost all of the other necessary physical capacities for optimal performance, but who lack the postural characteristics needed for highly specialized events. The following two examples will illustrate this point. If a sprinter has all the other characteristics to run very fast, but does not have enough APT, then a minor postural modification may be made, so as to enable a slightly better 'driving angle' during the thigh extension phase of the running cycle, by tilting the pelvis forward. To do this the trunk extensor and thigh flexor muscles must be strengthened and at the same time the abdominal and thigh extensor muscles stretched. Also, agility athletes who need speed over a short distance can slightly increase their level of tibial torsion (inverted feet or 'pigeon toes') by strengthening the medial rotators of the hip joint and stretching the lateral rotators. It should be stressed again that posture modification will only occur with an *intense* intervention programme taking place, often over several years.

- *Dynamic* posture can also be changed with good skills coaching, and this has been done by enlightened coaches for the last half century, in technique-oriented sports such as track and field, gymnastics, diving, rowing, golf and swimming. These coaches know how to incorporate various postural positions into their athletes' techniques, such as tilting the pelvis, rounding the back, tucking in the chin, squaring the shoulders, everting the feet and so on. However, less attention has been paid to dynamic posture in team sports where agility is an important factor in the game and more specialization in various positions is becoming necessary. For example the footballer who is straight backed with little mobility in his spine has a poor posture for collision sports, where players are running into rucks, mauls and packs, or for closed field running, where tacklers are able to hit the ball carrier with little notice. The round-shouldered player has a natural advantage in this situation, because he is able to 'tuck in' or 'cover up' very quickly, whereas the straight-backed player is not in as good a natural position to take the heavy contact and can easily become injured. Well-informed coaches can develop this dynamic characteristic by intensive practice in the correct postural position, thereby making their players more physically effective and less prone to injury (Bloomfield et al., 1994).

Conclusion

In conclusion, it must be stressed again that there are a large number of physical, physiological, psychological and skill factors which contribute to top sports performance and that posture may only play a small role in some sports, or almost none at all in others. It is necessary, however, for coaches to be aware of the situations where posture is important and to be able to appreciate its value in their athletes. If a particular posture appears to be an essential characteristic for a highly specialized sport, then coaches need to have enough knowledge in order to better select their athletes, or to at least modify their postures so that they can improve their performance.

BODY PROPORTIONS AND THEIR EFFECT ON SPORT PERFORMANCE

Human proportionality has been observed for thousands of years, but it was not until the fifth century BC that a Greek named Polykleitos sculptured Doryphoros, the 'Spearbearer', which was representative of the ideal body form with the proportions of a champion athlete. This figure was then used as a proportional model by sculptors for many centuries.

It was not until the late eighteen hundreds and the first part of the twentieth century that various sport scientists and coaches began to realise that human proportions were important determinants of athletic performance. However, it was only in the last two decades that they began to understand that performances could be significantly improved by modifying the individuals' techniques, and this was done by lengthening or shortening their levers during a skilled performance.

Significance of proportionality modification in sport

Even the casual observer will have noted that human body proportions vary greatly from person to person. These variations play an important part in the self-selection process for various sports and events, and it is obvious that there is little that can be done to alter some anatomical body proportions. With this limitation in mind, it is up to coaches to modify their athletes' technique when their proportions are not suitable for various sports skills, either by shortening or lengthening the various levers of the body in order to obtain an optimal performance. This is the essence of high-quality coaching, where coaches cater for each individual and are able to formulate the most efficient technique for their athletes. How to achieve this will be fully discussed later in this chapter.

Effect of growth on proportionality

During the growth period, every individual undergoes various proportionality changes to a greater or lesser extent, and it is important for coaches to realize this, because there will be times when allowances will need to be made for such changes.

The following information will enable the coach to understand the growth process better from a proportionality perspective:

- Figure 4.11 illustrates the changes which occur during the growth of various parts of the body in males, but females follow a similar pattern. The head is well advanced at birth while the trunk is reasonably developed, with the arms and legs lagging well behind the head and trunk.
- From birth, girls are usually more advanced than boys in relation to height. Their height spurt commences at approximately 10.5 years of age and reaches its peak height velocity (PHV) at approximately 12 years of age, with boys following girls by roughly 2 years (Tanner, 1989). Bone maturity in boys compared to girls is also approximately 2 years behind.
- Malina and Bouchard (1991) stated that 'maximum growth is obtained first in the tibia and then the femur, followed by the fibula and then the bones of the upper extremity. Maximum growth of stature occurs, on the average, more or less at the same time as maximum growth of the humerus and radius.' They further stated that 'in early adolescence a youngster has relatively long legs, because the bones of the lower extremity experience their growth spurts earlier than those of the upper extremity'. Many coaches have observed this 'long-legged' phenomenon and realize that they simply have to wait for the trunk to develop before their athlete has balanced proportions.

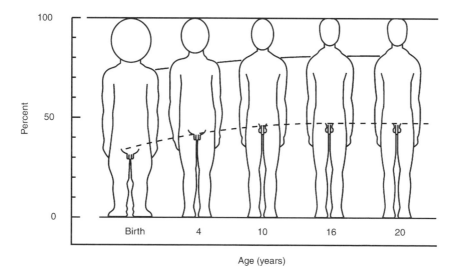

Figure 4.11: General changes in body proportions with age (adapted from Hills, 1991).

Kinanthropometric assessment

Human size and proportions are assessed by the use of anthropometry. The most common anthropometric measures are those which assess the lengths, widths, girths and volumes of body segments, using precision instruments. Anthropometric variables are often expressed as indices to allow a more meaningful description of physique to be made. For example the relationship of the length of the leg (foreleg or lower leg) to the thigh, i.e. the crural index, can be calculated in the following way:

$$crural\ index = \frac{(lower)\ leg\ length \times 100}{thigh\ length}$$

Similarly, the brachial index, which demonstrates the length of the forearm in relation to the arm (upper arm), may also be calculated:

$$brachial\ index = \frac{forearm\ length \times 100}{(upper)\ arm\ length}$$

When various anthropometric measures have been taken and the indices computed, then it is possible to make meaningful comparisons between individuals.

Individual comparisons of athletes

For many years individual comparisons have been made by comparing the raw anthropometric scores of one athlete with those of another, or with the average of one team against another. If coaches are very aware of the significance of the raw measures, for example when comparing the heights and weights of two eight-oared rowing crews, or the heights and weights of two rugby packs, then this method of comparison is of value.

The above system, although useful, has a limitation when the magnitude of the differences between individuals or groups, or when data over time, are compared. A number of strategies have been proposed including the somatogram (Behnke and Wilmore, 1974) and the unisex phantom, (Ross and Wilson, 1974; Ross et al., 1988) which have enabled sports scientists and coaches to view data from another perspective.

The somatogram

The somatogram, where the individual's percentage deviation from the mean value of the population is plotted on the gram, is a useful way to compare data. If the anthropometric proportions of an individual conform to the mean of the population, then all the values would fall on the central or zero line. This system however, does not account for variations in body size.

The phantom

Dimensional scaling of anthropometric measures with an adjustment for stature using a 'unisex phantom', is a method which can facilitate meaningful comparisons of individual proportions. In this system, raw data are compared with phantom values and the resulting deviations, in the form of Z-scores, are the basis for analysis. The phantom stratagem has been used to compare the growth of individuals over time, as well as the comparisons of individuals with specific group data.

Proportionality applied to sport performance

Lever lengths

The basic laws of physics as they relate to leverage, play an important part in sport, and bone lengths can be either an advantage or a disadvantage depending on the physical demands of the sport in which the individual competes. These lengths are absolute when the individual has reached full maturity and cannot be altered.

In some sports such as weight-lifting, for example, athletes with short levers will have an advantage over those who possess long levers, because the weight only needs to be lifted through a shorter distance (Hart et al., 1991). In other sports such as diving or gymnastics, where the body rotates rapidly in a given distance, short levers will also be an advantage to the performer. On the other hand if an athlete requires a long powerful stroke such as in swimming, canoeing or rowing, then a longer lever, provided it is accompanied by the muscular power to propel it, has an advantage in these types of sports. The same point can also be made in other sports where hitting or throwing are important. For example velocity generation for a tennis serve, a volleyball spike or a baseball pitch will all be higher for long-levered athletes, if they have the muscle power to rotate the longer segments (Bloomfield et al., 1994).

Insertion point

Although the gross bone length is usually referred to as the *lever*, this is only a general concept in sport to differentiate athletes with long or short levers from one another. However, it is the insertion point of the tendon as it attaches to the bone which is the main determinant of the lever's effectiveness. If this point is further away from the joint (axis of rotation), then it will positively affect the muscle function, giving that person a mechanical advantage, thus making him or her stronger and/or more powerful. Many coaches during their career will have observed two athletes who are similar in size, body shape, lever lengths and muscle mass, yet one is more powerful than the other. This is usually due to the tendon insertion position and/or muscle fibre type (Bloomfield et al., 1994).

Trunk and extremity indices

In general, individuals with long extremities and relatively short trunks are physically weaker than people with short extremities and long trunks.

Coaches for decades have used the above general statement in order to assess the strength, power and speed potential of their athletes and have mostly found it to be a useful guide. However, although it is generally accurate, it needs another dimension added to it which would enable coaches to make more accurate forecasts of their athletes' potential. This additional factor relates to the indices of the trunk and the upper and lower extremities, as well as the indices of the extremities themselves. This will be fully discussed in the following section.

Proportionality characteristics of athletes

One sometimes hears the statement, that 'athletes are born and not made' and in the case of proportionality or 'lever advantage', this is largely correct. It is very clear to those persons who have carried out research on, or spent a great deal of time with, various types of athletes, that some people are greatly advantaged by their body segment lengths, while others are not.

However, one should not overestimate the importance of this physical capacity, because there are many other important factors which go to produce an optimal performance. If one uses a high jumper as an example to illustrate the above point, it is clear that as well as having the optimal height and body shape, i.e. long lower limbs compared to the jumper's trunk, and long lower legs in comparison to thighs, the following characteristics will also be necessary:

- sufficient muscle mass with a high proportion of fast twitch muscle fibre compared to slow twitch fibre and tendon insertion points which give a greater mechanical advantage;
- a high level of skill which will enable the jumper to coordinate his or her body segments to 'smoothly' clear the bar;
- psychological control which will assist the athlete to focus on each jump in order to attain the best result.

All performances in sport consist of a multiplicity of variables, therefore it is important not to stress any one as being much more important than the others. However, the athlete's proportions are vitally important in ballistic events where explosive power and speed are necessary.

Specific proportionality characteristics

Racquet sports (tennis, badminton, squash, racquetball). Being agility athletes, racquet sports players have variable proportions because of the multi-faceted demands of their games. No definitive research has been carried out on these athletes; however, coaches state that they are a variable group of individuals. Because the shots used in racquet sports are executed with the upper extremities, knowledgeable coaches can help a player to compensate for an inefficient lever system. For example, the forearm can be flexed at the elbow to facilitate greater control when volleying, while it must be fully extended to enhance service technique. Two hands may be used for groundstrokes to compensate for a lack of strength, but if the athlete is powerful enough, then it may be best to use one hand, because a longer lever, provided enough force can be applied to the stroke, will increase racquet head velocity. This will increase the speed of the ball as it rebounds from the strings of the racquet. Further, while longer levered athletes may structure their basic game on high-velocity shots, shorter players must be agile and fast around the court in order to compensate for their lack of power because of their shorter levers (Bloomfield et al., 1994).

Aquatic sports. Swimming. Swimmers, at the highest levels of competition, have been increasing in height and weight for the last 30 years (Carter, 1984; Ackland et al., 1993). Elite level swimmers are generally heavier, taller and have a more robust upper body (Figure 4.12), and larger feet than lower-level competitors. Even among top-level swimmers there are special characteristics which differentiate them from one event to another. If a comparison is made between sprint and middle distance swimmers, the differences are quite marked. For example, sprint swimmers have a higher brachial index than middle distance swimmers because of their longer forearms and shorter upper arms, while sprinters also have low crural indices (i.e. a short lower leg length in comparison to their thigh length) which tends to give them a mechanical advantage over middle distance swimmers for freestyle kicking (Bloomfield and Sigerseth, 1965). Within strokes the freestyle and backstroke swimmers are taller than those competitors in the other strokes and have longer limbs, while butterfly swimmers were found to have longer trunks than the others. Breaststroke swimmers on the other hand were found to be very robust and powerful in the trunk region (Ackland et al., 1993).

Water polo.   Both male and female world class *water polo* players (Ackland et al., 1993) are tall and well built; however, there are significant proportionality differences within this sport when players in the various positions are compared with one another. Centre forwards and centre backs are larger and more robust than the other players, mainly because their greater size enables them to use their bodies very effectively in both attack and defence.

Figure 4.12: High-level swimmers are tall and have powerful trunks, as portrayed by this world sprint swimming champion.

Goalkeepers, on the other hand, are tall, less bulky and long limbed compared to the other players. They have a high skeletal mass, with lower upper body girths and are basically more ectomorphic. Ackland et al. (1993) suggested that this attribute gave them a reduced upper limb inertia which would facilitate relative quickness of movement to protect the goal.

Rowing and canoeing. High-level *oarsmen*, especially those rowing in eight oar crews, are tall and heavy with an average height of approximately 189 cm and an average body mass of 91 kg (Railton, 1969). Carter's (1984) statistics on oarsmen from four Olympic Games show a continuing trend with increases in both height and body mass. *Canoeists* also display similar developmental trends to rowers both in height and body mass, but are not as tall or as heavy as oarsmen (de Garay et al., 1974; Carter, 1984).

Gymnastic and power sports. *Gymnasts* are relatively short and light with long bodies and short legs, giving them a low lower limb/trunk ratio. They also possess a low crural index (Cureton, 1951). *Divers*, on the other hand, are taller than gymnasts but with similar trunk and leg ratios (Cureton, 1951; de

Garay et al., 1974; Ackland et al., 1993). Male and female world class divers are a reasonably homogeneous group; however, 10 m platform divers are less robust in physique than springboard divers, with relatively longer lower extremities. Ackland et al. (1993) stated that this characteristic was advantageous to the 10 m diver because 'the decreased moments of inertia are afforded by smaller absolute and proportional limb girths and segment breadths and these may provide an advantage in the performance of aerial manoeuvres'. It may also be possible that a more precise knife-like entry can be made by a more linear diver. When the top 10 divers were compared with the other competitors in the 1991 World Championships, they were found to be leaner than the other group; however, no other major differences were apparent.

Weight-lifters (Figure 4.13) have similar proportions to throwers, possessing powerful arms and shoulders. They also have long trunks with short thick and powerful legs, i.e. a lower limb/trunk ratio; and they generally have a low crural index.

Track, field and cycling.

Sprinters. These athletes are relatively short and muscular (especially in the region of the buttocks and the thighs) compared to middle distance runners, but of medium height (with mean heights of 176 cm for males and 166 cm for females) when compared to other track and field athletes. They have normal trunk lengths with short lower limbs (Figure 4.6), i.e. a low lower limb/trunk ratio (Tanner, 1964; Bloomfield, 1979). Dintiman and Ward (1988) stated that the champion male sprinter approaches 5 steps/s at full pace, while females average 4.48 steps/s. Such rapid leg movements can only be made by a relatively short limb (a shorter lever generally has a lower moment of inertia or resistance to movement than a longer one), which gives a greater 'ground strike rate' thus giving more propulsive force to the sprinter. It should also be noted that the crural index of sprinters is average.

High hurdlers (Figure 4.7) in many respects resemble sprinters, but are taller and possess longer legs (Cureton, 1951; Tanner, 1964) with proportions which are similar to 400 m runners.

Middle distance and distance runners. *Middle distance runners* are tall, linear and long legged with a normal length trunk, i.e. with a high lower limb/ trunk ratio and an average crural index (Figure 4.9). This contrasts with distance runners, who are progressively shorter as the race distance lengthens (Figure 4.14). They also have short lower limbs in comparison to their trunks i.e., with a low lower limb/trunk ratio and below average crural indices (Cureton, 1951; Tanner, 1964; de Garay et al., 1974).

Jumpers. All athletes who take part in jumping events, particularly the *high jump* and the *triple jump*, need to be tall and have long lower limbs relative to their trunk lengths (Figure 4.15) i.e. they should have a high lower limb/trunk ratio (Cureton, 1951; Tanner, 1964; Eiben, 1972; Bloomfield, 1979) as well as a high crural index (Cureton, 1951).

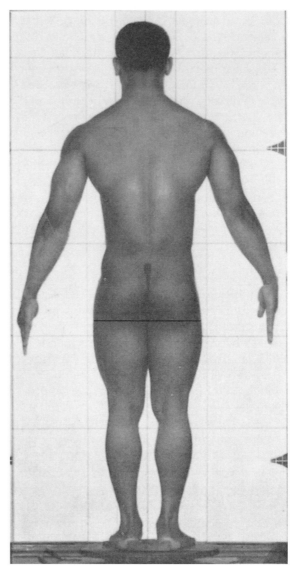

Figure 4.13: The proportions of a weight-lifter.

Throwers. These athletes are tall and heavy with powerful shoulders and arms and are becoming gradually larger each Olympiad (Cureton, 1951; Carter, 1984). Their legs and trunks are of normal length for their height; however, many of them have extremely long thick arms, especially the discus throwers (Figure 4.16). In contrast to the male athletes, Eiben (1972) stated that female throwers had long trunks and a low crural index.

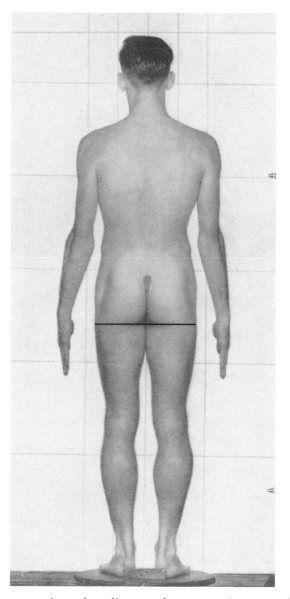

Figure 4.14: The proportions of an elite marathon runner (courtesy of Tanner 1964).

Cycling. Like many other athletes, *cyclists* are steadily increasing their height and weight (Carter, 1984). It is well known that track cyclists are more robust and powerful than road cyclists; however, cyclists are a reasonably homogeneous group as far as their other proportions are concerned. It should also be noted that anecdotal evidence from coaches indicates that

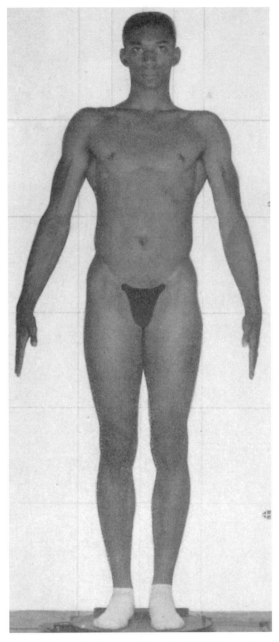

Figure 4.15: The proportions of a former Olympic high jump champion (courtesy of Tanner 1964).

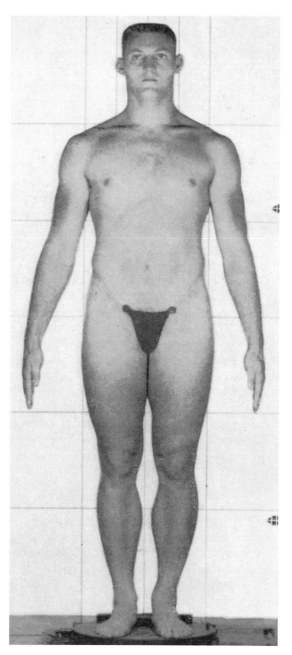

Figure 4.16: An elite discus thrower with typically long arms (courtesy of Tanner 1964).

high-level track cyclists have short thighs, giving them a high crural index which increases their mechanical advantage while pedalling.

Mobile field sports (field hockey, soccer, lacrosse).   Individuals in this group have differing proportions because of the multifaceted demands of their games. As with racquet sport players, little research has been done on proportionality in mobile field sports and one would not expect that a great deal will be done in the near future because the intelligent coach can use the already existing data from agility athletes and sprinters. This can quite easily be applied to athletes in these particular sports, who need speed or power and agility in the various specialized positions (Bloomfield et al., 1994).

Contact field sports (rugby, Australian football, American football).   Athletes in these sports, because they must be powerful, agile and fast, also need to be classified according to the position they occupy on the field. The winger or backfield player who requires speed should have similar proportions to a track sprinter, while a forward or a lineman will need proportions, bulk and agility similar to that of the field games thrower (Figure 4.17). Coaches in all games must determine the skills which are appropriate for each specialized position in contact sports at the elite level, then identify the proportionality characteristics which will satisfy them. This is the very essence of intelligent coaching.

Set field sports (baseball, cricket, golf).   As for the racquet sports and the mobile field sports groups, the proportionality of *cricketers, baseballers* and *golfers* is variable. As in racquet sports, intelligent coaches can compensate for an inefficient lever system in these athletes, since many of the skills they use are set or closed, with little or no forward body motion taking place while the skill is being performed. For example, technique modifications may be made in a golf swing or baseball pitch to compensate for an inefficient lever system.

Court sports (basketball, netball, volleyball).   The games of *basketball, netball* and *volleyball* are agility sports which partially rely on leaping skills. To do well in these sports the player must be extremely agile and able to jump, so special proportions are needed to do this. These players must be tall, have long upper limbs, lower limbs, and trunks and display a high crural index, i.e. long lower limbs in comparison to the length of their thigh.

Martial arts
    Wrestling and judo.   Participants in these sports have powerful shoulder girdles and arms, with long bodies and short lower extremities, i.e. a low lower limb/trunk ratio. They often have heavy lower limbs and possess a low crural index (Figure 4.18). All these features combine to give them a low centre of gravity, which makes it difficult to force them off balance (Cureton, 1951; Tanner, 1964).

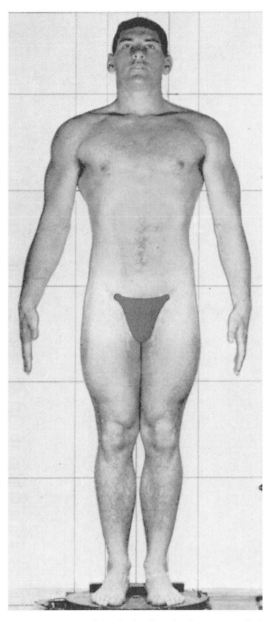

Figure 4.17: The proportions and body bulk which are needed for a forward in contact football.

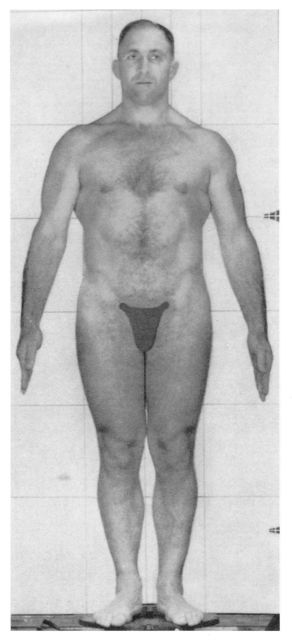

Figure 4.18: The bulk and proportions which are needed for an international heavyweight wrestler (courtesy of Tanner 1964).

Boxing. Athletes in this sport are variable in their proportions and do not have the same basic lever system as individuals in the grappling sports. Because there is a high degree of variability in their proportions, especially in the weights classes, it is up to the coach to compensate by modifying the fighter's technique.

Racial characteristics

Physical anthropologists and coaches have observed for some time that there are basic differences in the proportionality characteristics of the major races of the world. Africans (currently in or originally from Africa) have longer upper and lower extremities than Europeans (currently in or originally from Europe), while Asians (currently in or originally from the south-eastern and western Asian regions) have shorter extremities than both Africans and Europeans. It is interesting to note that Europeans cover a greater range of proportions than either of the other groups. In many cases they have proportionality requirements which suit certain sports admirably, but at the extremes of the range there are fewer individuals with the optimal lever systems for some specialized sports. They therefore find it difficult to compete against persons of other races who have larger numbers of their population with more suitable proportions (Bloomfield et al., 1994).

Special racial differences

Field and court sports. In the majority of these sports, there are many variables which contribute to high performances and although proportionality is one, this can be partially compensated for by intelligent coaching to modify the individual's skills. Therefore, except for very specialized positions, racial proportionality differences should not affect performances in these sports a great deal.

Track and field sports. Tanner (1964) in his definitive work on Olympic athletes, demonstrated conclusively that Africans have longer upper and lower limbs (relative to their stature), narrower hips and more slender calves than Europeans competing in the same event (Figures 4.19 and 4.20). He has also suggested that in sprinting the lighter calves of the former group produce 'a lower moment of inertia in the leg, and this would permit a more rapid recovery movement, that is a faster acceleration forwards, of the trailing leg'. Tanner (1964) further suggested that the original east African was more successful in the middle and long distance races, while the west African performed very well in the sprints. However he did not point out the reason for this difference, which has become more obvious recently, and this is that the tall slim Nilotic east African is physically suited to middle

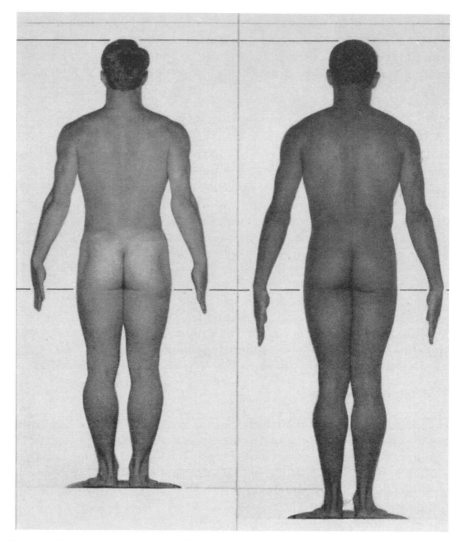

Figure 4.19: A comparison of a European and an African American sprinter who have identical trunk lengths (courtesy of Tanner 1964).

distance and longer events and the shorter, muscular west African is more suited to power (sprint) events (Bloomfield et al., 1994).

Gymnastic and power sports.   Many coaches have pointed out that individuals with long trunks and short upper and lower limbs do well in gymnastics and we are now seeing more gymnasts and divers who come from Asian countries. It would appear that Asians are well suited to these events, as well as to weight-lifting. Tanner (1964) also suggested that the proportions

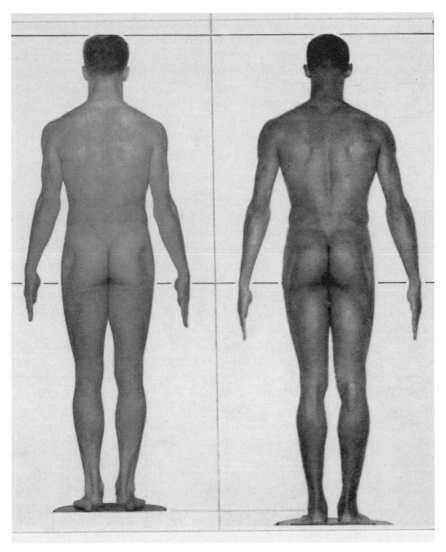

Figure 4.20: A comparison of a European and an African American 400 m runner who have identical trunk lengths (courtesy of Tanner 1964).

of this group are well suited to power sports, especially weight-lifting, where the upper and lower limbs are strikingly short in successful competitors of all races.

Body modification

The specific proportionality requirements for various athletic events have already been discussed in this chapter and they clearly demonstrate the important role of this capacity in high-level performance. However, except under extenuating circumstances, human proportions cannot be modified in the same manner as the other physical capacities by a simple intervention programme, because the mature athlete's bone lengths are absolute and cannot be changed, and therefore they are significant parameters in the process of self-selection for various sports and events.

As a matter of interest, some athletes' bodies have been deliberately modified by doctors or coaches. However, on both moral and ethical grounds, these changes cannot be recommended under any circumstances. These modifications are as follows:

- *Growth plate compaction.* Anecdotal evidence suggests that in some eastern European countries, pre-adolescent and early adolescent weight-lifters were given very heavy weights to lift over prolonged periods of time in the 1970s and 1980s. It has been reported that this practice compacted the growth plates in the legs, inhibiting the long bone growth and thus shortening their legs. It has also been claimed that prolonged heavy weight-bearing exercise may develop thick bones with a high mineral content. If this were the case, a mechanical advantage and a more solid base of support would be obtained.
- *Tendon insertion.* Earlier in this chapter in the section on *Proportionality applied to sport performance*, the subject of tendon insertion was discussed with relation to an individual being more powerful if the distance between the insertion of the tendon and the joint (axis of rotation) is greater than normal. Again, anecdotal evidence suggests that power-lifters who have ruptured a muscle by pulling the tendon off a bone during various lifts, particularly a *dead lift*, have become stronger in that region of the body where the tendon was re-attached to the bone a little further away from its previous position. For example, Bill Kazmair, an international level strong man, who ruptured his triceps brachii muscle, found he was stronger in forearm extension after the tendon had been reinserted into the ulna further away from its original position (Bloomfield et al., 1994).

Technique modification

The only acceptable way in which proportions can be changed is by a process known as technique modification and the coach can play a significant role in this. By altering the individual's technique, it may be possible to modify the lever system, thereby enabling the athlete to perform the skill in a more biomechanically efficient way.

Technique modification, to suit each individual athlete, is the basis of good coaching, so that the skilled coach must know when the individual's proportions are unsuitable and which changes will be needed to improve his or her performance. The following examples from the various sports groups will illustrate this point:

- A *tennis player* (Figure 4.21) may have the majority of the motor skills and the psychological profile needed to perform well in this sport, but be of tall stature with a relatively weak musculature. As well as a strength training intervention programme which will no doubt assist the overall performance, the player's volleys and ground strokes may need to be modified by the coach. This can be done by flexing the forearm at the elbow, thus shortening the lever to produce a more powerful forehand ground stroke. The player may also adopt a double-handed backhand technique, which not only shortens the striking lever, but may also facilitate greater stability and a better technique to hit a top spin shot (Bloomfield, 1979; Bloomfield et al., 1994).
- A *swimmer* (Fig. 4.22) may have a large number of the variables which are essential for a champion, but lack the proportions and strength needed for an efficient pull in the freestyle stroke. In addition to increasing the swimmer's strength, the propulsive lever can be shortened by flexing the forearm more than is normal for most swimmers (Bloomfield, 1979).
- A female *gymnast*, in the early stages of adolescence, will undergo a major growth spurt during this time which will increase her linearity, but at the same time decrease her stability. At this stage of her development, the coach will need to compensate for this proportionality change, in events carried out on the beam, by having her flex more at the knee joints, thus lowering her centre of gravity in order to increase her stability.

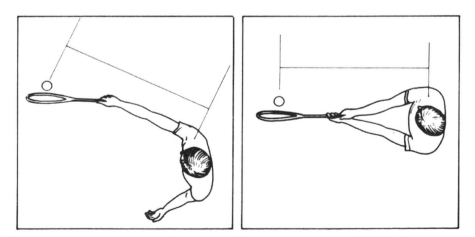

Figure 4.21: Shortening the effective lever using a two-handed backhand in tennis (courtesy of Bloomfield et al., 1994).

Figure 4.22: Shortening the effective lever in freestyle swimming (courtesy of Bloomfield, 1979).

- In *contact* and *combative* sports, athletes with long lower limbs should flex them at the knees a little more than shorter-legged athletes, in order to lower the centre of gravity and thus increase their dynamic stability.
- A *baseball* pitcher with a long upper extremity should flex the forearm more at the elbow than the shorter-limbed pitcher. This is done in order to make it easier to swing the arm forward in the early phase of the pitch prior to extending the forearm near ball release. This will increase the linear velocity of the hand, resulting in a faster ball being thrown.
- A *golfer* with long lower limbs should set up to the ball with a wider stance than a shorter limbed player, in order to prevent swaying laterally 'past the ball', which causes the club face to be slightly open at impact and may result in a push-slice being made (Bloomfield et al., 1994).

CONCLUSION

Human proportions cannot normally be modified using a physical intervention programme because individual bone lengths are finite, and under normal circumstances cannot be changed. Proportionality is a self-selector for various sports and events and some athletes are born with proportions which are highly suited to some sports but not at all suited to others. If an individual has many of the physical characteristics which are suitable for a particular sport, but lacks the leverage capacity to do this, then the intelligent coach can modify the athlete's technique to partially overcome this physical disadvantage.

REFERENCES

Ackland, T. and Bloomfield, J. (1995) Functional anatomy, in *Science and Medicine in Sport*, 2nd edn, (Eds. J. Bloomfield, P. Fricker and K. Fitch), pp. 2–31, Blackwell Scientific, Melbourne.

Ackland, T., Mazza, J. and Carter, J. (1993) Summary and implications, in *Kinanthropometry in Aquatic Sports—World Championships 1991* (Eds. J. Carter and T. Ackland), Human Kinetics, Champaign, IL.

Alter, M. (1988) *Science of Stretching*, pp. 43–50, Human Kinetics, Champaign, IL.

Behnke, A. and Wilmore, J. (1974) *Evaluation and Regulation of Body Build and Composition*, pp. 75–77. Prentice Hall, Englewood Cliffs, NJ.

Bloomfield, J. (1979) Modifying human physical capacities and technique to improve performance, *Sports Coach*, **3**, 19–25.

Bloomfield, J. and Sigerseth, P. (1965) Anatomical and physiological differences between sprint and middle distance swimmers at the university level, *The Journal of Sports Medicine and Physical Fitness*, **5**, 76–81.

Bloomfield, J., Ackland, J., and Elliott, B. (1994) *Applied Anatomy and Biomechanics in Sport*, 2nd edn, pp. 40–261, Blackwell Scientific, Melbourne.

Bloomfield, J., Fricker, P. and Fitch, K. (1995) *Science and Medicine in Sport*, pp. 2–31. Blackwell Scientific, Melbourne.

Brodecker, P. (1952) *Physical Build vs Athletic Ability in American Sports*, pp. 55–59. Athletic Ability Publications, Chicago.

Carter, J., (ed.) (1984) *Physical Structure of Olympic Athletes*, pp. 56–63. Medicine and Sports Science, 18, Karger, Basel.

Cureton, T. (1951) *Physical Fitness of Champion Athletes*, pp. 28–50, 379–441. The University of Illinois Press, Urbana.

de Garay, A., Levine, L. and Carter, J. (1974) *Genetic and Anthropological Studies of Olympic Athletes*, pp. 28–48, 83–146, Academic Press, New York.

de Vries, H. (1986) *Physiology of Exercise*, pp. 83–97. Wm. C. Brown, Dubuque.

Dintiman, G. and Ward, R. (1988) *Sport Speed*, p. 14, Leisure Press, Champaign, IL.

Eiben, O. (1972) *The Physique of Women Athletes*, pp. 181–184. Hungarian Scientific Council for Physical Education, Budapest.

Hart, C., Ward, T. and Mayhew, J. (1991) Anthropometric correlates of bench press performance following resistance training, *Sports Training, Medicine and Rehabilitation*, **2**, 89–95.

Hills, A. (1991) *Physical Growth and Development of Children and Adolescents*, pp. 33, 73–84. Queensland University of Technology, Brisbane.

Krogman, W. (1951) The scars of human evolution, *Scientific American*, **185**, 54–57.

Lorenzton, R. (1988) Causes of injuries: intrinsic factors, in *The Olympic Book of Sports Medicine I* (Eds. A. Dirix, H. Knuttgen and K. Tittle), pp. 376–389, Blackwell Scientific, Oxford.

Malina, R. and Bouchard, C. (1991) *Growth, Maturation and Physical Activity*, p. 260. Human Kinetics, Champaign, IL.

Marshall, R. and Elliott, B. (1995) Biomechanical analysis, in *Science and Medicine in Sport*, 2nd edn (Eds. J. Bloomfield, P. Fricker and K. Fitch), pp. 51–69, Blackwell Scientific, Melbourne.

Napier, J. (1967) The antiquity of human walking, *Scientific American*, **3**, 38–48.

Railton, J. (1969) *International Rowing*, p. 64. Amateur Rowing Association Publication, London.

Rasch, P. and Burke, R. (1978) *Kinesiology and Applied Anatomy*, pp. 361–387. Lea and Febiger, Philadelphia.

Ross, W. and Wilson, N. (1974) A stratagem for proportional growth assessment, *Acta Paediatrica Belgica*, **28**, 169–182.

Ross, W., De Rose, E. and Ward, R. (1988) Anthropometry applied to sports medicine, in *The Olympic Book of Sports Medicine I* (Eds. A. Dirix, H. Knuttgen and K. Tittle), pp. 233–265, Blackwell Scientific Publications, Oxford.

Tanner, J. (1964) *The Physique of the Olympic Athlete*, pp. 103–113. George Allen and Unwin, London.

Tanner, J. (1989) *Foetus into Man*, p. 15. Castlemead, Ware, Herts, UK.

Webster, F. (1948) *The Science of Athletics*, p. 331. Nicholas Kaye, London.

$$\boxed{5}$$

STRENGTH AND POWER TRAINING IN SPORT

W. Ritzdorf

German Sport University

INTRODUCTION

Strength and power development are integral parts of training in almost every sport. Free weight training in athletics, guided weight training with machines in swimming, specific strength training with additional loads in gymnastics, strengthening through the use of body mass in sport games, just to give a few examples, illustrate the scope of strength and power training in sport.

The objectives of training, however, are as different as the contents, methods and procedures used. This is only partially for methodological or organizational reasons. Traditional exercises, former experiences and dominant prejudices continue to affect daily training practice. Training of soccer players is often based on partner exercises as in former times, swimmers traditionally prefer strength training with so-called 'isokinetic' pull-devices, and track-and-field athletes predominantly use the free barbell with exercises adapted from weight lifting. Additionally, traditional prejudices such as 'strength training makes you slow' are deeply rooted in the perception of many athletes. However, it must be admitted that knowledge of sport sciences is not that advanced that detailed event-specific suggestions for training practice are available in every situation. There still remains much to be learned in the basic and applied understanding of what occurs in the neuromuscular system.

On the other hand, new aspects of strength and power training have appeared with the diversification of sports. Strength training is no longer limited to competitive sport. Strength training for prevention and

Training in Sport: Applying Sport Science. Edited by B. Elliott
© 1998 John Wiley & Sons Ltd

rehabilitation, as well as strength training as a leisure time activity in gyms, is now quite common.

Strength training was, and still is, a major part of athletic training with the aim to improve performance. In every sport where segment masses and/or implements must be accelerated, it is an integral part of daily training programmes. However, as the limits of load tolerance of the passive movement apparatus are reached, in many sports a parallel increase in the importance of strength training from a prophylactic point of view can be observed. Peak forces of more than 10 times body weight in the jumping events of athletics, 30 times the force of gravity in downhill skiing, large physical impacts in many body contact sports, physical capacities of performers such as muscular imbalances have all led to the acceptance of strength training as an important tool to prevent athletes from overload and overuse injuries. This aspect of strength training which is in part discussed in Chapter 3 will not be dealt with in this chapter.

The classical approach to a discussion of strength training (strength, power and strength endurance) will be related in this chapter to the demands of different groups of sports. The systematics of form and objectives of application of force then lead to the questions of components and influencing factors of strength and power and their forms of training. All applications of force in sport aim at accelerating or decelerating masses or to keep them in a defined position. These are the only common factors. Masses can vary markedly (more than 200kg in weight lifting to a few grams in badminton) and the final joint centre velocities may range from less than 2 m/s in weight lifting to more than 20 m/s in the racquet sports. The time periods lie between less than 100 ms in the support phase of sprinting to several minutes in rowing, while the starting conditions range from a static posture (weight lifting) to highly dynamic movements (long jump) and so on. Therefore, it is extremely doubtful whether all these demands can be reduced to the three dimensions of strength development mentioned above. As there is no form of motion that does not require some kind of force, all sports could be considered to benefit from strength development. This is of course not generally the case. For example, sports in which the metabolic energy supply is the predominant factor, as is the case in long-distance running, will not gain from weight training, while weight training in sports such as rhythmical gymnastics would also be inappropriate.

SPORTS WITH LONG-LASTING APPLICATIONS OF FORCE

Classification

A first group of sports is characterized by two aspects: the duration of force application is continuous and the applied forces are high but not maximal.

Within this very global distinction there is a wide spectrum of different demands and objectives. Sports such as rowing and short-distance swimming form one end of the spectrum. They are characterized by the fact that the duration of all single applications of force sum up to approximately one or more minutes. The ultimate aim of these sports is to produce a high velocity of the boat or the body over a reasonable period of time. Typically the applications of force are purely concentric with alternating tension and relaxation phases. Despite the amount of force applied, the energetic support of the musculature is an important limiting factor for athletic performance. It is therefore impossible to maximize every single impulse, as the total exercise time is too long. This is different to the situation seen for example in the acceleration phase of the sprint. Due to the rather short duration (6–7 seconds) of this phase, a maximization of each single impulse is logically required. Further discussion of this form of movement will occur later in this chapter.

Ice skating is another activity that on the surface appears quite similar to the previous examples. However, there is one important difference in that the contraction phases include a high isometric component and the release phases are rather short. Muscle contractions are even shorter in downhill skiing where the form of contraction is predominantly isometric. Although it is no problem even for untrained persons to assume the downhill skiing position for a short time, it is extremely difficult for this position to be held for the duration of the event (approximately 2 minutes) as this requires a high level of strength and local muscle endurance.

Sports which also include near maximal isometric contractions are found at the opposite end of the spectrum. However, due to rather small muscle groups or extremely unfavourable lever arms the required force is so high that the performable exercise time is reduced to a few seconds. Hang positions in free climbing or some elements in gymnastics (pommel horse, rings) belong to this group.

General structure

The aforementioned examples are basically different from other applications of force in sport. Normally a maximization of a short single impulse is demanded and questions of energy support need not be taken into account. High-level muscular contractions with a duration of several minutes, also place maximal demands on aerobic and anaerobic endurance and are typified by a marked production of lactic acid. As high isometric tensions suppress the blood circulation, energetic support must be maintained by the local energy depots. These circumstances must be taken into consideration when analysing the role played by strength.

In the one subgroup where the sum of impulses over an extended period is predominant, not every single impulse can be maximized. An increase of maximal strength is beneficial in this situation. As the activation of all muscle fibres at the same time is not required to achieve effective performance, a greater muscle cross-sectional area and a better recruitment always means a lower strain for the single fibre and an improved energy supply. If one assumes that in a concentric movement a given level of strength and endurance of about 70% of maximal strength may be produced for a given time, then an increase of maximum strength allows an application of force for the same time (or number of repetitions) with a greater absolute strength. Similar considerations are valid for sports with the demand of near maximal isometric contractions. Finally, the observation that the downhill tuck position in skiing can be maintained longer than the holding of the crucifix position on the rings in gymnastics can only be explained by the fact that the relative load for the activated musculature is markedly smaller. That is the mass of the relevant muscles is greater and the body positions and lever arms are more favourable. If this idea is pursued in downhill skiing, an increased level of strength must reduce the relative load and therefore, permit longer phases of isometric contraction.

In the gymnastic example the importance of maximum strength is directly evident. Exercises such as the single arm support on the pommel horse or crucifix on the rings can only be executed with a high level of maximum strength. In these exercises a defined body position can be held for a few seconds only if all fibres are not activated at the same time. Maximum strength is therefore a major aspect in these sports.

Maximal strength production is determined by biological, neuromuscular and mechanical factors.

Biological factors mainly refer to muscle cross-sectional area (CSA) and fibre typing. The physiological muscle cross-sectional area (PCSA) represents the amount of contractile elements within the muscle. It should be noted that even in muscles with parallel fibres the anatomical cross-sectional area (ACSA), measured as the largest extension of a muscle in one single position, is not a valid estimation of the whole CSA. Firstly the ACSAs of different muscles vary significantly along their proximo-distal axes. Secondly, within a muscle group (for example triceps surae) the maximum ACSAs of individual muscles (m. soleus, m. gastrocnemius) are often at different levels (see Roy and Edgerton, 1991, p. 116).

The classification of fibre typing is usually based on histochemical criteria. Although the correlation between histochemical classes and parameters of contraction has not yet been completely explained the following tendencies can be noted. Type I fibres are slow-twitch fatigue-resistant fibres used for long-lasting, low-level force production. Type IIA fibres (fast-twitch, fatigue-resistant) contribute to prolonged and relatively high force output. Type IIB fibres (fast-twitch, fatigue sensitive) are suited for short duration high force production. Type IIC fibres, an intermediate type, are ranked between slow- and fast-twitch fibres (for further information see Noth, 1992).

Neuromuscular factors refer to the firing rate and the recruitment of motor units. With an increasing discharge rate of motor units the forces generated by each impulse summate. As a consequence force output is positively related to the firing rate of a motor unit (Figure 5.1). This is one method of grading force production.

The other method is the recruitment of more motor units. The order of recruitment is determined by the size principle, first discovered by Hennemann, Somjen and Carpenter (1965). According to this principle the recruitment threshold of motor units increases with their size (Figure 5.2). As motoneurones with a high threshold innervate large fibres there is a positive correlation between recruitment threshold and force production.

The fact that the last fibres to be recruited are the large type IIB fibres is of special interest to strength training. These considerations are valid for non-explosive productions of force only. There is some evidence that they change in highly explosive contractions (see below).

Mechanical factors are related to the mechanisms of muscle action, the muscle length and the velocity of contraction. Maximum force production is achieved in eccentric contraction (Figure 5.3). Maximum strength values are between 10% and 40% higher than isometric maximal strength values. As maximal eccentric contractions are performed quite slowly it is inconceivable that reflex mechanisms are responsible for this observation. Maybe the lengthening of the activated muscle–tendon system produces elastic tension that is added to the strength produced by the voluntary contraction. Isometric maximal strength on the other hand is 10% to 15% higher than maximal concentric strength. With increasing loads the concentric maximum comes closer to the isometric maximum.

Muscle length–tension relations follow the general rule that maximal force is produced near the relaxed muscle length. This permits a maximum rate of actin–myosin cross-bridge production and an appropriate pretension of the

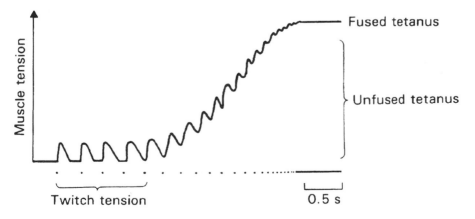

Figure 5.1: Firing rate and muscle tension (from Noth, 1992).

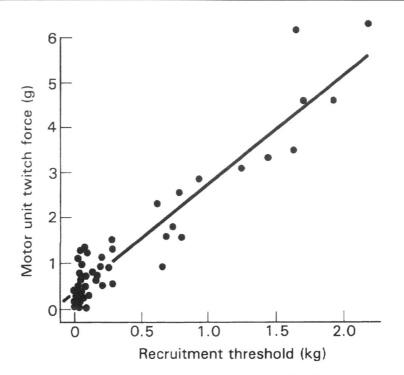

Figure 5.2: Motor unit twitch force and recruitment threshold (From Desmedt, 1981).

serial elastic structures. This knowledge has been used more or less successfully in designing strength training equipment (variable radius cams).

Finally the force produced depends on the movement velocity. With increasing velocity the maximal force decreases (Figure 5.4). Small loads enable the muscle to react with high shortening velocities, heavy loads require most of the cross-bridges for lifting the load rather than accelerating it.

However, care must be taken as the externally visible velocity for example of a barbell does not refer to the internal velocity of force production.

General adaptations

Adaptations in strength training refer to muscle hypertrophy as well as to the improvement of neuromuscular functions. Hypertrophy is of course the most obvious effect of strength training, which is the very reason for the primary prejudice against strength training. Therefore, it should be noted that an increase of maximal strength is always combined with an increase in relative strength (strength per kilogram bodymass). There are two distinct theories about the stimulus responsible for an adaptation of muscle CSA. The 'stimulus-tension theory' (Rasch and Pierson, 1964; Hettinger, 1968)

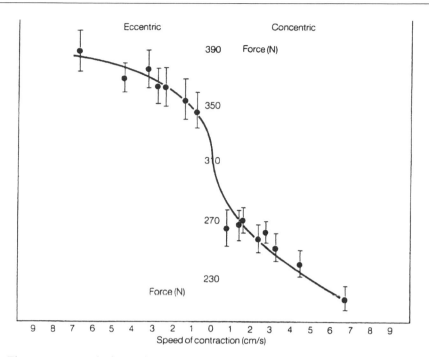

Figure 5.3: Muscle force, form and velocity of contraction (From Komi, 1973).

assumes that the intensity and the duration of muscular tensions are responsible for the excitation of hypertrophic effects. In contrast to this concept the 'ATP-debt theory' (Meerson, 1967; 1973) suggests that, during muscular exercises with submaximal loads, an ATP-debt occurs that is responsible for the adaptation. Findings by Goldspink (1978), however, indicates that even in completely exhausted muscles no ATP-debt can be determined. A debt situation can only occur by a decreased ATP-flux rate and this seems to be very unlikely. However, experiences from training practice have shown that by training with submaximal loads marked effects of hypertrophia and increases in strength can be provoked. Almost all training of bodybuilders is based on training with submaximal loads. The apparent contradiction might be explained in two ways; either the muscle reacts with the same adaptation independent of the actual degree of tension above a certain tension threshold, or different tensions lead to different adaptation mechanisms although the externally measurable result is identical.

In both cases an increase in muscle CSA can be observed. This is the result of an increase of contractile proteins. The surface of the myofibrils as well as their number increases. Satellite cells along the muscle fibres are stimulated for proliferation. Whether there is a proliferation not only of the myofibrils but of the whole fibre (i.e. a hyperplasy) is still being debated, although most studies reject this effect (for further details see Macdougall, 1992).

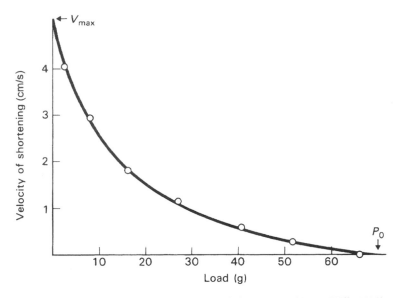

Figure 5.4: Muscle force and velocity of shortening (From Hill, 1938).

Although hypertrophy is the most obvious effect of strength training, there are some other very important neuromuscular adaptations. As these adaptations refer mainly to power they will be discussed later in this chapter.

Specific structure and demands

Rowing

Rowing may be used as an example of those sports with repeated submaximal applications of force over an extended time span. Rowing aims at minimizing time for a given distance. This means a maximization of mean velocity and therefore, a summation of accelerating impulses. A very brief movement analysis illustrates the following structure; the total race can be separated into a starting phase, an intermediate phase and the finish. In the first part of the starting phase lasting (10–15 seconds) the boat is accelerated with 8–10 strokes from the rest position to a maximal velocity of about 6 m/s. Each stroke is executed with maximal strength and the stroke frequency is approximately 44 strokes/min. This maximal velocity remains constant for the following 20–30 seconds with stroke frequencies between 40 and 44 strokes/min. This high velocity, which cannot be maintained for the complete race is reduced in the intermediate phase to about 5.2 m/s and this level is maintained for the next 3–4.5 minutes. The stroke frequency in this phase is around 32–38 strokes/min and is slightly raised in the final phase.

The total number of strokes during the race is about 240. Within a time span of little more than 6 minutes, 10 maximal and 230 submaximal applications of force (about 70% of maximum strength) are executed. In female rowers the percentage is about 80% of the distance and therefore, the total time is shorter. Maximal forces measured at the rowlock are about 1000 N in the long oar and 500 N in the scull and the time for a single stroke is about 1 second. Although there are brief eccentric and isometric contributions the major portion is the concentric contractions of the musculature. Rowing therefore, places high demands on maximum strength and strength endurance. The rate of force development is of minor importance to the maximum strength. The slow-twitch and intermediate fibres are therefore, predominantly addressed.

This structure of demands must be addressed in the rower's training. Strength endurance training takes place on the water as well as out of the boat. On the water the resistance may be varied with respect to the objective. It may be raised by enlarging the blades, by a brake or by rowing with half the crew. It may be lowered by shortening the outboard length of the scull. Strength endurance training out of the boat is normally done in circuit training. The total number of repetitions in one circuit is identical to the number of strokes in rowing (240) divided into 10–12 exercises. Within each exercise the frequency of contraction and relaxation should be 25–45 repetitions per minute and thus equals the frequency in rowing. Maximal strength training which aims at an enlargement of muscle CSA, particularly of the slow twitch fibres, is organized in sets comprising 6–8 repetitions.

Downhill skiing

The strength requirements in downhill skiing and also in ice skating are clearly indicated by the body musculature of the athletes. A marked hypertrophy of the quadricep, hamstring and gluteal muscle groups reflect the specific demands of this sport. Nevertheless the structure of the demand is quite complex. Producing very high force–time curves requires extremely high concentric maximal strength to be applied in a short time. Uneven surfaces and landings after jumps also place a high demand on eccentric and reactive strength. Finally, well-defined isometric strength is necessary to maintain the typical downhill position for about two minutes. As an increase of body mass is advantageous to performance, strength training is a basic part of athletic training in downhill skiers. Strength training therefore aims at hypertrophy, in addition to an improvement of recruitment and innervation frequency. It is then completed by isometric strength endurance training.

Gymnastics

The demands in gymnastics are as diverse as the elements of the sport. In this context emphasis will be placed on long-lasting isometric applications of force as they occur in exercises on the pommel horse, rings and, occasionally, on the horizontal bars. As in rowing, strength must be optimized and not maximized in gymnastics. In rowing it was argued that the maximal development of strength and endurance was contradictory. The argument in gymnastics is different as the required amount of strength can be determined quite precisely. Athletes must be able to keep their body in a defined position for a certain time whilst in positions of poor mechanical advantage. These would include the single-arm support phases in the pommel horse or during performance of the crucifix on the rings. If the high strength necessary for these elements is available, a further improvement of strength does not necessarily lead to an improvement of performance. Additionally gymnasts must limit their body mass and maintain high levels of flexibility, which places further restrictions on the development of strength. Consequently strength training in gymnastics is distinctly different from other sports. It follows the principles of 'learning by doing' and 'step by step approximation'. 'Learning by doing' means that the required strength is developed by the repeated application of the specific gymnastic element. 'Step-by-step approximation' means that the final element is achieved by an external support due to lack of strength. This support is reduced step by step until the final position (e.g., the crucifix) can be reached without any assistance. Isolated strength training is not yet a commonly used form of training in gymnastics.

General training methods and planning of training

The discussions on the specific demands have repeatedly led to the combination of maximum strength and strength endurance. It must be noted that these are not independent dimensions of strength. Maximum strength is a basic quality of strength endurance. On the other hand, differences in strength endurance can not be explained completely by maximum strength parameters. This knowledge has led to some uncertainty in practical training. Two contradictory approaches can be observed. According to one theory maximum strength and general endurance are developed separately and combined to produce strength endurance effects during the latter part of every year's training during actual competition. In the second approach strength endurance is trained in a complex manner with its own exercise regime. As in most of the above-mentioned examples in which the rate of force development is not decisive, maximum strength training is executed as a training for hypertrophy.

Aim	Improvement of strength
Method A	submaximal workouts
Intensity load	80%
Repetitions	8–10

Sets	3–5
Rest interval	3 min
Typical exercises	deep squats, half squats, bench press, lying snatch pull

Method B	pyramid workouts
Intensity load	70, 80, 85, 90%
Repetitions	12, 10, 8, 5
Sets	1, 2, 3, 4
Rest interval	2 min
Typical exercises	squats, cleans, bench press, lying snatch pull

Commentary: Within a training year, strength training usually begins in the general preparation period by using method A. After 4–8 weeks it is replaced by pyramid training. It must be noted that there is no definite proof that training with submaximal loads is in fact the best method to improve muscle CSA. As long as adaptations were explained by the ATP-debt theory there was some evidence for this assumption. Although the stimulus-tension theory does not basically contradict this approach the contribution of load intensity is more dominant. Even with training of bodybuilders, who primarily follow method A, there is no clear indication for the advantages of this method. The extreme exhaustion and 'burn out' regimes also used by bodybuilders would certainly lead to marked adaptations independent of the method used. On the other hand the rather high number of repetitions with medium velocity combined with the demands of these sports almost guarantee a high specificity of training loads. We can assume that this kind of strength training mainly applies to the slow-twitch and intermediate fibres so that the important aspect of energetic supply is also addressed. Nevertheless an occasional phase of training with high loads is also favoured. Training exclusively with submaximal loads leads to the effect that the real potential of the musculature cannot be achieved as specific adaptations for maximal loads have never been trained. The difference between the maximum load in a single repetition and in 10 repetitions is obvious. A 2–4 week training period with high loads markedly increases the maximum load in a single repetition. Subsequently, 80% intensity can be defined on a new level.

Very little scientific basis is available for strength endurance training. Very few studies have systematically dealt with this training method. Consequently, the methods are based more on experiences of training practice.

Aim	Improvement of strength endurance
Method A	**medium workouts**
Intensity load	40–60%
Repetitions	15–25

Sets	3–5
Rest interval	0.5–1.5 min
Typical exercises	all exercises for the trunk muscles, curls, butterfly, step-ups

Method B	**circuit training**
Number of stations	8–12
Workout time	30–60 s
Rest intervals	
between stations	15–60 s
Series	3–5
Rest interval	
between series	2–5 min

Commentary: The discussions on strength endurance training focus on the following considerations. Strength endurance is a combined quality composed of both strength and endurance. For the isolated training of these components there are more effective methods available than for the combined result. The question is whether the combination leads to a new quality and thus requires a combined training or whether the isolated development with a subsequent combination automatically leads to well-defined strength endurance. Rowers, for example, would therefore develop their levels of strength and endurance separately and then combine them by strength endurance training in the boat. Downhill skiers optimize their strength by isolated exercises and improve the strength endurance by simulation of the downhill position. An alternative to this approach would be where a training of strength endurance with medium loads and long workout times is executed over the full year. Both methods exist in training at an elite level. One conclusion based on practical experience would be that the higher the level of performance and the number of years of training the greater the domination of the isolated approach.

Training with junior athletes

The aforementioned sports put high demands on the technical and general physical abilities of the athletes. Therefore, at the commencement of athletic training the priority should be placed on training of movement technique. However, the strength requirements are so high from the involvement in performance, it is assumed that it is a specific stimulus for strength development. Rowing, downhill skiing and gymnastics certainly improve strength in children. Therefore, additional strength training is not necessary at this early age. General circuit training can be executed to improve the general 'athletic base'. During the juvenile age the proportion of strength training can be increased and the techniques used in basic exercises with the barbell learned.

SPORTS WITH SHORT-DURATION, HIGH CONCENTRIC APPLICATIONS OF FORCE

Classification

In contrast to previously discussed applications of force, the second group of sports consists of those in which the applications of force are brief and very powerful. The musculature generally functions in a purely concentric manner. These activities usually involve a mass (sport implement, own body) which has to be accelerated to a maximum or when the duration of a movement is to be minimized. In these sports the external loads are quite diverse and these variations influence the required level of force.

One end of the spectrum is characterized by maximal weights, as in weight lifting. In the pull phase the mass has to be accelerated a given distance from a stationary position to where the athlete can place himself/herself under the bar. The body has to be stretched when the weight is fixed (snatch) or a further acceleration of the mass ensues until the complete stretch is reached (clean and jerk). The middle of the spectrum comprises medium implement masses such as in the throwing disciplines of athletics. As speed is the most decisive factor with regard to performance, it is necessary to accelerate the throwing implement to a maximum velocity for release. This is what the athlete attempts under consideration of the following general strategies. There is always a pre-acceleration of the entire body system or sports implement. This occurs by means of a turn in discus throwing, a run-up in javelin, or a glide in shot put. The recruitment of supplementary large muscle groups (lower limbs, trunk) supports the final acceleration by the shoulder and arm musculature. Furthermore, this musculature is prestretched and put under pre-tension by going into an arched position (javelin) or by twisting the body (discus throw, shot put). At the other end of the spectrum which comprises very light weights, such as the ball in sport games or the implement in fencing a further modification of forces is necessary. Here, it is necessary to make distinctions between two different aims. Either the implement has to be accelerated to a maximum as in the case of a tennis serve or an attacking shot in volleyball, or a given distance has to be covered by an athlete within a minimal period of time in order to make the defensive reactions of the opponent more difficult, as in boxing or fencing. This requires different forms of applications of force which are explained below. Many types of sport require an acceleration not of an implement but of the body from a stationary position. In some cases this occurs with a preceding counter movement (e.g. block jump in volleyball), in other cases without a visible counter movement (e.g. take-off in the ski jump).

A separate chapter deals with accelerations of the body with existing initial energy and rapid eccentric–concentric take-off movements as they form an independent category of applications of force.

General structure

What the aforementioned examples have in common is the fact that a certain mass, whether it be a sporting implement or the athlete, has to be accelerated to a maximum. For this purpose there is negligible initial energy available and the musculature works almost primarily concentrically. Time minimization does not play any role with the exception of combat sports. Unlike the group of sports explained before, the focus is not on the maximization of sums of impulses within a longer period of time, but rather on the maximization of a single impulse. Consequently, the question of energetic supply to the musculature is generally unimportant. The muscular recruitment of as many muscle fibres as possible is required and this should ensue as quickly and as powerfully as possible. Thus it is a matter of power performance capacity of the musculature in a classical sense. It is no coincidence that the starting position before the release of the implement in the throwing disciplines in athletics is called the 'power position'. In general, power is characterized by the ability of the neuromuscular system to produce an impulse which should be as strong as possible within the shortest possible time. The following force–time history, representing a concentric extension movement of the legs, can be helpful in order to specify the global definition.

Impulse is equal to the area beneath the force–time curve (Figure 5.5). This area could be increased by increasing time. However, given a set distance this leads to a decrease of force in the case of movements within a single joint. In complex movements the possibility of increasing the time by means of a lengthening of the acceleration path is also useful. Thus there are two other possibilities to enlarge the impulse; an increase of the maximal force and/or an increase in the rate of application of the force. The incline of

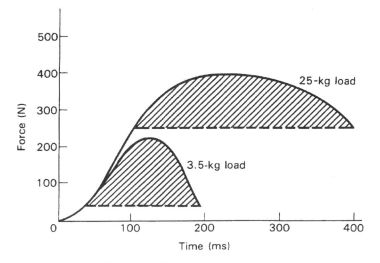

Figure 5.5: Components of power.

the force–time curve is governed by two parameters which can be considered as components of power. The starting power represents the value of force that is attained after 30 ms. It gains special significance when the objective is to cover a given distance within the shortest possible time (boxing, fencing). Explosive power is defined as the instant of the steepest inclination of the force–time curve. The significance of explosive power increases with the magnitude of the weight to be set in motion. As a result of this differentiation the question arises which determinating factors of power can be identified.

Maximal strength and its previously explained influencing factors undoubtedly play a decisive role. In terms of the biological factors of strength it is, however, crucial in many sports to pay particular attention to the CSA of specific muscles. For example there are different weight classes as in boxing and wrestling which demand maximum strength and power with a minimum body mass and in situations where the body must be accelerated; for example, in jumping or in sport games, total body mass must be carefully evaluated. Sports with maximal demands on power without any limitations of body mass (e.g. weight lifting in the upper weight class, shot put in athletics) also show an international tendency towards reducing the body mass. To compensate for reduced mass top athletes in these events show extraordinary results for example in vertical counter movement jumps as an indicator of power. Another indication that CSA is a necessary, but not perfectly related adjunct of power is given by bodybuilders. Despite their extraordinary body mass their power production is quite poor.

While muscle CSA is crucial, fibre typing is also of major importance. According to our present knowledge no alteration from slow-twitch to fast-twitch fibres can be expected, and therefore all efforts in training are made to improve the performance of type IIB fibres. In this manner the neuromuscular components of force production are addressed. As mentioned previously neuromuscular factors refer to the firing rate and the recruitment of motor units. Maximal recruitment of almost all fibres is required for a high level of starting strength and where high initial speed is required. High take-off or release velocities on the other hand do not depend only on the number of motor units involved but also on the force of contraction and the contraction speed of the fast-twitch fibres. The speed component must therefore, also be taken into account.

This refers to the above-mentioned mechanical factors. Either the force–velocity curve must be shifted upwards in its upper part where high external loads must be accelerated or to the right in its lower part with high velocities (Figure 5.4). As power production in the mentioned sports is always concentric the demand of a maximal impulse also refers to the muscle length–tension relationship. The voluntary prestretching of the muscles involved contributes to the maximization of the initial power during the shortening phase. But a continuous acceleration is dependent on the muscle's ability to also produce high forces at the end of extension.

The importance of the above-mentioned biological, neuromuscular and mechanical factors is dependent on the load that must be accelerated. This is discussed below.

General adaptations

In order to understand adaptations and training methods it is necessary to point out that power consists of both force and velocity components. It makes a great difference whether a barbell with a mass of 150 kg or a ball with a mass of several hundred grams has to be accelerated. Therefore, it is misleading to assume that there might be general adaptations or training methods. On the contrary the general rule must be that specific stimuli provoke specific adaptation reactions. Exact limits between the contributions of either force or velocity also do not exist. There is a spectrum which on the one side is force-orientated and on the other side velocity-orientated. As a matter of fact force and velocity are not independent of each other, even if the exact correlation in general is unknown.

The greater the force contribution to a movement, the more important is maximal strength. It is obvious that the available contractile mass influences the development of force. If one accepts this, the question then arises as to whether strength training automatically improves power. This statement is not generally proven. There are two reasons why an increase of maximal strength predominantly caused by hypertrophy is crucial. On the one hand this causes a significant increase in body weight which leads to problems previously mentioned, while on the other hand the critical arguments refer to the training method. An enlargement of the muscle CSA in particular is caused by using submaximal loads. In this training method approximately 8–12 repetitions are carried out per set with medium loads (approximately 80% of the maximal load), at relatively slow velocities. This results in corresponding adaptation reactions: muscle hypertrophy will occur as well as an improvement in the maximal force value, which can be attained if there are no limitations in time. However, the rate of force development (i.e. the inclination of the force–time curve) does not show any significant improvement.

The reason for this can be given by the fact that in the case of using submaximal loads and carrying out the movement in a non-explosive way the slow-twitch muscle fibres are recruited first. The tension can be successfully maintained by the repeated unloading at the same low frequency of the respective motoneurons. However, the capability of slow-twitch fibres to develop tension quickly is limited. Therefore, an improvement of the maximal force value can be observed whereas the steepness of inclination in force development remains unchanged, despite a significant muscle hypertrophy. To overstate this situation, repetitions of 10 do not improve anything except the performance in repetitions of 10. Consequently, it is not surprising that in high-level sport maximal strength training is carried out in most cases by training with near maximal loads, the corresponding limited number of repetitions and an explosive execution of the movement. The higher the load to be accelerated, the more significant is the explosive strength and as a consequence the recruitment and the firing rate of the motor units. Both of these factors are required while training with maximum loads. It is often postulated that such intramuscular coordination training makes no sense if it is carried out for a period of more than approximately six weeks because after that improvement in the existing musculature would be exhausted as no further enhancement in recruitment would be possible. However, this statement contradicts experiences gained in training practice. Weight lifters, among others, carry out year-round training with explosive applications of force within a range of high to highest intensities. It must therefore, be assumed that besides adaptations of recruitment and firing rate there must be other reactions of the biological system. First indications were given by Goldspink (1992) who showed changes in the field of molecules in the sense of 'fast' and 'slow' myosins.

To summarize: In power events with high external loads to be accelerated, strength training is of major importance. The training methods used must focus on the rate of force development. This requires high intensities in strength training.

The theoretical reflections are more difficult in those cases where the load is lower and as a consequence the movement velocities are higher. It is well known that with decreasing loads the realizable maximal strength gains also decrease. This can be explained by the fact that with high contraction velocities the number of possible cross-bridge linkages per time unit decrease. Moreover, experimental investigations have often confirmed that subsequent to a training session in which movements were executed at high velocities, the power of quick movements is more improved than that of slow movements (Moritani, 1992; Sale, 1992). Movements which are executed at high external velocities, however, require submaximal loads. As mentioned above there are several indications that in the case of explosive applications of force the fibres recruited do not follow the size principle. Due to the maximal, central innervation order ('neuronal drive') all motor units are involved in the contraction from the very beginning. This occurs with maximal frequency of innervation. This addresses another important component, that of firing rate. Maximal isometric applications of force are already reached at a firing rate of approximately 50 Hz, whereas a maximum firing rate of up to approximately 120 Hz has been measured in explosive applications of force (Desmedt and Godaux, 1978). They do not actually improve the maximal value but rather the rate of force development (see Figure 5.6).

Another important consideration, that of pre-movement silence, was reported by Sale (1992): 'little or no motor unit activity is present just prior to

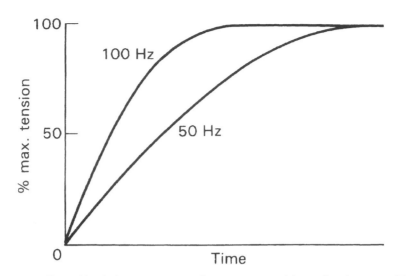

Figure 5.6: Effect of high-frequency stimulation on rate of force development (From Sale, 1992).

ballistic (brief, high velocity) actions . . . The brief silent period may bring all motoneurons into a non-refractory state, allowing them to be more readily recruited and brought to the possible maximum firing rate' (Sale, 1992, p.255). In practice the problems of velocity versus force as aspects of power are well known and have led to different training strategies. Sprinters use pull resistance and pull support regimes, shot putters, discus and javelin throwers execute the competition movement with lighter or heavier implements, tennis players train for serving with additional weights or with the racquet in the cover. The variety of the applied methods illustrate the existing uncertainty.

Specific structure and demands

Weight lifting

Weight lifting serves as the most typical example of sports in which very heavy weights have to be accelerated. The total mass to be accelerated consists of the mass of the barbells and the athlete's segment masses above the knee joint. For a successful lift, in the snatch the total mass has to be accelerated to approximately 1.8 m/s. This requires a recruitment of all muscle fibres. An exact observation of the start phase is helpful. In the starting position hip and knee joints are markedly flexed and the upper limbs extended. It is important that in this position the joints are fixed in such a way that the strength at the beginning of the stretch in the knee joint and later the hip joint is conveyed immediately to the barbell. This fixation of the joints at a very high isometric tension demands a strong activation of the flexor musculature. The explosive stretch must ensue from this very high isometric tension. In view of the low velocities involved, it is probable that all the muscle fibres including the slow-twitch ones contribute to a successful lift. Preparation of the weight lifter is certainly aimed at this recruitment. Internationally there are typically two different training systems. On the one hand there is the Bulgarian system whose entire year-round training is orientated towards handling the maximum weight. In five specific training exercises (snatch, power snatch, clean and jerk, power clean and jerk, front squat) the athletes use the respective maximum weight in every training session with single repetitions. There is no classical periodization. Weight lifters of other countries subdivide training into different periods. A 4–8 week period of preparation concentrates on enlarging the muscular CSA. The five to eight repetitions per set during this special period of preparation reduce to two repetitions per set during competition. In addition, training with submaximum weight (approximately 70%) occurs once a week, a session in which the velocity of movement should be maximized.

Shot put

There are clear differences between preparation for the shot put and weight lifting. First, the weight to be accelerated in the shot put is not maximal. Furthermore, the actual movement does not ensue from a stationary position, but follows a pre-acceleration pattern. Moreover, the final stretch in the elbow joint is prepared by a preceding stretch in the knee joint and in the hip joint. As a consequence a release speed of approximately 13 m/s can be attained. Application of force summates from the knee, to the hip and then to the upper limb. The extension at the knee joints and the acceleration of almost the entire body mass is predominantly a one-legged action which occurs without the benefit of vertical pre-acceleration. This puts very high demands on the maximum strength of the athlete. As the acceleration path is limited, application of very high strength in a short time is required. The extension and rotation of the hip follows shortly after the extension at the knee. At the end of the extension of the knee and hip, the velocity of the shot amounts to approximately 3.5 m/s. Therefore, pectoral and tricep muscles must accelerate a system that is already moving. A further acceleration of the shot is then only possible when the velocity of extension is greater than the velocity of the shot. Hence, the velocity of contraction plays a decisive role at this point. This is reflected in the training of the shot putter. Training of maximum strength of lower and upper limb musculature takes place mainly in the area of very high intensities and as explosively as possible. The classical exercises of weight lifting as well as use of the bench press exercise serve this purpose. However, emphasis must also be placed on velocity training. Puts with lighter shots should be part of training regimes. In other throwing events in track and field, special training and diagnostic equipment for discus and javelin throwing have been developed in training bases of the former German Democratic Republic, which enable direct control of velocity in the discipline-related movement process. Here too, training is often carried out using lighter implements. Its use is linked with the hope that the possible higher velocities in this process are then realizable with the competition implement. A phenomenon also emerges in throwing disciplines that has long been known in sprinting: despite clearly improved maximum and explosive strength, no higher movement velocities result. Stored and highly automated patterns of activation are probably resistant to changes in strength and power. They must first be destroyed and then rebuilt using the new muscular capability. These experiences from training practice confirm the assumption that aspects of velocity cannot be explained only through components of strength.

Tennis serve

The tennis serve is representative of the type of sports where the mass to be accelerated is very light. There are basically two variations in this type of sport; that is there is either permanent contact to the external weight (throw in American football, in handball, etc.), or a body segment (leg, arm) is accelerated to the maximum with, or without a racquet before the impulse is transmitted to a ball (e.g., soccer, baseball, tennis). The impulse produced with a given mass is therefore directly proportional to the segment's or racquet's velocity. Therefore, the maximization of velocity determines performance subject to a maintenance of precision.

The resulting velocity of the racquet head in the tennis serve is approximately 30 m/s. In combination with an optimal contact on the racquet this results in a post-impact speed of the ball of approximately 160 km/h. Shoulder, elbow, hand and racquet head reach their maximal velocity in a sequential order (see Figure 5.7).

About half of the resulting velocity arises in the last 100 ms before contact by the extension in the elbow (internal rotation of upper arm—not shown) and hand movement. The high velocities and light weights involved have for a long time been the reason for the opinion that special strength training in sport games is not necessary. Unlike javelin in athletics, for example, where the strength component of the sport was highlighted to the detriment of velocity training, the concept of power in sport games is generally completely neglected. The only exception for a long time was the use of minimal additional weights such as heavier balls in handball, heavier racquet in badminton or serving in tennis with the racquet in the cover. A small increase in weight is adequate on the one hand to alter and slow down the kinematic structure of a movement. But on the other hand it can hardly be

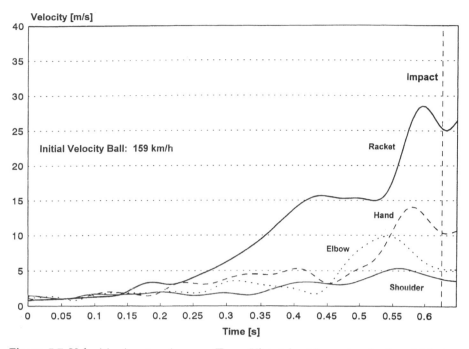

Figure 5.7: Velocities in a tennis serve (From Kleinöder, Neumaier, Loch and Mester, 1994).

enough to produce training effects in terms of power. The subjective feeling that the movement is subsequently easier with the regular sport implement is deceiving. In the most favourable case the former velocities are attained but higher levels are not achieved. If the components of power are to be improved then the previously mentioned methods for increasing explosive strength have priority. The velocity components must be trained in parallel to that without any additional weight. This frequently leads to a problem in training practice. As any form of experience including systematic strength training is lacking, it is not possible to begin directly by training with very high weights and explosive strength application. A phase of training with submaximal weights must precede the above, for the purpose of developing load tolerance over a period of some weeks. This requires the classical application of medium weights with smooth movement execution. As a result, however, the contraction velocities of the musculature could worsen for a short duration. This frequently leads to the cessation of strength train-ing and to the reputed confirmation of the prejudice that 'strength training makes you slow'. There are two possible solutions to the problem. Firstly, in the annual training plan it must be taken into account that the desired training effects are to be expected only after a period of many weeks. It makes no sense to start strength training shortly before the beginning of the competition period or shortly before particularly important matches. Secondly, there is no necessity to only move submaximal weights in a smooth tempo. Rapid executions of all repetitions are possible and appropriate here when the primary goal of strength training is not purely hypertrophy.

Boxing

Unlike the types of sport mentioned above, the goal in boxing, as in fencing, for instance, is not only a maximization of velocity, the primary goal is to minimize time. Thus starting power is decisively important. Figure 5.8 shows the force-time history of three world-class athletes.

The differences between the boxer, the weight lifter and the shot putter are evident. The boxer's curve shows the steepest incline in strength and reaches the maximal value very quickly, although this maximum is rather small. This reflects the specific boxing situation. On the one hand the demands on the maximal strength are so high that the boxer is compared with a weight lifter or a shot putter, a comparison that would not be made with a tennis player, for example. Conversely, the demands on the movement velocity are maximal, which is not required of a shot putter.

However, with respect to training method we see the main differences to the tennis player in the higher amounts of maximal strength training. An increase of maximal strength through explosive applications of force against very high and submaximal weights is supplemented by training of the movement velocity without additional weights.

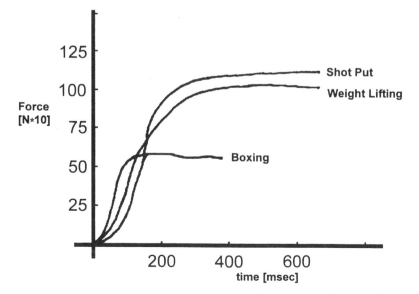

Figure 5.8: Force–time curve of elite athletes in different sports (From Bührle, 1985).

Jumping

Apart from those jumping movements further discussed under the stretch–shortening cycle section, there are two other groups of jumps which aim at a maximal acceleration of the body mass. In squat jumps the take-off follows from a deep body position. In the case of counter movement jumps a preparatory lowering of the centre of mass precedes the upward acceleration. The squat jump is similar to the movement found in ski jumps. During the descent in the ski-jump the ground reaction force rises to approximately twice the body weight. This necessitates an increased activation of the entire hip and leg musculature. The take-off begins with the departure from the curved section of the ramp. Depending on the ramp, about 0.2 seconds is available for the take-off. The take-off movement must be ended exactly upon reaching the edge of the ski-jump table. Performance in the squat jump can be improved basically by an increase of maximal strength. As an increase in maximal strength always implies a simultaneous improvement of relative strength it is not surprising that weight lifters, for instance, achieve outstanding results in the squat jump. However, as an increase of body mass involves considerable disadvantages for the ski-jumper in the flight phase, which far outweigh the possible advantages of a more powerful take-off, this method of training is not applied in ski jumping. An improvement of the take-off impulse must subsequently be achieved through other methods. On the one hand this is achieved by a steeper incline in the rate of force development, and on the other by a continuous force production until departure from the ramp. The first component can easily be achieved through an improvement of explosive strength by means of training against heavy weights. The second component comprises very technique-related training. Towards the end of take-off the velocity of the body is already quite high. An additional acceleration is hence only possible at high power applications. However, the musculature must produce this from an inconvenient length ratio as the joints are already relatively stretched and the musculature is correspondingly shortened. Hence the demands contradict the strength–velocity curve as well as the strength–length curve. Adaptation processes in this area can only be achieved when training takes exactly these conditions into account, as in the case of a take-off with and without additional weight.

The demands in counter movement jumps such as the block jump in volleyball are basically the same. The high initial tensions at the beginning of the stretching movement do not in fact result from an isometric contraction but from the breaking of the counter movement. The demands on the stretching phase are identical with a steep incline of the force ascent and maintenance of a high strength level until the end of stretching. Special training is required to simulate these conditions. It is not necessary, for instance, to carry out half squats with continuous velocity. The concentric phase can ensue significantly faster than the eccentric phase. It must be clearly emphasized that counter movement jumps are determined by the power capacity of the musculature and not by parameters of the stretch–shortening cycles. For this reason, forms of training like those used in strength training of jumpers (e.g. depth jumps) do not represent any specific form of training for counter movement jumps.

Summary

In sports with maximal applications of force in a short time power plays the decisive role. It can be assessed by the rate of force development and the movement velocity. Power is not an independent dimension of strength but it is determined to a high degree by maximal strength. It is, therefore, misleading to assume that a long-lasting improvement of power is possible without raising maximal strength. However, maximal strength is not a sufficient component to explain varying demands on power performance in sports. The importance of the velocity component which is not automatically improved by way of raising maximal strength increases with a decrease in the weight to be accelerated. It must be trained separately.

General training methods and planning of training

The training methods of a weight lifter, a ski jumper and a tennis player are so different that it is not possible to define common training rules. The differences refer to the general significance of strength training within the entire training regime and to the specific requirement with regard to power and to the periodization of training depending on the different periods of competition. Therefore, training methods have to be structured according to specific needs. One concept, however, fundamentally applies to all power training. Training with weight machines cannot serve as a substitute for training with free weights and there are several reasons for this. Firstly, training with machines does not generally lead to a strengthening of the whole body musculature involved in the movement. In the most unfavourable case (e.g. leg extension) training occurs only about a single joint. Thus the coordination of the stretching movement, which is a major aspect in all power exercises, is omitted. Secondly, the important consideration of stabilization of an active joint is missing. If the lower leg and the thigh are fixed, as in case of leg extension, stabilization of the knee is not necessary. In the real situation however, the latter is very important due to the fact that joint receptors provoke inhibitory impulses especially during quick movements. Thirdly, the dynamics of the movement are missing. As a rule high movement velocities cannot be reached by training with machines. For this reason alternatives for power training other than using the barbell or other free weights are limited. Furthermore, eccentric workouts will not be emphasized because they are of minor significance in training practice. They are undoubtably fundamentally appropriate, but as the help of a partner is necessary in practical application they are rarely taken into account. Under these circumstances the training contents can be systemized as follows.

Aim	Improvement of strength (recruitment)
Method	Maximal or near maximal workouts
Intensity load	90–100%
Repetitions	3–1
Sets	4–6
Rest interval	3–5 min
Typical leg exercises	squat, half squat

Commentary: The application of high loads leads to an improvement of strength without a significant increase of mass. It requires training exercises to be performed correctly. As a matter of course it is necessary to prescribe the range of intensity; however, it seems to vary around 95%, 97%, or 100%. The form of an athlete varies from day to day to such an extent that it is impossible to select the respective, corresponding weight. Athletes and coaches often underestimate the strain of this training method because of the relatively low sum of repetitions within one training unit. Nevertheless it represents an extreme strain for the central nervous system and therefore requires quite long periods of regeneration.

Aim	Improvement of explosive strength (rate of force development [RFD])
Method A	Maximal or near maximal workouts
Intensity load	90–100%
Repetitions	3–1
Sets	4–6
Rest interval	3–5 min
Typical exercises	power clean, snatch, power snatch
Method B	Submaximal workouts with maximal velocity
Intensity load	70%
Repetitions	5–1
Sets	2–4
Rest interval	3–5 min
Typical exercises	quarter squats, power cleans, hang cleans, power snatches, barbell squats

Commentary: The choice between methods is not an 'either–or decision'; each has its special functions that have to be used with appropriate emphasis according to the type of sport and the training period. In practice the evaluation of method A often causes misunderstandings which arise from mixing up the RFD with the externally visible velocity of the barbell. Despite the explosive RFD the barbell's velocity is slow as a consequence of the high weight. All exercises focus on explosive application of force. In order to reach this aim the above-mentioned exercises are even more appropriate than squats. Frequently, due to limited arm power, cleans and snatches are only beneficial if the initial RFD of the leg musculature is maximal and the barbell is accelerated to such an extent that a catch is possible. Thus the success of the execution of the movement enables us to draw direct conclusions on the RFD. This is more difficult with method B. The best success can be achieved with this method when the attained velocity can be measured. In cases of almost identical paths and straight-line accelerations of the barbell it is generally sufficient to measure the time of movement. In view of either the short acceleration distance or the highly specific movement process, quarter squats, hang cleans, and barbell jumps aim at the RFD towards the end of the stretch process.

Aim	Improvement of movement speed
Method	Unloaded or facilitated specific workouts
Repetitions	5–10
Sets	3–5
Rest interval	3–10 min
Typical exercises	sport specific

Commentary: According to our analysis of sports there is need to improve the movement speed independent of the RFD. Training exercises need to aim at adaptations of the neural system. This requires unloaded or even facilitated conditions. Shot putters use lower shot weights, sprinters run downhill, ski jumpers do a lot of jumps with their own body weight and so on. The relevance of low additional loads during the execution of the complex movement was discussed before and found to be of no advantage. Also in these exercises the effect of training is increased, if some kind of monitoring is used. Measuring of distances, times or velocities puts some pressure on the athletes to maximize their efforts.

In training practice the question still remains whether the different methods should be used in the sense of block training or combined training. In block training for a defined period (2–4 weeks) the focus is on one specific aspect, which is then replaced by the next. This model more closely follows the classical periodization scheme. In the complex training regime two different methods are considered within a single training unit. For example, puts with lighter weights are carried out after a short strength training session within the same training unit. Although there are many individual differences which depend on the specific type of sport, one trend can be stated in the following way to simplify matters: block training dominates in junior training and in the training of novice athletes, whereas complex training is more appropriate for elite sportspeople.

Power training with junior athletes

A variety of different goals specific to the sport must be included within the training units. For obvious reasons the thought arises that if 'real strength training' is not possible, the use of some additional weights should at least be taken into account. However, this is even less effective for children than in elite sports. This process provokes an early development of slow time programmes, which despite the later improvement of the power level, are able to resist changes because of their stability. Systematic general training already causes an improvement of power before puberty, but this fact is mainly the result of coordinative adaptations.

However, the training of the strength components with high loads puts a great deal of strain on the athletes. Minimal prerequisites for this kind of training are a marked strength of the trunk musculature and a very good technique for exercising with barbells. Both these prerequisites are absolutely necessary for training regimes with heavy weights. They can be trained very early and can be improved by a preceding hypertrophy training regime starting at an age of 13/14 years. Real power training should not begin before the end of puberty. The danger of damage, particularly with regard to the passive movement apparatus, is too high because of the heavy weights. In addition to this it is questionable whether the subdivision into strength and power training is of any significance at the beginning of the training process. The first adaptation subsequent to strength training with medium weights does not ensue as a result of the expected hypertrophy, but rather due to an improvement of the nervous regulation with regard to recruitment, firing rate and interaction of agonist and antagonist muscle groups. Thus in the beginning there is always an improvement of power irrespective of the load intensity.

SPORTS WITH APPLICATIONS OF FORCE IN THE STRETCH–SHORTENING CYCLE

Classification

In many sports the applications of force are characterized by a concentric phase which is preceded by a rapid eccentric contraction or by a very rapid sequence of eccentric–concentric combinations. As the eccentric phase is characterized by a stretching of the muscles and the concentric involves a shortening of the muscles, movements of this kind are described as a 'stretch–shortening cycle' (SSC).

The support phase in sprinting is a typical example. Imagine the objectives of minimization of support time, minimization of landing decelerating and maximization of the horizontal accelerating impulses. Therefore, the foot plant with the forefoot occurs with an ankle joint as rigid as possible and the lower limb should be almost fully extended. Support time can only be reduced if the musculature of the lower limb is activated before ground contact. Due to the high impact force the contracted musculature is stretched against its resistance. In the early support phase minimal flexion occurs in the ankle and knee joints, before the concentric push-off phase occurs in the latter support period. The entire support phase lasts less than 100 ms.

Conditions for all jumps that have a preceding starting movement are quite similar. Starting movements can be categorized by a maximum run-up velocity as in all jumping events in athletics, a short run-up for jumps in sport games, or a starting movement such as a flic-flac in preparation for the flight phase in gymnastics. The basic mechanics employed are identical. Kinetic energy is developed which is first amortized in the touch-down phase before the actual take-off occurs. The support times are always less than 200 ms. They vary between approximately 120 ms in gymnastics and in long and triple jumps, approximately 140 ms in the high jump, and 180 ms in a jump to dunk the ball in basketball.

Another example that would not appear typical at first sight is the phase of swing initialization and control in alpine ski racing. Due to the relatively long duration of a swing in slalom or giant slalom no SSCs might be expected. A more detailed analysis shows that a swing in slalom or giant slalom does not consist of a single edging action and turn of the skis, but rather an extremely rapid sequence of several regulating eccentric–concentric cycles. It is their function to regulate the swing with the aim of minimizing sliding.

General structure

The common structure of the aforementioned examples except for skiing therefore follows a general pattern. The stretch–shortening cycle of the activated musculature follows a general body movement in a very short time with the objective of maximizing the acceleration impulse. In this process the concentric acceleration phase can last less than 100 ms. Minimizing time and maximizing impulse are two requirements which are essentially contradictory. As an impulse is defined as the product of force and time, the reduction of time requires greater force to reach the same impulse. Therefore, it is extremely important to consider both factors for detailed analysis in each different sport.

In view of the special starting conditions and the extremely short periods of time the classical parameters for the description of strength and power are not adequate to explain the processes during an SSC. It is, therefore, legitimate to introduce a new dimension of strength; so-called reactive strength. Reactive strength describes the ability of the neuromuscular system to produce high concentric forces after a preceding rapid eccentric phase within a very short time span. The characteristics of reactive strength are related to two major aspects; the use of reflex-induced activities and the storage and recoil of energy. Both are connected with the rapid combination of eccentric and concentric contraction. They can be explained on the basis of the classical example of the depth jump. Here the starting energy results from the initial elevated position of the body. At the moment of touch-down a stretching of the leg extensor muscles and the related muscle spindles occur. This stretching leads to reflex activities in the musculature involved (see Figure 5.9).

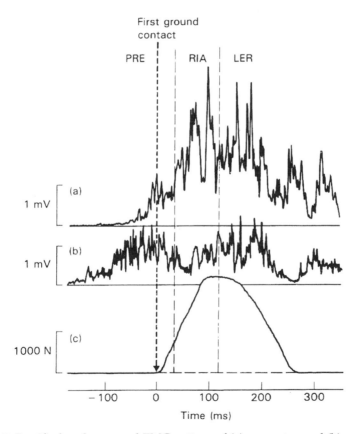

Figure 5.9: Rectified and averaged EMG pattern of (a) m. vastus and (b) m. gastrocnemius, and (c) vertical ground reaction forces from drop jumps. PRE, preinnervation phase; RIA, reflex-induced area; LER, late EMG response (from Schmidtbleicher, 1992).

Under favourable conditions the additional reflex activation is switched on to the maximum level of voluntary activation. Favourable conditions refer to three important aspects influencing the shaping of these reflex activities. First, there must be a high pre-activation of the extensor muscles before ground contact (Dietz et al., 1981; Komi, 1990). An effective release of the reflexes is only possible when a muscle is activated. Second, inhibitory mechanisms that can be observed in non-elite athletes must be reduced (Schmidtbleicher, Dietz, Noth and Antoni, 1978). Finally, a third important condition for the use of the reflex activities is the rapid initial stretch of the musculature. The velocity of the stretch, particularly at the beginning of the eccentric phase of touch-down, is considerably more important than the degree of the stretch (Schmidtbleicher, 1991).

In addition to reflex activity the second important aspect of reactive strength is the storage of energy in the parallel and series elastic components (e.g. Komi and Bosco, 1978). Muscles and especially tendons are capable of storing energy for a short time and partially putting it to use in the subsequent concentric phase. In this process the storage capacity of the tendons is approximately ten times larger than that of muscles (Alexander and Benet-Clarke, 1977). However, storage is only possible when two conditions are met. Stretching should not be too great and the combination of eccentric followed by concentric contractions must ensue in a very short time. Under these premises additional power is available in the push-off phase.

This addresses the problem of stiffness regulation (for further details see Carew and Ghez, 1985). The adjustment of stiffness is the field in which the athlete can voluntarily modulate the sequence of movement. Stiffness is determined as the quotient of change of tension to enforced change of muscle length and represents the actual control value of the organism. Two components can be regulated; first, the so-called set point, defined as the first point at which the musculo-tendonous system reacts with an increase in tension when the length increases. In a relaxed muscle the set point is extremely late, that is a change in length is not mirrored by a change in tension. Second, the rate of tension increase may be varied. The higher the quotient, that is the steeper the curve, the more tension will be developed against the enforced change in length. Stiffness adjustment is realized according to an optimum trend with respect to performance capacity of the nerve–muscle interface and the musculature. It ranges from very soft to very firm. In top athletes the optimum tends to a very firm adjustment. In general no effective storage of energy will be possible when stiffness adjustment is too soft. In this case, muscles and tendons will not store energy, as few cross-bridges are linked in the muscles, and the tendons are not tensed. Additionally, the necessary pre-activation of the musculature is missing and reflex potentials remain extensively inactive.

A firm stiffness adjustment has the following consequences. If the cross-bridges formed by the actin–myosin complex remain linked during impact a minimum change of muscle length occurs (i.e. minimal joint motion). The consequence for the concentric push-off is that a minimum acceleration path is available. The storage and the release of energy are then important factors influencing athletic performance. There is some evidence that this happens in take-offs with minimum support times. If support times are around 120 ms, as in gymnastics or in long jump, the contribution of an active voluntary contraction cannot achieve the desired result. The elastic and the spring qualities of tendons and muscles must be used. This however, requires a firm stiffness adjustment. In some cases, especially in beginners, too firm a stiffness adjustment leads to a breakdown of the biological system. The high impact forces cause the cross-bridges to tear. In spite of a significant change of length the related change of tension is very weak and more importantly, delayed. A reflex potentiation is also no longer possible.

The significance of reflex-induced activities and of elastic energy storage is so great that the significance of maximum strength decreases with an increasing degree of performance level. The provision of a high degree of maximum strength is, of course, an indispensable premise at the beginning of a training process that lasts several years because it is evident that only the existing contractile components can be used by way of reflex activation and energy storage. Furthermore, the possibility of stabilizing the joints is of tremendous importance, especially in very rapid movements. However, with increasing performance levels, the reactive strength becomes less dependent on maximum strength. Differences between athletes in reactive strength can then no longer be explained by differences in maximum strength. Therefore strength, while always important in sports with SSC, does not have to be at maximum levels. Simply, it is indeed important, for example, that a triple jumper is able to execute half squats with very high loads. But it is unimportant whether this occurs with 180 kg or 200 kg. This does not lead to an improvement of the reactive strength. This has been confirmed in a number of investigations, such as with national level high jumpers (see below).

Differences in reactive strength can be verified by reviewing force–time histories after depth jumps. This enables the determination of support and flight times as well as providing an analysis of the impulse form. Athletes with good reactive strength skills generally show a tendency towards greater flight times which have emanated from decreased support times (Ritzdorf, 1987) (Figure 5.10).

Substantial information can be gained from the force–time curve shape, where athletes with well-trained reactive strength when completing medium depth jump heights show an impulse curve that corresponds closely to a triangle. When there is a deviation from the triangular shape at modest heights, reactive strength is not sufficiently developed. Figure 5.11 shows the impulse forms of two female high jumpers after depth jumps from 30 cm. Table 5.1 also shows some corresponding kinematic indicator values.

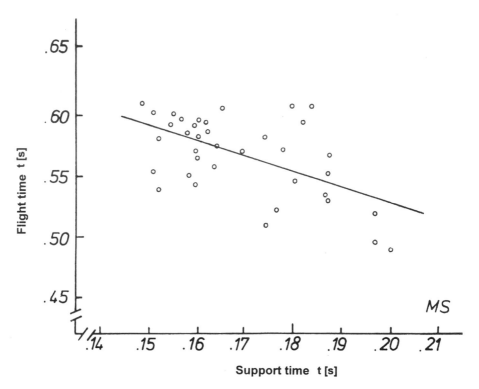

Figure 5.10: Support and flight times of a top female high jumper.

Table 5.1: Descriptive kinematic values for jumpers A and B

	A	B
Support time (ms)	163	202
Minimal knee angle (°)	159	148

Angular velocities
Ankle joint angular velocity
    eccentric (rad/s)
    concentric (rad/s)
	
	10.1
	13.4
		
		7.0
		12.5

Knee joint angular velocity
    eccentric (rad/s)
    concentric (rad/s)
	
	6.1
	12.2
		
		10.6
		12.8

Hip joint angular velocity
    eccentric (rad/s)
    concentric (rad/s)
	
	2.5
	7.6
		
		6.1
		6.3

Height of flight (cm)	48.1	41.0

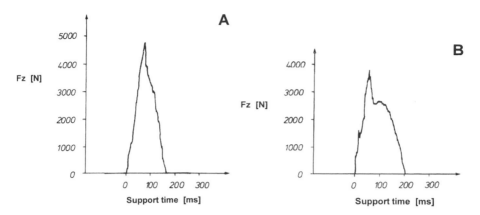

Figure 5.11: Force–time curves of two top female high jumpers after a depth jump from 30 cm.

Athlete A demonstrated a shorter support time with the classic triangle form impulse curve than athlete B, who did not manage a bouncing take-off. Angular velocities show that athlete A recorded a higher value during the eccentric phase in the ankle joint than B. By contrast, athlete B, who could not amortize the impact in the ankle joint using the calf musculature, recorded higher eccentric angular velocities as measured at the knee joint compared to A. The greater flexion in the knee joint for B not only leads to a lengthened take-off time, but also to a less effective take-off. As maximum power of the two athletes was also recorded, it could be stated that the differences found in jumping abilities could not be explained by differences in strength. In training practice there are also a number of tests that record reactive strength as horizontal or vertical take-off power. In the horizontal plane the alternate leg bound (five jumps) with an approach run is often used with the aim of reaching a maximum distance. In this case it is not necessary to limit the length of the approach run. Based on training experience, the difference to the alternate leg bound from a standing position is more interesting than the absolute distance itself. When the difference of the two test values is greater than 4 m for women and 4.5 m for men, this demonstrates a good reactive strength. In the vertical direction the reach-and-jump test after a depth jump is a suitable test procedure. It is remarkable that only elite jumpers attain better results in this case than in a counter movement jump. This also indicates that reactive strength is an independent aspect of power.

General adaptations

As a result of there being no completely general reactive strength capacity there are also no general adaptations and forms of training. Therefore, we must classify adaptations and methods of training. In this case a definition of the objective is helpful.

The aim of the adaptation process ensues from the requirement structure. Three distinct aims can be differentiated; impulse maximization without time minimization, impulse maximization with time minimization, and velocity and precision of the regulation process.

In the case of *impulse maximization without time minimization* the focus is based upon an optimum maximum strength level, the use of reflex activities and the utilization of stored elastic energy. As mentioned above, the reflex activities depend on the pre-tension of the musculature. This pre-tension shows a typical characteristic in the case of less trained athletes in that it relaxes shortly before ground contract, which means that the biological system is more softly adjusted. This is important for the untrained, especially as a protection mechanism of the tendons against overstress reactions. A reflex switch to voluntary activities is inevitably insufficient. An important consideration in training, therefore, consists of switching off these inhibitory impulses. In terms of a training method a step-by-step approach to continually higher impact forces can be adopted that finally approaches competition levels. It must be mentioned here that these forms of training are connected with high levels of strain on the body. Impulse maximization remains the goal. Forms of training are subsequently judged on whether impulse remains at least the same within the tolerable time span. This can be approximately estimated from the jump distance or height. Therefore, such reactive forms of training which show the attained distance (e.g. alternate leg-bound) or height (e.g. the height of the obstacles to be overcome in vertical jumps) are suitable in the training process as a measurable criterion. There is negligible conclusive evidence about training adaptations of the muscle–tendon system with respect to their storage capacity. However, there is some evidence that the elasticity and the stretchability of the tendons can be an important criterion. The better the tendon can accept changes in length, the smaller the danger of the muscle stretching beyond the area of short-range elastic stiffness and a subsequent tearing of the cross-bridges. This is the reason why the stretchability of the tendons is regarded not only as an important measure for preventing injuries, but at the same time as a means of contributing to increased performance. As adaptation of bradytrophic tissue, such as in tendons, ensues slower than adaptation of the muscle, special stretching must be a daily part of training. In this connection there is a widely held erroneous assumption that tendon forces also increase with increasing intensity (e.g. running velocity). Komi (1992, p.172) for example was able to demonstrate that the Achilles tendon force at approximately maximum running velocity (9.92 m/s) is less than at medium velocity (5.78 m/s). It is also a false assumption that this tendon force is less on softer grounds than on hard surfaces.

The adaptation processes sought are considerably more complicated when an *impulse maximization with time minimization* is necessary. In terms of a purely physical perspective these are two contradictory conditions. If the same impulse is to be achieved in a shorter time then the force must be higher. Another component complicates the matter further. Considered from a kinematic perspective and with the assumption of an already existing maximum shortening velocity, the shortening of the support phase is only possible when the maximum flexion of the joint in the amortization phase is reduced. However, a consequence of this is a decreased available acceleration path. Nevertheless, the force must be higher in the concentric phase. Despite this obvious discrepancy, experienced jumpers and sprinters show precisely this tendency. As mentioned before, the flight time achieved increases with decreasing support times after depth jumps. Of course this only applies within the measurable range of support times. One reason possibly lies in the fact that shorter support times require a harder stiffness adjustment and higher pre-activation. This then raises reflex activity and increases the energy uptake of series elastic components.

However, there is much to be said for the fact that, besides the force component, central nervous factors also play a dominating role. According to investigations by Voss (1991) human beings possess highly automated, stored time programmes that are very constant regardless of changing strength capacities. A similar observation in sprinting is known as a 'motor stereotype'. Experiences and measurements in training with top athletes confirm this. The female high jumper previously discussed (Figure 5.11B) showed slow time programmes irrespective of the movement form and the external force recorded in the process. Even in the case of simple hopping on the spot with minimal impact forces, support times were clearly prolonged and were generally above 180 ms. They hardly changed in the case of greater depth jump heights. Therefore, if the sport demands shorter time programmes all attempts to achieve these through modification of strength components fail. The nervous system must learn to react in the field of shorter time programmes. Scientific investigations in the area of training, together with practical experience, confirm the fact that this concerns a central nervous and not a conditional learning effect. Thus, we have been able to prove the following: When an athlete manages to get into short time programmes by means of external pull support (elastic bands) and manages to stabilize this, these short time programmes are subsequently found when the pull support is removed. Voss and Krause (1991) managed to achieve a similar result with electric stimulation, provoking a forced release of a corresponding movement programme. Although in the end it remains unclear what 'learning of the central nervous system' means, these findings, which have been repeatedly confirmed, have important consequences in training practice. Impulse maximization is no longer the only focus of training methods, but time minimization is of at least equal value. This leads either to other training exercises than the above-mentioned examples or to further modification of training principles. Alternate leg bounds cannot only be carried out with the objective of maximizing distance, but also with the objective of minimizing time (e.g. 30 m alternate leg bound with a maximum of ten jumps and with the objective of shortening the total time). The same applies to vertical jumps. Rating criterion is then the time required for a series of five hurdle jumps, for example, and not the hurdle height. Furthermore, there is a multitude of reactive training forms which include high movement frequencies. The varied adaptation processes in impulse

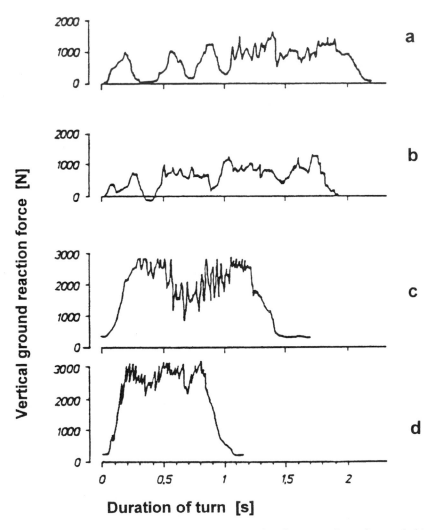

Figure 5.12: Ground reaction forces in a skiing turn (a = beginner; b = advanced skier; c = female world cup skier; d = male world cup skier).

maximization versus time minimization require the setting of an exact definition of objectives before certain training forms are applied.

There is one other category differing greatly from these two classes of SSCs. In the case of swing control in ski racing, in wind surfing, and in surfing on waves, the objective is to keep the skis, the sail, or the surf board in a definite position. Due to unevenness of the ground, changing wind or varying water conditions, fast changes of resistance are expressed with the consequence of very rapid SSCs of the highly activated musculature. These SSCs must then be re-regulated. Thus, no kind of impulse maximization is required here, but rather control is required for the *velocity and precision of the regulation processes*. Beginners only manage this with considerable time delays and with enormous activation–deactivation processes. Well-trained athletes can make high-frequency regulatory changes while maintaining a high degree of muscle activation.

Another condition that must be considered apart from the repeated impacts that requires special adaptation mechanisms is the rapid stretchings which occur almost randomly so that the athlete continually reacts instead of acting in a pre-set manner. In view of the extremely short time, however, these reactions cannot be consciously programmed. It seems to be a rather highly automated, very rapidly proceeding correction. The objective of these corrections is not the maximization of the shortening proportion of the SSC, but rather its optimization. In the approach used until now this means adjusting stiffness to as soft a level as possible during the maximum isometric contraction in order to use the absorbing capacities of parallel and series elastic components as much as possible. Furthermore, the intermuscular coordination of agonistic and antagonistic muscles plays an even more important role than in the aforementioned examples.

Specific structure and demands

Running

As a special chapter in this volume is devoted to running and sprinting this topic will be explained only very briefly. While in sprinting performance maximum strength is vital to the attainment of high levels of positive acceleration, reactive strength predominates in the phase where maximum velocity is recorded. During very short support times of less than 100 ms it is necessary to maximize the horizontal acceleration of the entire body, while at the same time vertical accelerations of the body should be minimized. In terms of movement technique, this means shortening the deceleration phases. The negative influence of footstrike is increased if a runner overstrides and where a large velocity difference occurs between the centre of mass (CM) of the foot and the body. The negative effect of these two factors can be reduced by accelerating the foot in a downwards–backwards motion before ground contact and by landing relatively close to the vertical projection of the CM of the body. This requires a fast, but non-reactive contraction of gluteal and the hamstring muscles. The foot plant occurs on the forefoot and the heel does not make ground contact. This technique emphasises the reactive strength of the calf musculature. When the two aforementioned conditions with respect to the vertical and horizontal deceleration components are met, then the eccentric phase within the SSC is very short and the induced peak forces are rather smaller than recorded for jumps. However, in view of the very minimal support times, it is doubtful whether reflex-induced activity peaks can be effective at all as the time of mono-synaptic reflexes are approximately 40 ms and a delayed mechanical effectiveness also accounts for 40 ms. Therefore, it appears to be more important to use the elastic capacities of the tendomuscular system. This assumes a maximum stiffness of the musculature of the lower leg and a high fixation of the ankle joint. In sprinting, therefore, the reactive strength component is limited to the muscles of the lower leg. The m. quadriceps femoris is not involved in this quick stretching, as the relatively low vertical impact force has to be amortized by the musculature of the lower leg. Otherwise the support phases would be too long. For this reason the reactive forms of training must also concentrate on these muscle groups. As classical forms of reactive strength training (alternate leg bounds, one-leg bounds, hurdle jumps) are related to relatively longer support phases, which hinder the training of very rapid time programmes. Simple bouncings would be a better training exercise as would sprinting and jumping movements with pull support.

Jumping

A basic distinction has already been made between squat jumps, counter movement jumps and drop jumps. From the point of view of reactive strength, however, this is not the most important distinction. All previous considerations have repeatedly shown that reactive strength has a highly specific structure. If this thought pattern is continued, it is possible to distinguish between the different kinds of drop jumps. With regard to practical training there are important differences in the nature of take-offs (one-legged, two-legged), take-off directions (horizontal–vertical) and surfaces (solid–elastic).

A typical example of one-legged horizontal jumps from a rigid surface is the long jump. The requirements of the long jump can be clearly defined as impulse maximization and time minimization. The necessity of minimizing time is based on the following consideration; the flight distance of the body's CM results from the take-off velocity and the take-off angle. This velocity has a horizontal component which is the result of the run-up and a vertical component produced during take-off. The significance of this vertical component fundamentally distinguishes the long jump from the sprint. The run-up velocity is the most important performance-limiting factor. High run-up velocities, however, are only relevant if the loss of horizontal velocity at take-off is low. This automatically leads to short take-off times with low amortization in the ankle, knee and hip joints. On the basis of this high horizontal velocity, the vertical take-off impulse must then be maximized. As the two goals of impulse maximization on the one hand and time minimization on the other hand ultimately contradict each other, the relationship between run-up velocity and take-off must be optimized in training. Strength-oriented jumpers tend to attach too much importance to take-off angle instead of run-up velocity. Velocity-oriented jumpers run the risk of 'overrunning' take-off, where take-off time is not long enough to be able to generate sufficient vertical impulse. This in turn results in an inadequate take-off angle. These points should be taken into consideration when training reactive strength. As soon as training of general reactive skills is no longer necessary (such as the reduction of inhibitory impulses prior to touch down), highly specific jumping forms must be chosen. The minimum training requirement is one-legged and horizontal take-offs. In top athletes two-legged, vertical depth jumps help to improve long jump take-offs as much or as little as squats with the barbell. When the level of performance improves the jumps must be carried out with increasingly high horizontal velocities. Depending on the type of jumper the focus then lies on impulse maximization or time minimization. The differences have already been described within the context of alternate leg bounds. Extreme stress is presented in jumps with take-off levels that are lower than run-up levels. For training purposes such conditions can be reproduced by creating a 10 cm high ramp for the last three to five run-up strides with take-off occurring from the ground. The reverse is problematic. Higher take-off positions change the kinematics and dynamics of a take-off so significantly that they hinder the development of the reactive strength which is so necessary for the long jump. The same applies to the bad habit of performing take-offs after short run-ups. This completely changes take-off characteristics and does not significantly contribute to improve take-off after a full approach.

The characteristics in training methods for the long jump can therefore be systematically classified as follows. All two-legged jumps, vertical jumps and horizontal jumps from a standing position require specific preparation. Specifically increases are required in the case of one-legged horizontal jumps with a low run-up velocity and one-legged horizontal hops with landings on the take-off leg. All one-legged horizontal jumps performed with a high run-up velocity and landing on the free leg have the greatest need for specific preparation.

The high jump is a typical example of a one-legged vertical jump from solid surfaces. The aim here can be clearly defined as impulse maximization as time minimization is not essential, although it can be observed as a trend in top jumpers. The height during flight of the CM depends solely on the vertical take-off velocity. This in turn, depends on the vertical impulse and the mass of the jumper. The total vertical impulse is derived from two factors. One part is needed for deceleration at touch down, the remaining part determines the vertical take-off velocity. In order to use as few parts as possible for deceleration athletes try to minimize the vertical touch-down velocity.

The horizontal component of the take-off velocity determines the take-off angle but not the height of flight. Normal take-off angles of 45–55° in the high jump mean that the vertical component of take-off velocity is identical to (45°) or slightly greater (>45°) than the horizontal velocity. Take-off in the high jump is therefore distinctive in that the run-up velocity is decelerated dramatically during take-off. Why then do high-jumpers have such a fast approach? The reason for the high run-up velocities must be based on the fact that athletes succeed in using parts of their run-up energy during take-off in order to optimize the vertical velocity component. This makes two aspects particularly significant for reactive strength training; the storage capacity of the muscles and tendons, and the radical change in movement direction. Unlike earlier high jump techniques where deceleration occurred mechanically with a foot plant using the heel, this deceleration is achieved by muscles in the case of the flop technique.

Compared to the long jump, the eccentric phase therefore becomes more important. A rigidly adjusted total system absorbs the run-up energy. The strong pronation in the take-off foot, which is a result of the curved run-up, promotes the storage of energy. The medio-lateral movement in the ankle joint increases the tension in the muscle–tendon system. If the stored energy is to be used then the body must be in a suitable position. A very fast, active hyperextension of the hips and subsequent fixation guarantee that the body moves from a backward lean into an upright position. Improving elastic and spring capacities is one central aspect concerning the reactive strength training of high jumpers. Two-legged and one-legged depth jumps from low heights (approximately 30 cm) with a purely bouncing take-off fulfil this requirement. The knee-bend is minimal, the jumps occur 'like springs' merely from the ankle joint. The training is supplemented by one-legged vertical jumps, for example, over hurdles. Landings normally occur on the take-off leg. The greater the distance between the hurdles, the greater is the horizontal velocity.

The last important group comprises two-legged take-offs from elastic surfaces such as in diving from a 3 metre board, trampoline jumps or in gymnastics. As an example, take-offs for vaults in gymnastics are very different to take-offs from rigid surfaces. It is nearly impossible to distinguish between the eccentric and concentric phase of the take-off. In chronological order, athletes try to generate maximum initial energy, to stiffen the biological system and then to use the elastic properties of the board. Unlike in the high jump, the touch-down velocity should be as high as possible. The literature would suggest high run-up velocities of 9 m/s.

When jumping in springboard diving the lower extremities are accelerated against the board to the maximum capacity. At touch down on the board the knees are almost fully extended. In the first phase of touch down a slight knee bend of less than 10° occurs. The system is stiffened to a maximum capacity and in this state, awaits the return of the generated energy. Extension occurs in the final phase of take-off when the system has made use of the flexible capacity of the base. This is where the requirement structure fundamentally differs from other take-offs. Here, the maximum stiffness adjustment, the maximum energy input and the chronological coordination of the final extension have priority. Special training exercises are necessary because the contribution of active extension is significantly reduced. Depth jumps can be performed from relatively high positions with the aim of touching down with maximum stiffness as a method of improving the stiffness adjustment. The athletes climb onto a high box, bend their knees slightly and fall and land as rigidly as possible in this position. The actual take-off does not occur. In other words, only the eccentric phase is trained. As for all the other take-off exercises, it is useful to practise this on the surface where performance will occur. An improvement in the coordinative part with the correct sequence of body segment movements is only successful if the same ground conditions available in competitions are also used in training.

Skiing

Skiing presents other fundamental demands on reactive strength than was the case in previously mentioned examples. It is not a matter of impulse maximization, but rather a high frequency regulatory maintenance of a defined position of the skis. In the downhill race and also in the slalom or giant slalom, this position is constantly threatened by external forces as a consequence of surface unevenness. During a slalom turn, up to ten of these disturbances occur, each of which corresponds to one SSC. However, the demand is inverse. The reflex-induced activation and possible storage of energy should not be used. On the contrary, their influence should be minimized. As already mentioned this cannot ensue by means of deliberate, conscious correction programmes. Based on our present knowledge three factors are of major importance. First, despite the high isometric requirements in strength, stiffness must be adjusted rather softly. In complete contrast to the conditions described for gymnastics, the absorbing characteristics of the muscle–tendon system must be used. Secondly, the intermuscular coordination has to be at the highest level. Over-regulated reactions are avoidable only through the high-frequency interaction of agonist and antagonist muscles. Thirdly, many variable and automatic central correction programmes have to be available. These abilities cannot be improved as a high level through classical reactive strength training. The real situation is very difficult to simulate with respect to training methodology. Reactive strength training on various surfaces (different floor coverings) and on hard uneven surfaces (forest paths, uneven grass surfaces) are feasible possibilities. The starting position should be similar to competition, that is with firm knee bending, and take-off should not cause a complete knee extension. Furthermore, the starting condition can be reversed; that is, the weight moves instead of the athlete. For example, in a supine position with bent knees, a falling weight (e.g. the partner) can be caught with the slightest possible amount of movement without subsequently pushing back.

General training methods and planning of training

It is essential to realize that reactive strength is the capacity that is the most difficult to change through training. It is fundamentally less trainable than strength and power. The first consideration must therefore be on the relevance of reactive strength to the particular sport. The answer is simple in the previously mentioned examples. Reactive strength is such an important performance-limiting factor that as a matter of fact it has high priority in training. The situation is different, however, in sport games. A discussion on its relevance is currently in progress in volleyball, caused by the increasing frequency of one and two-legged jumps from the backcourt. Classically the take-off in volleyball corresponds to a counter movement jump with a marked lowering of the CM and a relatively long take-off time (approximately 300 ms). In the last few years quick reactive take-offs have taken place parallel to this. As both variations are successful there is no urgent necessity for reactive take-offs. Under these conditions it is unnecessary to urge strength-orientated players to a long-lasting, time-intensive reactive strength training in order to change their take-off characteristics.

On the other hand, in sports in which the highest performance cannot be reached without a high level of reactive strength, then this must be a permanent part of training. This contradicts the classical periodization models in which reactive strength training exists almost exclusively in special periods of preparation and in competition. This does not make any sense in the preparation of elite athletes. If reactive strength is a relatively autonomous dimension of strength and is of decisive importance for competitive performance, then it must be trained all year. An isolated eight weeks of maximum strength training at the beginning of the preparation period, before the new level of strength is to be 'utilized' by reactive training methods, is not suitable for top athletes. The fact that intensity increases towards the competition period is trivial. The strain on the movement apparatus and the central nervous system during reactive strength training is so high that maximum loads are not realizable all year. A correct understanding of the term 'intensity' is important in this context. High intensity does not only mean 'as far as possible' or 'as high as possible'. 'As fast as possible' can also lead to the highest intensity.

The planning of all-year training is accompanied by decisions concerning block training versus complex training. Experience would dictate that combined training should be preferred. This means that in one training session not only one skill (e.g. maximum strength) is trained in isolation, but several capacities are combined (e.g. strength and reactive strength). In a practical experiment with top female high jumpers the question of which training contents might be best combined and which training contents are disadvantageous for subsequent reactive strength training in the afternoon session was investigated. Apart from a number of individual characteristics two uniform trends were seen. A muscle hypertrophia-stressed maximum strength training and training of speed endurance always lead to a short-term worsening of reactive strength. However, there were good combination possibilities with high intensive maximum strength training and speed training. Both coincide within a training section before reactive strength training. Based on observation, the significance of training volume (number of repetitions) was overestimated in practice. Recommendations of 250–300 reactive jumps per training session are completely unrealistic if the quality of the execution of the movement is not to suffer. Based on experiences the directional values given in Table 5.2 are useful.

Table 5.2: Types of reactive jumps and proposed number of maximum repetitions

Type of jump	Max. number of sets	Max. repetitions per set	Total number per session
Bouncing	10	12	120
Alternate leg bound horizontal	10	10	100
Single-leg hop horizontal	8	10	80
Two-legged vertical	8	2×5	80
Single-leg vertical	8	2×5	80
Drop jumps	8	5	40

Bouncing may be combined with the exercise of one other group.
In summary:

(1) As reactive strength is highly specific, reactive strength training must also be specific.
(2) Maximization of impulse and minimization of support time are different aims. They require different training methods.
(3) The surface chosen for training should be identical to the surface in competition. Attempts to use softer surfaces in training in order to minimize high impact forces at landing are misleading.
(4) If the focus is on the muscles of the lower leg there is no need to use maximum distances or heights in the exercises.

(5) Different forms of reactive strength training are an integral part of training throughout the year. They can be combined with high intensity strength training and speed training.

(6) The number of repetition sums is often overestimated in practice. Always remember that maximum effort and concentration is required in all take-offs.

Reactive strength training with junior athletes

Reactive strength training is inevitably associated with high mechanical strains of associated body segments. The landing phase is strain intensive with peak forces of up to ten times body weight absorbed by the body. These forces can lead to injuries when bone ossification is not complete, when too many repetitions are performed, and when muscular stabilization of the joints is insufficient. The early application of highly intensive forms of training has in the past often led to an early end to the careers of highly talented jumpers. This emphasizes the necessity of a long-term, systematic training structure in the jumping disciplines. A few athletes in the high-force discipline of the triple jump have proved that with appropriate physical capacities and a systematic training regime long-term careers are possible. Saneyev, Markov and Banks are triple jumpers who dominated this discipline over many years.

However, these considerations do not mean that children and youths should not go through any form of jumping. Jumping is an elementary form of movement which has place in training at all age levels. What is decisive is the choice and sequence of jumping exercises. For children between the ages of 10 and 14 years the focus should be on jumps which contain a variety of movement experience and rhythm training. These include alternating jumps, light hops, two-legged bouncing on the ground, varied rhythms in a jumping series, jumping relays, on-box jumps and so on. It is important that attention is not put on height or distance maximization in the training exercises. They not only negatively affect the passive biological structures, but also contain one other important disadvantage. There is every reason to believe that important movement programmes are learned and stabilized at this age before puberty and this applies to the repeatedly mentioned time programmes. When children execute too many training jumps with the goal of impulse maximization, the lack of muscle mass and maximum strength will result in the training of slower time programmes which are ultimately highly resistant to change. The same applies to the use of soft and absorbing surfaces. It can frequently be observed that children use training exercises similar to those used by adults but execute them on soft, absorbing surfaces (e.g., soft gymnastic mats). As a result the mechanical peak forces are indeed reduced. Nevertheless, this procedure promotes the training of a slower movement programme with slow, strength-stressed take-offs. As a result the reactive strength is not trained at all. Consequently, at this age velocity is in the foreground in all jumps. At junior ages between 15 and 18 years the reactive forms of training can be increasingly incorporated into training. It must be emphasized once again that reactive strength at the highest performance level is indeed independent from maximum strength. However, this statement assumes a high existing level of maximum strength. This cannot and must not be assumed in the case of youths and the parallel development of maximum strength is therefore, also an important component of training. Under this circumstance we can identify the general categories in jumping strength training shown in Table 5.3.

DIAGNOSTICS OF STRENGTH AND POWER

From a practical point of view there are at least two arguments for the diagnostic assessment of strength and power. Firstly, intensity loads in strength training are usually expressed as percentages of the maximum load in a single repetition. This requires a knowledge of the 100% level. Secondly, in most sports strength is an important factor in performance. Detailed information on the deficiencies of individual athletes is necessary for the planning and regulation of training. Assessment of strength and power may be executed with motor tests or with appropriate biomechanical devices. In general the precision of diagnostics must be greater than the differences to be measured. In the beginning of a training process simple motor testing may therefore be sufficient. With increasing level of performance and decreasing interindividual differences and intraindividual progress, scientific diagnostic assessment that differentiates at least similar physical capabilities is required. It is important to note that the diagnostic procedure used will

Table 5.3: Mechanical loads and rank-order of different reactive jumping exercises

Mechanical load	Horizontal jumps	Vertical jumps
Low	Standing long jump	Jumping on boxes Bouncings
Medium	Alternate leg bound without run-up	Two-legged hurdle jumps One-legged hurdle jumps with landing on lead leg
High	Alternate leg bound with run-up Single leg hops without run-up	One-legged hurdle jumps with landing on take-off leg Two-legged drop jumps
Very high	Single leg hops with run-up Take-offs from deeper plane	Single-leg drop jumps

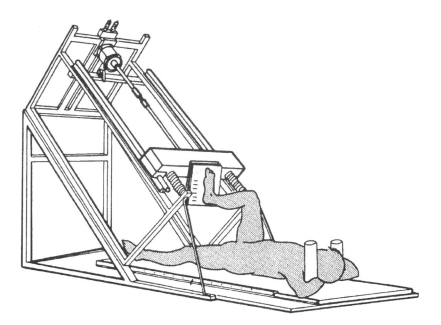

Figure 5.13: Measurement device for the registration of force–time curves (From Schmidtbleicher, 1992).

highly influence the results and their subsequent interpretation. If for example power is determined by using isometric measurements, the important aspect of velocity is neglected and the function of strength will be overestimated, whereas, if jumping ability is determined by using a jump and reach test the reactive strength components will be eliminated. So some kind of jumping ability is measured but not the specific form required in most jumping events.

Diagnostics of strength

The most simple procedures for strength diagnostics are motor tests that determine the maximum load in a single repetition in specific exercises. The precise control of the starting and final positions is of major importance. If for example the maximum load in a half squat is assessed then variations in the knee angle of 5° will modify the result. The consequences for further training would therefore be misleading. Please remember that this procedure may not be used for unskilled persons. In leisure sports and in junior athletes the one repetition maximum should not be used in assessment. It is sufficient to determine the 10 RM. In elite sport a better diagnostic tool in the assessment of strength is a force platform or similar force transducers. It is important to note whether the measurement refers to a single joint rotatory movement or a multiple joint translatory movement. Although single joint measurements can more precisely determine the strength of an isolated muscle (e.g. m. quadriceps femoris) than multiple joint measurements, they fail to give relevant information in elite sport. As there are no single joint movements in sport and as the direction of extension is different to that often recorded during movement the data gained may have no practical meaning. Studies with 10 national level female high jumpers were clear proof of this statement. The results of the single joint diagnostics only correlated with the athletes' overall body mass. Multiple joint measurements using a leg press device (see Figure 5.13), however, showed a very high correlation with the level of performance.

For multiple joint diagnostics the control of the starting position is extremely important. For example, the diagnostics of leg extensor strength is dependent on the body position. In a sitting position the force–angle curve is ascending–descending with a maximum at a knee angle of about 130°. In a lying position the force–angle curve is continuously ascending until almost complete extension (Hay, 1992, p.203). This starting position is typical for most sports.

Diagnostics of power

Power assessment is often performed in the same way as the diagnostic measurement of strength. The registered force–time histories allow the determination of starting strength and explosive strength as components of power. Starting strength is represented by the force after 30 ms, explosive strength matches the steepest incline of the curve. A power index may be determined as the quotient of maximum force divided by the time required to reach this value. All parameters can be determined under isometric and dynamic conditions. For a sport-specific diagnostic it is advisable, however, to use similar loads and directions of stretching as in the real situation. This prevents an overestimation of the role played by strength. In training practice a lot of motor tests are used to analyse power. For the leg extensor muscles, standing long jump or vertical counter movement jumps are typical examples. The height of flight is determined either in a jump and reach test or by measuring the flight time using a contact mat. Shot putters, for example, test their overall power with two-handed backwards throws of a shot. As a good coordination of this movement can be assumed for top athletes, differences in the distance reached can be explained by differences in power. While in untrained persons strength and power show high correlations, this is no longer valid for highly skilled homogenous groups. If all athletes show an extraordinary level of strength then strength no longer differentiates between varying power levels. This phenomenon is well known from other areas. For example, there is generally a good correlation between run-up speed and jumping distance in the long jump. However, no significant velocity correlation can be found within the group of 8 m jumpers. The run-up velocity of all these jumpers is both high and very similar so that differences in performance can no longer be explained by small differences in the run-up velocity.

REFERENCES

Alexander, R. McC. and Benet-Clarke, H.C. (1977) Storage of elastic strain energy in muscles and other tissues. *Nature*, London, **265**, 114–117.

Bührle, M. (1985) Dimensionen des Kraftverhaltens und ihre spezifischen Trainings-formen, in *Grundlagen des Maximal- und Schnellkrafttrainings* (Ed. M. Bührle), pp. 82–111. Hofmann, Schorndorf.

Carew, Th.J. and Ghez, C. (1985) Muscles and muscle receptors, in *Principles of neural sciences* (Eds E.R. Kandel and J.H. Schwarz), pp. 443–456, New York.

Desmedt, J.E. (1981) The size principle of motoneuron recruitment in ballistic or ramp-voluntary contractions in man, in *Progress in Clinical Neurophysiology, Vol. 9, Motor Unit Types, Recruitment and Plasticity in Health and Disease* (Ed. J.E. Desmedt), pp. 250–304, Karger, Basel.

Desmedt, J.E. and Godaux, E. (1978) Ballistic contractions in man: characteristic recruitment patterns of single motor units of the tibialis anterior muscle. *Journal of Physiology*, **264**, 673–693.

Dietz, V., Noth, J. and Schmidtbleicher, D. (1981) Interaction between preactivity and stretch-reflex in human triceps brachii during landing from forward falls. *Journal of Physiology*, **311**, 113–125.

Goldspink, G. (1978) Energy turnover during contraction of different types of muscles, in *Biomechanics VI A* (Eds. E. Asmussen and K. Jorgensen), pp. 27–39, University Park Press, Baltimore.

Goldspink, G. (1992) Cellular and molecular aspects of adaptation in skeletal muscle, in *Strength and Power in Sport* (Ed. P.V. Komi), pp. 211–229, Blackwell Scientific Publications, Oxford.

Hay, J. (1992) Mechanical basis of strength expression, in *Strength and Power in Sport* (Ed. P.V. Komi), pp. 197–207, Blackwell Scientific Publications, Oxford.

Henneman, E., Somjen, G. and Carpenter, D.O. (1965) Functional significance of cell size in spinal motoneurons, *Journal of Neurophysiology*, **28**, 560–580.

Hettinger, T. (1968) *Isometrisches Muskeltraining.* Thieme, Stuttgart.

Hill, A.V. (1938) The heat of shortening and the dynamic constants of muscle. *Proceedings of the Royal Society B*, **126**, 136–195.

Kleinöder, H., Neumaier, A., Loch, M. and Mester, J. (1994) Untersuchungen zur Variation im Aufschlag, in *Tennisvermittlung als Interpretation und Auswertung sportwissenschaftlicher Erkenntnisse* (Eds. P. Koch and P. Maier), pp. 41–64, Academica Verlag, St Augustin.

Komi, P.V. (1973) Measurement of the force–velocity relationship in human muscle under concentric and eccentric conractions. *Medicine and Sport, Vol. 8: Biomechanics III*, pp. 224–229, Karger, Basel.

Komi, P.V. (1990) Relevance of *in vivo* force measurements to human biomechanics. *Journal of biomechanics*, **23** (suppl. 1), 23–24.

Komi, P.V. (1992) Stretch-shortening cycle, in *Strength and Power in Sport* (Ed. P.V. Komi), pp. 169–179, Blackwell Scientific Publications, Oxford.

Komi, P.V. and Bosco, C. (1978) Utilization of stored elastic energy in leg extensor muscles by men and women. *Medicine and Science in Sports and Exercise*, **10**, 261–265.

Macdougall, J.D. (1992) Hypertrophy or hyperplasia, in *Strength and Power in Sport* (Ed. P.V. Komi), pp. 230–238, Blackwell Scientific Publications, Oxford.

Meerson, F. (1967) *Plastische Versorgung der Funktion des Muskels.* Nauka, Moscow.

Meerson, F. (1973) Mechanismen der Adaptation. *Wissenschaft in der UdSSR*, 7, 425–433.

Moritani, T. (1992) Time course of adaptations during strength and power training, in *Strength and Power in Sport* (Ed. P.V. Komi), pp. 266–278, Blackwell Scientific Publications, Oxford.

Noth, J. (1992) Motor units, in *Strength and Power in Sport* (Ed. P.V. Komi), pp. 21–28, Blackwell Scientific Publications, Oxford.

Rasch, P., Pierson, W. (1964) One position versus multiple positions in isometric exercise, *American Journal of Physical Medicine*, 43, 10–16.

Ritzdorf, W. (1987) Aspekte der Trainingssteuerung im Mikrozyklus, in *Brennpunkte der Sportwissenschaft: Trainingsoptimierung* (Eds. H.J. Appel and J. Mester), pp. 208–217.

Roy, R.R. and Edgerton, V.R. (1991) Skeletal muscle architecture and performance, in *Strength and Power in Sport* (Ed. P.V. Komi), pp. 115–129, Blackwell Scientific Publications, Oxford.

Sale, D.G. (1992) Neural adaptations to strength training, in *Strength and Power in Sport* (Ed. P.V. Komi), pp. 249–265, Blackwell Scientific Publications, Oxford.

Schmidtbleicher, D. (1991) Neuromuskuläre Effekte sportlicher Belstungen, in *Sportliche Bewegung und Motorik unter Belastung* (Eds. N. Olivier and R. Daugs), pp. 29–44, dvs publications, Clausthal-Zellerfeld.

Schmidtbleicher, D. (1992) Training for power events, in *Strength and Power in Sport* (Ed. P.V. Komi), pp. 381–395, Blackwell Scientific Publications, Oxford.

Schmidtbleicher, D., Dietz, V., Noth, J. and Antoni, M. (1978) Auftreten und funktionelle Bedeutung des Muskeldehnungsreflexes bei Lauf- und Sprintbewegungen. *Leistungssport*, 8, 480–490.

Voss, G. (1991) Zur Ausbildung elementarer neuromuskulärer Bewegungsprogramme. *Leistungssport*, 11, 47–50.

Voss, G. and Krause, Th. (1991) Zu den Beziehungen zwischen elementaren Bewegungsprogrammen als einem Ausdruck der Schnelligkeit und grundlegenden neuromuskulären Voraussetzungen. *Leistungssport*, 11, 24–28.

6

FLEXIBILITY IN SPORT

J. Bloomfield

The University of Western Australia

G. Wilson

Southern Cross University

Flexibility can be simply defined as the range of possible movement in a joint or in a series of joints (de Vries, 1986). It is developed by stretching the soft tissue, primarily around a joint, and is of great value to the athlete in many sports, because it can improve the overall performance significantly. The purpose of this chapter is to demonstrate the advantages or disadvantages of flexibility in sport and to present, with caution, the methods which will improve an athlete's potential to perform in various sports and events.

THE VALUE OF STRETCHING

During the last two decades coaches and sport scientists have increasingly realized the value of stretching for their athletes. In some sports, such as swimming and track and field, stretching has been extensively used for over 50 years, but coaches in the majority of sports have not been aware of the specific benefits until recently (Bloomfield et al., 1995).

Training in Sport: Applying Sport Science. Edited by B. Elliott
© 1998 John Wiley & Sons Ltd

General benefits

Many coaches and sport scientists now believe that flexibility exercises are of more value than was previously thought. In the past they have been used as part of the warm-up programme for various sports, but their value in the development of superior technique and for increasing the explosive power in a movement has only recently been realized. Stretching therefore has become a very important part of the modern training programme, in a similar way to that of strength, power and speed (Bloomfield et al., 1995).

Specific benefits

Improvement in performance

All well-informed coaches today are aware of the role played by stretching, if high levels of performance are to be reached. Sigerseth (1971) stated in the early seventies that certain skilled performances could be enhanced by increasing or decreasing the range of motion around various joints. Since that time coaches have realized that there are three main areas where improvements can be made and these are as follows:

- When an athlete is able to *increase the range of motion* in any skill in a ballistic sport, the potential to produce more force or velocity becomes possible, because a greater range of movement increases the distance and the time over which a force can be developed (Ciullo and Zarins, 1983). This in turn increases the velocity of the racquet, club, bat or projectile and a more powerful hit, throw (Figure 6.1) or kick can be made. Sports such as water polo, tennis, golf, cricket, baseball, football and some field sports are good examples of this. In fact, Jobe and Moynes (1986) reported that highly skilled golfers had twice the range of trunk rotation when they were compared to less skilled players.
- Being able to *increase the range of various movements throughout the body has enabled athletes to place themselves into more aesthetic positions in almost all sports.* In many cases these positions are accompanied by a more technically sound performance and moreover they are very pleasing to watch. For example in a high hurdles race, where the competitors stride smoothly over the hurdles rather than partially jumping them; or in a butterfly race, where instead of swimmers 'climbing' out of the water and then sinking back into it, they appear to glide over it. Further, in sport disciplines which are judged, such as gymnastics, diving or ice skating, the participant is expected to reach certain set positions in order to score high artistic marks. Without a high level of flexibility athletes are not able to match their very supple opponents (Bloomfield et al., 1994).

Figure 6.1: By increasing the range of motion of the throwing arm, this highly flexible water polo player is able to increase the velocity of the throw.

- For some time observant coaches have hypothesized that *a stretched muscle can produce a greater contractile force than a non-stretched one.* This is because the pre-stretched muscle stores elastic energy and then releases it as it is shortened. Wilson et al. (1992) demonstrated that flexibility training significantly increased the elasticity of the musculo-tendinous unit and thereby enhanced the utilization of elastic energy. This finding has supported the subjective opinions of coaches referred to above and will have a significant effect on the utilization of the explosive power concept in the future. There is no doubt that in the sports where explosive power is used, athletes can benefit greatly from its development through flexibility training (Figure 6.2).

Figure 6.2: This flexible golfer is able to store elastic energy in the musculo-tendinous units during the backswing and release the body, arms and club with great force on the downswing.

Prevention of injury

A low level of flexibility is a component of fitness that is frequently associated with muscular injury and many sports scientists and sports medicine doctors have suggested that stretching exercises may decrease the incidence, and severity of musculo-tendinous and joint injury. Moreover flexibility is currently seen as one of the best ways of avoiding these injuries. There are two mechanisms which account for the strong relationship between the flexibility of the musculature and its predisposition to injury. The first of these (Shellock and Prentice, 1985) is based on the effect of flexibility on the range of motion about a joint, while the second is based on the relationship between flexibility and the elasticity of the musculo-tendinous units (Wilson et al., 1991c).

Relief of muscular soreness

Muscular soreness can occur immediately after exercise and last for several hours, or be delayed for up to 24 hours or in some cases even longer. Static stretching for both types of soreness has been strongly recommended by de Vries (1986). He suggested that a brief period of static stretching (10 minutes) can be done after a work-out, so as to alleviate immediate soreness. If a muscle or group of muscles become sore at a later time, the athlete should again use static stretching, with stretch times of up to 2 minutes. This can be repeated two or three times a day.

Muscular relaxation

One of the important benefits of a stretching programme is the promotion of relaxation. When a muscle stays partially contracted for a period of time 'contracture' develops. This syndrome, plus chronic muscle tension, can shorten the muscle and make it less supple. As a result, undue muscular tension can produce excessive muscle tightness. Static stretching combined with a relaxation programme is of great value to alleviate this condition (Bloomfield et al., 1994).

RANGE OF FLEXIBILITY

Coaches need to understand that, as in the normal population, the range of flexibility within the competitive sporting population is extensive. Flexibility is a continuum with little movement at one end of the range, while at the other there can be a great deal. The former creates a very restricted range of movement, while the latter can cause excessive instability, leading to partial (subluxation) or in some cases, complete dislocation. It is necessary therefore, for the coach to decide the athlete's optimal level of mobility and to make sure that this is attained and then maintained.

Hypermobility

Hypermobile individuals with loose joint capsules, loose ligaments and in some cases abnormally small bony articulating prominences have commonly been labelled as 'double-jointed' and contortionists who performed in circuses or vaudeville in the past were basically hypermobile. In some sports such as gymnasts, swimming and diving, this may be an advantage, providing it is not extreme. However, in contact sports, where the game is played at a high speed and collisions with other players often occur, it can be very dangerous, particularly in contact games such as the football codes.

Hypermobility is not only a problem in sport as it relates to injury, but it can also be very detrimental to technique. Athletes who are partially hypermobile often exhibit too large a range of movement during the backswing and follow-through phases of a movement. This can place them in an awkward position to perform the next shot, or it may take them out of the play in some agility sports for a split second while they are recovering. In highly technique-oriented sports like swimming, for example, a degree of hypermobility is of value in freestyle or butterfly, but quite detrimental in backstroke, because if the swimmer has a hypermobile shoulder joint, the arm may enter the water directly behind the head, instead of level with the shoulder. The first part of the pulling stroke is then lateral, creating an equal and opposite movement of the hips, which causes a high degree of lateral frontal resistance. The type of action therefore reduces the efficiency of the stroke.

There are various tests for hypermobility. Figure 6.3 demonstrates them with the fourth position in each test showing hypermobility. If an athlete needs to decrease the range of movement in one or several joints, an *intensive* strength training programme should be undertaken in order to tighten the musculo-tendinous units, thereby giving more support to the joint itself. If possible this should be done during the adolescent growth spurt, as the athlete will not build up muscle and connective tissue in pre- or post-adolescence as quickly as during adolescence (Bloomfield et al., 1994).

Hypomobility

Joint stiffness or unusual soft tissue tightness often occurs in primary mesomorphs. It can be due to abnormally large bony prominences in the joint, very 'tight' joint capsules, or a large and 'bulky' musculature.

With hypomobile or inflexible athletes, stretching exercises must be commenced conservatively and carried out with caution and if this occurs over an extended period of time, their mobility will significantly improve. Each individual should be carefully evaluated and decisions made on which tissue should be stretched and to what degree. In contact games such as the tackle football codes, the coach should be aware that shoulder joints need to be 'tight', as do the hip and knee joints. Flexibility exercises to lengthen the musculo-tendinous units, especially in the areas of the hamstrings, quadriceps and calves, must be carried out carefully, with no exercises being performed which might loosen the ligaments and joint capsules of the athlete (Bloomfield et al., 1994).

SPECIFICITY IN FLEXIBILITY

There is a common belief that if athletes are flexible in one joint, then they will have a similar range of movement in others. However de Vries (1986) stated that 'an individual is a composite of many joints, some of which may be unusually flexible, some inflexible and some average'. Flexibility

Flexibility Rating Form

Name: _____   Date: _____

Movement	1	2	3	4	Rating
Arm horizontal extension					
Arm abduction					
Forearm flexion					
Forearm hyper-extension					
Hand flexion					
Hand extension					
Trunk flexion					
Trunk hyper-extension					

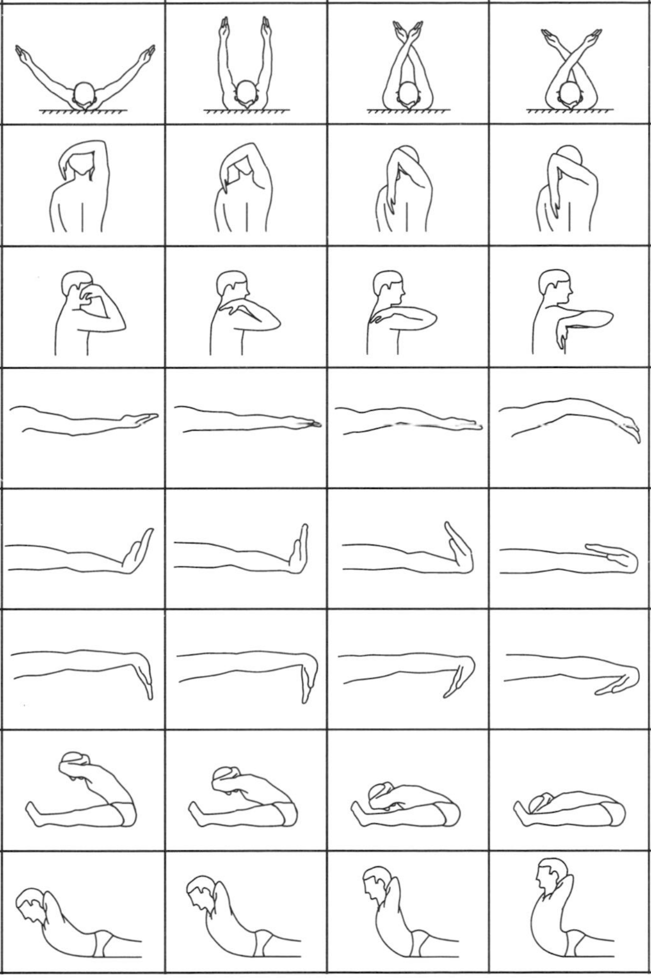

Figure 6.3: (and overleaf) Flexibility screening test (courtesy of Bloomfield et al., 1994).

therefore is joint-specific and depends not only on the 'tightness' of the ligaments, muscles, tendons and joint capsules, but also on the size and shape of the bones and how they are articulated. This is demonstrated in people who have dysplasia, where one or several parts of the body are disproportionately larger or smaller than the others. Examples of this would be a square-shouldered male with a large and protruding acromion process

Movement					Rating
Trunk lateral flexion					
Thigh flexion					
Thigh extension					
Leg flexion					
Leg hyper-extension					
Foot dorsi-flexion					
Foot plantar-flexion					
Comments:					

which makes the shoulder joint reasonably inflexible; or a female with a flat back and buttocks. In the first case this individual would make a reasonably poor butterfly swimmer, unless the technique is modified to accommodate this partial handicap, possibly by using side breathing. In the second example, a flat back and buttocks would not assist this person to easily perform a trunk hyperextension manoeuvre in gymnastics, even though levels of flexibility were above average in the other joints.

FACTORS AFFECTING FLEXIBILITY

Age

Research at this time is divided on whether there are periods in individual's lives when they are more flexible than at other times. Corbin and Noble (1980) suggested that flexibility increased in a child until adolescence, when there appeared to be a plateau effect, followed by a steady decrease in mobility as the individual aged. Research by Phillips (1955) and Kirchner and Glines (1957) did not support this finding and both stated that elementary school aged children become less flexible as they grew, reaching a low point between 10 and 12 years of age. From this time on, flexibility appeared to slightly improve until late adolescence. There seems to be no dispute in the literature, however, about the fact that from young adulthood there is a steady decline in flexibility until death. If a well-planned intervention programme aimed at increasing flexibility is carried out during childhood and adolescence, then extreme ranges of mobility can be obtained particularly in females; however, these ranges are more difficult to achieve in post-adolescence.

Critical training periods

The literature is confusing on this subject, with some researchers maintaining that it is during childhood and early adolescence that the best flexibility training results are obtained, while others disagree with this. Regardless of the exact time for optimal benefit, flexibility exercises can be done at any period in an athlete's life and are not dangerous, provided certain safeguards are adhered to. These will be discussed in detail later in this chapter.

Childhood and adolescence

Because individuals are undergoing rapid growth during childhood and adolescence, the coach must be careful not to overstress the musculo-skeletal system of a young athlete. Early in a child's life, the bones have not yet fully formed and the bone modelling process is rapidly occurring. This means that cartilage, which is steadily being replaced by bone, is very vulnerable to overuse syndromes and trauma. Well-planned strength and flexibility training will not cause injuries, but overtraining will. Further information on the types of injury which can occur with overtraining will be discussed in the section on the effect of growth on flexibility. It should also be noted that during periods of rapid growth a loss of flexibility can occur, as the bones may grow at a faster rate than the muscles around them. Consequently it is often necessary for children to perform flexibility exercises during the adolescent growth spurt, to maintain reasonable levels of flexibility at this time.

Post-adolescence

As the individual ages, muscles, tendons and connective tissue shorten and calcification of some cartilage occurs, with a resultant loss in the range of movement. This usually appears first in the lumbar region, followed by the knees, then in other joints. It can be minimized with a well-planned stretching and strength-training programme, provided the individual does not overstress the musculo-skeletal system (Bloomfield et al., 1994).

Gender

Research by Phillips (1955) and Kirchner and Glines (1957) found that elementary school aged girls were more flexible than boys of a similar age. From adolescence onward, females appear to be more flexible with smaller bones and less musculature than males; however, these observations, made by a large number of health professionals, teachers and coaches, have not been conclusively supported by research at this time.

Environmental conditions

There is general agreement that a warm-up must precede a stretching session. When soft tissue, particularly the musculo-tendinous unit is heated, it can promote relaxation which allows safe stretching to be performed. De Vries (1986) stated that flexibility was improved by 20%, by the local warming of a joint to 45°C (113°F) and was decreased by between 10% and 20% by cooling it to 18°C (65°F). In facilitating flexibility, warming up has the effect of reducing muscular injury and enhancing the performance of athletic activities. Safran et al. (1988) reported that the performance of a warm-up increased the force that was required to be exerted against rabbit musculature prior to the occurrence of injury. These researchers also reported that the warm-up increased the elasticity of the musculature. Asmussen et al. (1976) reported that the height achieved in maximal vertical jumps was reduced from 42 cm to 30 cm when the muscles of the lower limb were cooled by immersion in cold water.

Psychological effect

When team members warm up and stretch together they can serve as models and guides for one another. In a social situation, it is possible for a cohesive and co-operative group to achieve better results than if they had worked individually. It should be pointed out, however, that partner activities can be detrimental if the element of competition is introduced and that it is important for team members not to compete with one another, as this can be dangerous, and overstretching will injure the muscles and joints. Flexibility is a highly individual capacity and must be treated as such by all athletes.

LIMITATIONS TO THE RANGE OF MOVEMENT

When examining the range of movement (ROM) in any athlete, it is important for the coach to understand the anatomical and physiological limitations which are placed on the individual. The following sections illustrate this point.

Anatomical limitations

Connective tissue (soft tissue)

Connective tissue is widespread in the body and plays an important role in determining an athlete's range of motion, as it covers the end of the bone at each joint like a sleeve. It is also basically responsible for binding together various structures and consists of both fibrous connective tissue (collagen) and elastic connective tissue (elastin). Some joints in the body are supported by more of the elastic tissue and this is one of the factors that determines their range of motion.

Fascia

This is a band of fibrous like tissue which binds many structures in the body. The deep fascia which envelops the muscle is known as the *epimysium* and within the muscle can be found the *perimysium, endomysium* and the *sarcolemma*, all of which bind various components of the muscle. This tissue has limited stretch and soon resists movement.

Muscle

The contractile nature of skeletal muscle is reasonably well known, but is only of academic interest in an applied chapter on stretching. What is of importance with relation to muscle tissue is that although it is not able to lengthen of its own accord, it can be stretched externally. By doing this the myofilaments can slide further apart and an elongation of the muscle can occur. When a muscle is stretched under tension, for example during an eccentric contraction, the myofilaments slide apart and elastic energy is stored in the cross-bridge linkages between the actin and myosin filaments. The greater the muscular tension the more actin and myosin filaments are linked. As a result of this, more elastic energy will be stored.

Tendons

Tendons join muscle to bone and are normally cordlike, but they can also be flat; when flat or ribbon shaped they are known as aponeuroses. Tendons consist of closely packed collagenous bundles which have a longitudinal striation. Their structure ensures that they have little stretch and this quality enables them to transfer a muscular contraction directly to the bone to which they are attached. Nevertheless tendons do possess some elasticity, particularly the longer ones such as the Achilles tendon and are major storage sites for elastic energy (Alexander, 1987).

Ligaments

These are strong bands of connective tissue joining bone and their main function is to support a joint. They consist of bundles of collagenous fibres which run parallel to one another and have a structure which is similar to tendons, but they are usually flatter in shape. Their level of stretchability is also similar to that of tendons, in order to allow some limited movement at the joint, but they are strong enough to bind bone to bone, resisting moderate trauma or overstretching.

Soft tissue stiffness

It should be remembered by individuals who conduct stretching programmes that caution must be used at all times. The above-mentioned tissues are up to a point elastic by nature and are designed to return to their normal length after being stretched. If the force which is applied is too great, however, and the stretch is overdone, these tissues may rupture and the joint or joints being stretched may become unstable.

Bone tissue

It is obvious that the bone structure at the joints plays a restrictive role in flexibility. It is well known that individuals with large bony prominences at the ends of their bones have a finite limit on their joint mobility and any amount of stretching of the connective tissues around the joint will not alter this.

Physiological limitations

Sense organs or proprioceptors are involved in all movements where precision is required and are found in the muscles, tendons and joints. When stretching, two types of sense organs come into play, namely the *muscle spindles* and the *Golgi tendon organs* (GTOs). These organs pick up changes in the muscle length, or its velocity or force, and transmit them by electrical signals to the central nervous system (CNS), where they are processed and the appropriate response is made.

Muscle spindles

These are the primary stretch receptors in the muscle which respond to changes in length and rate of stretch. They run parallel to the muscle fibre and are enclosed in a fusiform-shaped spindle, and are known as *intrafusal* fibres. They should not be confused with *extrafusal* fibres which are the contractile units of the muscle itself.

Golgi tendon organs (GTOs)

These sensory receptors are located in the tendon close to the musculo-tendinous junction and respond to force or tension in the muscle. Their function is basically inhibitory and because they have a higher threshold than the muscle spindle, they only come into play after the muscle is vigorously stretched.

The stretch reflex (myotatic reflex)

If an individual stretches a muscle or group of muscles with a *ballistic* motion, the muscle spindles come into play and the *stretch reflex* is initiated. The magnitude of this reflex is dependent upon the amount and rate of stretching of the muscle, so that dynamic ballistic stretches invoke the maximal stretch reflex response. When this reflex fires, the muscle, which is close to being overstretched, suddenly contracts, reducing further extension of the limb. In this way the stretch reflex serves as a mechanism to protect the limb from being overstretched. Individuals should not take part in exercises which are strongly ballistic or bouncy, because this type of action will activate the stretch reflex when the muscle is at full stretch, increasing tension, which should be avoided because a better result will ensue if the muscle is stretched in a relaxed state.

The inverse stretch reflex (inverse myotatic reflex)

This is also known as *autogenic inhibition* and occurs when a *slow* contraction or stretch on a tendon exceeds a critical level. This causes an immediate reflex action which inhibits any further muscular contraction or stretching and the tension is quickly reduced. This reduction of tension acts as a protective mechanism which prevents the muscles and tendons from injury and is only made possible by the inhibitory impulses of the GTOs, which override the excitatory impulses from the muscle spindles.

The *inverse stretch reflex* can be used however, if it is carefully controlled, to assist individuals to reach high levels of flexibility. This is done by slowly stretching a muscle group to a point where the tension suddenly dissipates and the muscle relaxes. When this occurs the stretch can be slowly recommenced until the tension reaches another critical point and a further relaxation phase occurs.

Finally, it should be remembered that there is a risk associated with this technique if it is being carried out intensively, because it develops tension in the muscle, which may result in soreness and/or injury. Consequently care must be exercised when using the inverse myotatic reflex to achieve extreme ranges of motion.

ELASTIC PROPERTIES OF MUSCLES AND TENDONS

The majority of movements are the result of eccentric contractions, where the musculature lengthens under tension (the backswing, wind-up or counter-movement), followed by a concentric contraction, where the musculature shortens under tension (the forward swing or upward movement). Such movement sequences are seen in activities such as running, jumping, throwing, hitting and in most resistance training exercises. This movement sequence is commonly referred to as a *stretch shorten cycle* (SSC), as the musculature is stretched prior to being shortened. For example, prior to throwing a ball an individual will extend the arm backwards, stretching the musculature around the shoulder girdle and then bring the arm rapidly forward, shortening the musculature.

SSC movements augment the concentric phase of the activity, resulting in an increase in power when compared to similar movements performed without prior stretch. The ability of the SSC to enhance human movement has been known since the pioneering research of Marey and Demeny (1885), who observed that in two successive jumps the second was higher than the first, because it involved a more intense eccentric muscular action than the first. The augmentation to performance derived from use of the SSC is ascribed to a combination of the recovery of stored elastic energy from the musculature, the fact that concentric activity begins with tension in the muscles and additional, reflexively induced, neural input due to the stretch reflex.

The mechanisms underlying the use of elastic strain energy in SSC activities is a relatively simple process. During a resisted eccentric contraction, or counter-movement, the elastic regions of the musculo-tendinous unit are minutely stretched and consequently store elastic energy. On movement reversal (i.e. the concentric contraction) the extended regions recoil to their original form and during this process a portion of the stored elastic energy is recovered to produce kinetic energy that may augment the performance of the activity. The elastic regions of the musculo-tendinous unit include the tendon, epimysium, perimysium and endomysium and the crossbridge linkages between the actin and myosin filaments of the muscle. Of these regions, the tendon has been shown to be the dominant site for the storage of elastic energy (Alexander, 1987).

Most sporting activities utilize the SSC sequence because it uses elastic energy and the stretch reflex to contribute to the performance; however, there are several additional points which need to be considered. They are as follows:

- If a delay period occurs between the eccentric and concentric phases of an SSC movement, then the use of elastic energy in the movement will be reduced. In order to maximize this energy in SSC movements the delay period should be minimized and the movement should rapidly proceed from the eccentric to the concentric phase (Wilson et al., 1991a).
- Elastic energy stored in the muscles and tendons is rapidly released during the concentric phase of motion and contributes for only the initial few tenths of a second of the movement (Wilson et al., 1991a).
- The elasticity of the musculo-tendinous unit is a very important determinant of how much elastic energy is used in SSC movements. For relatively slow movement, such as a heavy bench press lift, it is evident that a very elastic musculo-tendinous system maximizes the use of elastic energy in the movement (Wilson et al., 1991b).
- Research performed by Wilson et al. (1992) has demonstrated that flexibility training increases the elasticity of the muscles and tendons, which serves to enhance the performance of SSC movements by increasing the contribution of elastic energy to the movement.
- Pousson et al. (1990) reported that strength training tended to increase musculo-tendinous stiffness, while Wilson et al. (1992) found that flexibility training tended to reduce the stiffness of the muscles and tendons. *These findings strongly suggest that athletes should perform flexibility exercises in conjunction with their strength training to maintain the elasticity of their muscles and tendons.*

FLEXIBILITY AND INJURY

There are many causes of sports injuries, but coaches have known for a long time that either a lack of flexibility, or in some cases hypermobility, can cause injury.

Injury prevention

Moynes (1983) suggested that stretching exercises were of value in the prevention of injury if they were carried out in conjunction with a suitable warm-up and strength training programme. However, this general statement, although correct, needs to be further discussed.

Range of motion

It is well known by elite level coaches that highly flexible joints and musculo-tendinous units will help reduce severe muscle strains or joint sprains when they are accidentally overstretched (de Vries, 1962). This mechanism has also been described by Shellock and Prentice (1985) who stated '. . . flexibility is important for injury prevention. There are many situations in sport where a muscle is forced to stretch beyond its normal active limits. If the muscle does not have enough elasticity to compensate for this additional stretch, it is likely injury will occur to the musculo-tendinous unit.'

Such an injury would occur in most individuals if they were to jump up and land in the splits position. However, if very high levels of flexibility are achieved, the performance of this movement would not result in injury. Thus it is important that coaches and athletes are able to judge the extreme ROM which their athletes will need in their sports and work towards this in training. A gymnast, swimmer or hurdler may need an extreme ROM in various parts of the body, while a tennis player or basketballer may need to be flexible, but not to an extreme.

Elasticity of the musculo-tendinous unit

Many muscular injuries which are related to flexibility do not occur as a result of overextension during an activity. For example, the majority of ruptures of the pectoralis major muscle occur during the performance of the bench press lift (Kretzler and Richardson, 1989), an exercise which is performed within relatively normal movement ranges. Similarly, pulled hamstring muscles commonly occur in athletes with poor flexibility; however, they are generally not caused by an overextension of the lower limbs. Thus it is apparent that a second mechanism underlying the relationship between flexibility and injury may exist. Such a mechanism was proposed by Wilson et al. (1991c) who observed a significant relationship between flexibility and muscular stiffness. These researchers demonstrated that individuals who were inflexible tended to possess stiff musculo-tendinous units. As external forces were imposed upon these units they were less able to attenuate the forces and consequently the incidence of muscular injury was greater, when compared to more flexible individuals who possessed musculo-tendinous units which were more elastic. These researchers stated that 'the musculo-tendinous unit represents the link between the skeletal system and muscular structures. As an external force is imposed on the musculature, a compliant system will extend to a greater extent allowing the applied force to be absorbed over a larger distance and greater time as compared to a stiff system. As such, the cushioning effect of a compliant system reduces the trauma on the muscle fibres decreasing the incidence of muscular injury as compared to a stiff musculo-tendinous system' (Wilson et al., 1991c). Thus the second mechanism underlying the relationship between flexibility and muscular injury is based on the significant association between flexibility and the elasticity of the musculo-tendinous unit, and the effect that this elasticity has on the incidence of muscular injury.

Many sports, however, do not demand extremely high levels of flexibility, so the coach must 'tailor' the stretching programme to suit each individual. Almost all athletes need a reasonable level of flexibility which can be of great value to them when they are trying to relax, even though they may not directly need it for their sport. Athletes involved in contact sports however, must be very careful not to overstretch joints, as they become unstable and, as a result, easily injured.

Prevention of muscular soreness

De Vries (1986) discussed the phenomenon of muscle soreness which occurred after training, and suggested that certain types of activity were more likely to cause soreness than others. They are as follows:

- eccentric contractions which will occur in plyometric jumping or downhill running;
- vigorous contractions, carried out while the muscle is in a shortened condition;
- muscle contractions which involve jerky movements or repetitions of the same movements over a long period of time;
- bouncing movements which involve stretching.

He further suggested that on many occasions it was not possible to avoid muscle soreness, but recommended that a 10 minute period of static stretching after exercise can bring about a significant degree of pain prevention.

Injury rehabilitation

Stretching is frequently used in the rehabilitation of muscle tissue. The muscle must be very slowly returned to its original length with gentle stretching exercises, which will encourage it to re-form in its long state, thus reducing cross adhesions. At the same time as the above process is occurring, proprioception and tension will be returning.

Where muscle soreness becomes a problem 24–48 hours after exercise, gentle *static stretching* should also be used. The athlete should hold each stretch for approximately 2 minutes and the exercises can be repeated two or three times a day until the soreness subsides.

THE EFFECT OF GROWTH ON FLEXIBILITY

Childhood and adolescence

In humans, various systems of the body grow at differing rates and this is the case with the skeletal and the muscular systems, as the former can lead the latter by as much as 6 months (Tanner, 1963), thus causing imbalances between the systems. Added to this phenomenon, and mentioned earlier in this chapter, is the bone modelling process which further complicates the individual's training programme. This is because there is still a small amount of cartilage in various parts of the skeleton, especially around the growth plates, which in some cases do not close until late in adolescence.

Problems occur during the many minor growth spurts in a child's life when the long bones grow rapidly and increase the tension of the musculo-tendinous unit (Leard, 1984). This causes tightness around the joints and often places a considerable amount of stress at the epiphyseal attachments. In some cases this causes an avulsion fracture to occur (i.e. the tearing away of a bony landmark to which a muscle is attached) when too much stress is placed on the apophysis (a projection of a bone to which a muscle is attached) by a forceful contraction of a muscle or group of muscles (Watson, 1992). Watson (1992) further stated that the most common avulsion fractures in children involve the following muscles and their attachments:

- the forearm flexors attached to the medial epicondyle of the humerus;
- the sartorius muscle attached to the anterior superior iliac spine;
- the rectus femoris muscle attached to the anterior inferior iliac spine;
- the iliopsoas muscle attached to the lesser trochanter of the femur;
- the abdominal muscles attached to the iliac crest;
- the hamstring muscles attached to the ischial tuberosity;
- the patellar tendon attached to the tibial tuberosity;
- the Achilles tendon attached to the calcaneus.

These injuries are most commonly seen in throwers, sprinters, jumpers, footballers and other agility athletes and occur when a sudden violent contraction is made. With relation to the above problem, and other less specific injuries, Leard (1984) suggested that if stretching exercises were started early in an athlete's career, flexibility should be maintained and many injuries would be prevented.

The reader should also be aware that various musculo-tendinous syndromes occur from lack of flexibility during childhood and adolescence and that in certain stages of development, the skeleton and the ligamentous and capsular tissues within the joint may not all grow at the same time. This may cause a degree of either hypermobility or hypomobility if there is too little or too much ligamentous tissue at various stages of the child's development. Leard (1984) further pointed out that low levels of flexibility were now thought to be the primary cause of several overuse injuries. These were as follows:

- Tightness of the structures in the popliteal region which prevents full leg extension, was often a characteristic of young athletes with chondromalacia.
- Decreased mobility and weakness in the cervical region and the shoulder girdle is sometimes the predisposing factor which causes medial epicondylitis (little league elbow) and lateral epicondylitis (tennis elbow). Pain in these regions can sometimes be the result of nerve impingement from the neck and can be alleviated if this area becomes more mobile.
- Lack of mobility in the thigh flexors and extensors and the lumbosacral region can result in chronic low back pain caused by poor posture.

Finally, it is important to understand that with children and adolescent athletes, all muscle groups must be in balance (i.e. antagonists and agonists), both from a flexibility and strength perspective. However, it is very dangerous to overstretch the immature skeleton, which still has much cartilaginous material in each joint. Because the body is very pliable at this time, it may appear that flexibility levels are rapidly improving but there can be long-term deleterious effects on the joints if this is overdone. Coaches should carefully supervise their athletes in order to ensure that no static stretching is done to the point of pain, especially during puberty, when changes are occurring in the musculo-skeletal system at a very rapid rate (Bloomfield et al., 1994).

Middle and old age

Older athletes must understand that as they age, their muscles shorten and connective tissue becomes stiffer and tighter. Cartilage steadily calcifies, becoming thinner because of wear and tear and as a result cannot absorb the pressure it could tolerate when the individual was considerably younger. All this leads to a steady reduction of mobility, but if regular stretching is continued, which is not overly stressful, then reasonable levels of flexibility can be maintained. Alter (1990), made an additional interesting point when he stated that 'stretching stimulates the production or retention of lubricants between the connective tissue fibres, thus preventing the formation of adhesions.'

Veteran or senior athletes should be careful of the knee joints and the lumbar region of the spine when they stretch, especially the L5–S1 joint and the facet joints which are very susceptible to stress and strain. Osteoarthritis can affect these and other joints and this problem can be exacerbated by ballistic ('bouncy') stretching. Caution must therefore be shown with the type of stretching performed by senior athletes, but if they adhere to a static stretching routine which is not to the point of pain, they should avoid many of the problems which occur in less prudent individuals (Bloomfield et al., 1994).

FLEXIBILITY MEASUREMENT

Cureton (1951), was one of the first sport scientists to systematically measure the flexibility of champion athletes and several of the field tests he formulated are still used today. Flexibility testing was at first crude, but has become more sophisticated during the last two decades and because of its importance in sport, will become more so in the future.

Static testing

This method of measurement is carried out with the subjects in a non-dynamic situation, meaning that they are not performing a sport skill at the time, but rather having their range of movement assessed in a laboratory environment.

Field tests

These are tests where there is a small degree of subjectivity in the rating procedure; however, they are useful for coaches in the field. The assessment can be carried out quickly and a rating scale is used in order to give the subject a special numerical rating for each joint (Figure 6.3).

Other tests, which sometimes include several joints, have been used for some time and are only general indicators of regional flexibility. The most popular, despite its lack of validity, is the *sit-and-reach test*, where the subject sits on the floor with the legs extended in front and with the feet pressed against a box which supports a measuring stick. With the legs flat on the floor, the trunk is flexed at the hip joints and the arms are fully extended along the measuring stick. Three other tests which are sometimes used to gauge general flexibility are the *trunk-and-neck extension test* the *shoulder rotation test* and the *ankle flexion–extension test*.

Laboratory tests

There are various levels of sophistication in these tests, ranging from the use of a simple goniometer to sophisticated instrumentation. The most simple device for measuring static flexibility is the *goniometer*, which is a protractor with two moveable arms attached to it. It measures the angle between two body segments at the extreme ends of the ROM. The tester must be very careful to locate the axis of the bones which form the joint and be aware that the soft tissue around the joint can influence the accuracy of the measurement.

A more sophisticated goniometer known as the *electrogoniometer* or *elgon* incorporates a potentiometer at the axis of the two measurement arms. Changes in the joint angle are recorded as voltage fluctuations, providing an analogue display of joint motion. This device may therefore be used to provide measurements of static as well as functional flexibility. Recent advances in elgon technology have permitted the recording of three-dimensional movements without the previous encumbrance to normal athletic performance.

Rather than measure the angle between two body segments, the *Leighton flexometer* (Figure 6.4a,b), a device containing two rotating and weighted dials, may be used to record the motion of the single, isolated segment with respect to the perpendicular plane. The body segment is moved through its full range of motion and the flexometer records the angular displacement in degrees. More recently, a Plurimeter has been used to carry out the same type of angular displacement and because it is simpler and faster to use it will steadily replace the flexometer.

Functional testing

The athlete's flexibility during the execution of a closed skill has been generally neglected by coaches and sport scientists. High-speed cinematography or videography to provide a two-dimensional or three-dimensional reconstruction of athletic performance are used extensively in the field of biomechanics in technique analysis. These tools may also be used to measure functional flexibility during activity. It is important to have the subject perform with a minimum of clothing, so that the bony landmarks can be marked, then clearly seen, when each individual film or video is analysed. Such a system is advantageous in that the ROM in various movements which involve a combination of joints may be measured during actual athletic performance, but as yet it has not been fully developed and utilized to its full potential, mainly because of the time and cost involved (Bloomfield et al., 1994).

METHODS USED TO INCREASE FLEXIBILITY

The majority of stretching exercises which have been used in sport in the past have been *ballistic* in nature. Kiputh's (1942) text on swimming was one of the first to present a specialized series of flexibility exercises and this was

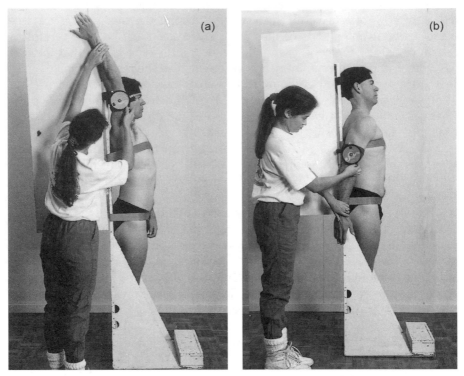

Figure 6.4:   Arm flexion–extension flexibility assessment—(a) flexion (b) extension (Courtesy of Bloomfield et al., 1994).

soon followed by others, especially for track and field athletes. When discussing methods to improve the ROM, de Vries (1986) stated that

> *conventional callisthenic exercises used for this purpose have usually involved hopping, bouncing, or jerky movements in which one body segment is put in movement by active contraction of a muscle group and the momentum then arrested by the antagonists at the end of the range of motion. Thus the antagonists are stretched by the dynamic movement of the agonists. Because momentum is involved, this system has been called the* ballistic method.

Ballistic stretching

Traditional stretching exercises which have been used in sport have generally been *ballistic* in nature. Although they have been in use for over 50 years, they were rarely questioned until two decades ago, when sport scientists and sport medicine specialists began to report that they may lead to injury and muscle soreness.

Disadvantages of ballistic stretching

Alter (1988) suggested that there were several reasons why ballistic stretching was not the best system to use and these are as follows:

- When connective tissue is rapidly stretched it does not have time to adequately adjust and this can result in soreness or injury.
- If a sudden stretch is applied to a muscle, a reflex action occurs which causes the muscle to contract. This then causes muscle tension to increase, making it more difficult to stretch the connective tissue. Further, with the muscle being stretched and contracted at the same time, the likelihood of injury is reasonably high.
- It has also been found that a quick stretch does not allow time for neurological adaptation to take place when one compares it to a slow stretch. This in itself will be a limiting factor in the improvement of flexibility.

Advantage of ballistic stretching

Some coaches still support ballistic stretching because they maintain that many movements in sport are ballistic in nature. Its supporters suggest that it is specific to sport and provided it is done with caution and the athlete does not overstretch, it can be an effective way to increase flexibility. When the sport has a strong agility component and the development of elastic energy is necessary, there is no reason why a certain number of exercises cannot be ballistic in nature, especially if they are very specific to the sport. However, it is of great importance that the musculature is thoroughly warmed up prior to performing ballistic stretching.

Static stretching

This method involves holding a static position for a period of time after the limb has already been stretched and it has become very popular over the last decade because it is both effective and relatively safe. Simply put, it involves a slow stretch (to inhibit the firing of the stretch reflex) almost to the point of resistance, where it is then held for 20–30 s or even up to 60 s if necessary. During this time the tension partially diminishes (due to the inverse stretch reflex) and the athlete slowly moves into a deeper stretch and repeats the above.

Advantages and disadvantages of static stretching

It is difficult to find any good reason why static stretching should not make up the majority of any worthwhile flexibility programme, despite the fact that some coaches feel that specific ballistic exercises are better for some sports. Currently there is strong support for static stretching among sport scientists and coaches, first because it gives very good results and second because it results in less muscle soreness and injury. Furthermore, slow stretching allows muscle relaxation to occur as a result of the firing of the GTOs, if the stretch is performed over a reasonable time.

Comparison of ballistic and static stretching

De Vries (1962) compared ballistic and static stretching methods and found that each type resulted in significant improvements in flexibility. He also found that neither system was better than the other in terms of the amount of mobility achieved, but stated that static stretching offers three advantages over the ballistic method. These were as follows:

- There is less danger of exceeding the extensibility limits of the tissues involved.
- Energy requirements are lower.
- Although ballistic stretching is apt to cause muscular soreness, static stretching will not; in fact the latter relieves soreness.

Proprioceptive neuromuscular facilitation (PNF)

This method is primarily based on Herman Kabat's (1958) PNF theory which was first adapted for use in physiotherapy, then later in sport. It was hypothesized that an increased ROM was promoted through the principles of successive induction, autogenic inhibition and active mobilization of connective tissues (Holt, 1974). Specifically it was suggested that greater muscle relaxation occurs after a significant contraction of the muscle. This may occur as a result of a reduced discharge of the muscle due to increased GTO activity.

There are many different combinations of PNF stretching and these can be found in Holt (1974), Alter (1988) and McAtee (1993), but the most common technique which is currently used in sport is as follows.

Contract–relax–contract technique

Sometimes known as scientific stretching for sport (3S), this is the most utilized method of the PNF techniques within the sport community and has been used with good results. For each exercise the muscle is initially placed in a lengthened position, then isometrically contracted against the immovable resistance of a partner for 6 s. This is followed by a *very brief* period of relaxation, after which the athlete contracts the appropriate muscle group, placing the body part into a new position. This movement is aided by the partner with *light pressure* which allows for a greater ROM to be achieved than in a static stretch (Figure 6.5a,b). The exercise is then repeated three or four times. It should be noted that a special computer-controlled flexibility system known as Flex.Sys has been recently developed in order to carry out the exercises without the assistance of a partner (Figure 6.6).

Figure 6.5: An elite gymnast using PNF stretching—(a) starting position (b) finishing position.

Figure 6.6: The FLEX.SYS computer controlled flexibility system (courtesy of FLEX.SYS).

Advantages and disadvantages of PNF

The supporters of PNF stretching claim that this technique increases the range of motion in a shorter time than several of the other techniques. This claim has been strongly supported by research performed by Wallin et al. (1985) who reported that PNF stretching techniques increased flexibility to a greater extent than ballistic stretching methods. The second advantage appears to be that there is a *slight* gain in strength at the same time that the ROM is being increased.

However, there are critics of the method who suggest that there is an increased chance of injury if the partner is incompetent and applies too much pressure. If care is taken, however, and the individual assisting the athlete is given clear verbal instructions, this should not occur.

Other techniques

Active stretching

The athlete alone is responsible for the stretching without the assistance of any external force, whether from a partner or from equipment (Figure 6.7). The individual should carry out this method slowly so that the stretch reflex is not initiated. There is no need, when using this method, for the athlete to stay at the full range of the stretch for more than 3 or 4 s.

Figure 6.7: An athlete using active stretching.

Passive stretching

Where athletes in such sports as gymnastics, diving, skating, track and field and swimming need an extreme range of flexibility in certain joints, the passive stretching system is of great value; however, it should be commenced in the pre-adolescent period if this is possible. When using this technique the athlete stays relaxed and makes almost no active contribution to the stretch, which should be done slowly and with care, because if it is carried out jerkily or outside the athlete's normal ROM an injury to a muscle and/or joint could occur. An external force is usually created by a partner (Figure 6.8); however, it can also be with a piece of equipment. The partner method is well known, but the use of equipment has only developed with the variable resistance strength training machines, which can place the muscle on passive stretch, with a slight change in posture near the end of each repetition (Figure 6.9). The advantages of this method are as follows:

- It allows the individual to stretch *well beyond* the active limit.
- It is effective when the agonist (the muscle group responsible for the movement) is too weak to initiate a movement which will move the limb through the full ROM.
- Because this technique is usually carried out in pairs it creates an enjoyable social atmosphere for the participants.

In some situations where athletes are attempting to recover the normal range of movement after a soft tissue injury, or wish to markedly increase their flexibility, *performance massage* (King, 1993) and light mobilization should be used before passive stretching is carried out. Those athletes who have experienced it attest to its definite value. As well, performance massage, in combination with light passive stretching, is also being used after strenuous competition or even heavy work-outs, in order to relax the athlete as well as contributing to his or her flexibility.

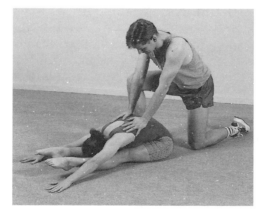

Figure 6.8: An elite gymnast undergoing passive stretching.

Figure 6.9: Passive stretching using a variable resistance machine.

STRETCHING GUIDELINES

During the last decade, informed coaches' attitudes have changed, first with relation to the value of flexibility and second with regard to the way it should be done. The old-fashioned approach was to stretch, often ballistically, to the point of pain and with an inadequate build-up. It is important for coaches to understand that stretching cannot be rushed and that it takes several years of flexibility training for an athlete to become proficient in carrying out these exercises.

As was previously mentioned, flexibility training is now an important part of many sport training regimes. It is also used extensively for the purposes of warming up and warming down. The following sections consist of guidelines which should be adhered to if the full benefits from flexibility training are to be obtained.

Preparation for stretching

The area where the exercises are performed should be reasonably comfortable and warm, and non-restrictive clothing which allows the athlete to stretch with ease should be worn. The individual should be in a relaxed state and warmed up before the exercises commence. At least a mild sweat must be reached before the stretching routine is started, otherwise an injury could occur.

Concentration during the exercises

During a stretching session the athlete must carefully monitor the amount of tension which is developed in the muscles. Each exercise must be commenced in a very relaxed state. Some coaches suggest that athletes visualize themselves in a particular situation which will help them to relax before each exercise. For example, they may be able to imagine themselves lying in a warm saline bath floating easily in a relaxed situation.

Athletes should also become aware of their breathing pattern and a useful technique is to slow down the breathing rate and increase the depth of each breath for the first five or six breaths in each exercise. A steady light pattern should follow the slightly deeper and longer breathing technique for the remainder of each exercise (Bloomfield et al., 1994).

Specificity of the exercises

When stretching to improve the ROM for any skill, the individual should carry out the stretch in the same postural position, the same plane of motion and through the same range of movement as the skill, if all of these are possible. If *ballistic stretching* is performed, then the stretch should be done in a similar way and at 75–80% of the speed of the skill, but *only after the muscle groups involved have first been warmed up and then stretched by the static method*.

Applying stretching principles

In order for the ROM to be improved in any part of the body, various stretching principles must be applied The actual stretching of the muscle group can be done for 20–30 s; however, this can last for up to 60 s if several 'small relaxations' are felt during the stretch. Each time one of these occurs the athlete is then able to stretch a little further. Between *four* to *eight* repetitions can be carried out for each exercise; however, this will depend on the amount of mobility training the athletes have already done during their competitive career.

Furthermore, the number of training sessions per day will be determined by the amount of improvement the athletes wish to make. One session a day, depending on its length, will result in an improvement in flexibility; however, two sessions are needed if any significant improvement is to be made in the short term. One of these is usually done in the morning and the other in the afternoon unless other training arrangements are more suitable. Once the appropriate level of flexibility has been achieved, one intensive training session per week has been shown by Wallin et al. (1985) to be adequate to maintain an established level of flexibility. It should also be mentioned that short warm-up and warm-down stretching sessions are not regarded as flexibility training per se, unless they are carried out for a prolonged period of time. They are in fact done as a preparation for normal training but in some cases, where a high degree of flexibility is not needed in the sport, they will provide athletes with enough stretchability to enable them to relax when needed. It should be emphasized that some athletes like gymnasts, divers, skaters, some swimmers and those competing in the field events will need specific flexibility training sessions, otherwise they will *never* reach the levels required for their sport (Bloomfield et al., 1994).

Intensity of the stretch

It cannot be stressed too often that although stretching exercises will produce a degree of discomfort, they should *not cause pain*. If the muscle vibrates or quivers and pain is present, then the athlete should cut down the force applied or limit the ROM. To force a joint past the point of discomfort will *finally result in an injury*.

Dangers involved in stretching

The notion that 'some stretching is good, so that more stretching is better' can be quite dangerous to the majority of athletes, especially those involved in collision sports and masters or veteran athletes, because excessive stretching can destabilize their joints, causing ligament or joint capsule injury. Athletes who have had a recent bone fracture, inflammation or infection, in or around a joint, a chronic sprain or strain, should be cautious with their programme.

The athlete should also perform stretching exercises in the correct postural position and not place limbs and the accompanying joints out of alignment. When malalignment occurs and the individual puts considerable pressure on the joint, an injury will almost certainly occur. Moreover, there are certain exercises which middle-aged sports people should not do and several of these have been well illustrated by Alter (1990).

SPECIFIC STRETCHING EXERCISES

In previous parts of this chapter a preference for the *static stretching* technique has been mentioned and much of the following section will be devoted to this; however, the PNF (3S) technique will also be described below.

Specific guidelines for static stretching

In this technique the muscle group is held on stretch for a period of 20–30 s, but can be held for 60 s if necessary (Anderson, 1980; Beaulieu, 1981; Alter, 1990) (Figure 6.10). This will basically depend, however, on whether one can utilize the 'small relaxations' which occur during the stretch.

- The *primary* stretch is held for approximately 10 s, after which a *secondary* stretch is made.
- The entire stretch (i.e. both *primary* and *secondary*) will usually take approximately 20–30 s to execute when the technique has been perfected, but could be slightly less or more depending on whether the desired result has been achieved.
- It is very important to hold the *primary* stretch until the inverse stretch reflex occurs and a slight relaxation is felt.
- The *primary* and *secondary* stretches must be done very slowly with no pressure or jerkiness. If this occurs there will be a rebound effect from the stretch reflex and some loss of control during the stretch.

Figure 6.10: An elite gymnast using static stretching.

- At the completion of the stretch the muscle group should be released slowly and under control.
- Approximately *four sets* of each exercise should be done during each work-out, although this may be too many in the early stages of a flexibility training programme. Those athletes wishing to become hyperflexible could increase to *eight sets* after a gradual build-up.
- It is important to keep agonists and antagonists in balance by stretching each group during a workout. The athlete should also keep each side of the body in balance, unless there is a logical reason not to do so.
- There is currently some disagreement as to the order in which the stretching routine should be done. Traditionally exercises have been alternated over the various regions of the body. More recently some sport scientists and coaches have suggested that the athlete should concentrate on one part of the body using several exercises, then move to another, then to another part and so on. There is currently no scientific evidence available which supports one method over the other.
- Flexibility training should be carried out each day in either one or two sessions depending on the sport. There should be *at least* one day off each week.
- It may be of value to use equipment or a partner for support purposes with some exercises. Others can be done quite effectively without them (Bloomfield et al., 1994).

General guidelines for PNF stretching (3S)

In this technique increased flexibility is gained by using an isometric contraction of the muscles to be stretched for 6 s, followed by a concentric contraction of the opposite muscle group, with *light pressure* being applied by the partner. The concentric contraction should last approximately 6–10 s (Figure 6.5).

Each exercise should be repeated *three* or *four* times during each training session and up to *two* training sessions per day can be done. At least *one* day each week should be used for rest and no flexibility training should be carried out.

There is no hard or fast rule with relation to the order of the exercise routine; however, most athletes adopt the alternating regional system.

SPECIFIC EXERCISES

Many books on flexibility show exercise routines which can be done on an individual basis or with a partner. Those shown in Bloomfield et al. (1994) are highly suitable for all the sport stretching programmes which are used in the remainder of this chapter.

FLEXIBILITY AND SPORT PERFORMANCE

Flexible joints and stretched muscles are of great value in the majority of sports. Stretching exercises will assist an athlete in the following ways:

- By increasing the metabolism in muscles, joints and the surrounding connective tissue.
- By increasing both the range and speed of movement around a joint or several joints.
- By promoting general muscle relaxation over the entire body.
- By increasing the elasticity of the musculo-tendinous unit and in so doing facilitating the use of elastic energy.
- By reducing injury due to the tearing of muscle or its musculo-tendinous junction.

The remainder of this section will discuss the type and amount of mobility which is needed for various sport groups and the specific sports and events within them.

Racquet sports (tennis, badminton, squash)

From a movement viewpoint, racquet sports are ballistic in nature, and high levels of flexibility are needed in order for athletes to place themselves into positions where they can hit the ball more powerfully, so as to be able to accelerate the racquet through a greater ROM when executing the shot. Furthermore, they will also be able to produce a greater contractile force, because a stretched muscle stores elastic energy and then releases it when it is shortened. During the last decade, high-level coaches have begun to realize the value of total body stretching, and are now giving more stretching exercises to racquet sports athletes than ever before.

Specific regions of the body to be stretched

Shoulder girdle.   Arm flexion–extension flexibility is an essential capacity of the racquet sports player, as the overhead strokes play an important part in these games.

The following exercises should be carried out to achieve this: tricep stretch, circular shoulder stretch, arm extensor stretch, arm adductor stretch.

Trunk.   Trunk flexion–extension, lateral flexion, and rotation are important movements which are carried out by all racquet sports players. The following exercises should be performed to increase flexibility in the above movements: abdominal and hip stretch, upper back stretch, lower back and hip stretch, rotational trunk stretch, trunk lateral flexor stretch, trunk extensor stretch.

Pelvic girdle and legs.   Any agility athlete must have the thigh, leg and foot flexors and extensors well stretched. The following exercises should be performed to achieve this: groin stretch, hamstring stretch, quadriceps stretch, quadriceps–ankle stretch, calf stretch, Achilles tendon–ankle stretch, thigh extensor stretch, thigh flexor stretch (Bloomfield et al., 1994).

Aquatic sports (swimming, waterpolo, rowing, canoeing)

The mobility needs of *swimmers* and *waterpolo* players are almost identical, while *rowers* and *canoeists* need similar exercises for their shoulder girdles, trunks, pelvis and thighs. Swimmers in particular depend on high levels of flexibility in the shoulder girdle in freestyle and backstroke. This enables them to keep their bodies in a straight line, which cuts down on frontal resistance, and not 'break' at the hips or roll, which is the major retarding factor in the great majority of swimmers. Butterfly swimmers should have even more flexibility in the shoulder girdle than freestyle and backstroke swimmers, as they need to be almost hypermobile. This characteristic enables them to stay very 'flat' in the water, thereby avoiding the frontal resistance and associated wave drag created by excessive 'rise and fall'. If a butterfly swimmer lacks the amount of flexibility needed to perform at the elite level, then a side breathing technique can be used.

Breaststrokers do not need as high a level of shoulder girdle flexibility as swimmers in the other strokes, but a mobile shoulder girdle will assist them to relax in the recovery phase of the stroke cycle. They do, however, need high levels of flexibility in thigh extension and abduction. Finally, all swimmers need above average flexibility in the thigh flexors and extensors, with high levels of plantar and dorsi flexion.

It has already been mentioned that backstrokers can be too flexible in the shoulder and elbow joints and that this can increase frontal resistance. In this situation swimmers must not only modify their technique, but also reduce flexibility levels using strength training exercises. Backstroke swimmers, however, do need high levels of trunk hyperextension, which enable them to have their body enter the 'hole' which has already been opened by the hands and head during the push-off at the start of the race.

Canoeists, particularly those competing in kayaking events, need high levels of flexibility in all the joints, especially in the shoulder girdle, while *oarsmen* must have extensive mobility in the thigh, leg and foot flexors and extensors. It is not essential for oarsmen to have very flexible shoulder girdles, but they should be reasonably mobile in this region as well as the trunk, in order to relax this portion of the body as much as possible during each stroke.

Specific regions of the body to be stretched

Shoulder girdle. For freestylers, butterflyers, backstrokers, waterpolo players and kayakists, the shoulder-girdle region must be well stretched. Oarsmen can also carry out the same exercises but do not need as many of them. The following exercises should be performed to achieve a high level of mobility in this region of the body: tricep stretch, backward stretch, circular shoulder stretch, arm extensor stretch, arm adductor stretch.

Trunk. Swimmers, waterpolo players, canoeists and oarsmen can profit from flexibility exercises which increase trunk flexion–extension, lateral flexion and rotation. The following exercises should be performed for this purpose: abdominal and hip stretch, upper back stretch, lateral trunk stretch, lower back and hip stretch, rotational trunk stretch, trunk extensor stretch.

Pelvic girdle and legs. Swimmers, waterpolo players, oarsmen (and canoeists to a lesser extent), need the thigh, leg and foot flexors and extensors well stretched. The following exercises should be performed to achieve this: groin stretch, hamstring stretch, quadriceps-ankle stretch, calf stretch, ankle stretch, thigh extensor stretch, thigh flexor stretch (Bloomfield et al., 1994).

Gymnastic and power sports (gymnastics, diving, weight-lifting)

Gymnasts and *divers* need the highest level of overall flexibility of any of the sports. It is not possible to attain the aesthetic positions which are needed to gain high marks in the various manoeuvres unless the body is extremely flexible (Figures 6.11 and 6.12). For this reason a wide variety of flexibility exercises need to be carried out and a considerable amount of time spent in mobility training. Furthermore, modern gymnastics and diving have become very ballistic in nature and stretched muscles can produce the contractile force which is needed, because the pre-stretched muscle stores elastic energy which is released as it is shortened. If one asks top-level coaches which are the most important physical capacities for gymnasts and divers to attain, they will state very positively that the development of explosive power and flexibility is essential for elite levels of performance.

When one examines the traditional training routines of *weight-lifters*, high levels of flexibility were not seen to be important. However, Wilson et al. (1992) have recently demonstrated its value with experienced power lifters who improved their bench press performance by 5.4% after an 8-week flexibility training period. The above investigators concluded that the improvement was brought about by the additional elastic energy which had been stored in the musculo-tendinous units as a result of the training programme. Coaches should heed these important findings and strongly consider commencing flexibility training with their weight-lifters. However, because they

Figure 6.11: An aesthetic position achieved by a female rhythmic gymnast.

do not need the flexibility levels necessary for gymnasts and divers, weight-lifters should only carry out the routines which are very specific and which have been designed for those competitors who take part in the contact field sports.

Specific regions of the body to be stretched

Neck, shoulder girdle and forearms.   It is important for gymnasts and divers to keep the neck supple and the shoulder girdle, hands and forearms very

Figure 6.12: The pike position can only be attained if the diver has a high level of thigh flexion.

flexible. The following exercises should be performed to achieve this: neck stretch, backward stretch, overhead stretch, circular shoulder stretch, arm extensor stretch, arm adductor stretch.

Trunk.   In gymnastic sports, high levels of trunk flexion–extension, lateral flexion and rotation are essential. The following exercises should be performed to achieve this: abdominal and hip stretch, back roll stretch, upper back stretch, lower back and hip stretch, rotational trunk stretch, trunk lateral flexor stretch, split pike stretch, trunk extensor stretch.

Pelvic girdle and legs.   All gymnasts and divers must have *very high* levels of flexibility in the thigh, leg and foot flexors and extensors. Extreme thigh flexion is essential if divers are to reach the classic tuck position which is required of them (Figure 6.12). The following exercises should be performed to achieve this: groin stretch, side split stretch, hamstring stretch, split stretch, groin–trunk stretch, quadriceps stretch, quadriceps–ankle stretch, quadriceps–groin stretch, Achilles tendon-ankle stretch, ankle stretch, split pike stretch, trunk extensor stretch, thigh adductor stretch, thigh extensor stretch, hip flexor stretch.

Gymnasts and divers will probably need additional specialized exercises in order to reach the flexibility levels they need in these sports. They should also carry out passive stretching exercises with a skilled partner or with their coach (Bloomfield et al., 1994).

Track, field and cycling

For over 50 years, coaches in *track and field* have traditionally given their athletes intensive stretching. Until 10 years ago most of the exercises were of a ballistic nature, but a gradual change has been made towards the static stretching technique in the majority of countries. Because track and field incorporates a large number of individual events, it is not possible to cover each one of these in detail; however, basic stretching exercises for each sports group will be dealt with.

Running, hurdling and cycling

Good technique in *running*, whether in *sprints* or *middle distance* events, is very dependent on high levels of flexibility. The same statement can also be made for hurdling, only more so, because the trail leg must be almost hyper-mobile in order for the hurdler to stride over the hurdle rather than to jump over it. Furthermore, because sprinting and hurdling are very ballistic, many athletes are prone to soft tissue damage, usually in the form of muscle belly or musculo-tendinous unit tears. It is vitally important for the major muscle groups in the leg to be well stretched and in balance, both from an explosive power and a flexibility viewpoint.

Cycling on the other hand does not have a history of flexibility training when one compares it with the above sports. However, it has been obvious to sport scientists for some time that the heavy thigh musculature of the average-level cyclist needed stretching and this is now being recommended by some of the more enlightened coaches. Not only will flexibility training improve the muscular efficiency of cyclists, but it will assist them to store elastic energy, which is especially important for track cyclists, who need high levels of explosive power.

Specific regions of the body to be stretched

Shoulder girdle. In modern sprint running and hurdling the arms contribute greatly to the propulsive power of the movement. In middle distance running there is some assistance from the arms but they are principally used for balance. Many elite coaches believe that high levels of mobility in the shoulder girdle and trunk assist the athlete to relax during the event and they therefore prescribe stretching exercises for both running and hurdling. This is also true for cycling, and stretching should therefore be carried out by this group. The following exercises should be performed to achieve this: backward stretch, overhead stretch, arm extensor stretch, arm adductor stretch.

Trunk. The trunk of the runner, hurdler and cyclist must also be flexible if high levels of relaxation are to be attained while competing. The following exercises should be performed to achieve this: upper back stretch, lower back and hip stretch, trunk lateral flexor stretch, trunk extensor stretch.

Pelvic girdle and legs. Runners, hurdlers and cyclists must also have very high levels of thigh, leg and foot flexion and extension. The following exercises should be performed to achieve these levels: hamstring stretch, quadriceps stretch, quadriceps–groin stretch, calf stretch, Achilles tendon–ankle stretch, trunk extensor stretch, thigh extensor stretch. The exercises listed below are for hurdlers only: groin stretch, side split stretch, split stretch, groin–trunk stretch, split pike stretch, thigh adductor stretch.

Field sports (jumps)

Athletes involved in jumping events need a *very high* level of flexibility in all regions of the body in order to perform the jumps well.

Specific regions of the body to be stretched

Neck and shoulder girdle. The following exercises should be performed to attain a high level of flexibility in this region: neck stretch, tricep stretch, backward stretch, overhead stretch, arm adductor stretch.

Trunk. The exercises listed below will assist the jumper to attain high levels of flexibility in trunk flexion–extension, lateral flexion and trunk rotation. The following exercises should be performed to achieve these levels: abdominal and hip stretch, upper back stretch, lower back and hip stretch, rotational trunk stretch, trunk lateral flexor stretch, trunk extensor stretch.

Pelvic girdle and legs.   High levels of flexibility are essential in the thigh, leg and foot flexors and extensors for the jumps. The following exercises should be performed to achieve this: groin stretch, hamstring stretch, quadriceps stretch, quadriceps–ankle stretch, quadriceps–groin stretch, calf stretch, ankle stretch, thigh extensor stretch, thigh flexor stretch.

Field sports (throwing events)

As for the jumps, field athletes need high levels of flexibility in all regions of the body.

Specific regions of the body to be stretched

Neck, shoulder girdle and forearms.   Because an extensive range of movement and elastic energy is needed for any good throw, the neck, forearms and the shoulder girdle in particular need to be well stretched. The following exercises should be performed to achieve this: neck stretch, tricep stretch, backward stretch, circular shoulder stretch, hand–forearm stretch, arm extensor stretch, arm adductor stretch.

Trunk.   Because the trunk is an essential part of any ballistic throwing movement, it must be extremely flexible. The following exercises should be performed to achieve this: abdominal and hip stretch, upper back stretch, lower back and hip stretch, rotational trunk stretch, trunk lateral flexor stretch, trunk extensor stretch.

Pelvic girdle and legs.   High levels of flexibility in this region are important for throwers because they are relying on leg power in the initial part of the throw. In order to achieve this, the thigh, leg and foot flexors and extensors must be well stretched. The following exercises should be performed to increase mobility levels in this region of the body: groin stretch, hamstring stretch, quadriceps–groin stretch, Achilles tendon–ankle stretch, ankle stretch, thigh adductor stretch, thigh extensor stretch, thigh flexor stretch (Bloomfield et al., 1994).

Mobile field sports (field hockey, soccer, lacrosse)

In this group of sports, body contact occurs, but it is not as severe as in the contact field sports where whole body tackling, to impede the opponent's progress, is an important feature of the game. Athletes in the mobile field sports need an above average level of flexibility, but do not need to be excessively flexible in any specific region of the body. Like other agility athletes, all players in this group should understand that high levels of flexibility will enable them to accelerate their stick or leg through a greater range of movement, as well as being able to store elastic energy in their propulsive muscles. These two features will enable them to apply more force to the ball as they hit, throw or kick it.

Specific regions of the body to be stretched

Neck, shoulder girdle and forearms.   Movements of flexion and rotation of the neck, as well as flexion–extension of the arm and flexion of the hand are important. The following exercises will assist the athlete to attain this: neck stretch, overhead stretch, circular shoulder stretch, hand–forearm stretch, arm extensor stretch.

Trunk.   Because the trunk is constantly moving during a game, flexion–extension, lateral flexion and rotation are important movements carried out by all players. The following exercises should be performed to reach the level of flexibility needed by this group: abdominal and hip stretch, back roll stretch, upper back stretch, lateral trunk stretch, lower back and hip stretch, trunk extensor stretch.

Pelvic girdle and legs.   All agility athletes must have thigh, leg and foot flexors–extensors well stretched. To achieve this the following exercises should be carried out: groin stretch, hamstring stretch, quadriceps stretch, calf stretch, ankle stretch, thigh extensor stretch, thigh flexor stretch (Bloomfield et al., 1994).

Contact field sports (rugby, Australian and American football)

Players in these sports need strong joint capsules and musculature around the shoulder, knee and ankle joints so that these joints are not dislocated or easily injured. In the above regions they should have normal levels of flexibility; however, the abductors of the thigh, hamstrings, quadriceps and calf groups should be well stretched and in balance in order to avoid soft tissue injuries. The contact athlete must also be careful not to overstretch the knee or ankle joints with additional activities such as intensive freestyle kicking, which can cause cruciate ligament and knee instability in these joints.

Specific regions of the body to be stretched

Shoulder girdle and trunk.   The following exercises should be carried out for these regions but high levels of flexibility should not be striven for:

backward stretch, overhead stretch, abdominal and hip stretch, back roll stretch, upper back stretch, lower back and hip stretch.

Pelvic girdle and legs.   The following exercises will enable the adductors of the thigh, hamstrings, quadriceps and the calf groups to be stretched: groin stretch, hamstring stretch, quadriceps stretch, quadriceps–groin stretch, calf stretch, thigh extensor stretch, thigh flexor stretch (Bloomfield et al., 1994).

Set field sports (golf, baseball, cricket)

In these ballistic sports high levels of mobility are of great value, first because the storage of elastic energy which takes place in the well-stretched muscle will enable the player to hit, throw or bowl with a powerful action, but also because the player will be able to deliver the club, bat or ball in a pitch or throw through a greater ROM. The combination of these two phenomena will enable the individual to perform the skills of these games with considerable explosive power.

Specific regions of the body to be stretched

Shoulder girdle, trunk and forearms.   All the games in this group require very high levels of arm flexion–extension, trunk flexion–extension, lateral flexion and trunk rotation as well as extension of the hands. The following exercises should be performed to achieve this: backward stretch, overhead stretch, circular shoulder stretch, hand–forearm stretch, upper back stretch, lateral trunk stretch, lower back and hip stretch, rotational trunk stretch, arm extensor stretch, trunk extensor stretch.

Pelvic girdle and legs.   Because the thigh and legs are used in the performance of almost all of the skills in the sports in this group, high levels of flexibility are also necessary in thigh, leg and foot flexion–extension. The following exercises should be performed to achieve this: groin stretch, hamstring stretch, quadriceps stretch, quadriceps–groin stretch, calf stretch, Achilles tendon–ankle stretch, ankle stretch, thigh extensor stretch, thigh flexor stretch (Bloomfield et al., 1994).

Court sports (basketball, netball, volleyball)

Because these sports are highly ballistic, ROM and the storage of elastic energy are very important. As well one needs to be concerned with the prevention of injuries to athletes in this group and 'long' stretched muscles will not be injured as readily as those which are 'bunched' and tight.

Specific regions of the body to be stretched

Shoulder girdle.   Arm flexion–extension mobility is an important capacity for athletes in this group. The following exercises should be carried out to achieve this: overhead stretch, circular shoulder stretch, arm extensor stretch, arm adductor stretch.

Trunk.   The court sports player when leaping often twists while in the air and as a result needs not only a high degree of trunk flexion–extension, but also lateral flexion and trunk rotation mobility. The following exercises should be performed to increase flexibility in the above movements: abdominal and hip stretch, upper back stretch, lower back and hip stretch, rotational trunk stretch, trunk lateral flexor stretch, trunk extensor stretch.

Pelvic girdle and legs.   All agility athletes must have the thigh, leg and foot flexors and extensors well stretched. The following exercises should be performed to achieve this: groin stretch, hamstring stretch, quadriceps stretch, quadriceps–ankle stretch, calf stretch, Achilles tendon–ankle stretch, thigh extensor stretch, thigh flexor stretch (Bloomfield et al., 1994).

Martial arts (wrestling, judo, punching and kicking sports)

Combatants in many of the martial arts in the past have not been very flexible; however, the last decade has seen a very definite change to this training policy. There is now an understanding of the concept of the storage of elastic energy and the realization that serious injuries can be sustained in the grappling sports if the individual does not have a flexibility level well above average, especially in the upper body. Furthermore a supple wrestler or judoist is sometimes able to escape from a hold by 'slipping' out of it; however, high levels of strength and explosive power must accompany this mobility.

Specific regions of the body to be stretched

Neck, shoulder girdle and trunk.   All martial arts combatants require high levels of arm flexion–extension, trunk flexion–extension, lateral flexion and rotation. The following exercises should be performed to increase flexibility in the above movements: neck stretch, tricep stretch, backward stretch, overhead stretch, abdominal and hip stretch, back roll stretch, upper back stretch, lateral trunk stretch, lower back and hip stretch, rotational trunk stretch.

Pelvic girdle and legs.   Even though the legs only play a supporting role in the majority of the martial arts, participants should have high levels of thigh

Figure 6.13: A gymnast performing a highly specialized exercise.

and leg flexion and extension mobility. The following exercises should be performed to achieve this: groin stretch, hamstring stretch, quadriceps stretch, quadriceps–ankle stretch, calf stretch, thigh extensor stretch, thigh flexor stretch. The exercises listed below are for participants in the kicking sports only: thigh extensor stretch and thigh flexor stretch (Bloomfield et al., 1994).

ADDITIONAL SPECIALIZED EXERCISES

Where highly specialized exercises are required for elite level performers (Figure 6.13) such as gymnasts, divers and track and field athletes, the reader should consult texts which contain such exercises.

CONCLUSIONS

In conclusion, it should be pointed out that over the last two decades, high levels of flexibility have gradually become *very important* to the majority of athletes, who cannot compete at a high level without them. The three main reasons for increasing the range of flexibility are as follows. First the highly flexible performers are able to place themselves into a more technically correct position in most sports. Where the sport is judged, the competitors are not only expected to be technically correct but are also required to reach certain set positions in order to score high artistic marks. The second reason is that when an athlete wants to increase the ROM in a skill, the potential to produce more force or velocity becomes possible and this is an important factor in many hitting, throwing or kicking sports. Finally, observant coaches have noted for some time that a stretched muscle can produce a greater contractile force than a non-stretched one. This theory has been recently supported by research, which has demonstrated that flexibility training increases the elasticity of the musculo-tendinous unit and in so doing increases the utilization of elastic energy in the stretch–shorten cycle movement. This finding has very important implications for athletes competing in sports where explosive power is required.

REFERENCES

Alexander, R. (1987) The spring in your step, *New Scientist*, **114**, 42–44.

Alter, M. (1988) *Science of Stretching*, pp. 7–91. Human Kinetics Books, Champaign, IL.

Alter, M. (1990) *Sport Stretch*, pp. 6–18. Leisure Press, Champaign, IL.

Anderson, B. (1980) *Stretching*, pp. 12–98. Shelter Publications, Bolinas.

Asmussen, E., Bonde-Petersen, F. and Jorgensen, K. (1976) Mechano-elastic properties of human muscles at different temperatures, *Acta Physiology Scandinavia*, **96**, 83–93.

Beaulieu, J. (1981) Developing a stretching program, *The Physician and Sportsmedicine*, **9**, 11, 59–69.

Bloomfield, J., Ackland, T. and Elliott, B. (1994) *Applied Anatomy and Biomechanics in Sport*, Blackwell Scientific Publications, Melbourne.

Bloomfield, J., Fricker, P., and Fitch, K. (1995) *Science and Medicine in Sport*, pp. 2–31. Blackwell Scientific, Melbourne.

Ciullo, J. and Zarins, B. (1983) Biomechanics of the musculotendinous unit, in *Clinics In Sports Medicine*, Vol. 2. (Ed. B. Zarins) pp. 71–85. W.B. Saunders, Philadelphia.

Corbin, C. and Noble, L. (1980) Flexibility: A major component of physical fitness, *The Journal of Physical Education and Recreation*, **51**, 23–4, 57–60.

Cureton, T. (1951) *Physical Fitness of Champion Athletes*, pp. 84–93. The University of Illinois Press, Urbana, IL.

de Vries, H. (1962) Evaluation of static stretching procedures for improvement of flexibility, *Research Quarterly*, **33**, 222–228.

de Vries, H. (1986) *Physiology of Exercise—For Physical Education and Athletics*, pp. 462–488. Wm C. Brown Publishers, Dubuque.

Holt, L. (1974) *Scientific Stretching for Sport (3-S)*, pp. 1–8, 12–31. Sport Research Ltd, Halifax.

Jobe, F.W. and Moynes, D.R. (1986) *Thirty Exercises for Better Golf*, Champion Press, Inglewood, CA.

Kabat, H. (1958) Proprioceptive Facilitation in Therapeutic Exercise, in *Therapeutic Exercise* (Ed. S. Litcht) E. Licht, New Haven.

King, R. (1993) *Performance Massage*, pp. 23–40. Human Kinetics Publications, Champaign, IL.

Kiputh, R. (1942) *Swimming*, pp. 38–55. The Ronald Press, New York.

Kirchner, G. and Glines, D. (1957) Comparative analysis of Eugene, Oregon, elementary school children using the Kraus–Weber test of minimum muscular fitness, *Research Quarterly*, **28**, 16–25.

Kretzler, Jr. H. and Richardson, A. (1989) Rupture of the pectoralis major muscle, *American Journal of Sports Medicine*, **17**, 435–458.

Leard, J. (1984) Flexibility and conditioning in the young athlete, in *Pediatric and Adolescent Sports Medicine* (Ed. L. Micheli) p. 198. Little, Brown, Boston.

McAtee, R. (1993) *Facilitated Stretching*, pp. 13–92. Human Kinetics, Champaign, IL.

Marey, M. and Demeny, M. (1885) Locomotion humaine, mécanisme du saut, *Comptes Rendus Hebdomadaires des Scéances de l'Academie des Sciences (Paris)*, **101**, 489–494.

Moynes, D. (1983) Prevention of injury to the shoulder through exercises and therapy, *Clinics in Sports Medicine*, **2**, 413–422.

Phillips, M. (1955) Analysis of results from the Kraus–Weber test of minimum muscular fitness in children, *Research Quarterly*, **26**, 314–323.

Pousson, M., van Hoecke, J. and Goubel, F. (1990) Changes in elastic characteristics of human muscle induced by eccentric exercise, *Journal of Biomechanics*, **23**, 343–348.

Safran, M., Garrett, W., Seaber, A., Glisson, R. and Ribbeck, B. (1988) The role of warmup in muscular injury prevention, *The American Journal of Sports Medicine*, **16**, 123–129.

Shellock, F. and Prentice, W. (1985) Warming-up and stretching for improved performance and prevention of sports-related injuries, *Sports Medicine*, **2**, 267–278.

Sigerseth, P. (1971) Flexibility, in *Encyclopedia of Sports Sciences and Medicine* (Ed. L. Larson), pp. 280–282. Macmillan, New York.

Tanner, J. (1963) *Growth at Adolescence*, pp. 10–15. Blackwell Scientific, Oxford.

Wallin, D., Ekblom, B., Grahn, R. and Nordenborg, T. (1985) Improvement of muscle flexibility, *The American Journal of Sports Medicine*, **13**, 263–268.

Watson, A. (1992) Children in sport, in *Textbook of Science and Medicine in Sport*, (Eds. J. Bloomfield, P. Fricker and K. Fitch), pp. 436–466. Blackwell Scientific, Melbourne.

Wilson, G., Elliott, B. and Wood, G. (1991a) The effect on performance of imposing a delay during a stretch-shorten cycle movement, *Medicine and Science in Sports and Exercise*, **23**, 364–370.

Wilson, G., Wood, G. and Elliott, B. (1991b) Optimal stiffness of the series elastic component in a stretch shorten cycle activity, *Journal of Applied Physiology*, **70**, 825–833.

Wilson, G.J., Wood, G. A. and Elliott, B.C. (1991c) The relationship between stiffness of the musculature and static flexibility: An alternative explanation for the occurrence of muscular injury, *International Journal of Sports Medicine*, **12**, 403–407.

Wilson, G., Elliott, B. and Wood, G. (1992) Stretch shorten cycle performance enhancement through flexibility training, *Medicine and Science in Sports and Exercise*, **24**, 116–123.

$\boxed{7}$

SPEED TRAINING IN SPORT

N. Stein

German Sport University Cologne

INTRODUCTION

Speed is one of the most important performance requirements in sport. However, it should never be viewed as an isolated characteristic. It must be considered as a partial component of the complex requirements needed for sport performance. In combination with a high standard of movement technique and coordination, sport-specific in general or discipline-specific forms of the complex characteristic 'speed' are of major importance to success in individual or team sports.

The importance of speed to performance varies considerably depending upon the sport discipline and the field of application. For example, it is relatively unimportant in fitness and health-based sports when compared to factors such as endurance, strength and movement characteristics. General leisure sports, however, do require at least a fundamental level of certain forms of speed such as reactive speed. The importance of speed in elite sports cannot be universally assessed because the speed demands are determined by the requirements of the specific sport or discipline.

In the future we can expect a continued increase in the dynamic aspects of performance in most sports despite a simultaneously increasing requirement for performance quantity. This makes the qualitative improvement of speed capabilities particularly important. In sports such as athletics in which the primary aim is either time minimization or speed maximization over relatively short distances, or distance or height maximization in jumps and throws, better performances are influenced by speed. Optimum reactions and the ability to execute motor actions at high speeds are also dominant in

Training in Sport: Applying Sport Science. Edited by B. Elliott
© 1998 John Wiley & Sons Ltd

contact sports. Speed is also very important in many technical sports, especially in the execution of highly dynamic movement elements and combinations.

Speed in performance is also receiving increasing recognition alongside other athletic prerequisites in sport games. In this case it is important to recognize the game situation as quickly as possible and to rapidly execute your own manoeuvre in correspondence to the opponent's actions. Speed characteristics are very important even in many endurance sports, especially in terms of sub-distance performance.

SPEED AS A MOTOR PHENOMENON

Structural approaches to speed

Knowledge concerning the specific performance structure of certain sports or sport disciplines is required for planned and effective training. All the possible components of sport performance have been sufficiently discussed in the literature, however, the description of an 'internal' structure, as seen in the fields of strength or endurance, is distinctly lacking with respect to speed. Discussions of the 'motor programme' and general structure associated with speed are often contradictory and usually too superficial. If disagreements exist in the determination of the structure of individual components within sport performance then it's difficult for the overall character to be determined. Effective teaching of sports, therefore, remains partially a game of chance. If one considers that an increase in training volume is hardly possible in elite sports and an increase in performance can therefore only be achieved through training effectiveness, then there is a pronounced necessity for careful investigation of the nature of speed. Precise speed training can therefore open developmental reserves at all performance levels.

As mentioned previously there are already many different approaches and terms concerning the structuring of speed described in the literature. These have been largely influenced by the associated fundamental structural understanding or by the terminology used in training practice. This has resulted in more than 50 descriptions related to speed (Bauersfeld, 1983; Bös and Mechling, 1983). Systemizing models were originally derived from the track sprint (e.g., Klemm, 1930; Osolin, 1954) or based upon a division of relatively independent speed factors (e.g., Simkin, 1960; Zaciorskij, 1971). Recently speed characteristics have been more likely to be assigned higher elementary and complex criteria (e.g., Platonov, 1987; Grosser, 1991; Schnabel et al., 1994). A number of practically oriented and sometimes very generalized hierocratic systemization models are also evident in the literature (e.g., Harre, 1986; Letzelter, 1978).

The following components or forms of speed are mentioned by Bauersfeld and Voss (1992, p. 13) in an attempted classification system:

- reactive speed;
- active speed;
- locomotor speed;
- endurance speed;
- action speed.

Reactive speed relates to all forms of movement as it is the ability to react to a stimulus in the shortest possible time. Active speed only occurs together with non-cyclic speed requirements. Locomotor speed and endurance speed are related only to cyclic movements. They refer to speed primarily of performance rather than at a structural level. Action speed refers to an action-oriented determination of speed for certain sports or groups of sports. It is detached from the purely motor aspect and places greater emphasis on spatial and temporal factors dealing with subjective action requirements. In this case an important role is played by psychological factors such as perception, decision-making, emotions and motivation (Polster, 1987).

The integration of speed into the complex system of sport performance, which is represented by equally diverse terms, does not always occur in a standardized manner. Associations can be made either with coordination, with the fitness–coordination field or to the fitness–energetic field. Historically speed classification has been based upon the fitness characteristics of strength, endurance and speed localized at the functional level as it relates to these characteristics. It is scientifically proven that endurance, apart from its dependence upon metabolic processes is determined predominantly by the cardiovascular system and strength by the muscular system. For speed this role is assumed by the nervous system.

During training, speed is traditionally associated with fitness by most practitioners. This originally occurred for functional reasons. However, this implies not only a purely formal association but far more seriously the determination of the training means and methods. The teaching of fitness performance requirements in applied measures is different in principle to that of coordination performance requirements (Bauersfeld and Voss, 1992).

Therefore, even today speed training is conducted mainly on the basis of controlled fitness, that is primarily energetically determined performance requirements. A good example of this is the relationship between load and recovery in sprint-specific speed training, which is oriented mainly upon the time necessary to refill the energy store or even on the normalization of the pulse. Similarly, the optimum loading time in cyclic speed training, is often determined from the perspective of anaerobic alactic energy availability. However, if one is of the opinion that speed is primarily dependent upon coordination, then such methods are almost counterproductive.

If the question concerning the requirements for effective speed training is to be seriously answered then it is essential to initially consider various approaches to the structure of speed. While discussing this topic it will be mentioned that sport science and sport practice have conflicting ideas on this point. Sport science is concerned with explaining the structure of speed, however, it has not made much progress and sport practice is under pressure to succeed and can therefore, not wait for suggestions on training methods. As these are often missing, sport practice is frequently dependent upon coaching experience.

Speed as a fitness-energetic capability

This traditional approach is frequently seen in the sport medicine literature. If one observes the possible spectrum from a single speed strength contraction to maximum speed endurance, which may be up to 40 seconds long depending upon the definition used, then it is evident that speed performances are purely anaerobic loads. The alactic and lactic metabolic capacities are of equal importance because during a maximal loading time of 10–11 seconds such as in track sprinting, the individual lactate values may be as high as 17 mmol/l blood.

If one assumes that the decisive factor in speed performance is the metabolic turnover of energy per unit time, then the adenosine triphosophate (ATP) concentration within the muscle cell is the relevant parameter. Theoretically this supply (ATP concentration never sinks below 40% of its initial value; Hollmann and Hettinger, 1980) would be exhausted after about three maximum muscle contractions (1–2 seconds of work). The yield of this energy-rich phosphate resulting from immediate ATP resynthesis from decomposing creatine phosphate (Lohmann reaction) which is three to four times more abundant in the muscle cell than ATP, would permit maximal muscle work for 6–8 seconds (anaerobic–alactic metabolism). The energy requirements of a 100 metre sprint would therefore, not be satisfied. A high-energy flow rate can be extended for 20–30 seconds through an anaerobic lactate strategy, i.e. by splitting muscle glycogen into lactate. This permits an extended period of maximum intensity work. The temporal limit of work performed at maximum intensity, therefore, lies at 30 seconds.

Speed training based upon energetic factors would thus address an increased concentration of energy-rich phosphate, especially creatine phosphate and muscle glycogen, an increased phosphorylase activity, an improved stock and increased activity of glycolitic enzymes and a faster release of ATP.

Speed as a primarily neuromuscular capability

The approach presented here regards speed in sport as the capability to achieve the greatest possible reaction speed and movement speed through functions of the neuromuscular system combined with cognitive processes and maximum will-power. Apart from movement technique, the important parameters also include the resistance to be overcome, individual conditions and external influences. Speed is thus described as a complex psycho-physical capability (Grosser, 1991).

The classification of speed outlined in Figure 7.1 was structured in a phenomenological manner for the 'pure' or 'elementary speed' forms and in a theoretical manner, based upon experience of the 'complex' forms. The latter are forms of pure speed combined with strength and/or endurance. These will be described together with the differentiation between speed, strength and endurance capabilities after the discussion on 'pure' forms of speed.

- *'Pure' (elementary) forms of speed.*
  —*Reactive speed.* Describes the ability to react with a movement in the shortest possible time following a stimulus or information. The measur-

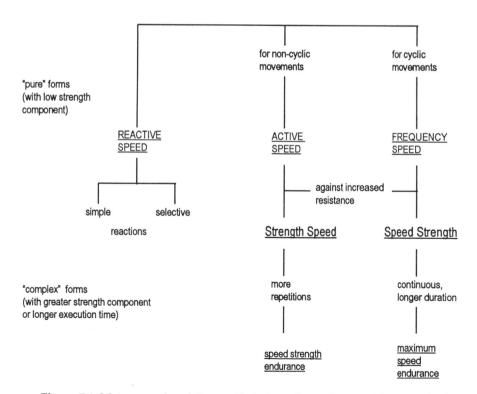

Figure 7.1: Motor speed and its manifestations (from Grosser, 1991, p. 17).

able reaction time is regarded as an indicator of the development of reactive speed. A division is made between simple reactions (e.g., swim start) and decision reactions (e.g., fencing or goal-keeping reactions). The performance relevant influencing factors identified for reactive speed (cf. Table 7.1) indicate the close association to action speed. A factor analytic investigation (Smirnov, 1974) showed no significant connection between reactive speed and other subcategories of speed.

—*Active speed.* This speed is characterized by the ability to execute non-cyclic movements at high speed against low external resistance (table tennis stroke, badminton stroke). If more than 30% maximum strength must be employed then it is defined as speed strength. Aspects of speed strength endurance become important in 'frequent repetitions of non-cyclic movements'. Highly developed movement technique is an essential requirement for a maximally developed active speed.

—*Frequency speed.* This relates to the same, repeated (cyclic) movement executed at the highest speed against low resistance (e.g., tapping, flying sprints, bicycle sprint). Frequency speed is closely related to movement rhythm.

Cyclic and non-cyclic forms of speed can appear in diverse forms and in elementary basic speed patterns. This is shown by the requirements

Table 7.1: Forms of speed and possible influencing factors (Grosser, 1991, p. 69)

Influencing Factors	Forms of speed					
	Reactive speed	Active speed	Frequency speed	Speed strength	Speed strength endurance	Maximal speed endurance
Talent	x	xx	xxx	xx	x	x
Sport Technique	xxx	xxx	xxx	xxx	xxx	xxx
Concentration	xxx	xxx	xxx	xxx	xxx	xxx
Anticipation	xxx	xxx		xx	xx	
Neural Activation	xx	xxx	xxx	xxx	xx	xx
Maximal Strength				xxx	xx	xx
FT-Fibers	xxx	xxx	xxx	xxx	xxx	xxx
Other Fibers			x	xx	xxx	xxx
Stiffness		xx	xxx	xxx	xxx	xxx
Anaerobic-lactic Energy stores					xxx	xxx
Anaerobic Energy stores					xx	xx

for maximum running speed in the track sprint. The cyclic portion, the step frequency, is a complex, sprint-specific manifestation of speed and the foot-tapping frequency is an elementary neuromuscular movement pattern. The non-cyclic portion is composed of the stance time which can again be regarded as a complex, sprint-specific form of speed and the ground contact time following deep jumps which depends upon individual elementary movement patterns and temporal programmes. The various forms of 'pure speed' can, therefore, also be described as discipline-specific real forms, and the elementary neuro-muscular programmes as the basic form which rarely occurs in sport practice.

'*Complex*' *forms of speed*. These forms of speed belong to the border regions between speed and endurance or speed and strength. The possibilities of developing them through training are far less restricted than for the pure forms of speed (Werchoshanskji, 1988).

—*Speed strength.* Describes the ability to produce the maximum possible impulse against a resistance in a defined time (e.g., maximal acceleration).

—*Speed strength endurance.* Describes resistance to a fatigue-related decrease in speed during maximum contraction velocities in non-cyclic movements with increased external resistance. This plays an especially important role in sport games.

—*Speed endurance* (maximal). Refers to a fatigue-related decrease in speed during maximum cyclic movements. The energy supply is predominantly anaerobic-lactic. Despite the high rate of lactate build up, this is defined as a form of speed because neural speed factors basically have a greater influence than endurance characteristics (Grosser, 1991). It is very important in the short sprint.

The relevant distinctions to pure strength and endurance capabilities are based upon three factors. The first factor is speed as the movements must be executed at the highest possible velocities. The second factor is percentage strength input which must be less than 30% of the present maximum strength and the final factor is energetic fatigue; at least externally there is to be no detectable decrease in movement velocity. Difficulties occur especially in the differentiation between speed and strength because of the mutual performance requirement of 'inter- and intramuscular coordination' which again indicates structural inaccuracies that prevent a sufficiently sharp distinction.

Motor speed is dependent upon many influential factors. However, the extent of their influence and their interaction is not fully clear at this stage. Figure 7.2 is a systemized representation of these factors.

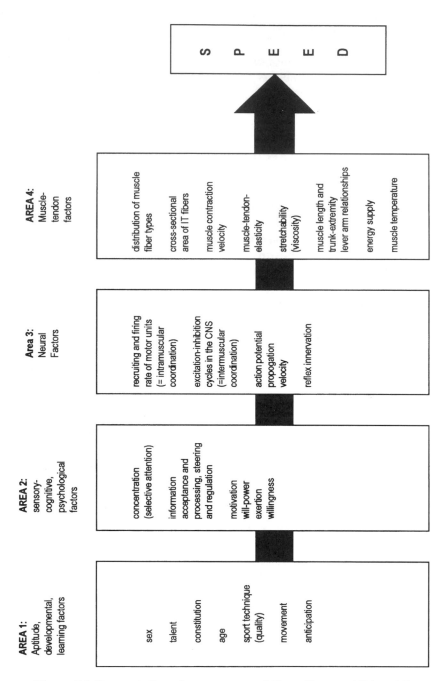

Figure 7.2: Factors influencing motor speed (from Grosser, 1991, p. 21).

Area 1: Aptitude and development factors

(1) An ideal trunk–leg relationship, psychological stability and a feeling for rhythm belong to the general characteristics of speed training. An above-average proportion of fast-twitch (FT) fibres, a good reactive speed and a strong will-power are special characteristics.

(2) The 'age' factor is especially important for the trainability of different influencing factors. It permits the determination of various sensitive phases, such as periods of particular trainability based upon the stage of biological development. An optimal trainability of reactive and frequency capabilities and optimal prerequisites for movement learning are seen between the ages of 10 and 12 years. This is due to a high plasticity of the central nervous system and a high excitability of the nervous steering ability at a stage when the differentiation inhibition is still low.

   The increase in muscle mass resulting from naturally increasing levels of testosterone or oestrogen during puberty (boys 13–17 years, girls 11–15 years) leads to an improved trainability of the strength components of speed. Initially the training of speed strength should be against low resistance; the maximum strength necessary for speed performances against greater resistance should not be given preference until later.

   As it is presently accepted that the percentage distribution of FT and slow-twitch (ST) fibres is not complete until the beginning of puberty, it appears logical to sacrifice premature endurance training in favour of developing speed. This is also important for the maintenance of developmental potential in endurance sports because special speed characteristics decide between victory and defeat at international levels.

(3) Speed is never an isolated capability, it is only one component of sport performance. An optimal application is not possible without a high technical standard (or action precision). Intermuscular coordination plays an important role. Special attention should be paid to technical schooling at this stage because there is an inversely proportional relationship between speed and action precision in beginners (Schellenberger, 1986).

(4) Anticipation is the psychological precognition of situations and actions. It permits a choice of set movement programmes and therefore a reduced reaction time in both simple and multiple reactions. This is where experience and control of the sensory cognitive areas play a deciding role. Anticipation belongs predominantly to action speed and is decisive in its application.

Area 2: Sensory-cognitive, psychological factors

(1) A good ability to concentrate in terms of a conscious control of attention and a strong will-power permitting the steering of psycho-regulatory

processes belong to the psychological foundations of speed. The ability to 'concentrate on the point' plays a decisive role in speed performances.

Area 3: Neural factors

(1) Intermuscular coordination is a prerequisite for the interaction of muscles and muscle groups active during a movement which also includes antagonist coordination. The neural capacity to produce a rapid succession of excitatory and inhibitory states and a simultaneous high-quality coordination is highly dependent upon the circuitry of spinal motor reflexes.

One of these reflexes is the stretch reflex which originates in the muscle spindle (the muscle length detector) and produces a muscle contraction after the muscle has been stretched. It can also result in a self-inhibition through the tendon spindle (Golgi tendon organ) following a strong muscle contraction. Further reflexes that must be harmonized for intermuscular coordination are the antagonist inhibition and antagonist excitation reflexes. The antagonist inhibition reflex also originates from the muscle spindle and results in relaxation of the antagonists whereas the antagonist excitation reflex originates from a reflectory circuitry of the tendon spindle, muscle spindle and further sensitive organs located peripherally and results in one extremity extending and the other flexing.

The vestibulo-cerebral system, the extra-pyramidal system and the pyramidal system must also be briefly mentioned here. The vestibulo-cerebral system produces modifications in muscle tension following variations in perceived balance, the extra-pyramidal system is responsible for the spatial and temporal control of automatic movements and the pyramidal system is responsible for steering arbitrary motor control and can be identified in movement programming.

These five motor-sensory functional systems are also termed the 'flexibility of the neural processes'. It is important to note for training practice that the potential for conducting motor-sensory corrections during high intensity movements is limited.

(2) Intramuscular coordination describes the recruitment and firing rate as regulating mechanisms of strength development (cf. chapter 5 on 'Strength training'). Recruiting is defined as the neural activation of muscle fibres. It follows a certain, set recruiting principle (based upon Hennemann et al., 1965). At low force levels relatively many small, slow motor units with low action potential thresholds are activated (ST fibres) and these permit a fine modulation of force development. During increasing contraction larger motor units with higher action potential thresholds are activated (FT fibres) which produce a greater relative force increase (Dietz, 1985). If as many motor units can be activated

(recruited) as rapidly as possible at the beginning of a movement then correspondingly high forces can be produced.

Firing rate refers to the depolarization frequency of the recruited motor units. This can also contribute to greater force being produced if the depolarization frequency of primarily the smaller motor units increases thus resulting in a greater force contribution. This also increases the total contraction velocity of the muscle (Dietz, 1985).

The importance of speed strength training to speed is therefore, obvious.

(3) Preactivation is especially important for running speed. During running increased gastrocnemius muscle activity can already be detected before foot strike. This can be interpreted as a protective mechanism but it also serves to provide advantageous conditions for force development at push-off. This is because most alpha-motor neurons are already activated or brought close to their depolarization threshold to improve the prerequisites for reflectory activity.

Area 4: Muscle-tendon factors

Muscle-tendon factors are here defined as the importance of the muscle–tendon structure or activity to speed performance.

(1) The development of force in muscles is morphologically dependent upon muscle fibre arrangement and muscle fibre type. Muscle fibre arrangement can be either fusiform or pennate. The latter can produce greater forces due to the greater physiological cross-sectional area. Pennate muscles can shorten more in the direction of pull and are therefore important for the range of motion of a joint. Muscle fibres are divided into 'white', thick FT fibres, 'red', thin ST fibres and mixed fibres. FT fibres are essential for speed-strength performance. The muscle fibre profile is determined both genetically and through environmental or training influences (Komi, 1989). Indisputable evidence is at present not available concerning the transformation of muscle fibres through training. It appears more likely that FT fibres may be transformed into ST fibres than vice versa.

(2) The elasticity and reactive tension ability of the muscle-tendon system are mainly responsible for the movement velocity of the stretch-shortening cycle, i.e. during reactive movements. A fast combination (<200 ms) of eccentric and concentric phases can lead to the storage of energy in the elastic components of the muscle–tendon system. This energy is then available for the concentric phase. In addition to this an increased reflectory activity occurs with initial stretching of the muscle–tendon system (e.g., of the gastrocnemius at foot strike) and in a trained athlete this leads to a tension level well exceeding a maximal voluntary contraction (MVC).

A special aspect is addressed by the following terms. 'Tension production dependent upon opposing forces' describes the fundamental principle that a muscle can only produce as much force as is opposing it through internal muscle resistance or external resistance. The 'inertial force dissipation effect' provides a movement velocity to an accelerating body through the delayed release of muscle force from elastic storage. *This results* in the body temporarily avoiding muscle forces due to its inertial properties (Lehnertz, 1987). These ideas explain it is more important in many movements that are to be executed as rapidly as possible to coordinate the kinematic chain so that the last segment of the chain (e.g., projectile or racquet head) achieves a maximum release or impact velocity. This can also be referred to as the coordination of partial impulses.

(3) A further important aspect of speed performances is associated with the term 'muscular imbalance'. This term, which originates from a health perspective, describes the functional imbalance between tonic and phasic musculature. An uneven development of agonists and antagonists is especially likely to occur in elite sports with one-sided (strength) training. This has a profound negative influence on the intermuscular coordination and integrity of the musculoskeletal system. An example of this is the commonly seen restricted hip extension resulting from very short hip flexors or shortened posterior thigh musculature leading to an increased injury risk. However, there are no precise indications as to what constitutes an ideal relationship from a health point of view or how it could be oriented towards the requirements of different sports, or whether these requirements may even coincide.

(4) The importance of the energy supply to the production of speed can be regarded as a fitness-energetic factor.

(5) A functional warm-up is extremely important to speed performances because of the high coordination and contraction requirements. An increased performance willingness of the complete organism and especially of the musculature is a prerequisite for fast movements. Further observations concerning the specific importance of warming up can be found in Section 7.3.

The possible influencing factors of the various forms of speed provide important information for specialized speed training.

Elementary neuromuscular movement programmes as foundations for speed

A promising recent investigation concerning the structure of speed has been published by Bauersfeld and Voss (1992) on 'elementary movement patterns'. This approach complements the characterizations discussed so far rather than contradicting them. Its approach, which sees the quality of elementary movement programmes as being determined by the performance of neuromuscular steering and regulating mechanisms, supports the work of Behrend (1988), Hauptmann (1990) and Lehmann (1991).

These authors regard speed as an elementary requirement for performance, which is neither primarily influenced by other performance determinants nor compensatable in elite sport performances. They unanimously categorize it as part of the neuromuscular system. They further assume that cyclic speed requirements are highly influenced by the quality of the individual cycle and therefore deduce that speed and its influencing factors are fundamentally non-cyclic (Bauersfeld, 1989). However, it is emphasized that there also appear to be cyclic programmes that influence, for example the leg-tapping frequency (Bauersfeld and Voss, 1992).

Elementary speed is seen especially in movements of extremely short duration and with extremely small external resistance. These movements, which are very rare in sports or can only be produced with technical constructions, are furthermore related to one or only a few joints (Schnabel et al., 1994). The developmental level of this form of speed is reflected in neuromuscular movement programmes or movement-specific 'time programmes'. In sport practice they generally occur in combination with other performance requirements without, however, being influenced by these.

The initially mentioned inaccuracies in the published structural approaches to distinguishing between strength and speed do not appear to apply to the factors of fatigue, velocity or external resistance.

What therefore is to be understood by 'elementary neuromuscular movement programmes'? Movements executed at high velocities generally occur without direct conscious control. They appear to be steered by conditioned and unconditioned reflexes or by programmes, yet their fundamental mechanisms are still not understood. However, very fast movements are seen especially in elite sport. These can be characterized either by a high complexity and high stability or by a high variability in terms of modified conditions and unstable functional systems (Voss, 1991b). Such movements can be explained by the engram theory of Bernstein (1988), because a single programme could not manage such a complex task. Regulation is achieved through a sequence of engrams but not through changes within a single engram. A movement parameter which is determined by an elementary movement programme stored in the central nervous system was apparently recognized within the stance time of drop jumps. The ground contact time, which in this case is a quantitative expression of the fundamental movement programme, can be described as a 'time programme' (Voss, 1991a,b). Time programmes are therefore innervation patterns that include the temporally determined neuromuscular impulse sequence of muscle activation and also the duration and ascending behaviour of bioelectrical activity. They are movement-specific, whereby structurally similar movements are steered by the same time programme (Bauersfeld and Voss, 1992).

Varying length time programmes must be distinguished. For jumps the limit for contact time is about 170 ms. The innervation patterns for a short, effective and a long, less effective time programme are illustrated in Figure 7.3. Short time programmes are characterized by a rapid increase in electrical activity even before ground contact and show no phase of reduced activity. The activity peak lies in the first third of the main phase. Shorter time programmes are regarded as essential prerequisites for world class athletes. They are largely ignored in youth training due to their compensatability.

It is also important that an increase in strength does not automatically lead to a transformation from long into short time programmes but that a transfer between structurally similar movements is possible. Time programmes therefore, appear to exist for whole classes of movements (Voss, 1991a,b).

The following structure could be used to combine the approach of Grosser with that of Bauersfeld and Voss:

(1) speed as an elementary ability in terms of the time programmes;
(2) speed as an elementary ability in combination with discipline-specific techniques (reactive speed, active speed, frequency speed);
(3) speed as a complex ability with motor aspects (e.g., speed strength, speed endurance and also sprinting speed) and from an action-theory point of view going beyond the purely motor perspective;
(4) speed as action speed.

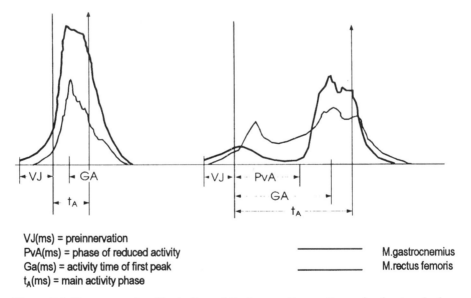

VJ(ms) = preinnervation
PvA(ms) = phase of reduced activity
Ga(ms) = activity time of first peak
t_A(ms) = main activity phase

———————— M.gastrocnemius
———————— M.rectus femoris

Figure 7.3: Representative illustration of the innervation pattern of a short and a long time programme (Bauersfeld and Voss, 1992, p. 19).

SPEED TRAINING—GENERAL ORIENTATIONS

A universally applicable speed training method can hardly be presented. This is because speed performance in different sports is too complex or technically too specific. This is also reflected in the training science literature, which generally presents speed training methods based upon examples of only a few sports, usually the track sprint. The following observations will therefore, be primarily restricted to training methodological orientations.

The relevance and execution of the warm-up in speed training

A special warm-up is indispensable before speed training because of both the high coordination and contraction demands placed upon the musculature and also because of the required level of psychological activation.

The first part of the warm-up should be used to stimulate circulation with the goal of increasing the core temperature, the muscle temperature and the metabolic and enzyme activity. After this it is recommended to perform a gymnastic exercise programme for all major muscle groups which should be interspersed with relaxation exercises. This should improve the elasticity of the muscles and effectiveness of the muscle spindles while also having a prophylactic effect against injuries. A further special portion involves influencing muscle tension, specific coordination and neuromuscular stimulation. Special jumping, strength and coordination exercises are of central importance. This should improve the excitability of the central nervous system, the performance speed, the contraction velocity and also attention and perception. A comprehensive warm-up programme should conclude with relaxation and concentration exercises. The total duration of the warm-up should be at least 25 minutes (cf. Grosser, 1991).

The training of elementary movement programmes

The speed performance potential of elite athletes often reveals no decisive deficits in biological requirements such as energetic capacities and motor nerve conduction velocity, motor reflex time and muscle fibre distribution or development. However, there appear to be large reserves available in the areas of neuromuscular steering and regulation. This is where the training of elementary movement programmes is applied. Contrary to 'classical' fitness training the intention is not so much to adapt the morphological system but rather to reorganize information processes. It would seem natural to perform speed training following the principles of technique training. These principles are based upon a trace modification theory (Kuhn, 1984 cited in Bauersfeld and Voss, 1992). Memory information, in this case movement programmes obtained for the first time, are modified and completed or perfected through continued learning. In technique training this is expressed by the intention of perfecting an ideal technique through the stages of rough form and ideal form. However, the usefulness of this theory can be doubted because an efficient removal of errors in set sport techniques is only possible at great expense or not at all. Elementary neural movement programmes should therefore, be trained based upon an alternative theory, the engram theory (Küchler, 1983; Bauersfeld and Voss, 1992). This assumes that part of motor learning, for example a motor programme, is initially saved as a dynamic, yet unstable engram. The dynamic engram is modified into a stable engram after only a few movement repetitions. The stable engram is difficult to modify. This is critical in the setup of speed training because it implies that an important role is played by those training methods that facilitate goal programmes through a variation of condition (cf. Voss, 1990). This is especially true since studies have shown that the support times (time programmes) achieved under less difficult conditions are later reproducible under normal conditions (Voss, 1985). The education of elementary movement programmes should occur in youth training (12–15 years) because the neuromuscular structures obtained through frequent practice can be only minimally modified at a later stage. This is further supported by the fact that goal programmes are usually established at this age and neuromuscular mechanisms can still be easily developed.

The aids that permit short time programmes to be achieved are based upon movement support or producing easier conditions during training. They are to be based upon the performance requirements which are not yet sufficiently developed to achieve the goal programme. In the youth field these are generally the strength capabilities. Examples of easier exercise conditions are:

- lighter equipment (throwing objects, balls, wrestling dolls, etc.);
- smaller equipment (apparatus settings, smaller paddles, thinner bars);
- body weight supports (e.g., take-off aids);
- modifications to competition conditions (smaller field, lower nets, etc.).

Training adjusted to the temporal aims of the time programme combined with immediate feedback information can also result in improved time programmes (Bauersfeld and Voss, 1992). If the easier conditions in training do not lead to shorter time programmes being learnt, then they have not been sufficiently goal oriented or other factors (e.g., genetic factors) have prevented the 'adaptation'.

As seen in technique training, a concrete suggestion for speed training is that it is not important to train into exhaustion but rather to guarantee a high degree of movement quality. This means that the goal programme should be realized in at least 60% of the repetitions; this is the decisive principle of speed training. Relatively few repetitions are generally sufficient. A total load volume of, for example, 140–300 repetitions for jumps or 40–100 seconds duration for cyclic loads with individual loading times not exceeding 8–10 seconds (6 seconds in youth training) spread over 4–6 weeks appears sufficient to effectively influence the elementary movement programmes. In terms of the load density, two training sessions (two or three series with complete recovery) per week appear sufficient (cf. Voss, 1991a,b).

Non-cyclic speed is a basic function for cyclic speed and should always be educated first. Concentrated non-cyclic and subsequent cyclic speed training should therefore, precede speed-specific sprint training.

However, short time programmes alone do not guarantee excellent speed performance. They must be incorporated into the complex competition movements and be specifically related to performance requirements in a goal-oriented manner. Complex speed training should therefore, be executed after training of the time programmes and this should place increasing emphasis on special movements and the competition movement. The goal is to utilize the conveying qualities of the elementary time programmes. This is only possible if the intended movement is executed at maximal intensity (Bauersfeld and Voss, 1992). This can only be achieved when training youth athletes with corresponding modifications under external conditions.

Reactive speed training

Reactions in sport are the response behaviour to signals which are perceived either optically, acoustically or tactilely. Depending upon the response behaviour a division can be made between either simple reactions in which only *one* previously determined response reaction is possible to a known signal or reaction choices where various reactions are possible to different signals. Reaction performance is influenced by a number of factors apart from attention regulation and pre-tension of the muscles. Thus long intensive stimuli lead to shorter reaction times. Fatigue, unaccustomed body positions, noise and diverse optical stimuli increase reaction times. As reactive demands in sport practice are usually followed by a movement or an action, the training of reactive speed should, as a rule, be combined with other performance demands. Martin et al. (1993) therefore regard reactive speed training predominantly as a part of technique training.

The trainability of reactive speed is very limited. It is generally assumed that improvements of 10–15% in simple reaction time and 15–30% in choice reaction time are possible. Despite many specialized studies it is still not known where these improvements occur. The psychological area, including information processing, anticipation and attention regulation appear dominant. Schnabel et al. (1994) regarded improved reaction performance as a result of 'reaction programmes' which are especially developed by practising standard situations. An increase in performance of reaction choices especially in sport games and contact sports is also associated with increased competition practice.

Many reaction exercises to optic, acoustic or tactile signals, both from rest or during movement, are possible in youth training to teach general reactive speed. Training should initially be performed under easier conditions followed then by increasingly more difficult and variable conditions (e.g., different starting positions and signals). According to Tabatschnik (1976) constantly recurring, identical (starting) signals lead to a stagnation of reactive speed. A rest of 2–3 minutes should be taken between the reaction exercises and no more than ten exercises should be executed. Catching games, relays and any ball games are also suitable for improving general reactive speed (e.g., Grosser, 1991; Geese and Hillebrecht, 1995).

The following three methods are preferred for improving reactive speed in simple reactions:

(1) *Repetitive method.* In track training this method involves reactive speed training of one to ten repetitions of competition specific starts over 10–30 metres. Here not only standard acoustic stimuli should be given as signals but also variations such as quiet clapping or stamping in order to place greater demands upon concentration. An additional inclusion of varying time intervals between individual commands is also useful in reaction training (Zaciorskij, 1968).

(2) *Partial method (analytical method).* This is based upon the fast reactive execution of single parts of the actual intended movement. If the track sprint start is again used as an example then reactive speed should initially be taught from the high start or take-offs should be executed slowly or without a signal. Grosser (1991) recommended 15 exercises for easier movement executions and six to eight for maximal executions, in both cases with 2–3 minutes rest.

(3) *Sensory method.* This assumes that an improved perception of reaction time will positively influence reactive speed. Firstly, the reaction times must be reported to the athlete in the form of objective and immediate feedback. The second step is to compare self perception of the reaction time with the objective information and then in a third step the athlete's reaction times are varied along guidelines provided by the coach (Matwejew, 1981).

There are also a number of possibilities for teaching reaction choices or complex reactions that are of special importance to performance in sports with suddenly changing action situations. The most obvious methods are the simulation of competition situations and a systematic participation in competition. However, these can not specifically influence individual factors of the complex course of the reaction. If certain characteristics of different reactive speed forms, within reaction choices, are simulated in training and conditions are created to reduce reaction times, then a positive effect can definitely be expected. For example, if the reactive speed towards a moving object (ball) is to be improved then Grosser (1991) suggests two steps:

(1) Firstly teach the ability to register the object in the field of view as soon as possible and also then develop the ability to anticipate possible object movements.

(2) Following this, greater demands should be placed upon speed of perception by including relevant stimulating factors. This can be achieved by including more balls, using a smaller playing field or increasing the number of opposing players. It is becoming increasingly popular to use electronic reaction devices. These include ball machines on which the frequency or speed of flight can be adjusted above those achieved in competition (cf. Matwejew, 1981).

Active speed training

In contrast to the training of non-cyclic movement programmes, this chapter presents active speed training in accordance with the terminology of Grosser (1991). It can be regarded as complementary to complex speed training discussed previously with elementary neural programmes.

Active speed rarely occurs in its pure form in sport because the technical level is such a major influencing factor. A specific training of active speed should therefore, consider all the abilities and skills that are responsible for movements executed at high speeds (Matwejew, 1981). It is therefore important to teach the athlete the ability to move not only as fast as possible but also as precisely as possible.

The fundamental methodological procedure for improving active speed is not only based upon the requirement of high movement quality but also upon the previously mentioned load orientation. As a rule all exercises should be of short duration (maximum 6 seconds) and initially executed sub-maximally prior to using maximal velocities. Additional loads should not be used.

General exercises to develop active speed can be any movement executed at high velocities. These include jumping, hitting and throwing exercises and also fast turns and falling–standing-up exercises; when combined with commands they can simultaneously contribute to an improved reactive speed.

The structure of specially designed exercises (all partial and complete forms of the technical exercise) must be the same as or similar to the competition movement. For example, if a technique and strength programme is designed for high jump then additional loads should not exceed 5% body weight, otherwise the dynamic structure of the movement would be disturbed.

The most effective method for improving active speed is the competition method. Its advantage is firstly that the movement is executed with its original structure and also that a maximum speed commitment is required which is hardly possible in training. However, as mentioned by Matwejew

(1981), if the competition method is frequently used while technical skills are lacking, then incorrect movement stereotypes can be developed and thus future performance development hindered.

The methodological procedures in speed training should thus be as follows:

- Teaching of movement techniques, first at middle competition speed (3–6 × 6–20 repetitions) then with sub-maximal and maximal competition speeds (3–5 × 6 repetitions) (Grosser 1991).
- Variable choice of exercise and execution velocity to prevent the development and reinforcement of a 'motor stereotype' which stops further speed development (Matwejew, 1981).
- Easier external conditions and body weight supports guarantee the realization of the required movement intensity and also prevent the development of movement stereotypes (Hauptmann and Nordmann, 1993).
- Modified competition situations and conditions (smaller action space and/or time restrictions, lower nets, fewer players, and so on) can also lead to increased speed if the technique is mastered (Schnabel et al., 1994).

The methods presented can be complemented by exercises with easier external conditions (e.g., lighter throwing objects, racquets) or decreased body weight (e.g., jumps with harnesses or elastic ropes). Therefore, similar methods may be used as in the teaching of short time programmes although the reasons for the choice of these methods are different.

Frequency speed training

Apart from the psychological, neural and muscle–tendon components of speed mentioned earlier the development of movement technique is as significant for frequency speed as it is for active speed. In addition to a highly developed central nervous system to enhance the excitation–inhibition cycle, the rhythm ability of intermuscular coordination also plays a major role. A good command of the refined form of the sport technical exercise is therefore a prerequisite for the teaching of frequency speed at a high level. The highest movement frequencies should always be sought, if necessary with decreased external resistance (see below). Increased loads are completely eliminated.

Apart from general development exercises such as one or two legged hopping and jumping, hopping and jumping runs, as well as different variations of running and specially designed (innervation) exercises are opportune. One of these is the 'sprint ABT' which includes exercises for active ankle work at different frequencies, skipping variations such as on the spot, while moving or over low obstacles (e.g., hats or children's hurdles), uphill and downhill. Further recommendations are special frequency runs (e.g., through laid-out gymnastics hoops), 'flying' sprints, such as maximal speed running over 20–40 metres after a run-up at individually chosen speeds, 'ins-and-outs' (speed changing sprints) and special coordination (technique) runs.

Various training methods are also used in the training of frequency speed in order to provide easier conditions (summarized in Stein, 1995). For example supra-maximal sprints aimed at improving frequency and running velocities are achieved by downhill sprints or sprinting in restrained circumstances (elastic ropes or special pulling systems). Training forms following the 'contrast method' are also employed by utilizing the 'after-effect influence' (Matwejew, 1981). In this case discipline specific exercises with increased resistance (uphill sprint, towing sled) are directly followed by movements executed under normal circumstances such as a subsequent free run or even easier conditions. This is based upon the utilization of a short remaining excitation of the nerve cells after a preceding high neural stimulation which results in an improved speed performance (Nordmann and Hauptmann, 1990).

The foundations for the methods employed are the same as for active speed training (cf. Grosser, 1991):

- All movements are to be executed at the maximum movement velocity.
- No fatigue is to occur during speed training.
- The athlete must be completely regenerated before training begins in some circumstances this may not be until 72 hours after the previous speed training session.
- The rest period between the series is to be chosen so that the frequency achieved in the previous exercise can again be attained in the next repetition.
- The duration of loading for elite athletes should be approximately 8–10 seconds, whereas with youth athletes a maximum of 6 second should be used.
- The best methods are the repetition method and the contrast method.

Complex speed capability training

'Complex' speed performances in sport-specific, technique-dependent forms of development are characterized by a close association of the speed capabilities with other performance requirements. Most training or competition movements which are executed at the greatest possible velocity have an obvious relationship with strength. The connection between neural and muscular requirements becomes stronger with increasing external resistance. This complexity is most obvious in acceleration capabilities which are strongly influenced by the individual developmental stage of maximum or speed strength. The ability to accelerate is in turn critical for the speed of the single movements or locomotor speed. This can be seen in the release velocity of sport projectiles, the take-off velocity by the jumper or the maximum speed achieved by sprinters.

Resistance to fatigue related speed decreases and speed strength are important in consecutively repeating non-cyclic movement actions in game or contact sports or acceleration actions. This field of 'speed strength endurance' which is no longer a part of speed capabilities will, however, not be covered in detail here. The ability to resist fatigue-dependent speed decreases is also important in longer duration cyclic movements which are to be executed at maximum contraction velocities, in this case in the form of 'maximum speed endurance'. The ability to maintain a high movement frequency is relevant for sprint disciplines (e.g., track, swimming, cycling) and for start performance, such as in rowing, kayak racing or speed skating and also in sport games which include many repeated acceleration phases. It is to be developed through relevant competition specific forms of training (see below).

The relationship between strength and speed

Firstly the role of strength in the various forms of speed must be clarified. Statements concerning the relevance of strength training for speed training can then be made on this basis.

Strength appears to play a quite minor role in the elementary neural movement programmes. A correlation between elementary time programmes and the stage of strength development could be determined neither in youth athletes in the most diverse sports nor in elite athletes. This is supported by the observation that even trained and untrained children already demonstrate short cyclic and non-cyclic time programmes (Bauersfeld and Voss, 1992). Therefore, pure strength training will presumably not result in shorter time programmes.

This fact can be partially compared to 'reactive strength' which, at least at high levels, can no longer be developed by increasing maximum strength. The teaching of maximum strength characteristics, especially concerning intramuscular coordination is, however, an important prerequisite in this case. The stretch–shortening cycle seen in many fast movements (e.g. , in all rapid take-off movements or in the support phases in sprinting which are only 100–130 milliseconds long) requires a high reactive tension ability in the relevant musculature. Although from a dimension analytical point of view this can be regarded as a relatively independent force component, it still benefits from a high initial level of maximum force (e.g., Komi, 1985; Bührle, 1989; Schmidtbleicher and Gollhofer, 1985). Strength training is also necessary to support and protect the passive musculoskeletal system when training elementary movement programmes and reactive strength capabilities for injury prevention reasons.

The role of strength training for active and frequency speed in a wider, sport-specific context is different because it is far clearer (cf. the approach of

Grosser proposed earlier). High strength peaks must be achieved in short time periods in many sports, for example track and field, sport games or martial arts. This is obvious in the starting action in sprinting or in the extreme speed strength movements of boxers or fencers. However, sport-specific speed strength in the form of sprinting, jumping, throwing, hitting or putting strength only achieves its full potential through exercises closely approximating the relevant technique. Here it is important to transfer the intramuscular training effect released by preceding maximum strength training to movements with decreased loads and to achieve greater contraction and shortening velocities in competition-specific conditions. Maximum strength training alone is not sufficient to optimally develop speed strength performance. Tidow (1993) referred to muscle biopsy results that showed that specific hypertrophic forms of maximal strength training result in some-times extreme transformations of FTG (IIb-fibres) into fast-twitch oxidative (FTO: IIa-fibres). Subsequent explosive forms of maximal strength training did not reverse this process. From a training methodology point of view, preparatory general developmental dynamic exercises for individual muscular development should be of central importance. For the development of a good muscle contraction ability this should occur with specifically designed (sport-specific) exercises. These include training exercises with and without additional loads which must be adapted to the movement structures of the competition discipline.

In summary the 'complex forms' of speed are especially speed strength and to a lesser extent maximum strength dependent. However, Grosser (1991) stated that the 'pure forms' can also be improved through maximal strength training as a result of better neural processes. He therefore defined maximum strength, speed strength and speed as a 'dynamic unit' in which the components complement each other. His statements appear to clearly contradict those of Bauersfeld and Voss (1992). However, this contradiction is removed if one recalls that the latter authors described speed as an elementary capability on the structural level, whereas the observations of Grosser were on the elite level. A comprehensive programme of speed training should take into account both approaches, with the training of the elementary movement programmes given greater emphasis.

No further observations concerning the theory of speed training and its contents are to be discussed here. Reference is made to Chapter 5 and also to the speed strength exercises in the presentation of 'speed training in selected sports'.

The relationship between endurance and speed

The combination of longer duration maximum cyclic movement frequencies with intensive, speed strength muscle contractions places great demands not only on the neuromuscular activation but also on muscle metabolism. The energy is provided by the storage of energy-rich phosphates and carbohy-drates in muscle and is generally provided only by anaerobic metabolism. As the anaerobic-lactate energy provision is only sufficient for a few sec-onds, even a maximum effort 100 m sprint results in considerable accumula-tion of lactate (e.g., Mader et al., 1983; Mahler, 1990; Schnabel et al., 1994). If the proportion of the lactic energy production is higher, then more inhibition processes occur in the central nervous system and neuromuscular regulation processes are disturbed. Consequently the movement frequency and strength capability decrease. This was shown by Jakowlev (1977) in a series of sprint tests. Martin et al. (1993) also reported that this programme fatigue (understood as diminishing differentiated control of the movement pro-gramme) was the primary limiting factor for the maintenance of the highest possible locomotor speed. From an energetic point of view large stores of creatine phosphate are therefore important prerequisites for maximum cyclic speed performances over more than 6–7 seconds. This further em-phasizes the significance of a high proportion of FTG (IIb-fibres) which contain approximately 50% more phosphate than ST fibres.

The short track sprint illustrates the significance of well-developed 'fre-quency speed endurance' both during the phase of maintaining maximum speed and in the deceleration phase when velocity decreases. When training this special sprint endurance it is important to have a sufficiently well-developed endurance base and to then exhaust the energy rich phosphates from this foundation with high-intensity short-duration loads (4–5 s, 30–40 m). This results in an adaptation of the storage capacity of the muscle to the loading. Repeated maximum loads beyond the phase of positive accelera-tion (40–80 m) stabilize the neural steering pattern and increase the glycolitic enzyme activity in the fast contracting muscle fibres. Overloading at max-imum intensity with the repetitive method (over 100–130 m) influences the substrate cycling in the session and thus leads to an increased glycolitic turnover and better tolerance of lactate production.

Complex action speed training

The primary aim of speed training in many sports (especially game sports and martial arts) is to increase not only the speed but also to enhance psychological and physical capabilities. Although the activity-oriented term 'action speed' (cf. Bauersfeld, 1983; Polster, 1987) was not further described in Section 7.2, the training of this complex form of speed will be briefly described here.

If complex movement actions are to be executed with optimal precision and greatest possible velocity then a close association is required between purer speed training with contents taken from technical and/or tactile edu-cation. Those cognitive, fitness, technical and coordinative requirements rel-evant to the action being trained must be taught in 'situation training' related to the competition conditions. Correct technique must be emphasized and the execution quality can not decrease during the training session (Hauptmann, cited in: Schnabel et al., 1994).

In this training method the volume of the fitness demands is only gradually increased alongside a simultaneous stepwise increase in the difficulty of the technical–tactile tasks. In this developmental process one of the major components of action speed is the reactive speed (reaction choice). Better anticipation, sport-specific knowledge and movement experience gained from increasing competition experience permit the training tasks to become more challenging. Finally, at elite levels the athlete must be taught to call upon available action programmes even in sport actions with a variety of solution possibilities. Training under time pressure, when tired, with a restricted field of view or with built-in disruptive factors, are all appropriate training ideas. Sufficiently long rest periods within the training blocks provide a good base for the set movement tasks to be performed quickly with full concentration while also ensuring safety and effectiveness.

In conclusion it will be mentioned that complex sport actions that build upon psycho-physical performance determinants must not always be performed in the shortest possible time and/or at maximum intensity. The example of faking or dummying in sports clarifies how a temporal delay between the cognitive and motor phases is necessary for an execution corresponding to the game situation. Harre and Hauptmann (1987) use the term optimal 'action velocity' and emphasize that the greatest reserves for a specific training of action speed lie in improving cognitive processes. There is restricted scope for removing deficits through 'motor' speed because 'psychological' speed occupies about 70–80% of the time required for the fastest possible solution of technical–tactile situations.

FOUNDATIONS OF PLANNING AND STEERING SPEED TRAINING

Genetic disposition and biological adaptation processes are significant planning factors when trying to develop the greatest possible performance ability of an athlete and to transfer this to competition. In the field of speed, neural and muscle–tendon adaptations are of primary importance. The repeated methodological steps to be employed in training should be oriented along steering and regulation processes determined by training science. Therefore, individual forms of speed or complex sport specific speed are today based on associations of the performance steering process illustrated in Figure 7.4.

The significance of speed in the planning of training is basically the same as other performance determining factors. A coach must determine which different speed capabilities or which forms (cyclic or non-cyclic) are dominant. A sport discipline analysis and the results of an essential state

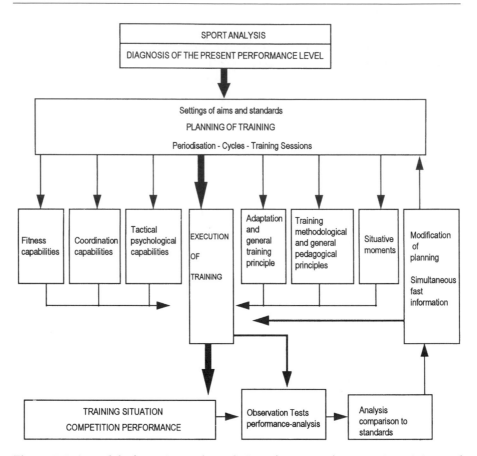

Figure 7.4: A model of steering and regulation of sport performance in training and competition (modified from Grosser, 1991, p. 145).

analysis will lead to the formulation of goals for the long- or short-term steering of speed training.

The planning and execution of optimal speed training is subject to specific methodological foundations and principles to a larger extent than normally seen in other fields of coordination-fitness training. The most important of these are summarized below (based upon: Dintiman and Ward, 1988; Grosser, 1991; Bauersfeld and Voss, 1992; Martin et al., 1993; Weineck, 1994; Stein, 1995).

General methodological foundations

Quality before quantity (less is often more!)

This implies that speed exercises should on the one hand be executed at maximal, or at least almost maximal movement velocities to ensure that no movement patterns directed at sub-maximal velocities are set. Speed training also places high demands on the hormonal and neural systems because a continuously high activity level is necessary. This prevents large overall training volumes and requires corresponding high regeneration times.

Speed training requires movements to be executed with great technical precision

The 'correct technical' movement execution is absolutely necessary because fast movements are 'program steered'. (That is, the great time pressure demands feedback mechanisms on a spinal rather than peripheral basis.) When choosing exercises, care must be taken not to make the demands too complicated and that complex movement forms are not performed at maximum speed until the correct technique is consistent.

Speed develops according to actions and demands

Speed capabilities are therefore trainable only through special exercises as opposed to general exercises. These special exercises should simulate the spatial, temporal, dynamic and energetic characteristics of competition as closely as possible. The various speed capabilities must be taught on the basis of a differentiated method at an early stage because the development of neuromuscular steering and regulation processes is action dependent and not influenced by natural maturation processes. In principle, non-cyclic speed loading should be realized before cyclic, and these in turn before complex demands.

The development of speed performance is dependent upon many different factors

Apart from ensuring optimal movement technique, maximum and speed strength capabilities must act as a 'dynamic unit'. In certain cases, particularly with cyclic speed loads, a highly developed specific endurance is also beneficial to reduce muscular elasticity and muscular imbalances are detrimental to speed-specific performance. In order to minimize internal resistance, special attention should therefore be paid to the elasticity of the active musculoskeletal system before each speed loading. A fast neural excitation-inhibition cycle of the active muscles and the stretchability of the antagonists are decisive for a highly developed intermuscular coordinative performance. Finally the importance of an increased body temperature produced by a well-directed 'warm-up' can not be underestimated (Stoboy, 1972).

Speed training at a high level must include constant feedback

Practical experience shows that an effective teaching of speed is associated with frequent objective feedback of performance results. This applies to a coupling of qualitative characteristics (fast information within 5–30 seconds, e.g. video) in the technique-coordination field. However, the development of a subjective perception of maximum speed through frequent time controls (e.g., with photoelectric beams) or estimated times in completed trials should also be provided.

Speed training depends upon high motivation

Conscious involvement of the athlete and the desire to achieve optimal performances determine the results of speed actions. Psychological mobilization and the ability to concentrate should have greatest priority in training.

Long-term steering of speed training

As mentioned above the neuromuscular steering process of speed training is not part of a natural developmental process. Depending upon the demands of the performance structure of the specific sport, the speed loads are generally set early in life. The period prior to biological maturity is especially favourable, because at this age the central nervous system addresses speed stimuli well and the muscle fibre profile can still be influenced to a certain extent (Hauptmann, 1994). A reduced trainability is to be expected after puberty because a 'setting' of biological performance conditions occurs. Bauersfeld and Voss (1992) and Lehmann (1993) are therefore justified in demanding the introduction into youth training of conditions which emphasize the development of elementary speed prerequisites. Here attention should be focused on the exploitation of the developmental stages with the greatest growth rates ('sensitive phases'). The ages from 7–9 years old prior to 12–14 years (girls) and 13–15 years (boys) generally require a diverse, goal-oriented basic education (Weineck, 1994).

A speed-oriented structuring of fundamental training (the first stage of long-term training) should produce important pre-conditions for later best performances. Firstly, different forms of speed (non-cyclic, cyclic and action speed) are taught in a differentiated manner. Secondly, high velocities are guaranteed in movements and actions through minimized strength and strength endurance demands (e.g., adapted children's competition equipment, field sizes, distances, competition duration).

The subsequent training stages (build-up and follow-up training) should include greater proportions of special exercises than the previous fundamental training. Complex, discipline-specific acceleration and speed training in connection with the coordination structure of the competition movement does not receive priority until the beginning of this phase. The development-dependent, increasing load acceptance permits more training of the fitness components of speed; primarily speed strength and speed endurance. The volume and intensity of the main training forms increase corresponding to an increased total training volume. However, the restriction of training exercises to a constant maximum intensity should be avoided to prevent the development of a 'motor stereotype' (i.e. a fixed central nervous movement programme) which is difficult to influence at later stages. A systematic variation between easier, normal and more difficult conditions in training is especially effective in preventing performance stagnation in terms of a 'velocity barrier'.

Finally, in elite training all methods, contents and means are to be associated with appropriate volume and intensity increases to aim at the highest possible individual speed performances. The goal-oriented development of special performance requirements, such as special strength to individual optimum levels, while maintaining the training of elementary movement programmes is vital.

A clear increase in competition activity not only requires speed but also differentiated measures in the periodization of speed training. A double or multiple periodization within a training year has become standard in elite sport in the speed and speed strength disciplines, irrespective of the competition calendar. In an annual cycle this allows the setting of an increasing load volume and the systematic increase in intensity (or, if appropriate distance) as foundation for a more rapid increase in performance (e.g., Tschiene, 1974; Tabatschnik, 1981). However, this is dependent upon the duration of the preparation and competition periods being matched in such a manner that the necessary discipline-specific characteristics can be adequately developed with general and special means (Stein, 1993).

Based upon the realization that a certain saturation effect occurs after a certain training time, Grosser (1991) recommended that speed should be steered through speed and speed strength training in periodization sections of 16–20 weeks. An initial 4–6 week basic endurance and general strength endurance training is followed by approximately 4–10 weeks of muscle development training, which is in turn succeeded by intramuscular coordination training of 3–6 weeks. Reactive and speed strength exercises should be included in the training from the start. Depending upon the sport this sequence is followed either directly by speed and technique training or not until about 2–3 weeks of speed strength training has been interspersed.

Upon the assumption that the development of strength and speed can be regarded separately, Werchoshanskij (1984) introduced the model of the 'long-term delayed training effect' (Figure 7.5). A half-year cycle is composed of a developing stage (A) followed by a concentrated strength training (B) which includes participation in competition and is succeeded by directed technique and speed training (C). The duration of the strength training phase and that of the long-term training effect (LVT) are usually identical and lie between 4 and 12 weeks.

The periodization models described for the development of different speed capabilities which are predominantly designed for the track sprint are

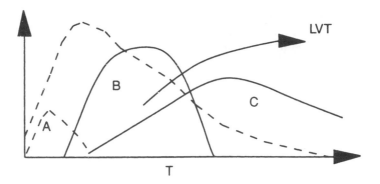

Figure 7.5: Model of training construction in cyclic sports (explanation in the text: after Werchoschanskij, 1984, p. 28).

not adequate for a comprehensive understanding of speed from a neuro-muscular perspective. The specific conditions of different sports also require a detailed planning of training.

More recent thoughts concerning training construction are also based upon an accentuated speed training spanning a complete year. Bauersfeld and Voss (1992) recommended that speed be trained in intensive training sessions of at least 14 days, independent of the performance structure demands in the relevant sport or discipline. This is in agreement with the present knowledge of training which bases long-term, cyclic training processes upon the following 'rule'. The accepted, general 'classic' periodization concept founded by Matveev (1965) is valid only for low and middle performance classes of individual sports. For elite athletes an event sequence of cycles and periods determined by the competition calendar should be employed rather than the normal sequence from general to special preparation. The reason given for this is that elite athletes possess an especially high performance level which can only be further improved by specific influence at precisely this level. Furthermore, these athletes are already training at the limits of their adaptation reserves and therefore, require special sport-specific training loads. Apart from the priority of specialized training, the representatives of the 'new' theory (Boiko, 1988; Werchoshanskij, 1988; Verkhoshansky and Lazarev, 1989) primarily demand that the method of 'directed load concentration' be employed. This refers to the division of training into focused content 'blocks' (e.g., technique or strength blocks) with high load volumes. A clear separation of the strength block from the phase of speed improvement is illustrated by the example of sprint disciplines (Figure 7.6). Speed training receives minimal attention within the macrocycles of concentrated strength training (shaded area). The special sprint speed training (v) is only commenced during the long-term delayed training effect of the strength load in the second macrocycle.

The load concentration method presented is not intended to replace the accepted periodization theory (Martin et al., 1993). However, it does show

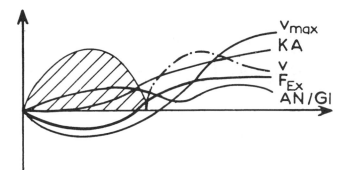

Figure 7.6: Block structure in sprint training; KA = strength endurance, AN/GI = anaerobic-glycolitic area, V_{MAX} = maximum speed development, F_{EX} = development of explosive strength (further explanations in the text: after Werchoshanskij, 1988, p. 134).

that it is important in training science to pay attention to alternate and maybe more rational solutions if the functional reserves are to be exploited through special load stimuli.

Short-term steering of speed training

Short-term steering of speed training in this context refers to the microstructure of the training plan, that is the weekly and individual session plans. It is important for the steering of load dynamics within the microcycle to take into account the fact that training sessions with different contents also have different after-effects. The hetero-chronology of the recuperation process is a complicated training methodological problem in speed training. Overlying training effects of successive training sessions can have either positive, negative or neutral effects on speed development. For example, Matveev (1985) found in a study of judokas that it was advantageous for a medium intensity strength training in the morning to be combined with a low-intensity speed training in the afternoon. A number of principle distinguishing possibilities in terms of the structure of microcycles are seen especially in elite sport and these indicate various training method approaches and associated different interpretations. This explains why there can not be a 'universal structure of microcycles' (Matwejew, 1981, p. 213). However, a general characteristic of a microcycle in speed oriented sports is the division between a loading phase and a repetition phase. An example taken from swimming shows the following phase structure (Figure 7.7).

The function of the microcycle is to ensure an optimal load–recovery relationship. A decisive role is played by muscular and central nervous system fatigue, especially in speed training. This applies particularly to the formation of individual training sessions. Martin et al. (1993, p. 170)

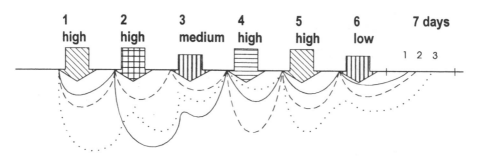

Figure 7.7: A scheme for the construction of a microcycle for highly qualified swimmers under consideration of the dynamics of the recuperation processes during (1) speed loading, (2) anaerobic and (3) aerobic loading (after Platonov, 1980, p. 143).

established that 'reduced muscular performance regenerates in the short term parallel to the creatine phosphate resynthesis'. Based upon this information muscular fatigue should hardly occur in speed training and the small loading volumes involved therein. This is especially true if anaerobic–alactic metabolism is primarily employed. According to Grosser (1991, p. 107) a 'fatigue-free' execution of pure speed exercises should be expected in the following loading processes:

(1) *Series principle*. Loading phases of less than five seconds duration (corresponding to 30–40 m sprints), three or four repetitions, recovery pauses of 1.5–3 minutes, three or four series with 10–12 minute pauses between series.

(2) *Repetition principle with individual loads*. Loading phases of 7–10 seconds (60–80 m sprints), three to five repetitions with pauses of 15–20 minutes.

However, according to the results of Hellwig (1991) the latter training principle may involve clear above-threshold lactate values which contradict the demand for a fatigue-free training. Similar loading durations of 8–10 seconds for cyclic exercises (maximum of 6 seconds for young athletes) are suggested by Bauersfeld and Voss (1992) and Weineck (1994). Non-cyclic speed actions should be employed as maximal single trials or only in small series whereby the summed time of the individual trials within one series should not greatly exceed the suggested times.

Concerning the required length of pauses within a training sessions it should be assured that the time, velocity or frequency of the previous loading is again achieved. For maximum intensity cyclic loads a reference value is 1 minute rest for every 10 m distance run.

The training orientations mentioned so far also take into account 'central fatigue' which, although actually caused by local changes in the musculature, is primarily seen as fatigue of the central nervous system (Hollmann and Hettinger, 1980). Rapidly occurring central fatigue can be traced back to a 'programme decrease of the motor impulse (Dietz, 1985, p. 26) which sets in immediately after the very high deactivation frequency occurs in sudden maximum contractions. Apart from a loss of velocity this is connected with limitations in reaction times, movement precision and concentration. Consequently, large volumes of maximum intensity movements within one training unit are not appropriate.

Training fatigue as a manifestation of both the central nervous and muscular systems probably evolves two phases during a typical load summation within a microcycle (Martin et al., 1993). In the first phase up until about mid-week, decreased performance after loading can be compensated relatively quickly, that is parallel to the replenishment of the energy store. In the second phase of 'complex', centrally originating fatigue the reduced fast coordinative performance due to loading can no longer be fully regenerated. Therefore, pure speed training under regenerative conditions should always be completed in the first days of a microcycle. Complex speed capabilities such as speed endurance which counteract programme fatigue are more practical in the second half of the week.

Grosser (1991) suggested approximately 48 hours for 100% recovery (compensation) as the necessary regeneration time for maximal speed loading and 72–84 hours for achieving a higher performance potential (super compensation). From this it can be concluded that two or three training sessions of highly intensive speed work are recommended in one microcycle. An example of a microcycle structure for high overall intensity sprint training is illustrated in Figure 7.8.

A final aspect of short-term steering concerns the sequence of training contents. Up until now the following rule was used if different performance determining capabilities were being taught in one training session: 'Pure' forms of speed and technique training *before* strength and strength *before* endurance (Grosser et al., 1986). Experience from training practice (e.g., Allmann, 1985), however, indicates positive after-effects of maximum strength training (intramuscular strength training) followed by subsequent speed training. This mainly subjective observation originates from an increased neuromuscular performance preparedness. Such a 'utilization training' should, however, be completed within 5–20 minutes of the strength training. Martin et al. (1993) recommended this combination one or two times within the first half of the week.

Conclusion

The presented possibilities of speed training structure are to be regarded as proposals. They should under no circumstances be uncritically adopted. As speed performances are always connected to certain sport techniques or

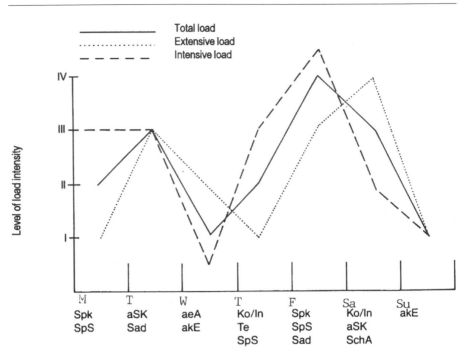

Figure 7.8: Micro-cycle in sprint training from the stage of special preparation with a high overall intensity lying close to the limit (Letzelter, 1978, p. 75). Explanation: Ts: training session; Spk: sprint strength; SpS: sprint speed; aSK: general speed strength (especially jumping strength): Sad: sprint endurance; aeA: aerobic endurance; akE: active recovery; Te: specific technique training (starts, etc.) Ko/In: specific coordination and innovation exercises; SchA: speed endurance.

embedded in specific action sequences, they must also be trained in connection with the sport-specific techniques and situations. Each sport must therefore, implement its own concept for a meaningful planning and steering of speed training.

PERFORMANCE DIAGNOSTIC PROCEDURES IN SPEED TRAINING

Performance diagnostics analyse and assesses the movement characteristics important to a specific sport or discipline and also the demand parameters relevant to performance. The use of performance diagnostic procedures represents a considerable step towards understanding the complex characteristics of speed training. The observation and assessment of complex performance is, however, in most cases not sufficient. Differential techniques to objectively assess sport performance are required, especially in speed-dependent sport movements in which the competition result is often decided by 1/100 second. The time, velocity and frequency are commonly used as parameters.

The information content of the specific sport motor test procedures is often sufficient to determine the present state of the performance ability and also to proceed with a rough assessment of training effectivity. At the elite level the methodologically more complicated biomechanics and sport medicine procedures and diagnosis possibilities are also employed. Such possibilities are only applicable in very limited fields of sport because they generally involve using high-quality apparatus (e.g., computer-supported measuring and information systems, interactive video).

General and sport-specific motor test systems

As standardized observation procedures for collecting characteristics of the specific motor-coordination ability level, sport motor tests must not only fulfill the known criteria of validity, reliability and objectivity but also satisfy the demands of an adequate differential diagnosis. It is not always immediately possible to identify the difference between a speed test and a speed strength test. A procedure can be termed a speed test if the external load does not exceed 30% of the maximal load (Kunz and Unold, 1991). Tests which include jumps with body weight are therefore, more correctly characterized as speed strength tests.

Speed test exercises can be subdivided into general and specific test forms. The former usually determine elementary speed capabilities whereas the latter determine complex speed performances. In practice a further division is made between procedures for controlling reactive speed, non-cyclic active speed and cyclic speed and cyclic frequency speed. Finally some 'test literature' differentiates between studying speed in whole body movements (e.g., running or skipping) and partial body movements (e.g., tapping, arm circling).

It is noticeable that in contrast to the significance of speed as a 'fundamental motor characteristic', the test theory in the field of speed is still in its infancy and the sport motor test procedures available have only gross diagnostic value. We are usually confronted with parts of heterogeneous test batteries or single tests. There is a complete lack of test batteries for a differentiated grasp of speed. Bös and Mechling (1983) stated that this is because on an operational level, speed can only be regarded in conjunction with other motor abilities.

Tests for reactive speed

In training practice reactive speed is measured as the time taken from the signal to the initiation of the movement (reaction time). In complex actions (sport games or martial arts) the time required for the complete action is determined. The possibilities of measuring reaction capabilities with sport motor test procedures are, however, limited. Firstly because these performances are largely anticipatory and therefore, difficult to measure and also because of the lack of suitable testing instrumentation (Martin et al., 1993). Therefore, only certain parameters of simple reactions or reaction performance are usually collected which must then be regarded and assessed in association with further movement actions.

An example of a general (non-specific) form of reaction test is the stick-dropping test, in which the athlete must grab a falling stick as quickly as possible with an open hand while in a seated position (Grosser and Starischka, 1981). Theoretically, the special reaction capabilities of complex sport actions are possible only in competition-like conditions, but this is not presently possible as competition situations can only with great difficulty be simulated in the laboratory. Appropriate tests, usually reduced to simple actions and directed at reaction choices with optical signals, have been experimentally investigated in contact sports (e.g., Stulrajter, 1987; Zukowski, 1988) and sport games (e.g., Alain and Proteau, 1982; Juwu, 1990). The specific question of the effect of ball colour on reaction times was studied by Rogers et al. (1991). Tests concerning boxing can be found in Kirchgässner (1981) and Grosser and Starischka (1981) and information concerning sport games in Konzag (1983).

Tests for active and frequency speed

Control of active and frequency speed usually occurs in the form of single tests. The following examples of tests are usually used for the range of non-sport-specific diagnosis (summarized amongst others from Grosser and Starischka, 1981; Hess, 1985; Grosser et al., 1986): high starts and running over 10–40 m (accelerating ability); 20–30 m flying sprints (locomotor speed); skipping test (movement frequency); 'Japan test' (non-cyclic speed).

The majority of sport motor test procedures aiming at controlling maximum non-cyclic or cyclic manifestations of speed clearly lack appropriate validity. As a rule not only 'pure' speed capabilities but also (or even especially) the levels of other speed performance components are being measured. This criticism can be demonstrated by the cyclic accelerating ability in sprinting which is predominantly based upon strength capabilities. The time or velocity measurements commonly used to objectively analyse non-cyclic fast actions or the distance and height measurements in certain sport motor tests also have this fault. In these situations classic speed strength tests such as the triple hop, five hop, standing long jump, Abalakow test (jumping harness test), jump and reach test or medicine ball putting are used (cf. Chapter 5).

Tests for complex speed

Appropriate multi-functional tests (complex single tests or test profiles) are used for diagnosis because complex sport specific speed usually includes a combination of different fundamental speed capabilities. These tests are related to the movement demands of the relevant sport as much as possible. The influence of technique on the fitness characteristics must, however, be taken into account when interpreting the test results.

Examples of such sport motor test procedures, which are also popular as forms of training are (after Gerisch and Reichl, 1978; Grosser and Starischka, 1981; Neumaier, 1983) slalom running for sport games (sprint agility); dribbling test for footballers (sport specific speed and dribbling ability in a non-game situation); and the 9-3-6-3-9 test (line running on a marked court) for volleyballers (maximum cyclic and non-cyclic speed).

Diagnostics for elementary speed requirements

Corresponding to the importance of elementary speed requirements, performance diagnostics should not be restricted to the mentioned speed capabilities but should also assess the quality of the neural movement programme at the basis of fast movements. Hauptmann (cited in: Schnabel et al., 1994, p. 179), however, saw problems in diagnosing elementary speed capabilities ('basic speed') because at present the secured 'inner parameters' for the central nervous and neuromuscular requirements are missing.

The objectivity and determination of the quality of elementary non-cyclic speed requirements of the lower extremities is frequently based upon determining the ground contact time in the stretch–shortening cycle of low/high jumps (Bauersfeld and Voss, 1992). Stance times less than 170 milliseconds are defined as an indication for good non-cyclic speed prerequisites.

In order to assess elementary cyclic speed capabilities of the lower extremities, Lehmann (1992, 1993) recommended a frequency determination during alternating foot tapping in a seated position. Frequencies greater than 12 Hz (contacts per second) are regarded as a favourable neural prerequisite for high movement velocities.

There are also attempts to analyse elementary speed capabilities in complex performances, especially in specific exercises or competition exercises (Bauersfeld and Voss, 1992). These determine the usefulness of elementary speed capabilities, that is the transfer of performance differences to special movements. For example the performance in throwing a lighter apparatus is compared with that using the competition apparatus or the tapping frequency with skipping frequency or the sprint performance over 15 m with the sprint performance over the same distance with a ball.

In summary, it can be concluded that practical sport (sport motor) tests are more appropriate for the diagnosis of the momentary performance and training level. The tests described for the estimation of fundamental speed parameters can not be realized without employing biomechanical measuring equipment. They form the bridge to the training science diagnostic procedures which are covered in the following section.

Biomechanical measuring and control systems

Speed performances that are based upon maximum movement velocity can only be precisely registered with the precision-measuring technology offered in biomechanics. Sport motor tests with their gross diagnostic demands are no longer adequate.

Procedures such as cinematography, dynamometry and electromyography are employed for the assessment of speed capabilities. Acceleration capabilities and locomotor speed are determined primarily with photoelectric beam systems and speedographs. Measurements of the velocity on the (competition) stretch to identify strengths and weaknesses in specific sections has become a routine process in sprinting, alpine skiing or the run-up in athletic jumping events. The time diagrams constructed upon the basis of reference runs contain information concerning the development of speed, for example in swimming, speed skating or hurdle sprints (Baumann et al., 1986). In the sport science field the application of high-speed video systems plays an important role in determining kinematic characteristics such as displacement velocity, angular velocity or support time. The recent development of continuous velocity measurements with laser systems is of particular interest (Figure 7.9).

The measuring systems employed in dynamometry, such as force-measuring platforms, force sensors or accelerometers, provide information

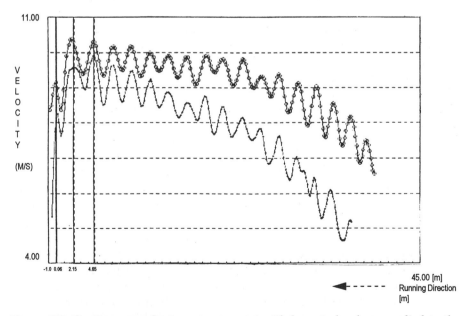

Figure 7.9: Continuous velocity measurement with laser technology applied to the run-up structure of two female long jumpers (Dickwach and Perlt, 1995).

concerning force–time patterns and force peaks in combination with acceleration performance. Furthermore, force platforms and contact mats are appropriate testing instruments for the diagnosis of elementary speed capabilities (see Chapter 3).

The possibility of electromyographic analyses will also be mentioned, although these are not without their problems in highly dynamic locomotor movements. They have been successfully used in non-cyclic movements, such as the determination of EMG–time curves in the stretch–shortening cycle in elementary speed capabilities.

Physiological measurements of performance

Physiological measurements have been employed in speed training to only a limited extent. As a rule they act as control of the training load from a metabolic perspective. Their use therefore lies predominantly in assessing maximum speed endurance and regeneration ability after high-intensity loading. Tests of the twitch and innervation velocities of muscles/nerves have no practical meaning at present.

However, performance physiological studies provide important reference data concerning the steering of training loads in the maximal intensities set for speed training and the determination of the present performance level. Measurement of urea and creatinase concentrations in the blood serum a few hours after the conclusion of training help to determine whether the preceding load volume is appropriate. Subjective perceptions of the athlete can be supported or modified by these data. (According to Grosser et al. (1986) an increase of, for example, the serum urea to values greater than 8 mmol/l blood is an indicator of overtraining.)

There are only isolated conclusions concerning specific test procedures for determining, the individual lactate to performance relationship in short speed loading (e.g., Hellwig, 1991). They generally discuss the use of series loading for assessing the alactic and/or lactic performance capability. Muscle biopsy investigations for the quantitative determination of alactic capacity must be ruled out as routine procedures.

SPEED TRAINING IN SELECTED SPORTS

Speed has been described in the previous chapters as an unusually diverse complex of capabilities that manifests itself in different sports and disciplines in very different ways. This complexity and the sport-specific development of speed which is strongly dependent upon technique characteristics means that only certain examples of specific speed training methods and contents will be discussed here.

The development of speed in selected individual sports

Speed training in athletics (short sprint)

General structural demands.   The term 'speed training' traditionally refers almost exclusively to the teaching of sprint capabilities. This is partly due to the fact that reactive speed and especially cyclic speed manifest themselves to the greatest extent in the track sprint. The 100 m sprint has for a long time been the subject of numerous investigations.

Analyses of sprint performance structure indicate a complex association of neural, muscular and metabolic factors. The primary biomechanical indicators of sprint performance, stride length (spatial behaviour) and stride frequency (temporal behaviour) can only be improved by influencing coordination, strength, technique, flexibility and special forms of endurance. Figure 7.10 illustrates these performance limiting factors in sprinting. The question of whether stride length or stride frequency is dominant and their dependence based on age, sex and other possible factors has not been adequately answered at many performance levels. An individually optimized relationship between factors must therefore, be employed to develop maximum velocity.

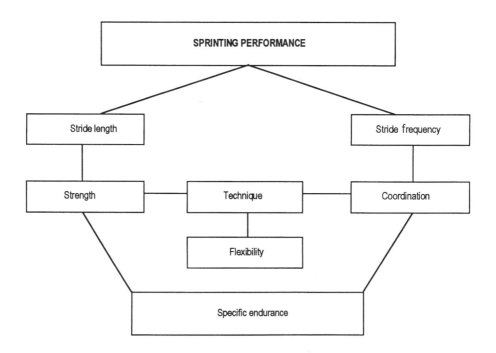

Figure 7.10: Performance limiting factors in sprinting (Jonath et al., 1995, p. 64).

On the basis of velocity–time curves the specialist literature differentiates between the following four phases in the 100 m sprint: the reactive phase, the acceleration phase, the phase of maximum velocity and the phase of decreasing velocity (e.g., Gundlach, 1963; Ballreich, 1969; Dick, 1988a,b; Hess, 1990). Factor analysis of the short sprint indicate that reactive speed, acceleration ability, locomotor speed and maximum speed endurance are relevant to performance in the different portions of the running distance and therefore also for the complete distance (e.g., Hess, 1991a). However, reactive speed and speed endurance behave differently when compared to the other factors, as they do not play a major role in differentiating between sprint performance levels (Ballreich, 1969).

Special structure of demands for speed capabilities in the short sprint

There are only minimal systematic differences between reaction times and sprinting performance for athletes with similar reaction times (e.g., Joch and Hasenberg, 1990). This speed prerequisite will therefore not be discussed further.

Earlier studies such as by Gundlach (1963) and Ikai (1967) concerning the sprinting behaviour of the best male and female sprinters in the world in part contradict previous data. The maximum velocities of the best sprinters during the 1987 and 1991 championships and the 1988 Olympic Games were not usually reached until between 50 and 60 m, or sometimes not even until the 70 to 90 m mark (Susanka et al., 1988; Brüggemann and Susanka, 1990; Ae et al., 1992). Speeds in excess of 11 m/s were achieved during the men's 100 m sprint and Lewis (USA) even reached a speed of 12.05 m/s.

In training structure, the acceleration ability is therefore regarded as the parameter with the greatest influence upon the competition result (e.g., Hess, 1991a). Maximum strength and speed strength are regarded as the most important prerequisites for acceleration ability together with a well-developed sprint technique. Non-cyclic time programmes are also important parameters.

Acceleration performance is to a certain extent relatively independent and cannot be compared to speed coordination aspects of speed. However, acceleration and sprinting speed are commonly trained in a complex manner with speed training because sprinting speed is completely dependent upon acceleration performance. One can only run at a velocity to which one has accelerated. A further distinction can be made for elite sprinters who initially accelerate (0 m to approximately 30 m) and then 'pick-up acceleration' takes place (approximately 30 m to 60 m) (after Dick, 1988b). Within a group of homogeneously highly qualified sprinters the superiority of the fastest is most marked in the pick-up acceleration phase (Bartonietz and Güllich, 1992). The aim in training locomotor speed is to maintain the maximum speed attained after the acceleration phase for as long as possible. This primarily involves coordination training (with decreased strength demands) because of the high demands placed upon movement control. Intermuscular coordination becomes dominant in the relevant sections of a 100 m sprint, especially the tension and relaxation ability of the musculature based upon the flexibility of the neural processes.

Kinematic characteristics such as support and airborne times in individual stride cycles are performance indicators at the highest speed levels which should not exceed 100 or 120 milliseconds respectively (Mero et al., 1982; Schwirtz, 1989). Further criteria are dynamic characteristics, such as a greater, horizontally directed acceleration impulse in the late stance phase or a lower horizontal braking impulse in the early stance phase. According to recent data, an important force factor in the sprinting movement lies in the 'pulling' action of the steps as occurs in a fast hip extension movement following an active foot touch-down. This reduces the importance of the leg extension which is important in the acceleration phase (e.g., Waser, 1985).

According to Tepper (1989), the following ideas must be incorporated into a training programme for improved performance in the 100 m sprint:

(1) Performance improvement in the short sprint requires an increase in the total velocity–distance function.
(2) Apart from an absolute higher intensity, over the entire race elite performers require both a longer acceleration phase and an increased maintenance of the maximum velocity.
(3) The performance structural portion of speed endurance capabilities decreases at higher levels. A clear distinction must be made between the performance structural and the training methodological functions of this capability.

Training of sprint capabilities

Sprint training must initially be based on both elementary and complex performance prerequisites (Figure 7.11). Secondly, a distinction must be made between training of acceleration ability (including reactive speed) and locomotor speed. The interchanging relationship between these performance factors must be taken into consideration in a complex education.

Reactive speed. Although reactive speed is relatively unimportant in a weighting of the speed determining characteristics of the short sprint (approximately 3%) it must still be considered in sprint training because of the small margin that often decides between victory and defeat. As a result of the minimal trainability of motor reactive speed in trained sprinters with whom extremely good reaction performances (little over 0.1 s) can be taken as a selection criterion, a stabilization of this ability should therefore be a primary aim. This is particularly so as variations in reaction times are

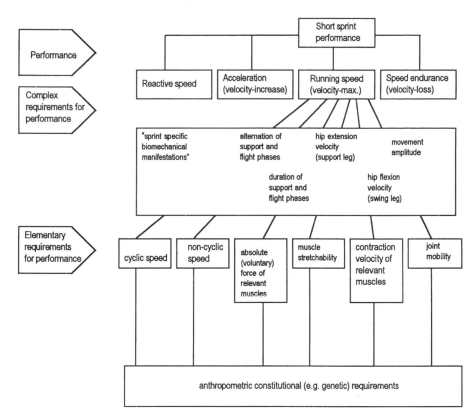

Figure 7.11: Structure and classification of the short sprint (Weineck, 1994, p. 419; after Lehmann, 1993, p. 12).

influenced by the momentary excitation state (pre-start state) or the physical/mental state of fatigue often experienced in practice. From a training method perspective a high degree of directed (selective) sensory attention should be developed with the aim of producing an increase in activity of the central nervous system. There are indisputable benefits of a general, fundamental teaching of reactions achieved through:

- reaction games (catching, tagging games), relays, ball games;
- diverse reaction exercises to optical acoustic and tactile signals;
- starts to diverse signals with different body positions.

Despite this, the specific teaching of reactions at higher levels should be executed in association with the competition movement (deep start) and the high levels of acceleration. By using a discipline-specific form of information (acoustic signal) the simple reaction required in sprinting should be trained by frequently practising the standard situation and its continuation with relevant variations. Examples of variable conditions are changing the standing position of the starter and irregular time intervals between the commands. Training should proceed primarily with the repetitive method with starts over 10–30 m, including partner starts or handicap starts in which one runner starts further back than the competitors. Tabatschnik (1976) recommended variations in the standard acoustic stimulus as a method of increasing the concentration performance to prevent stagnation of reactive speed. Zaciorskij (1968) and Matwejew (1981) supplement this training idea with the 'sensory method' aimed at improving time perception.

Acceleration ability.   The relevant muscle groups must be taxed at the highest intensity for the optimization of accelerating ability. The decisive parameter to be developed is the specific speed strength level which must be based on a very high level of maximum strength. Furthermore, the acceleration distances in training must be set such that maximum velocity can be reached. Whereas distances of about 20 m may be sufficient in youth training, distances of 45–60 m are more appropriate at elite levels. With respect to load, the number of repetitions and repeat series must be kept low. It should be remembered that the energy supply is in the anaerobic–alactic area which is highly dependent upon the length of rests. For example, Weineck (1994) recommended one minute rest for every 10 m run. Resistances must also be kept at a level at which the typical competition movement structure is maintained. The following special training contents are given as examples (summarized from Bartonietz and Güllich, 1992; Schnabel et al., 1994; Weineck, 1994; Jonath et al., 1995; Stein and Mäde, 1995):

- low/high starts under normal conditions up to 60 m (depending upon performance level);
- starts under easier conditions (downhill or while being pulled);
- starts under more difficult conditions (uphill or with pulling resistance);
- starts against competition or handicap starts (see above);
- ins-and-outs;
- relays;
- pushing trolleys, boxes, and so on.

The use of horizontal jumps has a particularly beneficial effect upon the accelerating ability. 'Short jumps' such as ankle jumps, one- or two-legged single/triple/five jumps are as effective as 'long jumps' (mainly jump runs to 80 m or jump runs against resistance).

Specialized strength training is extremely important (e.g., Allmann, 1982; Hawkins, 1984; Lopez, 1991). Maximum strength training with repeated maximal strength applications (especially in terms of intramuscular coordination) should initially precede special speed strength development. Dynamic force application methods receive priority in the following transition phase. These can be complemented by particularly effective variations of reactive (plyometric) strength training. More specific explanations of this phenomenon are found in the chapter on strength training.

Maximum cyclic (locomotor) speed.   Together with accelerating ability, loco-motor speed is the major factor in sprint performance with respect to train-ing structure. The maximum velocity achieved is regarded as the actual qualification criterion for sprinters. Training of maximum cyclic speed de-mands the highest intensities, low load durations, alactic or low lactic meta-bolic situations, long recovery pauses within the training units and a good neuromuscular preparedness of the athlete (Tepper, 1989). A further re-quirement is the improvement of intermuscular coordination, the quality of the movement technique and movement rhythm. However, if the exercises used for speed improvement are not sport-specific then they must initially be trained at submaximal levels. Training can only be started at maximal or supramaximal intensities with good control of the movement.

General developmental exercises composed of all non-cyclic and cyclic hopping, jumping, and sprint forms are useful in improving the locomotor speed, given that they possess 'certain similarities in the coordinative move-ment structure' to the competition discipline (Matwejew, 1981, p. 169). Spe-cially designed exercises for the track sprint teach specific movement technique and frequency speed on the basis of the competition movement. These include:

- coordination/innervation exercises from the so-called sprint ABC (e.g. dribbling (as ankle running on the spot); skipping; heel raises; all forms of 'short jumps' such as hopping runs, springing jumps, alternate jumps and running jumps);
- 'flying' sprints (maximum speed sprints over 10–30 m after preceding maximum acceleration);
- ins-and-outs (direction changing runs at highest velocity);
- speed increase runs with maximum velocity at the end;
- training of relay baton changes;
- coordination runs (technique-control running).

The use of 'supramaximal' sprints are of particular benefit especially when teaching elementary cyclic speed. Forced or simplified conditions pro-voke an increase in frequency or running velocity which is up to 10% higher than for a normal sprint. Prognostic velocities or time programmes can be achieved through:

- running downhill on a small gradient;
- pull-support runs (with elastic rope or special pulling system);
- sprinting on motor-driven treadmills.

The main training method to be used is the repetition method with the athlete primarily concentrating upon good technique, execution velocity and high acceleration levels with complete recovery pauses. In supramaximal training special attention should be paid to the loading of the neuromuscular system. Maximum (frequency) speed training should therefore not be used at the elite level, more often than two or three times in a microcycle. Kusnezow (quoted in Tschiene,1973, p. 197) preferred 'variable loading' rather than the solitary use of standard loads at maximum intensity, to prevent a neural stabilization which could lead to a velocity barrier.

Speed training in swimming

General structural demands.   Competitive performance in swimming is influenced by many related factors (Figure 7.12). Although swim-specific endurance is the most important requirement, the introduction of the 50 m sprint event has increased the importance of highly developed speed performance. In this shortest competitive distance both the maintenance of speed and especially the maximum speed must be improved. The maximum speed can be measured over short distances of 15–20 m. Until recently similar demands have only been seen in water polo.

Special structure of demands for speed capabilities in swimming.   As it is a new discipline the freestyle sprint places new and sometimes different biomechanical and physiological demands upon the competitors. The contents and planning of training must therefore, also adapt. An improved reaction time at the start, a higher movement frequency achieved through the contraction velocity of activated muscles and a rapid interchange of contraction and relaxation of the musculature necessary for the swimming movement are the main characteristics in the development of swimming technique. From a biomechanical point of view the successful execution of the swimming movement becomes more important when the body is moving in the swimming direction at greater velocities because the water resistance increases disproportionately to the movement velocity. An optimized technique is therefore, especially important in faster swimming to reduce water resistance. A successful biomechanical technique suitable for sprint swimming shows smaller intracyclic fluctuations in speed, a high average swimming speed and a constant average speed over the complete distance.

The biomechanical requirements and the physiological characteristics of optimum performance are important in the race tactics of sprint swimming. Races deviating from what might be termed optimal biomechanics may be a result of the biologically imposed quotient of energy flow rate/time resulting in a particularly noticeable decrease in energy production in the first 30 seconds. Wirtz (1995) concludes that even though the speed of the fastest

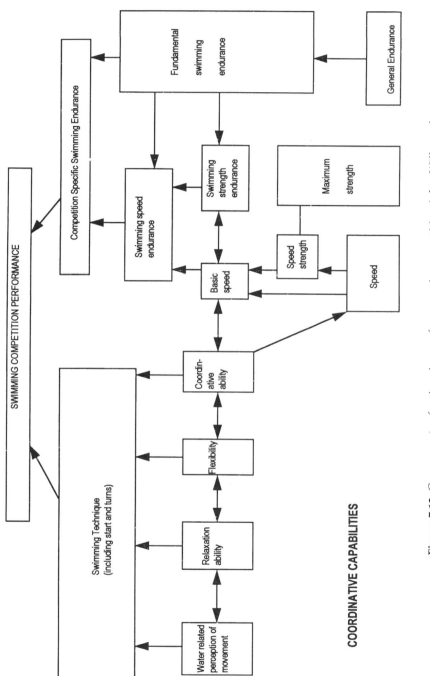

Figure 7.12: Components of swimming performance in competition (after Wilke and Madsen, 1988).

elite swimmings decreased over 50 m, the decrease was less pronounced than in weaker athletes (Figure 7.13). This may indicate a better cooperative function between the energy-producing mechanisms.

Swimming speed is reliant on the activation of specific muscle and muscle fibres. Training methods must therefore be developed which highlight the training of competition technique. This may be assisted through use of additional weights either to pull the swimmer in the swimming direction (Figure 7.14b) or against it (7.14a). There are many indications that sprint performance in the water is improved by pulling-induced hypermaximal swimming. Maglischo (1982) employed this training method by increasing the swimming speed with fins. Wilke and Madsen (1988) pulled a swimmer with a rope as another method of increasing the swim specific speed and the stroke frequency. No scientific studies of the semi-tethered method with

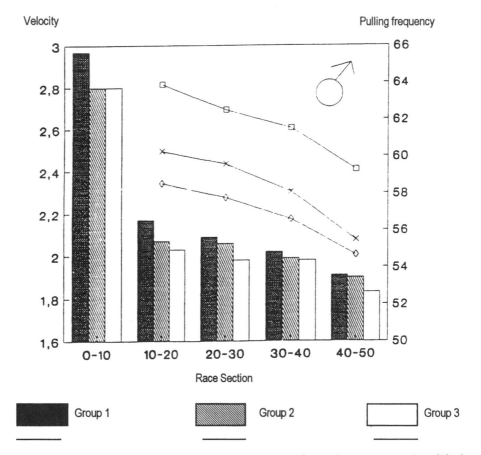

Figure 7.13: Velocity and stroke frequency in 50 m freestyle swimming (modified from Wirtz, 1995).

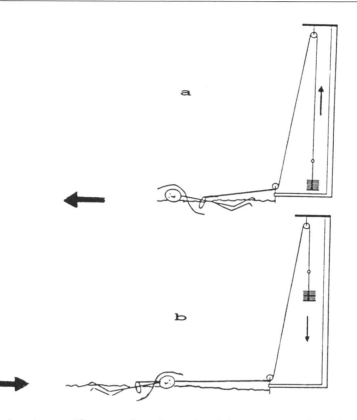

Figure 7.14: A swim-specific strength and speed training apparatus (modified from Wirtz, 1995).

hyper-maximal speed mentioned above have been applied to swimming. The greater movement velocity may improve neural mechanisms (Krüger, 1979).

The transfer of propulsive forces to the body during the execution of movements is especially relevant in sprint swimming. A clear distinction between speed and strength in training methodology may therefore not be possible. Studies relating the development of strength on land to sprint capabilities in water have shown only weak correlations at an elite swimming level (Costill et al., 1983; Sharp, 1986; Reilly et al., 1990). However, all these authors emphasized that development of a basic strength level is indispensable.

A greater specificity of strength demands in the water is achieved through tethered or semitethered methods. Studies by Hopper (1982), Costill et al. (1983), and Christensen and Smith (1987) indicated a close relationship between free swimming speed and strength training using a tethered approach where a defined force on the rope restrained the swimmer. Various other authors have also suggested this as a suitable training method for sprint swimming (Baldermann and Stichert, 1982; Sharp, 1986; Satori and Tschiene, 1987; Bollens et al., 1988).

Mobilizing the available strength potential is dependent upon the number of activated muscle fibres (recruitment) and the adaptation velocity (impulse frequency). As this mobilization is movement-specific it should be trained under competition conditions whenever possible. Therefore, the applicability to elite swimmers of intramuscular and intermuscular strength training on land is limited.

The following sequence of methods is suggested for speed training in swimming given that a general foundation of well-developed musculature and sufficient aerobic endurance is present:

- hypertrophy training of the relevant musculature; first on land then in the water;
- training of the relevant musculature against increased resistance with the primary aim of increasing fibre recruitment;
- hypermaximal swimming to increase the impulse frequency;
- the training of speed endurance.

So how can the various components of swimming speed be improved in practice? Firstly training the maximum speed performance should occur predominantly in those biological structures already possessing a certain level of coordination. Secondly the correct choice of training methods is important.

The following forms of training are available for improving reactive speed and the specific demands of swimming placed upon the non-cyclic (active) speed and the cyclic (frequency) speed.

(1) *Reactive speed*
    (a) Training in water
        (i)   starting dives and water starts from various positions with and without a start signal followed by a maximum sprint over a short distance (also with different signals given at varying intervals)
        (ii)   water games with a ball, at times in restricted areas
        (iii)   'little' games in the water for youth training.
    (b) Training on land
        (i)   general training of reactions by methods seen in athletics and sport games (e.g., ball return games, shadow running, sprinting on command).
(2) *Non-cyclic active speed*
    (a) Training in water
        (i)   starting dives with scrutiny of the imprint on the starting blocks

(ii)   various forms of turns with explosive push-offs from the wall
(iii) diving
(iv)   water games and obstacle swimming for youth training.
(b) Training on land
(i)   jumping and sprinting exercises with maximum intensity as seen in athletics
(ii)   throwing and pushing exercises (with complete body extension) with a medicine ball
(iii) maximum strength and explosive strength training with weight machines or free weights
(iv)   small games such as relays or ball games for youth training.
(3) *Cyclic frequency speeds*
(a) Training in water
(i)   all forms of exercises for improving technique
(ii)   complex and single movements in all swimming disciplines (short distances at highest movement frequencies)
(iii) starts followed by quick sprints
(iv)   training of turns (e.g., sprint—fast turn—sprint)
(v)   sprints with variations in frequency (ins-and-outs)
(vi)   swimming with propulsive and restraining aids (e.g., tethered and semitethered methods)
(vii) water polo technique (dribbling, game situations, accelerations and changes of direction on command—with and without a ball)
(viii) games with and without a ball in youth training.

The most appropriate method for the development of the above speed characteristics is the repetition method. The volume of training is kept small in order to prevent the unavoidable maximum loading intensities of an excessive anaerobic–lactate metabolism. The number of repetitions is high but the distance covered is short and long rest periods should be included.

The specific intensity parameters are as follows:

- Duration of individual repetitions is between 6 and 8 seconds.
- This represents a distance of 15 m (with starting dive) or approximately 12 m (with push-off from the wall).
- Duration of rest periods between 3 and 5 minutes.
- The number of repetitions per training session is 4–20.

A high level of anaerobic–lactic metabolism is produced when high movement frequencies and high strength demands are combined. Therefore, a specific maintenance of speed for competition performance is indispensable as a supplement to maximum speed capabilities in sprint swimming.

However, in this section the training of speed endurance in swimming will only be briefly mentioned.

Resistance to fatigue-related loss of performance should be trained by the repetition method and intensive interval training. Speed repetition training is employed only when in good training form and usually over distances (50 or 100 m) specific to the competition preparation. The distances lie between 25 and 75 m with swim times of 10–45 seconds. Between four and eight repetitions are executed at speeds of a minimum of 95% of the present fastest time. The rest periods, which if possible should be active (compensation swimming) should permit general overall recovery.

The use of intensive interval training especially in preparatory phases comprises distances of 25–50 m in two to four series of eight repetitions. The swimming speed is 93% of the present best time. The rest period between repetitions is approximately 60–90 seconds with rests between series of approximately 3 minutes (compensation).

A special form of training for speed endurance is the broken competition distance. In this form of competition and control method the competition distance is divided into sections, the sum of the swim times over the separate sections should be equal to, or marginally less than, the time aimed at over the complete distance.

It should be emphasized that specific measures must be taken for preparation and regeneration within training sessions concentrating upon the development of speed. These include an adequate warm-up swim, compensation swimming in the rest periods and also an active warm-down swim.

The improvement of speed in ball games

Speed training in tennis

General structural demands.   Tennis is a very complex sport with predominantly non-cyclic loading. Technique, tactics, psychology and physical capabilities influence the strength of a player. Even small physical advantages, especially in speed or endurance, can decide matches at the elite level. The importance of special fitness training as a component of systematic performance control is often underestimated. Weber (1985) stated that elite tennis placed greater physical demands upon players than in past years. The neglect of fitness training and therefore also speed training, seen mainly at lower levels, is the result of the widely accepted idea that 'tennis is played, not trained'. Another problem is the difficulty involved in determining the precise influence of various fitness factors such as speed on tennis performance.

Special structure of demands for speed capabilities in tennis.   The optimization of materials such as stiffer racquets and a need for varying abilities when playing on different court surfaces, combined with a more aggressive playing attitude, have unavoidably led to increasing demands upon the speed and explosive capabilities of tennis players. Although tennis is not a pure speed sport, the aim of correctly returning the ball one more time than the opponent is also dependent upon speed. In terms of speed requirements, the complex aim of the movement is one restricted to a simple sprint to the ball but also to a rapid comprehension of the game situation, the psychological construction of a tactical plan, the preparation of the shot, its execution and the attainment of an advantageous position in preparation for the next shot. The various speed demands required for this can either be characterized by a player's own game plan or consist of more passive reactions as seen in response to the pace of the game played by your opponent. A basic rule is that the faster one's game (by making shots early or hitting the ball with high velocities), the shorter the distance the ball and the player must travel and also the shorter the time available for the opponent to react. However, this may also result in a more difficult shot and consequently a higher error rate. Finally, a greater speed of movement requires more energy for muscular work.

Objective, quantitative analyses of the game structure and the reaction to loads in tennis (e.g., Weber, 1985) have shown that energy-rich phosphates are capable of providing sufficient energy for the majority of rallies in a game. The average time for rallies cited here was 10 seconds with a rest of approximately 20 seconds between rallies, which would permit a complete regeneration of the phosphogens. If one further considers that the distance that must be run to play a shot in tennis is at the most 14 m (on average about 4 m) it becomes clear that the metabolic requirements of tennis players are primarily dictated by a high phosphorylation potential for fast, explosive, short-duration movements. This is accompanied by high demands on tennis-specific coordination which increase even more with faster court surfaces or when an attacking tactic is used during play. The anaerobic, lactate steered speed endurance is less important because only rarely do lactate levels of 4–8 mmol/1 occur, for example in matches dominated by baseline play rallies may last longer than 15 seconds. Of greater relevance is that form of (aerobic) endurance that permits a player to maintain an optimal technique and maximum speed even in long matches. In this case a large reservoir of readily available carbohydrates plays an important role along with the previously mentioned ability to rapidly resynthesize energy-rich phosphates.

Specific speed training for tennis

Running, hitting and jumping movements are found most frequently in tennis. Movement studies based upon video analysis show that apart from reactive speed, the ability to accelerate (cyclic motor speed) and jumping and hitting speed (non-cyclic active speed) determine performance (Geese, 1985). Grosser (1992) suggests two steps towards the improvement of speed for tennis players. Firstly fundamental speed should be developed, for example by jump training following 'unweighting' which should then be integrated into complex game situations. Speed improvement for complex, tennis-specific performance is attempted through various forms of training for footwork and racquet handling. Exercises such as accelerations from standing, sprints, direction changing sprints, side steps, serve and volley actions, net playing actions and others should not exceed a maximum of 6 seconds. These exercises should be executed in series of 4–6 repetitions with rest periods of approximately 3 minutes between the series and rest periods of approximately 1 minute between repetitions to restore the creatine-phosphate reservoir.

Specifically structured weight training can be a useful supplement to speed training. The relationships between strength and speed of movement form the basis for a quite specific profile of demands for strength training in tennis. The fact that a decreased mass to be moved reduces the correlation between maximum muscle strength and movement speed whilst the coordination aspects become more significant, applies to all stroke movements in tennis but not to the acceleration of the player's own body such as in a sprint to the net. This is discussed in the instructions for speed training for sprinting in athletics.

Many training methods and contents are offered in practice for the improvement of reactive and movement speed in game sports. A selection of these relevant to tennis are presented here.

Reactive speed.   Letzelter (1978) defined the most common forms of reactions in game sports as distinguishing reactions, choosing reactions and reactions to moving objects. These forms indicate reaction times of 0.25–1 s. Decisive improvements in reaction skills of tennis players are dependent upon an optimization of the anticipation of game situations. As a result of the complex demands upon reaction skills, it is suggested that both reactive and the active speed are not trained in isolation but should be combined as a tennis-specific training complex. The teaching of reactions in complex game situations can be accompanied by exercises based upon simply choosing reactions to improve reactive speed and the ability to concentrate:

- short distance sprints with changes of direction dictated by optical signals;
- running games from track training, if possible with special demands placed upon the ability to react to optical inputs, such as returning games in a tight space;
- shadow running in pairs;

- volleys hit at very short distances from serves, returns or volleys with the back turned to the player hitting the ball and then turning around at the sound of the shot.

Running speed.   The distance run in one direction in tennis is a maximum of 14 m and in 70% of the cases less than 5 m. The maximum non-cyclic running acceleration therefore plays a dominant role, especially in game situations, such as those requiring a change of direction with an explosive start or certain game strategies seen especially in attacking tennis. The development of specific running speed (acceleration, braking, change of direction) together with maximum and reactive strength of the leg muscles must be trained at high levels. Kleinöder and Mester (1991) showed a positive effect result from an 8 week periodized strength training programme on tennis specific movement speed.

An optimal starting position (e.g. side stepping) from which the body can accelerate in various directions depending on the level of agility can be trained through running coordination. Absolute speed maximization is not of primary importance in a tennis match, but rather an optimally adapted running speed. The combination of a chosen running speed for various court surfaces is always a compromise between needing to reach the ball, being in a position to play an effective shot and the need to conserve energy. A stable stance position for the shot must also be attained which permits an acceleration in the opposite direction without sliding as a result of high running speeds (which may, for example occur on sand). The previously mentioned tennis-specific endurance is certainly also decisive for the speed performance over a complete match. We therefore arrive at the apparent paradox that speed in tennis is to a certain extent dependent upon endurance.

Examples for the improvement of special running speed are:

- running coordination exercises, e.g., skipping for about 5 m at a maximum frequency;
- flying sprints (with prior acceleration) over 10–30 m;
- high starts over 5–10 m, also in various directions;
- sprint starts from a prone position over 2–10 m;
- short sprints on a hill or against resistance;
- horizontal jumps (running jumps, one legged hops) from a standing position and as initial movements;
- fast side-steps and cross-steps along the line, also with changes of direction;
- 'potato picking' (balls deposited upon the line intersections of the court are individually deposited behind the baseline as rapidly as possible);
- pendulum runs from line to line;

- complex exercises, for example with racquet and ball: reaching a lob with a sprint, smashing and then sprinting to the net, or playing passing shots while running at maximum speed.

Stroke speed.   The speed of the tennis stroke and therefore also the velocity of the ball are dependent upon the acceleration of the racquet. As this piece of sporting equipment possesses only a relatively small mass, intermuscular coordination and the stroke technique rather than strength capabilities such as maximum strength are of major relevance. Geese (1985) is of the opinion that the majority of elite male tennis players possess sufficient muscular strength to hit tennis balls at such velocities that they can hardly be returned. The problem therefore, does not lie in a lack of specific strength but rather in the coordination of stroke execution. On the other hand many top international players show that the athletic characteristics in tennis have become more prominent. Mester and Weber (1990) partially explained this by the following fact: points won were the result of a serve or from powerful shots from the baseline or from midcourt more often than in the past. These authors regarded the development of explosive strength in terms of attaining a high force level in a short time as indispensable for an effective acceleration of the racquet in the serve or in a forceful groundstroke. Special attention was given to neural adaptation (recruitment and frequency). In addition to this, studies conducted on male and female tennis players of different playing standards have shown that even a considerable increase in maximum strength achieved through appropriate training will definitely not lead to a decrease in coordinated performance. This was shown through special coordination tests such as serving precision. If a tennis stroke is regarded as an overall movement in which a down–up motion of the body precedes the majority of strokes or in which approaching balls can only be reached and returned in conjunction with body movement, like jumping, then the above statement concerning the importance of maximum strength and reactive strength must be modified. Transfer of the additional specific strength to the appropriate movement (stroke) is easier for higher-class players with a greater level of movement automization (Kleinöder and Mester, 1991).

However, the velocity of the shot itself and especially the manner in which it is achieved depends not only upon strength and coordination capabilities but also on the general playing style and tactical behaviour in specific game situations. For example the velocity of a volley is achieved almost without racquet acceleration and depends upon the velocity of the opposition shot. Similar to the previous description of running speed, when contemplating the speed of a stroke an optimum speed of movement required for safety and length of the shot is also fundamentally more important than a maximum movement speed. The first serve, in which an ace is attempted, smashes and passing shots are some exceptions where high accelerations are required. The optimum speed of a stroke is also dependent upon the tactical requirement so that 'safe' shots with high levels of topspin are hit with relatively high vertical racquet velocity while 'penetrating' shots are hit with higher levels of forward racquet velocity. Training the speed of the stroke should be based upon a sound technique and discontinued in a training session if the accuracy of the shots becomes noticeably scattered.

Training examples.

- One-armed or two-armed throwing of medicine balls (also used for imitation of forehand stroke);
- imitating shots against increased resistance (weighted racquet, Deuser strap, hand weights, and so on);
- very rapidly executed serves, returns, 'killer forehands';
- fast shots in specific situations, e.g., passing shots while running near full speed or combining lobs and smashes;
- volleys under time pressure;
- drill training, e.g., two players at the net place pressure upon a player at the baseline who is attempting to hit a passing shot;
- shadow tennis with rapid stroke simulations;
- stroke simulations with the racquet in the cover, whereby special attention must be paid to racquet guidance;
- tennis shots with squash or badminton racquets and soft balls (can also be employed as a means of overcoming a speed barrier);
- 10 repetitions of four winning shots hit with the forehand and backhand from the half court.

SYNOPSIS OF SPEED TRAINING THEORY AND PRACTICE

The term speed is used in sport in many ways but often in a very imprecise manner. It is mainly used to characterize those performances in which speed is dominant but occurs in combination with other performance requirements.

The different approaches for differentiating speed can be summarized by firstly stating that people basically possess the general characteristic 'pure' speed. This is highly genetically disposed, can only be minimally trained and if it occurs in sport at all then only in very short reactive performances or with minimal external resistance. Alongside this there is also 'complex' speed that has various functions which are dependent upon further functional capabilities such as strength or endurance. Complex speed performances can be optimized by effective training of neural and muscular characteristics. The quality of the so-called 'elementary' movement programmes (in terms of 'short-time programmes') is regarded as a prerequisite for developing other forms of speed.

The final comment is that although one cannot call speed a universal characteristic, generally applicable instructions can be made concerning speed training. Sports science dictates that the path from practice to an analysis of demands and then further practice continues to be the most promising for fulfilling practical and effective speed training.

REFERENCES

Ae, M., Ito, A. and Suzuki, M. (1992) The men's 100 metres, *New Studies in Athletics*, **7**, 47–52.

Alain, C. and Proteau, L. (1982) Auswahlreaktionen bei Rückschlagspielen, in *Die Reaktionszeit des Sportlers* (Ed. A. Krüger), pp. 87–102, Bartels and Wernitz, Berlin.

Allmann, H. (1982) Sprintschnelligkeit und Kraft, *Lehre der Leichtanthletik*, **4**, 116–118.

Allmann, H. (1985) Maximalkraft und Sprintleistung—Maximalkrafttraining im Sprinttraining, in *Grundlagen des Maximal- und Schnellkrafttrainings* (Ed. M. Bührle), pp. 282–300, Hofmann, Schorndorf.

Baldermann, G. and Stichert, K. - H. (1982) Zum Stand des Krafttrainings im Sportschwimmen unter besonderer Berücksichtigung angewendeter Krafttrainingsöüngen und -mittel, *Theorie und Praxis des Leistungssports*, **2/3**, 215–225.

Ballreich, R. (1969) *Weg- und Zeitmerkmale von Sprintbewegungen*, Bartels & Wernitz, Berlin.

Bartonietz, K. and Güllich, A. (1992) Die Bedeutung der Pick-up-Beschleunigung bei Höchstleistungen im 100 m-Sprint: Ein Beitrag zu Leistungs- und Trainingsstruktur des Kurzsprints, in *Olympiastützpunkte im Brennpunkt praxisorientierter Sportswissesnschaft (Vol. 10)*, pp. 198–214, DSB, Frankfurt.

Bauersfeld, M. (1983) Studie zu ausgewählten Problemen der Schnelligkeit, *Wissenschaftliche Zeitschrift der DHfK*, **3**, 45–64.

Bauersfeld, M. (1989) Charakteristik der Schnelligkeit und deren Trainierbarkeit im Prozeß der sportlichen Vervollkommung, *Wissenschaftliche Zeitschrift der DHfK*, **3**, 36–47.

Bauersfeld, M. and Voss, G. (1992) *Neue Wege im Schnelligkeitstraining*, Philippka, Münster.

Baumann, W., Schwirtz, A. and Gross, V. (1986) Biomechanik des Kurzstreckenlaufs, in *Biomechanik der Sportarten Vol. 1* (Eds. R. Ballreich and A. Kuhlow), pp. 1–15, Bauer, Stuttgart.

Behrend, R. (1988) *Methodische Lösungen für ein schnelligkeitsorientiertes Sprungtraining im leichtathletischen Aufbautraining*, Diss. DHfK, Leipzig.

Bernstein, N.A. (1988) *Bewegungsphysiologie*, Barth, Leipzig.

Boiko, V.V. (1988) Die gezielte Entwicklung der Bewegungsfähigkeit des Sportlers, in *Informationen zum Leistungssport Vol. 6* (Ed. Deutscher Sportbund, Bundesausschuß Leistungssport), Frankfurt.

Bollens, E., Annemans, L., Vaes, W. and Clarys, J.P. (1988) Peripheral EMG comparison between fully tethered and free front crawl swimming, in *Swimming Science V* (Eds. B. Ungerechts., K. Reischle, and K. Wilke), pp. 173–182, Human Kinetics, Bielefeld.

Bös, K. and Mechling, H. (1983) *Dimensionen sportmotorischer Leistungen*, Hofmann, Schorndorf.

Brüggemann, G.P. and Susanka, P. (1990) Time analysis of the Sprint Event, in *Scientific Research Project at the Games of the XXXIV Olympiad – Seoul 1988* (Eds. IAF and IAAF). Final report, London.

Bührle, M. (1989) Maximalkraft – Schnellkraft – Reaktivkraft, *Sportwissenschaft*, **3**, 311–325.

Christensen, C. L. and Smith, G. W. (1987) Relationship of Maximum Sprint Speed and Maximal Stroking Force in Swimming, *Journal Swimming Research*, **2**, 18–20.

Costill, D.L., King, D. S., Holdren, A. and Hargreaves, M. (1983) Sprint Speed vs. Swimming Power, *Swimming Technique*, **20**, 20–22.

Dick, F.W. (1988a) Zur Entwicklung der Sprintschnelligkeit, *Lehre der Leichtathletik*, **28**, 1053–1054.

Dick, F.W. (1988b) Developing Sprinting Speed, *Athletics Coach*, **4**, 4–5.

Dickwach, H. and Perlt, B. (1995) Geschwindigkeitmessung mittels Laser, *Lehre der Leichtathletik*, **26/27**, 151–159.

Dietz, V. (1985) Neurophysiologische Grundlagen des Kraftverhaltens, in *Grundlagen des Maximal- und Schnellkrafttrainings* (Ed. M. Bührle), pp. 16–34, Hofmann, Schorndorf.

Dintiman, G.B. and Ward, R.D. (1988) *Sport Speed*, Leisure Press, Champaign, IL.

Geese, R. (1985) Kraft und Schnelligkeit im Tennissport, in *Konditionstraining im Tennis* (Eds. H. Gabler and B. Zein), pp. 36–46, Zwalina, Ahrensburg.

Geese, R. and Hillebrecht, M. (1995) *Schnelligkeitstraining*, Meyer and Meyer, Aachen.

Gerisch, G. and Reichl, A. (1978) Durchführung und Auswertung eines motorischen Tests im Sportspiel Fußball, *Leistungsfußball*, **9**, 23.

Grosser, M. (1991) *Schnelligkeitstraining*, blv, Munich.

Grosser, M. (1992) Schnelligkeit und Sportliche Leistung, *Tennissport*, **3**, 4–6.

Grosser, M. and Starischka, S. (1981) *Konditionstests*, blv, Munich.

Grosser, M., Brüggermann, P. and Zintl, F. (1986) *Leistungssteuerung in Training und Wettkampf*, blv, Munich.

Gundlach, H. (1963) Laufgeschwindigkeit und Schrittgestaltung beim 100-m-Lauf, *Theorie und Praxis der Körperkultur*, **12**, 4–6, 255 ff.

Harre, D. (1986) *Trainingslehre*, Sportverlag, Berlin.

Harre, D. and Hauptmann, M. (1987) Schnelligkeit und Schnelligkeitstraining, *Theorie und Praxis der Körperkultur*, **3**, 198–204.

Hauptmann, M. (1990) *Der Einfluß von geringen äußeren Bewegungswiderständen auf das Niveau der Schnelligkeitsfähigkeit und auf die Ausbildung von schnellen Bewegungsleistungen*, Diss. DHfK, Leipzig.

Hauptmann, M. (1994) Training der Schnelligkeit, in *Trainingswissenschaft* (Eds. G. Schnabel, D. Harre, A. Borde), Sportverlag, Berlin.

Hauptmann, M. and Nordmann, L. (1993) 'Erleichterte Bedingungen' im Training, *Leipziger sportwissenschaftliche Beiträge*, 34, Sankt, Augustin.

Hawkins, J.D. (1984) Specificity strength training as a factor in the improvement of shoulder strength and sprinting speed, *Track and Field Quarterly Review*, **2**, 55–59.

Hellwig, T.-A. (1991) *Das Verhalten der Blutlaktatkonzentration nach Sprintbelastungen unterschiedlicher Belastungsdauer und -intensität unter besonderer Berücksichtigung der Entwicklung einer speziellen Testmethodik zur sprintspezifischen Leistungsdiagnostik und Trainingssteuerung*, Hartung - Gorre, Konstanz.

Hennemann, E., Shahani, B. T. and Carpenter, D. O. (1965) Excitability and inability of motoneurons of different sizes, *Journal of Neurophysiology*, **28**, 599–620.

Hess, W.D. (1985) Tests zur Diagnostik der Schnelligkeitsfähigkeiten in der Sportmethodik, *Theorie und Praxis der Körperkultur*, **10**, 729–731.

Hess, W.D. (1990) Zur Biomechanik des Sprints und ihre Anwendung in der Trainingspraxis, in *Techniques in Athletics*, Keynote Symposia, Cologne, July 7–9, 24–48.

Hess, W.D. (1991a) Leistungsstrukturelle Aspekte des 100-m-Laufes und ihre Umsetzung in die Trainingspraxis, *Die Lehre der Leichtathletik*, **22**, 15–18.

Hess, W.D. (1991b). Sprint-Lauf-Gehen, Sportverlag, Berlin.

Hollmann, W. and Hettinger, T. (1980) *Sportmedizin—Arbeits- und Trainingsgrundlagen*, Schattauer, Stuttgart, New York.

Hopper, T.R. (1982) Measurement of power delivered to an external weight, in *Biomechanics and Medicine in Swimming IV* (Eds. A.P. Hollander, P.A. Huijing, and G. de Groot), pp. 112–119, Human Kinetics, Champaign, IL.

Ikai, M. (1967) Biomechanics of sprint running with respect to the speed curve, in *Biomechanics I. Proceedings of the First International Seminar on Biomechanics*, pp. 282–290, Karger, Basel and New York.

Jakowlev, N.N. (1977) *Sportbiochemie*, Barth, Leipzig.

Joch, W. and Hasenberg, R. (1990) Über den Zusammenhang zwischen Startreaktionszeit und Sprintleistung, *Leistungssport*, **1**, 36–39.

Jonath, U., Krempel, R., Haag, E. and Müller, H. (1995) *Leichtathletik 1 Lanfen*, Rowohlt, Reinbeck.

Juwu, Z. (1990) A study of correlation between extremities reaction time and performance of young Chinese women volleyball players, *Sports Science Beijing*, **2**, 70–76.

Kirchgässner, H. (1981) Ausgewählte Probleme der Bestimmung der Reaktionsfähigkeit in den Zweikampfsportarten unter besonderer Berücksichtigung experimenteller Untersuchungen im Boxen, *Theorie und Praxis der Körperkultur*, **8**, 586–600.

Kleinöder, H. and Mester, J. (1991) Krafttraining im Tennis—Auswirkungen auf die Bewegungsschnelligkeit? *Tennissport*, **2**, 2–6.

Klemm, O. (1930) Gedanken über Leibesübungen, *Neue Physiologische Studien*, **2**, 145–167.

Komi, P.V. (1985) Dehnungs–Verkürzungs–Zyklus bei Bewegungen mit sportlicher Leistung, in *Grundlagen des Maximal- und Schnellkrafttrainings* (Ed. M. Bührle), pp. 254–269, Hofmann, Schorndorf.

Komi, P.V. (1989) Skelettmuskulatur, in *Olympiabuch der Sportmedizin* (Eds. Dirix et al.), pp. 29–49, Sportärtze Verlag, Köln.

Konzag, G. (1983) Entscheidungstest—ein Verfahren zur Objectivierung des Resultats und der Zeit für taktische Handlungen von Sportspielern, in *Untersuchungsmethoden in der Sportpsychologie* (Ed. B. Schellenberger), pp. 129–146, Sportverlag, Berlin.

Kozlov, I. and Muravyev, I. (1992) Muscles and the sprint, *Fitness & Sports Review*, **6**, 192.

Krüger, A. (1979) Sprintvermögen und Informationsverarbeitungskapazität des Menschen, *Lehre der Leichtathletik*, **44**, 1398–1400 and **45**, 1436.

Küchler, G. (1983) *Steuerung der Muskeltätigkeit und begleitende Anpassungsprozesse*, Fischer, Stuttgart.

Kunz, H. and Unold, E. (1991) *Schnelligkeitstraining*, Eidgen. Sportschule, Magglingen.

Lehmann, F. (1991) *Zur Struktur und Entwicklung der maximalen Laufgeschwindigkeit in der Wechselwirkung von Schnelligkeit als neuromuskuläre Leistungsvoraussetzung und Kraft*, Habilitationsschrift, Leipzig.

Lehmann, F. (1992) Zur Beziehung zwischen Schnelligkeit als neuromuskuläre Leistungsvoraussetzung und maximaler Laufgeschwindigkeit im Sprint-Nachwuchstraining, *Leistungssport*, **4**, 12–19.

Lehmann, F. (1993) Schnelligkeitstraining im Sprint. Problemanalyse, neueste wissenschaftliche Erkenntnisse, Konsequenzen für das Kinder- und Jugendtraining, *Leichtathletiktraining*, **5/6**, 9–16.

Lehnertz, K. (1987) 'Kraftempfindungstraining' als Mittler zwischen Kraft- und Techniktraining, in *Theorie und Praxis des Techniktrainings* (Eds. H. Mechling, J. Schiffer and K. Carl), pp. 109–123, Cologne.

Letzelter, M. (1978) *Trainingsgrundlagen*, Rowohlt, Reinbek.

Lopez, V. (1991) An approach to strength training for sprinters, *Track Technique*, **115**, 3668–3685.

Mader, A., Heck, H., Liesen, H. and Hollmann, W. (1983) Simulative Berechnungen der dynamischen Änderungen von Phosphorylierungspotential, Laktatbildung und Laktatverteilung beim Sprint, *Deutsche Zeitschrift für Sportmedizin*, **34**, 14–22.

Maglischo, E.W. (1982) *Swimming Faster*, Mayfield, Palo Alto, CA.

Mahler, P. (1990) *Experimentelle Untersuchung zur Energiebereitstellung im Sprint*, TU, Munich.

Martin, D., Carl, K. and Lehnertz, K. (1993) *Handbuch Trainingslehre*, Hofmann, Schorndorf.

Matveev, L.P. (1965) *Problema periodizacii sportivnoj trenirovki*, Moscow.

Matveev, L.P. (1981) *Grundlagen des sportlichen Trainings*, Sportverlag, Berlin.

Matveev, S. F. (1985) *Postroenie trenirovocnych mikrociklov*, Kiev.

Mero, A., Luhtanen, P. and Komi, P. V. (1982) Zum Einfluß von Kontaktphasenmerkmalen auf die Schrittfrequenz beim Maximalsprint, *Leistungssport*, **4**, 308–313.

Mester, J. and Weber, J. (1990) Krafttraining im Tennis—Auswirkungen auf die Koordination? *Tennissport*, **5**, 2–6.

Neumaier, A. (1983) *Sportmotorische Tests in Unterricht und Training*, Hofmann, Schorndorf.

Nordmann, L. and Hauptmann, M. (1990) Kontrastives Training–Erkenntnisstand und trainingsmethodische Anwendung, *Theorie und Praxis der Körperkultur*, **6**, 420–427.

Osolin, N.G. (1954) *Das Training des Leichtathleten*, Sportverlag, Berlin.

Ozolin, E.S. (1990) The sprint, *Soviet Sports Rev*, **2**, 57–60, **3**, 142–144, **4**, 195–199.

Platonov, V.N. (1980) *Sovremennaja sportivnaja trenirovka*, Kiev.

Platonov, V.N. (1987) *Teorija sporta*, Kiev.

Polster, H. (1987) Handlungsschnelligkeit—Theoretische Bestimmung und experimentelle Befunde, *Wissenschaftliche Zeitschrift der DHfK*, **3**, 26–43.

Reilly, M.F., Kame, V.D., Termin, B., Tedesco, M.E., Ria, B., Falgairette, G. and Robert, A. (1990) Assessment of the Mechanical Power in the Young Swimmer, *Journal Swimming Research*, **3**, 11–15.

Rogers, D., McMorris, T. and Morris, T. (1991) Response Times of International Table Tennis Players to Different Coloured Balls and Backgrounds—A preliminary Invetigation, in *Applied research in Coaching and Athletics* (Eds. Simpson et al.), pp. 41–47, American Press, Boston.

Satori, J. and Tschiene, P. (1987) Die Fortentwicklung des Trainings, *Leistungssport*, **2**, 7–16.

Schellenberger, H. (1986) Handlungsschnelligkeit und Handlungsgenauigkeit im Sportspiel, *Theorie und Praxis der Körperkultur*, **6**, 427–429.

Schmidtbleicher, D. and Gollhofer, A. (1985) Einflußgrößen des reaktiven Bewegungsverhaltens und deren Bedeutung für die Sportpraxis, in *Grundlagen des Maximal- und Schnellkrafttrainings* (Ed. M. Bührle), pp. 271–281, Hofmann, Schorndorf.

Schnabel, G., Harre, D. and Borde, A. (Eds) (1994) *Trainingswissenschaft*, Sportverlag, Berlin.

Schwirtz, A. (1989) Läufe, in *Biomechanik der Sportarten* (Ed. K. Willimczik), pp. 127–148, Rowohlt, Reinbek.

Sharp, R.L. (1986) Muscle strength and power as related to competitive swimming, *Journal Swimming Research*, **2**, 5–10.

Simkin, N.W. (1960) *Physiologische Charakteristik von Kraft, Schnelligkeit und Ausdauer*, Sportverlag, Berlin.

Smirnov, K.M. (1974) *Sportphysiologie*, Sportverlag, Berlin.

Stein, N. (1995) Zielsetzungen und Formen von Widerstandsbelastungen im Schnelligkeitstraining, in *Widerstandsbelastungen im Schnelligkeitstraining* (Eds. N. Stein and U. Mäde), pp. 7–14, Leichtathletik – Verband Nordrhein, Duisburg.

Stein, N. and Mäde, U. (Eds) (1995) *Widerstandsbelastungen im Schnelligkeitstraining*, Workshopbericht, Leichtathletik—Verband Nordrhein, Duisburg.

Stein, R. (1993) Die Beschleunigungsfähigkeit bestimmt die Sprintleistung, *Leichtathletiktraining*, **5/6**, 33–36.

Stoboy, H. (1972) Neuromuskuläre Funktion und körperliche Leistung, in *Zentrale Themen der Sportmedizin* (Ed. W. Hollmann), pp. 16–42, Springer, Berlin–Heidelberg–New York.

Stulrajter, V. (1987) Reakcny cas e jeho vyuzitie v serme, *Teorie a Praxe tel. Vych.*, **2**, 107–112.

Susanka, P., Miskos, G., Millerova, K., Dostal, E. and Baral, F. (1988) Time analysis of the sprint hurdle events at the II World Championships in Athletics, *IAAF Scientific report*, Rome.

Tabatschnik, B. (1976) Zur Verbesserung der Reaktionsschnelligkeit von jugendlichen Sportlern, *Leistungssport*, **3**, 186–188.

Tabatschnik, B. (1981) Die langfristige Vorbereitung des Sprinters, *Die Lehre der Leichtathletik*, **45/46**.

Tabatschnik, B. and Sultanov, N.A. (1981) Differentiated methods of training sprinters, *Soviet Sports Review*, **1**, 45–46.

Tepper, E. (1989) Zum Entwicklungsstand und zum Trainingssystem des DDR – Frauenkurzsprints, *Lehre der Leichtathletik*, **23**, 655–658; **24**, 687–690; **25**, 721–722.

Thorstensson, A. (1988) Speed and acceleration in *The Olympic Book of Sports Medicine, Vol. 1*, (Eds. A. Dirix, H.G. Knuttgen and K. Tittel), pp. 218–229, Blackwell, Oxford.

Tidow, G. (1993) Lösungsansätze zur Optimierung des Schnellkrafttrainings auf der Basis muskelbioptischer Befunde, personal communication.

Tschiene, P. (1973) Leichtere Bedingungen im speziellen Schnelligkeitstraining, *Die Lehre der Leichtathletik*, **6**, 197–200.

Tschiene, P. (1974) Zur Doppelperiodisierung in DLV-Bereich, *Die Lehre der Leichtathletik*, 1017–1020.

Tschiene, P. (1977) Einige neue Aspekte zur Periodisisierung des Hochleistungstrainings, *Leistungssport*, **7**, 379–382.

Verkhoshansky, Y.V. and Lazarev, V.V. (1989) Principles of planning speed and strength/speed endurance training in sports, *Journal of National Strength and Conditioning Association*, **2**, 58–61.

Voss, G. (1985) *Zu Wechselbeziehungen zwischen Schnelligkeit und ausgewählten anderen Leistungsvoraussetzungen bei zyklischen Schnellkraftbewegungen und Möglichkeiten der Trainierbarkeit der Schnelligkeit*, Diss DHfK, Leipzig.

Voss, G. (1990) Zur Gestaltung eines azyklischen Schnelligkeitstrainings in den Sprungdisziplinen, *Die Lehre der Leichtathletik*, **32**, 21–22.

Voss, G. (1991a) Elementare neuromuskuläre Bewegungsprogramme—eine Leistungsvoraussetzung für leichtathletische Sprungbewegungen, *Lehre der Leichtathletik*, **2**, 40–44.

Voss, G. (1991b) Zur Ausbildung elementarer neuronaler Bewegungsprogramme, *Leistungssport*, **3**, 47–50.

Waser, J. (1985) Zum Techniktraining beim Laufen, *Leistungssport*, **1**, 34–38.

Weber, K. (1985) Stellenwert des Konditionstrainings im Leistungstennis, in *Konditionstraining im Tennis* (Eds. H. Gabler, B. Zein), pp. 9–17, Zwalina, Ahrensburg.

Weineck, J. (1994) *Optimales Training*, Perimed—spitta, Balingen.

Werchoshanskij, J.W. (1984) Der langfristig verzögerte Trainingseffekt durch konzentriertes Krafttraining, *Leichathletik-Magazin*, **30**, 25–28.

Werchoshanskij, J.W. (1988) *Effektiv trainieren*, Sportverlag, Berlin.

Wilke, K. (1992) Analysis of Sprint Swimming: the 50-m Freestyle, in *Biomechanics and Medicine in Swimming* (Eds. D. MacLaren, T. Reilly and A. Lees), pp. 33–46, E and FN Spon, London.

Wilke, K. and Madsen, O. (1988) *Das Training des jungendlichen Schwimmers*, Hofmann, Schorndorf.

Wirtz, W. (1995) *Apparative Entwicklung und Anwendung eines dreidimensionalen kinematischen Verfahrens im Kraulsprint*, Diss, German Sports University, (unpubl.)

Zaciorskij, V.M. (1968) Die körpelichen Eigenschaften des Sportlers, *Theorie und Praxis der Körperkultur*, Beiheft, 1, Bartels & Wernitz, Berlin.

Zaciorskij, V.M. (1971) Die körperlichen Eigenschaften des Sportlers, *Theorie und Praxis der Körperkultur*, Beiheft 2, Bartels & Wenitz, Berlin.

Zukowski, N. (1988) Wyniki sportowne w judo a czas reakcji roznicowej, *Sport wycznowy*, **12**, 32–34.

$\boxed{8}$

ANAEROBIC AND AEROBIC TRAINING

T. Reilly

Liverpool John Moores University

J. Bangsbo

University of Copenhagen

INTRODUCTION

In designing a training programme, it is important to assess the strengths and weaknesses of the athlete as well as the requirements of the sport. Factors such as duration, intensity and frequency of exercise are all influential in determining the extent and nature of the adaptation to a training regimen. It appears clear that regardless of the type of exercise, the cellular changes are restricted to the muscle fibres recruited during training. This chapter deals with effects of various types of training on performance and metabolism as well as the associated adaptations in the tissues. Extensive reviews of training on muscle metabolism can be found elsewhere (e.g., Saltin and Gollnick, 1983).

Various components of fitness training are illustrated in Figure 8.1. They distinguish between training for short-term (anaerobic) and sustained (aerobic) exercise. The strength of the training stimulus is related to the intensity of exercise: appropriate intensities during aerobic and anaerobic training are indicated in Figure 8.2.

Training in Sport: Applying Sport Science. Edited by B. Elliott
© 1998 John Wiley & Sons Ltd

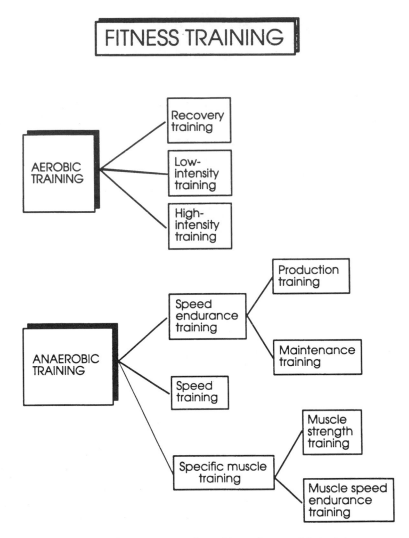

Figure 8.1: Components of aerobic and anaerobic training.

In order to set the necessary background for an understanding of training mechanisms, the production of energy during exercise is briefly described. Both anaerobic (without oxygen) and aerobic (with oxygen) sources of energy are considered.

ENERGY PRODUCTION DURING SPORT

In some sports continuous exercise is performed either at a very high or at a moderate intensity during the entire event; examples of these two extremes

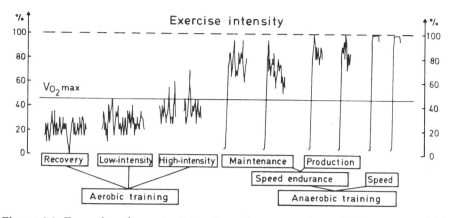

Figure 8.2: Examples of exercise intensities of a soccer player during games within aerobic and anaerobic training, expressed in relation to maximal intensity (100%). The exercise intensity eliciting maximum oxygen uptake and the maximal exercise intensity of the player are represented by the lower and the higher horizontal dotted line, respectively.

are a 100 m sprint and a marathon run, respectively (Figure 8.3). In other sports such as basketball the players perform many different types of activities, and the intensity of effort can alternate at any time and range from standing still to sprinting all out. The contribution from the various energy systems is dependent on the type and intensity of exercise. Therefore, in this section the production of energy as well as the utilization of substrates within different forms of exercise are discussed.

A unique property of skeletal muscle is its ability to transform chemical energy into mechanical work. The immediate source of chemical energy during a muscle contraction is derived from the hydrolysis of adenosinetriphosphate (ATP) with formation of adenosinediphosphate (ADP) and inorganic phosphate:

$$ATP + H_2O \rightarrow ADP + Pi + H^+ + energy \ (29 \ kJ/mol)$$

The restoration of ATP can be accomplished through either anaerobic or aerobic reactions. These are briefly discussed below (see Figure 8.4).

Anaerobic energy production

Creatine phosphate (CP) can be utilized to produce ATP according to the reaction:

$$CP + ADP + H^+ \rightarrow ATP + creatine,$$

which is mediated by the enzyme creatine kinase (CK).

A minor anaerobic energy contribution is obtained from the degradation of ADP to adenosine monophosphate (AMP):

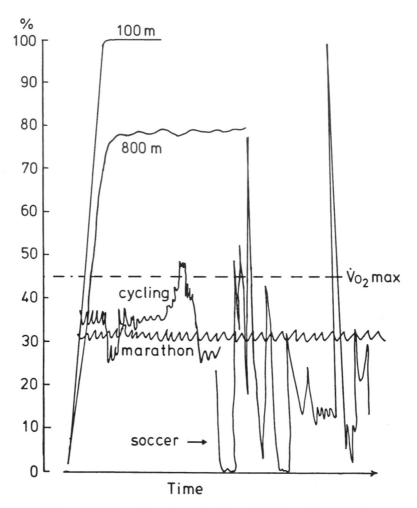

Figure 8.3: Examples of exercise intensities in various sports.

$$2\,ADP \rightarrow ATP + AMP,$$

which is regulated by the enzyme AMP kinase. The AMP can be further degraded to inosine monophosphate (IMP) and ammonia/ammonium (NH_3) through a process mediated by AMP-deaminase:

$$AMP + H_2O + H^+ \rightarrow IMP + NH_3.$$

The latter reactions occur primarily during heavy exercise and at the end of prolonged exercise.

A major anaerobic energy source for a muscle is degradation of glycogen or glucose to pyruvate. This process is referred to as glycolysis:

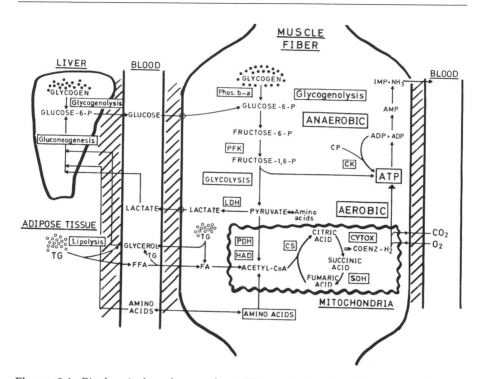

Figure 8.4: Biochemical pathways for ATP production in skeletal muscles and sources of substrates. The flux through a pathway is among other factors regulated by the activity of enzymes involved in the reactions. On the figure are given some of the key enzymes: CK: Creatine kinase; Phose. b-a: Phosphorylase (b and a); PFK: Phosphofructokinase; LDH: Lactate dehydrogenase; PDH: Pyruvate dehydrogenase; CS: Citrate synthase; SDH: Succinate dehydrogenase; CYTOX: Cytochrome oxidase.

$$\text{glycogen} \rightarrow \text{pyruvate} + 3\text{ATP},$$

in which phosphorylase a and b (Phos: glycogen to glucose-1- phosphate; *glycogenolysis*) and phophofructokinase (PFK: fructose-6-phosphate to fructose-1,6-diphosphate) are considered the key regulatory enzymes. The pyruvate may enter the mitochondria (see below), be used for formation of alanine, or be converted to lactate:

$$\text{pyruvate} + \text{NADH} + \text{H}^+ \rightarrow \text{NAD} + \text{lactate}.$$

Lactate production is in its turn mediated by the enzyme lactate dehydrogenase (LDH). Under physiological conditions lactate is almost fully dissociated:

$$\text{lactate} \rightarrow \text{lactate}^- + \text{H}^+.$$

Thus the production of lactate leads to an elevated muscle activity, if the protons (H^+) are not removed by buffering or released to the blood.

Aerobic energy production

The aerobic energy is produced in the mitochondria by use of oxygen, which is taken up from the blood. The substrate for this reaction may be formed through glycolysis, which refers to utilization of carbohydrates. Substrates may also be derived by catabolism of fat and, to a lesser extent, amino acids (protein).

The net reaction of carbohydrate utilization is

$$\text{Glycogen (glucose)} + 39(38)\ ADP + 39(38)\ P_i + 39(38)\ H^+ + 6\ O_2 \rightarrow 39(38) \\ ATP + 6\ CO_2 + 6H_2O.$$

Three of the 39 ATP molecules produced are formed anaerobically (see above). The carbohydrate for glycolysis is primarily in the form of glycogen stored within the exercising muscles, but glucose taken up from the blood can be used. The glucose is released to the blood from the liver, which forms glucose from the breakdown of glycogen (glycogenolysis), or from precursors such as glycerol, pyruvate, lactate and amino acids. The latter process is named gluconeogenesis.

The net reactions of utilizing a representative free fatty acid (FFA; palmitate) are:

$$\text{palmitate} + 129\ ADP + 129\ P_i + 23\ O_2 \rightarrow 129\ ATP + 16\ H_2O + 16\ CO_2$$

The substrates for fat oxidation are triglycerides (TG) stored within the muscles and fat carried in the blood. Substrate is primarily FFA released from adipose tissues and to a lesser extent TG.

The different processes related to energy production are summarized in Figure 8.4, where some of the key enzymes in the different reactions are also given. For a discussion about the regulation of the various pathways and the interplay between the energy systems during exercise, the reader is referred to reviews by Saltin and Gollnick (1983) and Bangsbo (1995).

Energy production during continuous exercise

When discussing energy production during continuous exercise, it is suitable to classify the exercise as submaximal and supramaximal exercise. These represent intensities lower and higher than that eliciting maximal aerobic power (maximum oxygen uptake), respectively (see Figure 8.2).

Submaximal exercise

The energy demand during submaximal exercise is linearly related to the exercise intensity. The relative contribution to the energy production from oxidation of carbohydrates is increased with increasing exercise intensities (Figure 8.5). Lactate appears to be produced at rest, but glycolysis leading to lactate formation contributes significantly to the energy production only at intensities above about 60% of maximum oxygen uptake ($\dot{V}O_2$ max; Figure 8.5). As exercise continues the glycogen concentration in the exercising muscles becomes progressively reduced, which leads to increases in fat oxidation and uptake of glucose from the blood.

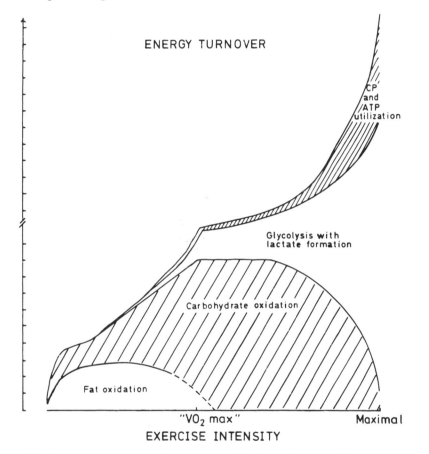

Figure 8.5: Energy turnover and energy contribution from aerobic and anaerobic energy sources at rest and during exercise.

Supramaximal exercise

The ATP stored in a muscle can be utilized very quickly, but the amount is limited and can only provide energy for some milliseconds. Nevertheless, during exercise the ATP concentration in muscles rarely becomes lower than 60% of the resting level. This means that ATP is rapidly restored during exercise. Breakdown of CP represents the immediate ATP source and CP in the muscle can be used up almost completely, but its storage is very limited.

Glycogenolysis and glycolysis (see Figure 8.4) appear also to be activated very soon after the start of exercise (Hultman and Sjöholm, 1983). For a 6 s maximal exercise bout ATP/CP and glycolysis each contribute about 50% of the total anaerobic energy turnover, whereas the corresponding values for a 30 s maximal exercise are around 20 and 80% (Boobis, 1987).

The aerobic energy production in the initial phase of exercise is limited, as there is a delay in the increase of the oxygen transport to the exercising muscles. However, O_2 bound to myoglobin (Mb) and haemoglobin (Hb) in blood within the muscle, and further O_2 dissolved in the muscles, constitute a direct O_2 source which can be used at the start of the exercise. This local oxygen store represents about 5% of the total energy turnover during the first 6 s of maximal exercise. The anaerobic energy production for a 30 s exercise bout contributes about 11% to the total energy turnover (Bangsbo, 1994).

The muscle's production of energy has also been determined during longer exercise periods. In one study subjects performed exhaustive knee-extensor exercise (approximately 3 minutes) at a work-rate corresponding to an energy production of about 130% of $\dot{V}O_2$ peak for the exercising muscles (Bangsbo, Gollnick, Graham, Juel, Kiens, Mizuno and Saltin, 1990). Based on muscle CP breakdown, changes in nucleotides, accumulation of glycolytic intermediates and lactate as well as release of lactate, the total anaerobic energy production was estimated to be 450 ml 'O_2-equivalent' $\times$ kg^{-1}. The oxygen uptake of the active muscles amounted to 550 ml·kg^{-1} active muscle, corresponding to 55% of the total energy production. This value is lower than the 70% suggested for exhaustive cycle exercise of similar duration (Medbø and Tabata, 1989). The difference is probably caused by a higher aerobic contribution from ventilation and involvement of muscles working submaximally during cycling and probably also by an underestimation of the anaerobic energy turnover during the cycling exercise.

Figure 8.5 shows the energy sources during exercise at various intensities. The relative aerobic and anaerobic contributions to the total energy turnover within a muscle during exercise at a constant intensity performed to exhaustion are shown in Figure 8.6.

Energy production during intermittent exercise

In many sports the exercise performed is intermittent and intermittent exercise training is used in almost all sports. It is therefore important to know how metabolism and performance during an exercise bout are influenced by previous exercise. Through the years this has been investigated systematically by changing one of the variables at a time. Such studies form the basis for understanding the physiology of intermittent exercise. It has to be recognized that in the laboratory studies the variations in intensity and

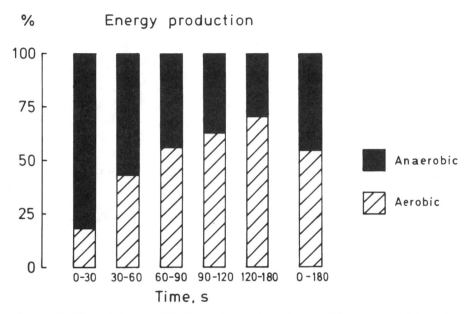

Figure 8.6: The relative contribution of aerobic and anaerobic energy yield during different stages of supramaximal exercise to exhaustion (left) and during the entire exercise period (right).

duration of the exercise are regular, whereas in many intermittent sports the changes in exercise intensity are irregular and can be almost random.

The duration of the exercise bouts in an intermittent exercise programme is important for the accumulation of lactate both in the blood and in the muscle. In a study by Saltin and Essén (1971) the ratio between exercise and recovery was kept constant (1:2). The muscle and blood lactate concentrations were only slightly higher than at rest when the exercise time was 10 and 20 s, whereas the concentrations were considerably increased with exercise bouts of 30 and 60 s duration.

The metabolic response during intense exercise is also related to the duration of the rest periods in between the exercise bouts. In a study by Margaria, Olivia, di Prampero and Ceretelli (1969), the subjects exercised repeatedly for 10 s at an intensity that led to exhaustion after 30–40 s, when performed continuously. Blood lactate increased progressively when the periods of exercise were separated by 10 s of rest, while it was only slightly elevated with 30 s of rest in between the exercise bouts.

In a study by Essén, Hagenfeldt and Kaijser (1977), the subjects performed continuous and intermittent cycle ergometry for 1 hour at the same mean intensity. The intermittent exercise alternated between 15 s rest and 15 s of exercise at a work-rate that for continuous cycling demanded maximum oxygen uptake. When the exercise was performed intermittently, the changes during the exercise periods were more pronounced. Only small alterations occurred in ATP and CP during the continuous exercise, while in the intermittent regimen considerable fluctuations in these variables were observed. After 5 min of the intermittent exercise protocol, the CP concentration was 40% of the resting level, and it was increased to about 70% of the initial level in the subsequent 15 s recovery period. Similar changes were found during the following 55 min of the intermittent exercise.

A marked difference in muscle fibre type recruitment was also observed between the two types of exercise protocols. While it was mainly the slow-twitch (ST) fibres that were activated during the continuous exercise, both ST and fast-twitch (FT) fibres were involved in the intermittent exercise (Essén, 1978). The different pattern of fibre type recruitment between continuous and intermittent exercise has important implications for training. By performing the training intermittently it is possible to train some muscle fibres (FT fibres) that would have been recruited only after hours of submaximal continuous exercise. This is particularly relevant for those sports in which high-intensity exercise frequently occurs. Intermittent exercise also allows a prolonged high metabolic stress without fatiguing the fibres recruited. Essén (1978) compared intermittent exercise with continuous exercise performed at the same power output (corresponding to $\dot{V}O_2$max). The continuous exercise led to exhaustion within a few minutes, while the intermittent exercise could be sustained for 1 hour without inducing fatigue. The rate of glycogen utilization and accumulation of lactate during the continuous exercise at the high intensity was greater than during the intermittent exercise. On the other hand, the rate of fat oxidation was considerably lower than during the intermittent exercise.

Several studies focusing on intense intermittent exercise have shown that performance was gradually impaired, and muscle lactate accumulation considerably decreased as the intermittent exercise was continued (McCartney, Spriet, Heigenhauser, Kowalchuk, Sutton and Jones, 1986; Spriet, Lindinger, McKelvie, Heigenhauser and Jones, 1989; Gaitanos Williams, Boobis and Brooks, 1993; Bangsbo, Graham, Johansen, Strange, Christensen and Saltin, 1992a; Bangsbo, Graham, Kiens and Saltin, 1992b). For example, when subjects repeated ten 6 s sprints on a cycle ergometer, Gaitanos and co-workers (1993) found a 33% reduction in peak power and a 27% reduction in mean power output. For the first exercise bout, net breakdown of ATP, CP, and energy release from glycolysis could account for approximately 6%, 44% and 50%, respectively, of the total anaerobic energy production, while the corresponding values for the tenth exercise bout were approximately 4%, 80% and 16% (Figure 8.7). An extended discussion of the causes of the lowered rate of glycolysis when intense exercise is repeated has been reported by Bangsbo (1995).

Oxygen transport

For activities that are sustained for longer than 60 s or so, the muscles are dependent predominantly on the supply of oxygen to sites of energy

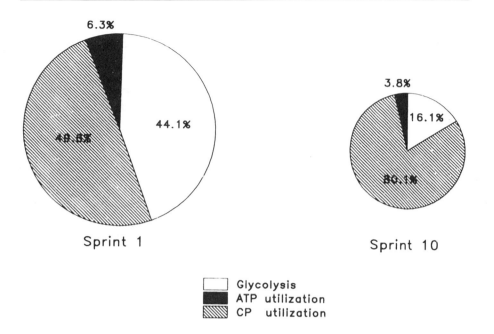

Figure 8.7: Relative contribution from breakdown of ATP and CP as well as glycolysis during the first and tenth 6 s sprint. Each of the 10 sprints was separated by 24 s of rest. Data by Gaitanos et al. (1993) used with permission from *Journal of Applied Physiology.*

utilisation. The oxygen transport system encompasses an integrated involvement of lungs, heart, oxygen carriage in the blood and utilization in muscle cells. The latter is influenced by the blood supply, the network of capillaries around muscle fibres, the mitochondrial number and content and the type of muscle fibres. Central factors, that incorporate pulmonary and cardiac parameters as well as blood volume and content, determine the amount of oxygen that is delivered to the active tissues. Peripheral or local factors refer to the ability of selected muscles to use the oxygen that is offered to them by means of the circulation. These factors are influenced both by heredity and by training.

Pulmonary ventilation refers to the process by which ambient air is brought into the lungs and exchanged with air passing through them. At rest approximately 250 ml of oxygen leaves the alveoli and enters the blood for each breath, whereas about 200 ml of CO_2 diffuses in the reverse direction to be exhaled during breathing. During heavy exercise over 20 times this amount of oxygen may be transferred across the alveolar membrane. The rate of pulmonary ventilation may increase from 6 l/min at rest to about 200 l/min in top class athletes during strenuous exercise. The primary purpose of ventilation during aerobic exercise is to maintain a constant and favourable concentration of O_2 and CO_2 in the alveolar chambers. This ensures effective exchange of gases before the oxygenated blood leaves the lungs for transport throughout the body.

Normally the lungs do not limit the performance of aerobic exercise but may do so under certain circumstances. Lung function may be restricted in athletes suffering from asthma. This is usually indicated by a subnormal value for the forced expiratory volume (FEV) which is measured in a single breath of forceful exhalation and reflects the power of the lungs. Voy (1986) estimated that around 11% of USA Olympic Games athletes at Los Angeles suffered from asthma or exercise-induced bronchospasm. Exercise-induced asthma is generally triggered post-exercise and recovery may take 30–50 minutes unless bronchodilators are employed to ease breathing difficulties.

The conventional view has been that pulmonary ventilation is not a limitation in aerobic performance at sea level but Dempsey (1986) provided evidence of oxygen desaturation in some top athletes undergoing intense exercise. This could occur due to anatomically narrow airways when all other aspects of oxygen transport are highly trained and can not be remedied by training.

The ventilation system can also be a limiting factor at altitude due to the lower environmental pressure compared to that at sea level. This leads to a drop in the partial pressure of oxygen within the alveoli and an inadequate loading of haemoglobin in the red blood cells with oxygen. This occurs once the oxygen-saturation curve of haemoglobin begins to fall steeply at an altitude of about 1.6 km. Normally at sea level the red blood cells are almost fully (98%) saturated with O_2; at an altitude of 3.2 km the saturation is reduced to 90% and at 6.4 km it is about 70%.

Performance is also limited by lung function in breath-hold divers. In this instance the relevant factors are vital capacity and the tolerance of hypercapnia (excess CO_2). The depth to which divers may go is influenced by the effect of pressure on lung volume and the diver may not go safely beyond the point where the air in the lungs is reduced to the equivalent of the residual volume. The breath-hold is normally terminated when CO_2 levels rise to stimulate the inspiratory centre in the medulla of the brain, although the duration of the breath-hold can be extended by training, as indicated by the performance of professional pearl divers.

Aerobic training can alter pulmonary ventilatory responses to exercise. As maximal oxygen uptake ($\dot{V}O_2max$) is elevated with training, there is an increase in the corresponding minute ventilation ($\dot{V}Emax$). At submaximal exercise there is a reduction in the ventilation equivalent of oxygen ($\dot{V}E/\dot{V}O_2$) so that less air is breathed at a given oxygen consumption (Rasmussen, Klausen, Clausen and Trap-Jensen, 1975). The expired air of trained athletes contains less oxygen than that of untrained individuals for a given $\dot{V}O_2$ (Tzankoff, Robinson, Pyke and Brawn, 1972). This reflects the capacity of trained muscle to extract more of the oxygen passing through the tissues in the local circulation. There is also an elevation in the ventilation threshold (Tvent) with endurance training which represents the exercise intensity at which VE starts to rise disproportionately to VO_2 in response to a progressive exercise test. This may be related to metabolic alterations but is specific to the exercise modality (running, cycling or rowing) used in training (Bunc and Leso, 1993).

The oxygen–haemoglobin dissociation curve determines the quantity of oxygen carried in the blood at a particular plasma oxygen tension (PO_2). At the normal alveolar PO_2 of 100 mm Hg, haemoglobin is 98% saturated and for each 100 ml of blood leaving the lungs, 19.7 ml O_2 is carried bound to haemoglobin whilst a further 0.3 ml is dissolved in the plasma. Increase in acidity, temperature or PCO_2 above normal values shifts the sigmoid-shaped curve downward and to the right, a shift referred to as the Bohr effect. This would represent a reduced effectiveness of haemoglobin to hold oxygen. The haemoglobin concentration is higher in males compared to females (average values are 14.6 and 13.0 g/dl, respectively) but it is the total amount of haemoglobin which is correlated with $\dot{V}O_2max$. Females are disadvantaged in this respect in that they have a lower blood volume compared to males. Carbon monoxide (CO) binds much more easily to haemoglobin than does oxygen and for this reason CO in cigarette smokers reduces the oxygen-carrying capacity of the blood. Cigarette smoking is therefore incompatible with aerobic training.

The unloading of oxygen from haemoglobin to the tissues is influenced by the substance 2,3-bisphosphoglycerate (2,3-BPG). Trained athletes seem to have higher levels of 2,3-BPG in their plasma than untrained individuals, a factor which would ease the release of O_2 to the active tissues. High-intensity exercise can cause significant increases in 2,3-BPG, confirming this adaptive response to assist oxygen supply to active muscles (Klein, Forster, Stewart and Wu, 1980). Females have higher 2,3-BPG levels in red blood cells compared to males of similar aerobic fitness, which may indicate that this is a compensatory mechanism for their lower haemoglobin concentrations (Pate, Barnes and Hiller, 1985). These low haemoglobin levels may be accentuated in female athletes with inadequate dietary iron or with low serum ferritin stores.

The amount of blood pumped from the heart, the cardiac output, is a function of the stroke volume and the heart rate. This may increase from 5 litres/minute at rest to 30 litres/minute at maximal oxygen consumption, depending on the capacity of the athlete. The cardiac output of Olympic endurance athletes may exceed this upper level. The major adaptations to endurance training are an increase in left ventricular chamber size and a consequent decrease in resting and submaximal heart rate, an increase in maximal cardiac output, a rise in maximal oxygen uptake and an increase in total blood volume. In the case of well-trained endurance athletes it is likely that the maximal ability to consume oxygen is limited by central factors (cardiac output) rather than peripheral factors (including oxidative capacity of skeletal muscle).

The improved endurance capacity of trained muscle is partly due to an increase in its capillary density. In athletes, values 20% greater than normal have been reported for the number of capillaries per muscle and in a given cross-section (Brodal, Ingjer and Hermansen, 1976). There was a corresponding difference in $\dot{V}O_2$max between endurance athletes and an untrained group. There are also metabolic adaptations in muscle that enhance oxidative capacity. There is, for example, an increase in both number and size of the mitochondria with enhancement of enzymes of the Krebs cycle and electron transport system (Holloszy and Coyle, 1984).

Individuals who excel in endurance sports seem to be endowed with a muscle fibre type composition that is appropriate to the demands of the sport (Bergh, Thorstenssen, Sjodin, Hulten, Piehl and Karlsson, 1978). For example, whilst the twitch characteristics of muscle fibres seem to be unaffected by endurance training, their histochemical properties are. Endurance runners demonstrate a predominance of slow twitch (ST) fibres as do cross-country skiers. In addition to high levels of mitochondria in these fibres, there is an abundance of myoglobin which gives rise to the naming of these fibres as red. Furthermore with endurance training the so-called intermediate (fast twitch) FTa fibres assume more of the biochemical make-up of ST fibres, showing increased oxidative enzymes and raised levels of myoglobin.

ANAEROBIC PERFORMANCE

Anaerobic performance is determined both by anaerobic power and anaerobic capacity. Anaerobic power represents the highest rate of anaerobic energy release, whereas anaerobic capacity reflects the maximal anaerobic energy production an individual can obtain at any exercise bout performed to exhaustion. These two aspects of anaerobic performance will be considered in this section, which will end with a discussion of the cause of fatigue during intense exercise and the effect of ergogenic enhancement of muscle CP and creatine.

Anaerobic power

The power produced by a muscle during dynamic contractions depends on both force and velocity factors. It is difficult to evaluate the force output of each single muscle in a movement. Instead the external mechanical power output during the movement can be measured.

In the past the maximal power generated over a period of time has been calculated from measurements made during vertical jumping (Sargent,

1924) and stair climbing (Margaria, Aghemo and Rovelli, 1966). Later, Bar-Or (1981) used a friction-loaded cycle ergometer to monitor a subject's maximum power output (peak power) and the time-course of the decline of power output (fatigue index) during cycling at maximum speed against a predetermined resistance related to body weight for 30 s. The test has become known as the 'Wingate test'. In recent years the test has been further developed by determining force output in 1 s intervals and by taking into account the acceleration involved (Lakomy, 1986).

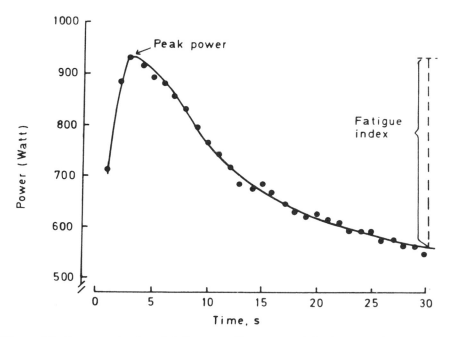

Figure 8.8: Power output and fatigue profile generated during a cycle ergometer sprint.

Anaerobic capacity

Several attempts have been made to determine the anaerobic capacity during whole-body intense exercise (Margaria, Edwards and Dill, 1933; Margaria, Cerretelli, di Prampero, Massari and Torelli, 1963; Monod and Scherrer, 1965; Medbø, Mohn, Tabata, Bahr and Sejersted, 1988), but so far none has been really successful. A close relationship between the oxygen deficit observed during intense exercise and anaerobic energy production, estimated from muscle metabolic measurements, observed in a study of one-legged exercise, suggests that the oxygen deficit can be used as a measure of the anaerobic energy turnover also during whole-body exercise (Bangsbo et al., 1990). However, several findings in studies of whole-body exercise indicate that the use of the oxygen deficit is questionable, if the energy demand during supramaximal exercise is estimated from a linear relationship between submaximal work-rate and oxygen uptake (Bangsbo, 1992). It is likely that the energy demand during high-intensity exercise is underestimated by this procedure, and more so the higher the work-rate with a consequent shorter exercise time to exhaustion. This limits the information obtained from oxygen deficit determinations and should be taken into consideration when comparisons are performed.

It has been suggested that blood lactate after intense exercise reflects the anaerobic energy production during exercise (Margaria et al., 1933; Margaria et al., 1963). The blood lactate concentration represents a balance between the rate of release of lactate from the active muscles and the removal of lactate from the blood. As the latter rate, among other things, is influenced by the athlete's endurance capacity (Donovan and Pagliassotti, 1990), peak blood lactate after maximal exercise is not a good indicator of the anaerobic energy turnover.

It appears that it is necessary to obtain biopsies and measure metabolites related to the anaerobic energy systems, if one wants to determine the anaerobic energy production accurately.

Fatigue during intense exercise

During maximal exercise the power output peaks within a few seconds and declines thereafter (Figure 8.8). Thus, fatigue, defined as a loss of force output, occurs even within 5 s of intense effort. What causes fatigue during intense exercise has to be understood before addressing the question of how fatigue might be delayed by training.

High-intensity exercise is associated with a large production of lactate and a concomitant elevation in acidity within the exercising muscles. Decreases in muscle pH from about 7.1 to 6.5–6.8 are often observed during intense exhaustive exercise (Juel, Bangsbo, Graham and Saltin, 1990); based on nuclear magnetic resonance (NMR) studies, it has been suggested that pH in individual fibres can be even lower (Vandenborne, McCully, Kakihira, Prammer, Bolinger, Detre, de Meirleir, Walter, Chance and Leigh, 1991). This may affect the muscle performance, as low pH has an inhibitory effect on various functions within the muscle cell (Edman, 1992).

It is generally believed that lactic acid accumulation and lowered pH causes fatigue (see Metzer and Fitts 1987; Sahlin 1986). However, lactate and pH may not be exclusive determinants of fatigue (Bangsbo et al., 1992a,b). For example, it has been demonstrated that performance was impaired when intense exercise was repeated after 1 hour of recovery even though muscle and blood lactate had returned to resting levels (Bangsbo et al., 1992a,b). In addition, fatigue occurred at a lower muscle lactate concentration during the second exercise bout. Findings by Sahlin and Ren (1989) are in accordance with the suggestion that lowered muscle pH is not always critical in the development of fatigue. They showed that despite persistently high muscle lactate concentrations, and probably lowered muscle pH, maximum contraction force was completely restored two minutes after a series of intense exhaustive isometric efforts.

If muscle lactate and pH are not, or at least not always, causally linked with a decline in muscle tension, what then is the cause of fatigue? It is difficult to identify a single factor responsible for the reduction in performance during intense exercise. It does not appear to be related to lack of energy, since muscle ATP is found to be relatively high at exhaustion during intense voluntary exercise (Bangsbo et al., 1992a,b). This proposition is in agreement with the observation that no fibre was totally depleted of ATP when single fibre analysis was performed on muscle biopsies taken immediately after exercise, even after electrical stimulation that resulted in a large decline in force (Söderlund, 1991).

There are various other suggestions for the cause of fatigue. Fatigue may be localized within the individual muscle cells. For example, it could be related to a failure in the coupling between stimulation and Ca^{2+} release from the sarcoplasmic reticulum (SR), or to a decreased rate of Ca^{2+} re-uptake to SR, which would slow the rate of relaxation (Donaldson, 1990).

Fatigue may also be caused by a reduced neural activation of the muscle. It could be cortically based, but it appears that in well-motivated subjects, a substantial component of fatigue can be localized in the muscle (Bigland-Ritchie and Woods, 1984). This is supported by the demonstration of a reflex inhibition in skeletal muscles at exhaustion (Bigland-Ritchie, Dawson, Johansson and Leppold, 1986). It is unclear what activates this reflex, but it may be the potassium accumulating in the interstitium of the active muscles. Another reason for failure of excitation–contraction coupling could be inhibited propagation of the action potential due to ion disturbances over the muscle membrane and a possible block in its propagation into the t-tubules. A role of potassium in the two latter hypotheses is supported by the findings that release of potassium into the blood declined at the onset of fatigue and that the venous potassium concentrations in the contracting muscles were the same at the point of exhaustion when intense exercise was repeated (Bangsbo et al., 1992a,b). Thus, a continuous efflux of potassium from the exercising muscle, together with a limited re-uptake and a reduced release to venous blood, probably lead to a progressive accumulation of potassium in the interstitium which may be implicated in the fatigue process.

The scheme which may prevail is that an elevated potassium concentration around the muscle fibres blocks prolongation of the action potential over some fibre membranes and possibly at the same time stimulates the sensory input, which causes inhibition of spinal motor nerves (Figure 8.9). This is likely to be a gradual process, and can at first be overcome by the drive from the motor cortex as the firing rates are elevated and new motor

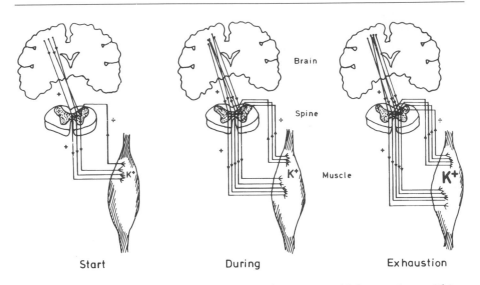

Figure 8.9: Theoretical scheme of how accumulating interstitial potassium within a muscle can cause fatigue.

units are activated. However, a point is reached when the number of new muscle fibres that it is possible to activate is considerably reduced and the reflex inhibition causes such a reduction in spinal motor activity output that the muscles are unable to maintain the exercise intensity.

The time needed to recover fully after intense exercise is dependent on a variety of factors such as the fitness of the subject, the activity in the recovery period, and the intensity and duration of the preceding exercise. The latter is illustrated by the findings of Balsom, Seger, Sjödin and Ekblom (1992). They observed that running time (approximately 5.5 s) was progressively increased when a 40 m all-out sprint was repeated 15 times, whereas in contrast, performance was unaltered in 40 sprints of 15 m (approximately 2.5 s). In both cases the sprints were separated by a 30 s rest period. Thus, it appears that 30 s was long enough to recover from approximately 3 s of maximal exercise, but not when the duration of the maximal exercise was about 6 s. Active recovery has a minor beneficial effect on performance in a subsequent exercise bout (Bangsbo and Saltin, 1993). This means that the muscles may return to a normal level more quickly when low-intensity exercise is performed between intense exercise bouts. This benefit of active recovery can be exploited within physical training programmes.

Effect of creatine on metabolism and performance during intense intermittent exercise

Ingestion of creatine has been shown to increase the CP and particularly creatine levels in muscles (Harris, Söderlund and Hultman, 1992; Greenhaff,

Bodin, Soderlund and Hultman, 1994). Greenhaff et al. (1994) found that five subjects increased their total muscle creatine level (CP and creatine) by 25% after a creatine intake of 20 g/day for five days. It seems that this dosage is optimal and effects may be maintained for about a month when this high intake for five days is followed by a lower intake (5 g/day). There appears to be an upper limit for storage of CP and creatine of about 160 mmol/kg d.w. (Harris et al., 1992; Greenhaff et al., 1994). The effect of supplementation was greatest in those individuals with the lowest initial total creatine contents, e.g. the largest increase was found in two vegetarians (Harris et al., 1992).

An elevated level of creatine and CP may affect CP resynthesis after exercise. Greenhaff et al. (1994) found a tendency towards an increased rate of CP resynthesis during the first 2 min of recovery from electrically induced muscle contractions, which almost depleted the CP storage, after subjects had ingested creatine (20 g/day) for five days compared to before the feeding period. A faster resynthesis of CP may have an impact on the ability to perform intermittent exercise (Greenhaff, Casey, Short, Harris, Soderlund and Hultman,1993; Balsom, Ekblom, Soderlund, Sjodin and Hultman, 1993a; Birch, Noble and Greenhaff, 1994). In the study by Balsom et al. (1993a) subjects performed ten 6 s high-intensity exercise bouts on a cycle-ergometer separated by 24 s of rest, after they had ingested either creatine (20 g/day) or placebo for a week. The group which ingested creatine had a lower reduction in performance as the test progressed than the placebo group. On the other hand, as one would expect, creatine ingestion appears to have no effect on prolonged (> 10 min) continuous exercise performance (Balsom, Harridge, Söderlund, Sjödin and Ekblom, 1993b).

Although creatine ingestion increases muscle CP and creatine concentration, it is likely that only in a limited number of sports will athletes benefit from using creatine, since creatine ingestion also causes an increase in body mass. This increase is most likely to be due to an increased accumulation of water. Nevertheless, a gain in body weight has a negative influence in most sports in which the athletes have to move their body mass against gravity. It has been proposed that creatine ingestion also improves performance during running, but the results so far are not convincing (Harris, Viru, Greenhaff and Hultman, 1993). Furthermore, it is unclear how ingesting creatine for a period influences the body's own production of creatine and the enzymes that are related to creatine/CP synthesis and breakdown, e.g. CK (see Figure 8.4). It may be that an athlete through regularly taking in creatine reduces the body's ability to produce CP and creatine. This may result in a reduction in the CP and creatine levels, when the athlete no longer is ingesting creatine. Regularly ingesting creatine may also lead to an impairment of the ability to utilize CP. In addition, very little is known about any possible side-effect of a frequent intake of creatine. High concentrations of creatine may have negative effects on the kidney, which has to eliminate the excess creatine.

One should also consider that ingestion of creatine can be viewed as doping. It may be argued that creatine is a natural compound and that it is normally contained in food. However, it is almost impossible to get doses of creatine corresponding to those used in the experiments which have shown enhanced performance, as the content of creatine in 1 kg of raw meat is around 5 g.

ANAEROBIC TRAINING

Training at an intensity higher than the work-rate corresponding to $\dot{V}O_2max$ is classified as anaerobic training (see Figure 8.10). This type of training is important in any sport in which the participants execute either a single bout or repeated bouts of high-intensity exercise. Anaerobic training can be sub-divided into programmes incorporating strength training and training programmes without external loads. This section will mainly deal with the latter type of training and results from strength training studies will only be included where appropriate. For a review of strength training see Chapter 5.

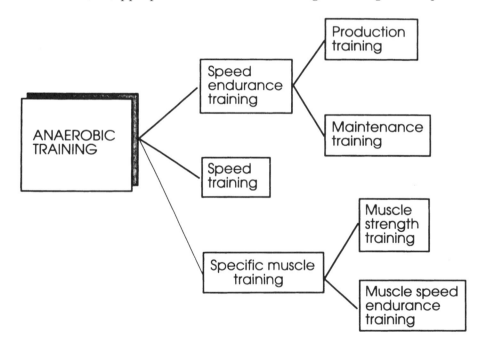

Figure 8.10: Components of anaerobic training.

Anaerobic training and performance

In several studies short-term sprint or interval training has been shown to result in improvements in performance during high-intensity tests (Table

8.1). For example, in the investigation by Nevill, Boobis, Brooks and Williams (1989) eight subjects carried out a training programme consisting mainly of 'supramaximal' exercise. The training resulted in improvements in mean and peak power of 6% and 12%, respectively, during a 30 s all-out sprint test. These changes were associated with higher muscle lactate accumulation after the training period. Similar findings were obtained by Sharp, Costill, Fink and King (1986) and Boobis (1987). The question is what muscle cellular changes occur with high-intensity exercise training that increase lactate production and what changes delay fatigue and thus improves performance?

Muscle cellular effects of anaerobic training

In this section the adaptations in muscle cells induced by training are described, as is their relation to improved performance (Table 8.1).

Muscle CP and ATP

Many studies have shown little or no change in the concentration of CP and ATP with high-intensity training (Table 8.1). However, in two studies a pronounced decrease in the muscle concentration of ATP was observed after a period of sprint training (Hellsten, Norman, Balsom and Sjödin, 1993; Stathis, Febbraio, Carey and Snow, 1994). The different response in the latter studies compared to earlier findings is probably due to differences in the form of exercise, training frequency and the total amount of work done. In the study by Hellsten et al. (1993) one group of subjects performed 6 weeks of sprint training three times per week and another group carried out sprint training twice a day for 1 week. The reduction in muscle ATP concentration for the two groups was 13% and 24%, respectively. The change in muscle ATP concentration was not caused by the last training session as the muscle ATP concentration was also lowered 72 hours after the end of the training. When the group that had trained for 6 weeks performed the same exercise as the other group for one week, no further degradation of muscle adenine nucleotides was observed. This lack of decrease in ATP was associated with an elevated level of adenine nucleotide and purine salvages enzymes (Hellsten, 1994). Thus, it appears that the muscle adapts to the frequent stimuli by diminishing the loss of ATP. Similarly, Stathis et al. (1994) observed that muscle ATP was lowered after a period of intense training and that the reduction in ATP during maximal exercise was less after the training period. The functional importance of the loss of muscle ATP is difficult to evaluate, as there was no difference in performance on a 30 s maximal exercise bout in the study by Hellsten et al. (1993), whereas Stathis et al. (1994) found an elevated performance level. Nevertheless, it appears that the improvement in performance observed after a period of anaerobic training

Table 8.1: Effect of high–intensity training in humans on performance, mitochondrial and glycolytic enzymes, as well as muscle substrates and fibre types measured in biopsies from m. vastus lateralis.

Type of training/ duration	Performance		Glycolytic enzymes				Mitochondrial enzymes				Glyco-gen	ATP	CP	Fibre types			Reference
	Peak power	Mean power	CK	PFK	PHOS	MK	CS	MDH	HAD	SDH				ST	FTa	FTb	
2–3/wk, 6wk 15+30 s sprints cycling	-2%	1%	8%	16%*	–	–	12%*	–	–	–	–	–	–	-9%	7%	7%	Jacobs et al. (1987)
3/wk, 6wk	8%	2%	13%*	16%*	–	–	1%	–	12%	–	–	12%*	–	-7%	12%	-6%	Hellsten et al. (1993, 1994)
14/wk, 1 wk 10 s sprints cycling	15%*	6%	10%	17%	–	–	9%	–	6%	–	-23%*	–	–	–	–	–	Hellsten et al. (1994, personal communication)
3–4/wk, 8 wk 6–30 s sprints + 110% VO_2max (running)	12%*	6%	–	–	–	–	–	–	–	–	10%	-11%	-1%	–	–	–	Nevill et al. (1989)
3–4/wk, 8 wk 5 s sprints (running)	9%*	–	36%*	–	–	20%*	–	–	–	–	–	-12%	6%	3%	3%	-3%	Thorstensson et al. (1975)
4/wk, 7 wk 6 s sprints	10%	15%	-1%	7%*	-5%	-1%	–	5%	–	3%	–	–	–	3%	5%	-2%	Costill et al. (1979)
30 s sprints (isokinetic)	11%	15%	15%*	22%*	8%*	13%*	–	14%*	1%	–	–	–	–	-1%	4%	-2%	
4/wk, 8 wk 30 s sprints (cycling)	26%*	–	–	47%*	10%	–	-2%	–	–	-2%	–	–	17%	–	–	–	Sharp et al. (1986)
8/wk 6 + 30 s sprints (cycling)	7.5%*	8.1%	–	–	–	–	–	–	–	–	36%*	-5%	-7%	–	–	–	Boobis (1987)
3/wk 30 s sprints (cycling)	17%*	12%	–	–	–	–	–	–	–	–	-19%*	8%	–	–	–	–	Stathis et al. (1994)

is not due to changes in the high phosphate energy stores as there is either no change or a decrease in CP and ATP caused by this form of training.

Muscle glycogen

Training at a high intensity increases the stores of glycogen within the trained muscles. For example, Boobis (1987) observed an increase of 36% in muscle glycogen following a period of intense training. In a study of rats the glycogen levels were 49%, 35% and 17% higher in soleus, red and white gastrocnemius, respectively, after an 11-week period of sprint training (Saubert, Armstrong, Shepherd and Gollnick, 1973). Thus, the increase in muscle glycogen (after a period of intense training) appears to occur in all muscle fibre types.

In the study by Boobis (1987) the increase in muscle glycogen was associated with an 8% increase in peak power during maximal cycling. It is unlikely that the elevated muscle concentration was the cause of the better performance, since it has been demonstrated in humans that performance as well as glycogenolytic and glycolytic rates during short-term intense exercise are independent of the initial muscle glycogen concentrations above about 50 mmol/kg w.w. (Bangsbo et al., 1992b).

Fibre types

The effect of high intensity exercise training on fibre type composition is not clear. In some studies no changes have been observed, whereas other studies have shown a significant increase in the relative number of histochemically determined fast-twitch a (FTa) fibres and a decrease in ST and fast twitch b (FTb) fibres (Table 8.1). The difference may be related to both the intensity and duration of the training; also the muscle biopsies obtained may not be representative of the whole muscle. Furthermore, the histochemical classification of fibre types should be used with caution, as many muscle fibres contain more than one myosin heavy chain (MHC) isozyme (Biral, Betto, Danieli-Betto and Salviati, 1988). Nevertheless, studies of muscle MHC-isoforms and strength training seem to confirm that the high intensity training can increase the expression of MHC type FTa at the expense of expression of MHC type FTb and perhaps MHC ST (Andersen, Klitgaard, Bangsbo and Saltin, 1994). Thus, it appears that the number of FTa fibres can increase and the number of ST fibres decrease with anaerobic training. This may be one of the explanations for the observed increase in peak power during maximal exercise after a period of anaerobic training, since MHC type FT fibres can develop force more rapidly than ST MHC fibres.

Muscle enzymes and myoglobin

Anaerobic training appears to elevate the level of enzymes related to the anaerobic production of energy (Table 8.1), while aerobic training seems to have no or only moderate effect on those enzymes. Several studies have shown a higher CK activity after a period of high intensity training, whereas Jansson and Sylvén (1985) observed no difference in the CK activity in thigh muscles (m. vastus lateralis) between endurance trained and untrained subjects. This may explain why top-class sprinters have a faster and more pronounced muscle CP breakdown during a 30 s maximal contraction compared with endurance trained and untrained subjects (Johansen and Quistorff, 1992). The differences between these groups may also be due to genetic factors. One of these could be that the sprinters had a larger number of FT fibres, which are known to possess higher CK activity and CP concentration than ST fibres (Jansson and Sylvén, 1985; Tesch, Thorsson and Fujitsuka, 1989).

In some studies of athletes, intense training has been shown to produce an increase in the glycolytic enzymes (Table 8.1). Hellsten (1994) found that the activity of PFK was elevated by 16% after six weeks of sprint training without a corresponding change in sprint performance. These findings suggest that an increase in the activity of glycolytic enzymes is not the main cause of the increased performance after a period of training. An increase in glycolytic enzymes implies that a certain change in an activator results in a higher glycolytic rate. The impact of these changes might be minor, as the activity of glycolytic enzymes is found to be at high levels in human muscle and only a partial activation of these enzymes is sufficient to initiate a rapid glycolysis. Nevertheless, the increase in the maximal activity of the glycolytic enzymes may partly explain the higher rate of lactate production after a period of anaerobic training (Sharp et al., 1986; Nevill et al., 1989).

Generally it requires a rather prolonged stimulus to change oxidative enzymes and myoglobin (Andersen and Henriksson, 1978). It is therefore not surprising that oxidative enzymes, such as citrate synthase (CS) and succinate dehydrogenase (SDH), were unaltered or only slightly elevated after periods of anaerobic training in which the actual exercise periods were relatively short (Table 8.1). Similarly, myoglobin has been found to be unresponsive to sprint training (Jacobs, Esbjörnsson, Sylvén, Holm and Jansson, 1987).

Muscle buffer capacity and lactate transport

Muscle buffering capacity may be determined by either titration of muscle homogenates with strong acid (*in vitro* determination) or it may be calculated from the estimated production of H^+, that is from lactate accumulation, and the observed change in muscle pH (*in vivo* determination). The latter method is influenced by transmembrane fluxes of ions, and it is assumed that the ratio between H^+ and lactate efflux is 1 to 1. As it has been observed that H^+ is released at a higher rate than lactate during intense exercise (Bangsbo, Graham, Johansen and Saltin, 1993), it is likely that the ratio between lactate accumulated in muscle and change in muscle pH overestimates the true buffering. The homogenate technique is not affected by ion fluxes and it does not include the buffering related to the CO_2/HCO_3 system. The differences between the two methods might explain the finding that, for the same subjects, the muscle buffer capacity determined by titration was lower than the estimated *in vivo* capacity (211 vs. 268 mmol/pH/kg d.w.) during exhaustive knee-extensor exercise (Juel et al., 1990).

The muscle buffer capacity determined *in vivo* in subjects trained for various ball games and for endurance trained athletes has been reported to be around 220 mmol/pH/kg d.w., which is higher than that observed for sedentary subjects (164 mmol/pH/kg d.w.; Sahlin and Henriksson, 1984). The difference may be related to the trained subjects having a higher muscle protein, such as carnosine and histidine, level which increases the buffering of H^+. Sharp et al. (1986) observed an increase in the *in vivo* muscle buffer capacity of 36% after eight weeks of sprint training. Similarly, Nevill et al. (1989) found that after eight weeks of sprint training four subjects had a greater lactate accumulation for the same change in muscle pH during a 30 s sprint. In the latter study the muscle buffer capacity determined by titration was unchanged. Thus, it cannot be excluded that the changes of the muscle buffer capacity *in vivo* in these studies were caused by alterations in ion fluxes and the ratio between H^+ and lactate release from the muscle. On the other hand, Fox, Henckel, Juel, Falk-Rønne and Saltin (1986) studied horses undergoing an 18-week interval programme and found a significant increase in the *in vitro* muscle buffer capacity. Similarly, Bell and Wenger (1988) reported that the muscle buffer capacity determined by titration was 16% higher after a period of training. Thus, it appears that the buffering capacity of muscle can be altered by training. This is supported by the observation that the buffering of a calf muscle, determined by titration, increased when training was performed at altitude (Mizuno, Juel, Bro-Rasmussen, Mygind, Schibye, Rasmussen and Saltin, 1990).

An elevated muscle buffer capacity will lead to a higher pH for a similar amount of lactate produced during high intensity exercise. Therefore, the inhibitory effects of H^+ within the muscle cell should be lessened, which may lead to improved performance. However, the role of pH in muscle fatigue is not well established, and a lowered pH within the muscle might not always be crucial in the development of fatigue (see p. 366). This is supported by the observation of a significant increase in performance after a programme of sprint training without any change in the muscle buffer capacity determined by titration (Nevill et al., 1989).

A higher rate of release of H^+ from the exercising muscles after training would also delay the fall in muscle pH during intense exercise. A lactate/H^+ carrier mechanism appears to account for a considerable part of the total efflux of lactate and H^+ (see Bangsbo et al., 1993), and it may be altered by training. In a study of rats, it was observed that the lactate transport capacity, studied in giant sarcolemmal vesicles from the calf muscles, was significantly elevated after seven weeks of training at an intensity close to or slightly above the intensity for $\dot{V}O_2$max (Pilegaard, Juel and Wibrand, 1993). On the other hand, prolonged swim training at a moderate intensity had no effect on the lactate transport capacity. Thus, it appears that the capacity to transport lactate and probably also H^+ can be elevated by high-intensity training. This is supported by a finding of a higher muscle lactate transport capacity in athletes competing in sports characterized by high-intensity exercise bouts compared to untrained individuals and endurance sports specialists (Pilegaard, Bangsbo, Richter and Juel, 1994).

Muscle Na⁺/K⁺ pumps

Muscle Na+/K+ pumps

The number of Na^+/K^+ pumps has been found to be elevated after a period of intense exercise training (McKenna, Schmidt, Hargreaves, Cameron, Skinner and Kjeldsen, 1993). In the study by McKenna et al. (1993) the subjects underwent sprint training for seven weeks, which resulted in an 11% increase in performance during four 30 s sprints on a cycle. The better performance was associated with a 16% increase in the estimated concentration of Na^+/K^+ ATPase. It is possible that the improved capacity of the muscles to take up potassium during intense exercise may be the cause of improved performance after a period of anaerobic training, since accumulation of potassium might be involved in the fatigue processes.

Principles of anaerobic training

Training at a fast pace is probably the best way to increase high-intensity exercise performance, as the greatest changes occur concomitantly with the highest rates of muscle contraction. Anaerobic training can be divided into 'speed training' and 'speed endurance' training, in addition to specific muscle training (Figure 8.10). The principle of speed training is covered in another chapter. 'Speed endurance' training can be separated into *production* training and *maintenance* training (Figure 8.10). The purpose of 'production training' is to improve the ability to perform maximally for a relatively short period of time, whereas the aim of 'maintenance training' is to increase the ability to sustain exercise at a high intensity.

In 'production training' the exercise intensity should be almost maximal, as it appears from studies in both animals and humans that this is the most effective way to elicit adaptations in the glycogenolytic and glycolytic enzymes (Costill, Coyle, Fink, Lesmes and Witzman, 1979; Jacobs et al., 1987). In order to maintain a high intensity throughout an interval training session, the duration of the exercise periods within the 'production training' sessions should be relatively short but long enough to stimulate the systems which limit performance. Costill et al. (1979) found that the activity of the glycolytic enzyme PFK in muscle was higher after training periods consisting of either 6 or 30 s of intense exercise bouts, but the activities of other anaerobic enzymes (phosphorylase, CK and myokinase) were elevated only after the training programme with 30 s exercise bouts. This indicates that 6 s might be too short to elicit major adaptations in the enzymes associated with anaerobic metabolism. On the other hand, very brief maximal exercise bouts, characterized as speed training, might increase the speed of neural transmission to muscle actions. In order to perform maximally in a subsequent exercise bout, the resting periods should be long enough for muscles to approximate to their pre-exercise state. Thus, exercise periods lasting 10–40 s, with the highest possible speed separated by rest periods of 0.5–3 minutes might be optimal for 'production training' (Table 8.2). During this type of training there will only be moderate increases in heart rate, as full adaptation of the oxygen transport system to exercise takes a while. Furthermore, due to a limited release of lactate from the exercising muscles, blood lactate will not reach very high values, even though the muscle lactate concentrations can be high.

Compared to 'production training', the exercise intensity in the 'maintenance training' is slightly lower but the duration of the exercise period is longer (Figure 8.11). The exercise duration should be between 30 and 90 s and the resting periods of similar length (Table 8.2). When the exercise periods are longer than 1 min, heart rate should approach maximal for each individual. The blood lactate concentration should increase progressively and it should be fairly high (> 10 mmol/1) after completing some exercise periods.

The adaptations caused by high-intensity training are mostly localized within the exercising muscles. Thus, it is important that the activities during the training session are similar to those experienced during competition. This can be obtained by performing activities similar to the sport or actually replicating the sport. Figure 8.11 shows examples of exercise intensities during 'production training' and 'maintenance training' performed as drills in soccer. Figure 8.12 includes an example of an exercise within 'production training' in basketball.

Table 8.2: Principles of anaerobic speed endurance training

	Exercise duration(s)	Rest	Intensity	Number of repetitions
Speed endurance training	Production 10–40	Five times the exercise duration	Almost maximal	2–10
	Maintenance 30–90	equal to exercise duration	Almost maximal	2–10

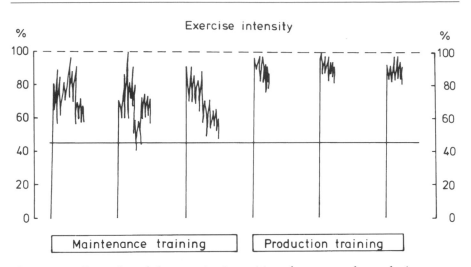

Figure 8.11: Examples of the exercise intensities of a soccer player during games within anaerobic training, expressed in relation to maximal intensity (100%). The exercise intensity eliciting maximum oxygen uptake and the maximal exercise intensity of the player are represented by the lower line and the higher horizontal dotted line, respectively.

Figure 8.13 shows an exercise entailing anaerobic 'maintenance training' in soccer. The figure also shows the heart rate and blood lactate concentration for one of the players taking part in the game. The high heart rate and blood lactate show clearly that the drill can be used for anaerobic 'maintenance training'.

AEROBIC PERFORMANCE

For decades the maximal oxygen uptake ($\dot{V}O_2$max) was deemed by exercise and work physiologists to be synonymous with aerobic fitness. It is recognized that in endurance sports a high ability to consume oxygen is a prerequisite for success. Maximal values over 80 ml/kg/min are noted in cross-country skiers, middle-distance and distance runners and professional cyclists (Reilly, Secher, Snell and Williams, 1990).

The $\dot{V}O_2$max has traditionally been measured whilst the athlete runs on a motor-driven treadmill or exercises on a cycle ergometer. The exercise intensity is raised in a progressive fashion until the subject reaches voluntary exhaustion. Expired air is collected during the test and the oxygen consumed calculated, the highest value attained constituting the $\dot{V}O_2$max. The availability now of on-line gas analysers (including facilities for breath-by-breath analysis) takes the technical tedium out of such assessments.

The limitations of the $\dot{V}O_2$max test for fitness assessment are now being recognized. The mode of exercise needs to be tailored to the specialism of

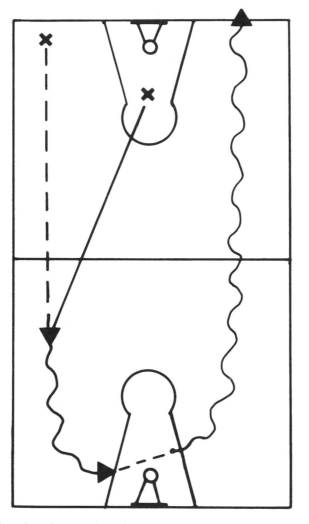

Figure 8.12: Speed endurance ('production training') game within basketball. The players receive the ball in a fast-break, hit the opponent's basket and are then dribbling the ball back to their own basket with maximal speed.

the athlete if it is to be of real value. A running treadmill fulfils the requirement for runners while a cyclist is best tested when appropriate devices are fitted to the individual's own racing bicycle (Firth, 1981). Competitors employing mainly upper-body actions in their sport are best tested on arm ergometers (Reilly and Secher, 1990).

The exercise performance during a test to measure $\dot{V}O_2$max may be a better indicator of performance potential than is the actual $\dot{V}O_2$max. Time to exhaustion in a graded treadmill test was found to be more highly correlated

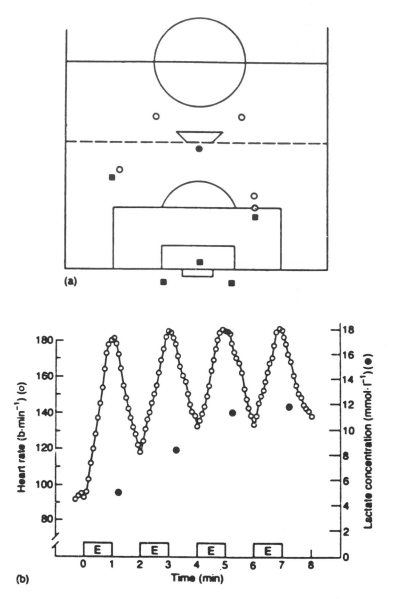

Figure 8.13: Speed endurance ('maintenance training') game within soccer. The players play 2 against 2 with man-to-man marking on one third of a field with two goals and two goalkeepers. They alternate between 1 min of exercise and 1 min of rest. Blood lactate (right) and heart rate (left) here are also shown.

with running time that was the $\dot{V}O_2$max (Noakes, Myburgh and Schall, 1990). The same high correlation has been found in international race-walkers (Reilly, Hopkins and Howlett, 1979).

In most aerobic sports, competitors do not operate at intensities corresponding to $\dot{V}O_2$max, for example, marathon runners race on average at about 80% of the maximal aerobic power. Whilst recognizing that $\dot{V}O_2$max may be a good indicator of potential, the ability to operate at a high fraction of $\dot{V}O_2$max is important for a successful endurance performance. This level depends largely on the oxidative capacity of the active muscles. Whilst the $\dot{V}O_2$max shows a modest response to endurance training regimens, the oxidative capacity of the muscles is elevated significantly. This is reflected in the exercise level corresponding to a reference lactate concentration (for example, 4 mmol/l) which shows a pronounced effect of training.

Consequently, the blood lactate responses to submaximal exercise are used as a basis for monitoring training status of endurance athletes in preference to $\dot{V}O_2$max. The test protocol may entail 3–4 submaximal exercise intensities after which a blood sample is obtained from an ear lobe, finger tip capillary or arm vein. For swimmers, a two-speed test has been used (Mader, Madsen and Hollmann, 1980).

The concept of a threshold for anaerobic metabolism has proved alluring. Disagreement among sports physiologists about the interpretation of the mechanisms underlying the accumulation of lactate during extended exercise has been aired extensively. Some authors have proposed the use of the inflection point in ventilation (VE) when plotted against $\dot{V}O_2$ under conditions of incremental exercise (Wasserman, 1986). This has been termed the ventilation threshold (T_{vent}) and it is normally highly correlated with the so-called lactate threshold (T_{lac}). The two curves have been dissociated by manipulating glycogen stores (Hughes, Turner and Brooks, 1984) or monitoring responses of McArdle's patients whose muscle enzyme deficiency leads to an inability to produce lactate. The claims by Conconi, Ferrari, Sigmo, Droghetti and Codeca (1982) that the deflection in heart rate response to increased exercise intensity reflects the point of dependence on anaerobic metabolism has also not been universally accepted.

The lactate response to increased exercise intensity demonstrates a curvilinear relationship and this curve is shifted to the right as a result of endurance training (Figure 8.14). This shift is a result of both increase of lactate clearance in blood and decreased production in the muscles. Monitoring of blood lactate response to exercise has been a useful tool in gauging submaximal responses to training. Usually a reference velocity or work rate such as the velocity corresponding to a 4 mm/l blood lactate value (V-4 mmol/l) is chosen.

An alternative concept is the maximal lactate steady state ($LaC_{max}ss$). This represents the velocity above which the blood lactate rises inexorably until fatigue occurs in the course of continuous exercise (Aurola and Rusko, 1992). Assessment is time-consuming and is of limited use and the procedure is unlikely to be adopted for routine use.

Blood lactate responses are dependent upon the test protocol and other factors. Therefore, they cannot be used to determine training intensity but

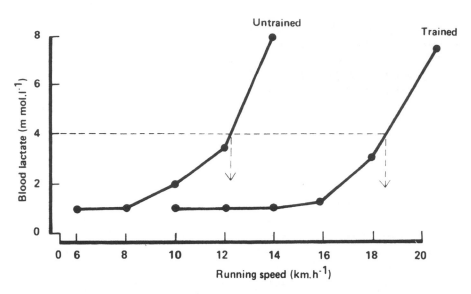

Figure 8.14: Schematic illustration of the changes in blood lactate responses to a graded exercise test produced by endurance training.

the effect of training can be determined by most tests. The lactate minimum concept refers to the point at which blood lactate reaches a minimum before rising in the course of an incremental test begun after inducing lactate production with a preliminary high-intensity bout (Tegtbur, Busse and Braumann, 1993). This has been correlated with the value of $Lac_{max}ss$ and, unlike the value of V-4 mmol/l, is seemingly not affected by glycogen depletion.

One of the chronic metabolic consequences of endurance training is that the oxygen consumption during submaximal exercise may be reduced. This represents in part an improvement in skilled factors such as optimal muscle fibre recruitment and pattern of neuromuscular stimulation. It is reflected in increased mechanical efficiency, that is the work done as a percentage of the energy cost. In many activities it is difficult to measure mechanical power output precisely and the oxygen cost for a given work rate is referred to as 'economy'. Running economy may be improved as a consequence of chronic endurance training and it is thought that running economy may be disturbed in the overtrained state.

Specificity of aerobic fitness assessment

Specificity is acknowledged as a fundamental principle in fitness training since effects are specific to the mode of exercise used and to the muscle groups involved. Aerobic training does entail central adaptations such as in heart function but local muscular factors may limit exercise performance.

The specificity concept has been acknowledged in attempts to match the ergometric task to the speciality of the sport.

Larrson, Larsen, Modest, Serup and Secher (1988) described the development of a kayak ergometer for use in winter training and for measurement of work capacity and $\dot{V}O_2$max. Their experience with Danish international paddlers led the authors to conclude that the ergometer was useful for both training and the evaluation of work capacity. This ergometer and commercially available rowing ergometers are based on wind turbulence generated by a flywheel. The amount of work done during each pull or stroke is displayed on the ergometer and a cumulative total is shown at the end of exercise. This feedback provides information that is useful both to the performer and to the sports scientist.

An alternative ergometer was validated for canoe and kayak specialists by Derham and Reilly (1993). The resistance was electromagnetic, the ergometer being modified from a swim-bench for application to kayak specialists. Peak $\dot{V}O_2$ values on the kayak ergometer demonstrated high correlations with performance in water tests that were not observed for $\dot{V}O_2$max when measured on a cycle ergometer using arm or leg exercise.

For swimmers, sophisticated swimming flumes are available in some of the national facilities, including Colorado Springs (USA), Rome (Italy), Otago (New Zealand) and Tsukuba (Japan). As an alternative, physiological responses to tethered swimming can be employed. More widely available are swim-simulators which were originally designed for fitness training of swimmers on land. The best simulators have a facility for recording power output on each pull. Research using adult swimmers has shown that monitoring of maximal power production may be of more relevance to swimmers than physiological responses to exercise on such simulators (McArdle and Reilly, 1993). Another criticism of the simulators is that leg muscle involvement on the exercise is neglected.

Test protocols and ergometric devices have been adapted for fitness testing of wheelchair athletes. Lees and Arthur (1988) described a friction-braked wheelchair ergometer which incorporated the use of the athlete's own wheelchair. The system was computer-linked for recording of power production and was suitable for assessment of both $\dot{V}O_2$max and anaerobic fitness according to requirements. Systems for application to wheelchair athletes have been regularly upgraded by research groups catering for special populations (Van der Woude Veeger and Dallmeijer, 1995).

Indirect assessment of aerobic performance

For purposes of testing large groups, particularly non-athletic populations, submaximal tests have long been in vogue. The exercise may be stepping onto a bench at a set frequency, running or cycling. The most widely used has been the cycle ergometer test of Åstrand and Rhyming (1954). In this test heart rate response to a single exercise intensity is used to estimate the $\dot{V}O_2$max. Despite corrections for the age and sex of the individual, the test has a large predictive error. Nevertheless, it is widely adopted for use in health education and health promotion programmes.

Determination of physical working capacity (PWC) entails a two- or three-stage test. From heart rate response to two or three steady-rate exercise intensities, the physical working capacity is computed as the power output corresponding to a heart rate of 170 (or 150) beats/min. The test has several limitations; for example, the individual with a large lower limb muscle mass has an advantage.

A variation of the step test used by Åstrand and Rhyming (1954) has been employed in the monitoring of aerobic fitness during pregnancy (Williams, Reilly, Campbell and Sutherst, 1988). The step-up was chosen as it resembles daily activities such as stair climbing. The step-height is fixed at 200 mm and the step-up rate varied. The rate of stepping is kept constant for 5 minutes and altogether three work stages are used with a rest intervening. The work rates are self-selected by the subjects to correspond to low, moderate and high exercise levels and attain target heart rates of 115, 135 and 155 beats/min. Metabolic as well as cardiac responses can be measured and PWC_{150} computed. Whilst a fixed height of stepping does not make allowances for subjects of different body sizes, nevertheless the test was considered useful for evaluating physical work capabilities of subjects with uncomplicated pregnancies.

For adults with modest exercise ambitions, walking has been advocated both for aerobic training and as a modality for testing. Brisk walking close to a maximal rate is necessary to ensure that a training stimulus to the oxygen transport system is provided. Field tests have been validated for a 1 mile (1.6 km) walk-test in the USA (Porcari, Ebbeling, Ward, Freedson and Rippe, 1989) and a 2 km walking test in Finland (Oja, Laukkanen, Pasanen and Vuori, 1989). The procedure is easy to administer, the task is suitable for mass testing (individuals set off in staggered starts) and it has immediate face validity. These tests represent a development of Cooper's walk–run test over 12 min which had been used for decades in both athletic and recreational sports groups (Cooper, 1968).

A more vigorous field test now adopted by sport practitioners and applicable to occupational fitness in heavy work (e.g., firefighting, military, police and so on) is the progressive shuttle-run test (Leger and Lambert, 1982). It comprises an endurance shuttle-run which progresses from walking pace to fast running pace, with subjects moving from one line to another 20 m away, reversing direction and keeping to a pace dictated by a sound signal. The pace gets faster every 2 min and the test is terminated when the subjects can no longer keep up with the required speed. The $\dot{V}O_2$max can be estimated from the exercise duration and norms are available for use with children

(Leger, Mercier, Gadoury and Lambert, 1988) as well as adults. The test has been adopted within the EUROFIT test battery by the European Commission of Experts.

The 'Yo-Yo' test is an alternative to the 20 m shuttle-run. It was designed to reflect the intermittent nature of activity in sports such as soccer (Bangsbo, 1994). The exercise intensity is varied and bouts of exercise are interspersed with periods for recovery.

AEROBIC TRAINING

Endurance training

General endurance is an important component of fitness for games or prolonged exercise, since individuals are more likely to commit errors and adopt techniques that may lead to injury as fatigue sets in and coordination declines. Endurance fitness is chiefly a function of the oxygen transport system and its consumption by the working tissues. It is particularly relevant where a high percentage of maximal oxygen consumption has to be utlilized for a prolonged period, such as in marathon running. All endurance training schedules are designed to improve aerobic capacity, the most pronounced effects being on the heart and involved skeletal muscles. In general, central and peripheral factors account approximately equally for the overall improvement. An increase of 25% in $\dot{V}O_2max$ is regarded as a good training effect but improvements in endurance performance may be much more pronounced than this. As the variability between individuals in $\dot{V}O_2max$ exceeds the typical training effects on the parameter, the conclusion is that genetic factors have a greater influence on the determination of top endurance athletes than does physical training.

Endurance training protocols fall into one of two categories, namely continuous or intermittent exercise. Continuous intense exercise (short high-speed distance or SHD work) is used in time trials, training for pace judgement or to increase tolerance to physical effort. Regular SHD work leads to a significant increase of the respiratory capacity of the active muscles. Because exercise is intense, risk of soft-tissue damage is prevalent, particularly in the muscles and tendons of the lower limbs in running. Long, slow, distance (LSD) work at moderate intensity is used by athletes specializing in prolonged duration events or as background conditioning for middle-distance events. Because enhancement of respiratory proteins involved in aerobic metabolism and located within the muscle mitochondria is related to the duration of exercise, this type of training is particularly effective. As a result of the high energy expenditure per workout, fat depots are trimmed and risk of muscle and tendon injury associated with repeatedly lifting 'excess deadweight' against gravity is reduced.

Because of the volume of work performed in LSD training, over-use syndromes may occur. The more common injuries include march fractures, lower fibular stress fractures, anterior tibial compartmental problems, chondromalacia patellae and trochanteric bursitis in runners. All too frequently inadequate footwear, hard surfaces and large ground reaction forces are implicated.

The jogger's training regimen also has LSD as the basic ingredient, though the duration of a typical session may be a mere 10% of that used by top marathon runners. The exercise intensity is usually around 60% to 65% of the maximal oxygen uptake with heart rates around 140 to 150 beats per minute. Joggers are more likely to sustain injuries if they attempt to emulate the daily training frequencies of club athletes. Five sessions per week is the recommended maximum for this group (Pollock and Wilmore, 1990).

Interval training

Interval training describes regimens where repeated work bouts 0.5–5 minutes in duration are interspersed with recovery periods of somewhat similar lengths. These schedules are used extensively by swimmers, cyclists, rowers and runners. High lactate levels may be induced by the exercise bouts and lactate levels in blood may rise progressively with each repeated effort. There is a suggestion that recovery from the intense efforts is improved as a result of aerobic training. This ability may be trained by maintaining an activity level at about 60% of the maximal heart rate in between the more strenuous efforts (see Figure 8.2). Active recovery between the successive exercise bouts enhances the removal of lactate from the blood. There is a linear relation between the intensity of the active recovery, and blood lactate disappearance up to an intensity of about 60% VO_2max (Gollnick and Hermansen, 1973).

The variables in interval training which the coach or athlete can manipulate include the number of repetitions, the duration of the effort, the exercise intensity and the recovery time between the efforts. Altering the duration of the efforts between days introduces variety into the training stimulus. The number of repetitions can be increased systematically as conditioning is developed whilst the pace can then be quickened. Finally, the recovery periods can be shortened; where these are inadequate to allow recovery, anaerobic endurance is also stressed.

In the form of 'interval training' originally developed in Germany in the 1930s, the optimum exercise intensity was deemed to be that which elicited heart rates of about 180 beats/min while recovery was terminated when the rate fell to about 120 beats/min. These rates were considered to provide the optimum stimulus for cardiac hypertrophy. This method of training is more likely to increase maximum oxygen uptake than is continuous submaximal exercise performance (Rusko, 1987). Placing an emphasis on high-intensity exercise is likely to cause recruitment of fast-twitch muscle fibres and so enhance training of peripheral as well as central factors.

Variations of interval training include fartlek, pyramid training and parlauf. Fartlek or 'speed play' entails sustained exercise in which the tempo is frequently altered, usually to coincide with the type of terrain. The intensity may be varied spontaneously from hard efforts to light exercise according to the athlete's disposition. This relative freedom makes fartlek enjoyable. The flexibility in the training stimulus ensures that all the major metabolic pathways are stressed at some time. Incorporating a fartlek session 3 times a week into the programme of elite distance runners has proved to be more effective than 20 minutes at the so-called 'anaerobic threshold' in improving 10 km time. Both programmes decreased the blood lactate response during submaximal exercise without increasing $\dot{V}O_2max$ (Acavedo and Goldfarb, 1989).

Pyramid training provides a formal means of varying the duration and intensity of exercise and the recovery intermission. Sessions may involve, for example, precise interval accelerations of 100, 200, 400, 800 and 1200 m for runners. The athlete then returns down the distances to finish with a sprint before warming down.

Parlauf or continuous relays can be introduced into training routines to stimulate club spirit for games players. It can engage two, three or four members per team for a period pre-determined by the coaching staff. In the two-per-team format, rest periods do not permit complete recovery so that performance may inevitably deteriorate. This type of regimen is suited for swimmers and middle-distance runners but can also be used for fitness training by games players.

Circuit weight training

Circuit training provides a good method of general conditioning but is mainly specific muscle endurance training. The individual athlete rotates around a series of exercises set out in a circle, usually 8 to 12 separate exercises being involved. Muscle groups engaged are varied between work stations, the purpose being that local muscular fatigue is avoided whilst stress is maintained on the cardiovascular system. This method lends itself to group involvement and so it is frequently applied for squad training, especially pre-season.

In circuit weight training the majority of the stations employ resistance or weights. Contemporary multi-station training systems are designed so that the athlete can use the machines for aerobic training as well as dwell at one station for specific muscular conditioning work (Reilly and Thomas, 1978). The stimulus to the oxygen transport system may be inadequate for many multi-station machines due to a predominance of arm exercises. In such a case the blood lactate will be higher than for the same oxygen uptake in leg exercises (Garbutt, Boocock, Reilly and Troup, 1994).

A varied programme of exercises is incorporated into the circuit shown in Figure 8.15. Employment of a higher number of repetitions in the large muscle group work and fewer repetitions of the arm exercises ensures that a high training stimulus is maintained for the oxygen transport system. Once the athlete is habituated to the exercises, it is likely that three sets of the complete circuit are required. As aerobic fitness develops, the loads can then be increased progressively and pace accelerated. Progress is readily apparent to the athlete who is then easily motivated by this form of training.

Aerobics

The form of exercise known as 'aerobics' grew out of the demand for exercise as a means of acquiring health-related fitness. Its popularity developed alongside 'sport for all' campaigns and promotional drives to participate in physical training for recreational purposes. There was also a recognition that exercise programmes, especially when married with dietary regimens, reduce the risk of cardiovascular disease and aid recovery from such problems as coronary heart disease.

The guidelines of the American College of Sports Medicine have been adopted world-wide for exercise prescription in health-related contexts. They specify that exercise training should engage major muscle groups in continuous activity for 20–30 minutes a day, 3 days a week. The intensity of exercise should be within 50–80% $\dot{V}O_2$max or in excess of 60% of the maximal heart rate. In calculating the exercise heart rate that elicits a training stimulus to the circulatory system, the formula of Karvonen (1959) has been adapted. This specifies that the exercise heart rate should be above 60% of the estimated heart-rate range (maximum minus resting heart rate). Thus for an individual with a maximum heart rate of 180 and a resting rate of 60 beats/min the training threshold is 132 beats/minute. Where the maximum heart rate is not known, it is estimated by the formula 220 – age in years, although in a majority of cases this over-estimates the ageing effect on the maximal heart rate. The heart rate response to exercise programmes has been used to assess its suitability for training the oxygen transport system in so-called 'aerobics' programmes.

Initially, aerobics consisted of a long sequence of exercises performed to music. High-impact exercises induced injuries and are generally eschewed in programmes tailored to individuals of low initial fitness levels. Commercially available videos provide exercise regimens for participants to follow in their own homes. Many of these are unergonomically designed and do not match the capabilities of those using them (Reilly, 1992).

Various exercise modes have been employed over the last decade for 'aerobics' training. These include cycling, jogging, swim-aerobics,

1. Squat

2. Bench Press

3. Lateral Pull Down

4. Sit-Up

5. Seated Row

6. Leg Press

7. Dead Lift

8. Shoulder Press

9. Back Extension

Figure 8.15: Circut of training exercises from Garbutt et al. (1994).

deep-water running, ladder-climbing and stepping. These have been sup-plemented by use of sports equipment such as rowing ergometers and ski-simulators. Their effectiveness depends on product design and flexibility for the individual to raise the exercise intensity. Ski-machines with the facility for passive actions are of little use for progressive training whereas those that permit dynamic movements and incorporate modifiable resistance set-tings do provide a good basis for training the oxygen transport system (Reilly, Kirton, McGrath and Coulthard, 1993).

Combined and cross-training

Sports, and games in particular, make demands on anaerobic pathways and on muscular strength as well as on the oxygen transport mechanisms. Whilst aerobic metabolism provides the main energy sources during soccer, for example, the critical aspects of performance may depend on anaerobic efforts (Bangsbo, 1994). Consequently aerobic training must be used in conjunction with other components of fitness in the preparation of such players for performance. For this reason intermittent regimens, especially if they are closely related to games drills, are relevant in training contexts.

There may be unwanted interactions between endurance and muscle strength. When endurance training gets complete emphasis in pre-season conditioning periods, muscle strength may be adversely affected (Hickson, 1980). If muscle strength programmes predominate for a prolonged period, the ensuing hypertrophy of fibres may lead to a lowered capillary to muscle fibre ratio. In this case oxygen supply to active fibres may be compromised. It is, therefore, important that the training programme is balanced according to the needs of players. It is essential also that the design of training should take into account the stage of the season and the competitive schedule. Rigorous and exhaustive training in the days leading up to competition will adversely affect performance. This is because of a reduction in muscle glycogen to below normal levels at the start of play and an earlier onset of fatigue during the game (Saltin, 1973).

The oxygen transport system must be trained for competition in sports such as distance running, cross-country skiing, cycling and so on. The tri-athlon event combines swimming, cycling and road-running into a single discipline and requires competitors to be proficient in each. Participants need to have a highly trained oxygen transport system and local muscular adaptations specific to each sport. Generally the greater gains in metabolic (mechanical) efficiency are obtained through swim training and the least in cycling. Each of the disciplines must be practised regularly; otherwise the biochemical adaptations specific to the muscle fibres recruited in the sport concerned are lost due to 'detraining'.

ENVIRONMENTAL FACTORS

Training and time of day

The term 'Circadian rhythms' refers to fluctuations in biological functions or in human performance that recur about every 24 hours. They represent an adaptation to the spin of the earth about its long axis which is completed once every solar day. The alternation of light and darkness linked with the solar day is manifested in the sleep–wakefulness cycle in humans. This cycle represents a continuum that ranges from the unconsciousness associated with deep sleep to a state of high excitement.

There are two major biological rhythms that are attributed to the ability of the organism to control its many systems with a circadian system. These are the clocks linked with sleep–wakefulness and that of core body temperature. The major structures in the brain that are associated with circadian rhythmicity are the pineal gland and the suprachiasmatic nucleus cells of the hypothalamus.

Many human performance measures show a circadian rhythm that is closely in phase with the curve of body temperature (Figure 8.16). For this reason body temperature has been regarded as a fundamental variable in circadian rhythmicity. The curve in human performance is evident in relatively short-term exercise. The circadian rhythm in swimming over 100 m and 400 m, for example, is greater than the effect of sleep disturbances on these measures (Sinnerton and Reilly, 1993). For this reason time trials or qualifying times are more easily achieved in the evening than in the morning.

Strenuous training programmes should be retained for afternoon or evening rather than in the morning. The reason is that a greater training stimulus can be applied when the body temperature curve is near to its peak time. Muscle and joint temperatures are low in the early morning and consequently the body is ill-prepared for exercise at this time of day. Morning sessions should be preceded by a systematic warm-up in which the joint's range of motion is increased by appropriate exercises and muscle temperature elevated. Even so, the exercise should be moderate and the more strenuous regimens should be preserved for later in the day. Non-elite and recreational athletes are subjected to a greater cardiovascular 'shock' when intense exercise is conducted in the morning than in the evening. Consequently individuals doing aerobic training for preventive purposes are better advised to exercise in the afternoon and evening than in the morning before going to work (Cabri, De Witte, Clarys, Reilly and Strass, 1988).

The normal circadian rhythm is disturbed when athletes cross time zones for purposes of training or competition. This can have an adverse effect on competitive performance, even when only two or three time zones are crossed. Team performance is affected after travelling from coast-to-coast to

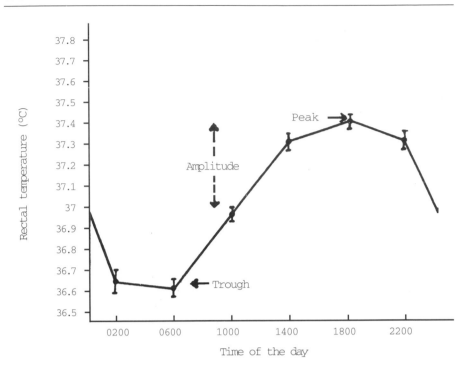

Figure 8.16: The circadian rhythm in core temperature.

play American Football matches, the deterioration being worst when travelling eastwards (Jehue, Street and Huizenga, 1993). A change of training times for some days in advance of travel to coincide with time at the local venue of competition can help to reduce the decrement in performance.

Training and competing in the heat

Athletes accustomed to a temperate climate may often be required to train and compete in other parts of the world which have a much higher ambient temperature. They may also have to cope with abrupt changes in temperature in their own country. Unless they are thoroughly prepared for such events they may encounter problems that range from discomfort and impairment of performance to serious medical emergencies associated with heat illness:

(1) Performance may be adversely affected by a rise in body temperature beyond an optimal level. The body core temperature is normally regulated at about 37°C and during exercise is thought to be optimal in the range 38–38.5°C. If core temperature rises much beyond this level, heat distress or heat injury of varying severity will be encountered. These

problems tend to be associated with endurance type sports such as distance running or extended strenuous training practices.

The ideal air temperature for a marathon race for top runners is about 14°C. When wet bulb temperature exceeds 28°C there is serious risk of heat injury in endurance sports. In such conditions the body is unable to maintain heat balance and strenuous training must be curtailed.

(2) Muscle cramps are associated with loss of body fluid and tend to occur in competition more than in training. Games players competing in intense heat may lose 2 litres of sweat per hour and marathon runners may lose 4–5 litres of fluid during a race. Although the body loses electrolytes in sweat, such losses cannot adequately account for the occurrence of cramps. These seem to coincide with low energy stores as well as reduced body water levels. Generally the muscles employed in the exercise are affected, but most vulnerable are the leg (upper or lower) and abdominal muscles. The cramp can usually be stopped by stretching the involved muscle and sometimes massage is effective.

(3) Heat exhaustion is characterized by a core temperature of about 40°C. Associated with this is a feeling of extreme tiredness, dizziness, breathlessness and tachycardia (increased heart rate). The symptoms may coincide with a reduced sweat loss but usually arise because the skin blood vessels are so dilated that blood flow to vital organs is reduced.

(4) Heat stroke is a true medical emergency. It is characterized by core temperatures of 41°C or higher. Hypohydration can be driven so far as to threaten life. Heat stroke is characterized by cessation of sweating, total confusion or loss of consciousness. In such cases treatment is urgently needed to reduce body temperature. There may also be circulatory instability and loss of vasomotor tone as the regulation of blood pressure begins to fail.

During exercise about 75% of the energy expended results in generation of heat. It is estimated that strenuous exercise would result in a 10°C rise in core temperature within an hour if the body did not have a facility for losing heat to the environment. The body may also gain heat by exposure to solar radiation and by re-radiation of heat from hot surfaces such as the road in road-running or concrete surfaces in games. Skiers and mountaineers may also gain heat by reflection from snow. Some protection is provided by cloud cover or shaded areas.

There are two main physiological mechanisms contributing to heat loss during extended training sessions. The first involves an increased blood flow to the skin: the body surface can lose heat to the environment (by convection and radiation) due to the extra warm blood being shunted through its subcutaneous layers. In strenuous exercise where the cardiac output is maximal or near it, it is possible that this increased cutaneous blood flow will compromise the blood supply to the exercising muscles and adversely affect performance. The second mechanism is sweating, which is the main avenue of heat loss during exercise in the heat. The sweat glands are stimulated when core temperature rises and they secrete a dilute solution containing electrolytes and trace elements. Heat is lost when the fluid evaporates on the surface of the body, no heat exchange occurring if the sweat drips off or is wiped away. In hot and very humid conditions evaporation is limited because the air is already highly saturated with water vapour and unable to take up much additional water: its ability to do so is dependent on the water vapour pressure gradient, which is low when humidity is high. Consequently hot humid conditions are detrimental to performance and increase the risk of heat injury.

A consequence of sweating is a reduction in body water. The body water present in the cells, in the interstices and in plasma seems to fall in roughly equal proportions. The fall in plasma volume may compromise the supply of blood to the active muscles and to the skin for thermoregulation. Although the kidneys and the endocrine glands try to conserve body water and electrolytes, the thermoregulatory mechanisms (sweating) override those controlling body water and the athlete may become dangerously dehydrated. This may happen within 30 minutes of intense exercise in certain combinations of environmental conditions, especially if the athlete is inadequately hydrated beforehand. It is therefore, important that athletes are adequately hydrated before undertaking training sessions in the heat, and where possible attempt to rehydrate during the training session. The body does not adapt to training repeatedly in a dehydrated state so delaying the provision of fluid is unnecessarily risky.

The higher the state of aerobic fitness the lower is the thermal strain on the athlete since the well-trained individual has a highly developed cardiovascular system to cope with the dual roles of thermoregulation and exercise and also an increased rate of sweat production. The highly trained individual acclimatises more quickly than one of poorer fitness. Training will also improve exercise tolerance in the heat but does not eliminate the necessity for heat acclimatization.

Heat acclimatization

The main features of heat acclimatization are an earlier onset of sweating (sweat produced at a lower rise in body temperature) and a more dilute solution from the sweat glands. The heat-acclimatized individual sweats more than an unacclimatized counterpart at a given exercise intensity. There is also a better distribution of blood to the skin for more effective cooling with acclimatization.

Heat acclimatization occurs relatively quickly and a good degree of adaptation takes place within 10–14 days of the initial exposure. Further adaptations will enhance the athlete's capability of performing well in heat stress conditions. Ideally, therefore, the athlete or team should be exposed to training in the climate of the host country for at least 2 weeks before the event and train in that climate. An alternative strategy is to have an acclimatization period of 2 weeks or so well before the event with subsequent shorter exposure nearer the contest. If these suggestions are not practicable, attempts should be made at some degree of heat acclimatization before the athlete leaves for the host country. This pre-acclimatization may be achieved in various ways:

(1) The athlete may be exposed to hot and humid environments, seeking out the hottest time of day to train at home.
(2) If the conditions at home are too cool the athlete may seek access to an environmental chamber for periodic bouts of heat exposure. It is important that the athlete exercises rather than rests under such conditions. Repeated exposure to a sauna or Turkish bath is only partially effective. About 3 hours per week exercising in an environmental chamber should provide a good degree of acclimatization.
(3) The microclimate next to the skin may be kept hot by wearing heavy sweat suits or windbreakers. This will add to the heat load imposed under cool environmental conditions and induce a degree of adaptation to thermal strain. Dawson, Pyke and Morton, (1989) showed that training in sweat clothing in cool conditions can provide the same improvements in heat tolerance as training in hot humid conditions.

On transfer to a training camp in a warm climate, sports participants should be encouraged to drink copiously. They should drink much more fluid than they think they need because thirst is often a very poor indication of real need. The osmolality of the urine can be used to indicate the state of hydration but requires baseline data under normal conditions for purpose of comparison. When the athletes arrive in the hot country they should be discouraged strongly from sunbathing as this itself does not help acclimatization except by the development of a suntan, which may help to protect the skin from damage via solar radiation. In Australia or other hot countries this exposure is dangerous, being linked with high levels of skin cancer due to a reduced ozone layer. Adaptation of the skin to sunbathing is a long-term process and is not helpful in the short term but the negative effects of a sunburn can cause severe discomfort and a decline in performance. Athletes should therefore be protected with an adequate sunscreen if they are likely to be exposed to the sun.

Initially training should be undertaken in the cooler parts of the day so that an adequate workload can be achieved and adequate fluid must be taken regularly. If sleeping is difficult arrangements should be made to sleep in an air-conditioned environment but to achieve full acclimatization some of the day should be spent exposed to the ambient temperature other than in air-conditioned rooms. Although sweating will increase with acclimatization, there should be no need to take salt tablets, provided adequate amounts of salt are taken with normal food.

In the period of acclimatization the athlete should regularly monitor his/her body weight and try to compensate for weight loss with adequate fluid intake. Alcohol is inappropriate for this purpose since it acts as a diuretic and increases urine output. Athletes are reminded that they should also ensure that the volume and colour of urine is normal. If these indications are satisfied, the training load can be increased gradually as acclimatization is effected.

When training or competing in the heat, especially in endurance events, it is important to be hydrated adequately before the start. Cool water can be ingested up until 15–20 minutes pre-start. The warm-up should be restricted in intensity and conducted in the shade so that body temperature is not raised substantially before competition.

During exercise liquid refreshment should be taken where rules permit this. Recommended intakes are about 150–200 ml every 15–20 minutes since the intestine cannot absorb any more than this. Runners may find it easier to drink on the move if they sip through a straw rather than drink from an open cup. Taking in fluid is less of a problem for cyclists who are not exposed to the repetitive jolts that runners experience on each footfall. The fluid helps to reduce the rise in body temperature during exercise. Guidelines for energy and electrolyte content of drinks have been presented by Maughan (1991). Salt tablets should be avoided since they draw water into the gut whilst being absorbed.

The body will not lose heat by evaporation if sweat drips off the skin. So, sweat should not be wiped off the body unless it is a hindrance, for example, to vision.

As the body loses some heat by convection when air currents cool its surface, the wearing of light, loose clothing helps in this respect. The larger the surface area of the body that is exposed for cooling the better.

Clothing of natural fibre such as cotton (or at least a cotton–polyester mix) is desirable under warm and radiant environmental conditions. Clothing of synthetic fibre such as nylon and polyester does not absorb sweat: the humidity in the clothing microclimate increases, evaporative efficiency decreases and body temperature rises as a result.

Wearing headgear can be a useful practice for some athletes when the sun is shining. This helps to reduce the penetration of heat to the head and prevents a rise in brain temperature that would adversely affect performance. This explains why marathon runners may choose to wear sun hats when racing in hot countries. Such lightweight sun-caps are generally available in sports shops.

Training and competing in the cold

Many athletes have to train and compete in cold conditions, outdoors in winter months. They may also have to travel overseas to climates that are more variable than at home and that may be colder than they are accustomed to. In cold weather conditions athletes who have poor aerobic fitness and who are unable to sustain an exercise intensity sufficient to remain in thermal balance may be in danger of hypothermia. Additionally, long-distance runners and cyclists may be at similar risk if improperly clad for the cold, wet and windy weather. The same caution extends to skiers and climbers as conditions on the mountain slopes can change quite suddenly.

Early symptoms of hypothermia include shivering, fatigue, loss of strength and coordination and an inability to sustain work rate. Once fatigue develops, shivering may decrease and the condition will often worsen. Later symptoms include collapse, stupor and loss of consciousness.

The key factor prior to exposure to cold conditions is planning. There are few physiological adaptations to cold that will be helpful, so behavioural alterations are extremely important. Suitable clothing for cold and cold–wet conditions should be worn. Attention should also be directed to boots, gloves and headgear as well as to choice of garments and undergarments.

Clothing of natural fibre (cotton or wool) is preferable to synthetic material in cold and in cold–wet conditions. The clothing should allow sweat produced during exercise in these conditions to flow through the garment. The best material will allow sweat to flow out through the cells of the garment, whilst preventing water droplets from penetrating the clothing from the outside. If the fabric becomes saturated with water or sweat, it loses its insulation and in cold–wet conditions the body temperature may quickly drop.

Athletes training in the cold should ensure that the trunk area of the body is well insulated. The use of warm undergarments beneath a full tracksuit may be needed. Dressing in layers is well advised since the outer layers can be discarded as body temperature rises and if ambient temperature increases.

When layers of clothing are worn, the outer layer should be capable of resisting both wind and rain. The inner layer should provide insulation and should also wick moisture from the skin to promote heat loss by means of evaporation. Polypropylene and cotton fishnet thermal underwear has good insulation and wicking properties and so is suitable to wear next to the skin.

The blood supply to the head is not reduced in the cold as is blood flow to the limbs: as a consequence the body may lose much heat through the head unless appropriate headgear is worn. Thermal socks help maintain foot temperatures in the comfort zone and gloves help to maintain manual dexterity. In cold–wet and windy conditions exposed areas should be well protected against frost-bite.

Immediately prior to competing in the cold the athlete should endeavour to stay as warm as possible. A thorough warm-up regimen (performed indoors if possible) is recommended. It is thought that cold conditions increase the risk of muscle injury in sports involving intense anaerobic efforts;

warm-up exercises may afford some protection in this respect. Competitors may need to wear more clothing than they normally do during their event.

Aerobic fitness does not directly offer protection against cold. Nevertheless it will enable game players to keep more active when not directly involved in play. The distance runner (or cyclist) with a high level of aerobic fitness will also be able to maintain activity at a satisfactory level to achieve heat balance. On the other hand the individual with poor endurance may be at risk of hypothermia if the pace of activity falls dramatically. Shivering during activity signals the onset of danger.

There is no evidence that the body acclimatizes to cold in a major way. Consequently training in cold conditions will not be helpful to compete in a cold climate.

Altitude training

Altitude poses a variety of challenges to those that enter this environment. Apart from the difficulties presented by the terrain, there are the environmental hazards associated with temperature, weather, air velocity and so on. The ultimate obstacle is often a shortage of oxygen in the air to fuel the body's energetic processes. This is due to the drop in atmospheric pressure which in turn affects the partial pressure of oxygen in the lungs and pulmonary diffusion. Its effects on exercise performance are evident at moderate altitudes such as at Mexico City, Johannesburg or the mountain training camps in Colorado and Font Romeu (France).

Another question is posed about the advantage that high-altitude dwellers may have compared to sea-level people. It should be noted that there are no permanent human settlements above 5.9 km and stays at this altitude or above lead to progressive physiological deterioration. Stays above 3 km are unlikely to be of any benefit for athletic performance at sea level. At this altitude the saturation of red blood cells with oxygen is down to almost 90% compared with 97% at sea level and at higher altitudes the saturated value falls steeply. Finally the advantages possessed by distance runners from the East African highlands seem to be more related to racial and training factors than to altitude per se.

The problem of coping with hypoxia was faced by Olympic participants at the 1968 Games in Mexico City which is located at an altitude of 2280 m. Its impact on performance was underlined in track and field athletics by the results of the distance races; all medallists in events from 1500 m upwards were either trained or dwelt at altitude. A more contentious question followed in the wake of these statistics and the recent dominance of East African runners brought up at altitude. That is, whether the physiological adaptations associated with training at altitude benefits subsequent performance at sea level?

These issues demand an understanding of the nature of the adaptations that take place, how they depend on the degree of hypoxia, the duration of exposure to altitude and the timing of the return to sea level. Additionally, the characteristics of the sport and individual differences in responding to altitude are also relevant. The state of training of the individual and the training done at altitude seem to be crucial factors.

Our understanding of the physiological responses to exercise at altitude was furthered by the numerous experiments that were conducted before and after the Olympic Games at Mexico. Later the emphasis shifted to the high mountains and the possibilities of climbing the Himalayan peaks without oxygen support. The main altitude studies in the 1980s consisted of measurements on the slopes of Everest and a simulation of an Everest climb in a hypobaric chamber. The main study in the 1990s was on Pikes Peak in Colorado at an altitude of 4300 m: this was concerned largely with metabolic and hormonal responses at this height. The most relevant studies concerned with the efficacy of altitude training camps have followed athletes during sojourns at mountainous locations and their responses after returning to sea level. Collectively these studies have contributed to our knowledge about physiological stresses at altitude and adaptations to hypoxia, but underline that prescriptions about altitude training are still inexact.

There is very little effect of altitude on exercise performance until a height in excess of 1500 m is reached. There is a suggestion from recent research that physiological responses may be affected, albeit to a minor degree, at altitudes as low as 610 m (Gore et al., 1995). Despite the pressure drop, the haemoglobin in red blood cells is still almost completely saturated with oxygen so the active muscles may not be adversely affected and some athletes cope well with altitude exposure up to 2000 m. Altitude training camps below this level are unlikely to provoke the kind of adaptations that are needed to boost oxygen transport and utilization. Intense exercise at an altitude above 3000 m is likely to provoke unwanted medical conditions and scheduling of major competitions or training sessions is not recommended for such heights.

The body's primary method of coping with hypoxia associated with exercise at altitude is by increasing the frequency and depth of breathing. One consequence is that this leads to the blood becoming more alkaline. Within a few days the kidneys restore blood acidity towards normality by excreting bicarbonate. This reduces the body's alkaline reserve. On return to sea level it may be unable to cope as well as before with an influx of acid to the blood from the active muscle. Consequently, performance in sports making large demands on anaerobic mechanisms would be adversely affected but for the improvement in buffering capacity that occurs (Mizuno et al., 1990). Of course, anaerobic efforts that require locomotion (running, jumping, cycling and so on) and throwing are improved at altitude for physical (reduced air resistance due to its lower density) rather than for metabolic reasons. It has been calculated, for example, that Bob Beamon's world record jump at Mexico had a 31 cm contribution from the effect of the prevailing atmospheric pressure and wind conditions and most importantly the increased run-up speed that the reduced air density permitted (Ward-Smith, 1986).

The pioneering research work on the adverse effects of altitude on aerobic performance, conducted a quarter of a century ago, is confirmed by current work on Scandinavian skiers (Ingjer and Myhere, 1992). The maximal oxygen uptake is reduced by about 10–14% on first exposure to 2.3 km height; it improves a little but after 3–4 weeks is still 7–9% below sea-level values. The fall in maximum oxygen uptake is about 1% for every 100 m above 1500 m. The pumping power of the heart muscle is reduced and the active muscles rely more on anaerobic sources at high exercise intensities. The anaerobic capacity is unaffected by altitude but at given exercise intensities (e.g. running at 20 km per hour) more lactate is produced by the active muscles and accumulates in the blood.

The improved ventilatory capacity and lung perfusion at altitude only helps to cope with exercise at altitude and is of little benefit on return to sea level. At altitude the increased pulmonary ventilation helps boost the loading of oxygen into the circulation. At the lower pressures that apply in unloading of oxygen to the active cells, the transfer is improved by increased levels of 2,3-bisphosphoglycerate (BPG), a substance which reduces the affinity of the red blood cells for oxygen. The effect of increased 2,3-BPG is lost quickly once the sojourn to altitude is over. The decreased affinity of the red blood cells for oxygen and the better uptake by active muscles are evident on immediate return to sea level and are reflected in a decreased blood lactate response to a set exercise intensity.

In view of the elevated ventilatory and lactate responses to exercise at altitude, the training intensity will need to be lowered for the first few days at altitude. This is not necessarily a great disadvantage to well-trained athletes who can accept the period at altitude for consolidating training effects (rather than further high-intensity training) or occasionally drop to a lower altitude level for the more intensive training efforts.

The distinctive response to altitude training that might help to improve aerobic performance at sea level lies in the adaptations of the oxygen transport system. This has been clarified to experiments using blood doping (transfusional polycythaemia) and a synthetic version of the renal hormone erythropoeitin (EPO). Each of these raises the amount of oxygen delivered to the active cells and can dramatically improve both aerobic parameters and endurance performance. The hormone EPO is stimulated by hypoxia, such as occurs at altitude, and increases production of red blood cells in the bone marrow. This process is stimulated on early exposure to altitude and the effect is evident within a week. The effect is most pronounced after 3–4 weeks and is reflected in an elevated total body haemoglobin. This response continues to improve oxygen transport, although the effect on the sea-dweller moving to altitude never quite matches the blood profile of the native. If this response to altitude exposure was the sole concern, then a clear case could be made for supporting the use of altitude training by endurance athletes. Inevitably, the complexity of the physiological responses, the particular environmental considerations and the characteristics of the individual complicate the issues.

In the early days of exposure there is a pseudo-increase in haemoglobin, to which oxygen is bound in the red blood cells. This is due to a decrease in plasma volume. Gradually the plasma volume is partly restored (complete restoration takes at least 2 months) and red blood cell production increases, stimulated by EPO action. The elevation in serum EPO increases with the level of hypoxia; at about 1900 m it reaches 30% higher values than at sea level within 2–3 days but at 4500 m this increase is about 300%. Serum EPO concentrations show a decrease after about one week and this may be linked with an increased oxygenation of the tissues due to 2,3-BPG. Meanwhile the average true increase in haemoglobin at altitudes between 1.8 and 3 km is about 1% per week.

It has been estimated that optimal haematological adaptations to altitude take about 80 days (Berklund, 1992). This may be accelerated by periodic visits to higher altitudes, say up to and just over 3 km, but without training there. The subjects with low haemoglobin and haematocrit prior to altitude exposure benefit more from training camps at altitude. It is also important that adequate iron is stored in the body prior to altitude exposure. There may be a case for iron supplementation prior to and during the stay at altitude. Low iron stores may explain why some athletes have failed to benefit from altitude training.

On return to sea level the hypoxic stimulus is no longer present and some physiological effects are quickly reversed. Red blood cell formation is depressed and 2,3-BPG levels fall, for example. It may take several days for bicarbonate levels in cerebrospinal fluid to return to normal. Two months following return to sea level, total blood volume and red cell volume may fall to below normal pre-altitude levels, by which time the beneficial effects of altitude stays will have been lost. There is therefore a risk of decreased endurance performance at sea level some months after altitude training.

Some physiological adaptations to hypoxia may help cope with exercise at altitude but have dubious value for subsequent performance at sea level. The main benefits that carry over to sea level are adaptations in the oxygen-carrying capacity of the blood. These cannot be induced fully by using portable altitude simulators that reduce the inspired oxygen. A continuous 10-week period at moderate altitude or repeated periods of shorter exposure are necessary for optimal effects. Schedules for accentuating increases in red blood cell mass comprise 3–4 weeks at moderate altitudes on 3–4 separate occasions with an interval of 1 week between the sojourns. This approach may be more suitable for skiers than runners but has proved effective also in middle-distance runners. Attention is directed to diet since there is an increased dependence on blood glucose at altitude. Considerations should be given also to iron supplementation in order to support the increased production of red blood cells. Long-term stays at altitude produce changes at cellular level (notably increased mitochondrial enzyme activities and improved capillarization) that in part resemble responses to endurance training. Altitude exposure cannot substitute for endurance training since the muscles actually engaged in exercise must have the oxidative capacities to exploit the enhanced oxygen delivery. Coaches must appreciate the cautions of scientists towards altitude camps being prescribed as the panacea for healing imperfections in training and fitness.

OVERVIEW

It is clear that it is very difficult to establish what causes improvements in performance with physical training. Nevertheless, appropriate training delays onset of fatigue and shortens periods of fatigue experienced during competition.

The training programme must place demands on the metabolic pathways stressed in competition. The activity must be matched to that of the sport concerned, since training effects are specific to the mode of exercise. Anaerobic training must take into account the duration and the frequency of intense efforts during competition. Adaptations to speed work include neuromuscular as well as biochemical mechanisms.

Aerobic training engages central and peripheral factors linked with oxygen transport and utilization by the active muscles. Physiological alterations provoked by endurance training depend on the intensity of exercise, the duration of training, the exercise mode and the training frequency. Adaptations to submaximal intensities may be more important than are maximal responses in determining endurance performance. So-called 'aerobics' training has relevance for health-related, rather than elite, performance. Irrespective of the standard of the individual, environmental factors (such as time of day, temperature and pressure) will have an impact on the performance. They must be taken into consideration when the overall training schedules of the athlete or team are being planned.

REFERENCES

Acavedo, E.D. and Goldfarb, A.N. (1989) Increasing training intensity effects on plasma lactate, ventilatory threshold and endurance, *Medicine and Science in Sports and Exercise*, **21**, 563–568.

Andersen, J.L., Klitgaard, H., angsbo, J. and Saltin, . (1994) Myosin heavy chain isoforms in single fibres from m. vastus lateralis of soccer players; effects of strength and detraining, *Acta Physiologica Scandinavica*, **150**, 21–26.

Andersen, P. and Henriksson, J. (1978) Capillary supply of the quadriceps femoris muscle of man: Adaptive response to exercise, *Journal of Physiology*, **270**, 677–690.

Åstrand, P.O. and Rhyming, I. (1954) A nomogram for calculation of aerobic capacity (physical fitness) from pulse rate during sub-maximal work, *Journal of Applied Physiology*, **7**, 218–221.

Aurola, S. and Rusko, H. (1992) Does anaerobic threshold correlate with maximal lactate steady state?, *Journal of Sports Sciences*, **10**, 309–323.

Balsom, P.D., Seger, J.Y., Sjödin, B. and Ekblom, B. (1992) Physiological responses to maximal intensity intermittent exercise, *European Journal of Applied Physiology*, **65**, 144–149.

Balsom, P.D., Ekblom, B., Soderlund, K., Sjödin, B. and Hultman, E. (1993a) Creatine supplementation and dynamic high-intensity intermittent exercise. *Scandinavian Journal of Medicine and Science in Sports*, **3**, 143–149.

Balsom, P.D., Harridge, S.D.R., Söderlund, K., Sjödin, B. and Ekblom, B. (1993b) Creatine supplementation per se does not enhance endurance exercise performance, *Acta Physiologica Scandinavica*, **149**, 521–523.

Bangsbo, J. (1992) Is the oxygen deficit an accurate quantitative measure of the anaerobic energy production during intense exercise? *Journal of Applied Physiology*, **73**, 1207–1208.

Bangsbo, J. (1994) The physiology of soccer with special reference to intense intermittent exercise, *Acta Physiologica Scandinavica*, **151**, Suppl 619, 1–155.

Bangsbo, J. (1995) Regulation of glycogenolysis and glycolysis during intense exercise—in vivo studies using repeated intense exercise, in *Biochemistry of Exercise X* (Eds. R. Maughan and S.M. Shirreffs), pp. 261–275, Human Kinetics, Champaign, IL.

Bangsbo, J. and Saltin, B. (1993) Recovery of muscle from exercise, its importance for subsequent performance, in *Intermittent High Intensity Exercise*: Preparation, stresses and damage limitation. (Eds. D.A.D. Macleod, R.J. Maughan, C. Williams, C.R. Madeley, J.C.M. Sharp and R.W. Nutton) pp. 49–69, E. & F.N. Spon, London/New York.

Bangsbo, J., Gollnick, P.D., Graham, T.E., Juel, C., Kiens, B., Mizuno, M. and Saltin, B. (1990) Anaerobic energy production and O_2 deficit–debt relationship during exhaustive exercise in humans, *Journal of PhysiologyS*, **422**, 539–559.

Bangsbo, J., Graham, T.E., Johansen, L., Strange, S., Christensen, C. and Saltin, B. (1992a) Elevated muscle acidity and energy production during exhaustive exercise in man, *American Journal of PhysiologyS*, **263**, R891–R899.

Bangsbo, J., Graham, T.E., Kiens, B. and Saltin, B. (1992b) Elevated muscle glycogen and anaerobic energy production during exhaustive exercise in man, *Journal of Physiology*, **451**, 205–227.

Bangsbo, J., Graham, T.E., Johansen, L. and Saltin, B. (1993) Lactate and H+ fluxes from skeletal muscles in man, *Journal of Physiology*, **451**, 205–222.

Bar-Or, O. (1981) The Wingate anaerobic test; characteristics and applications, *Symbioses*, **III**, 157–172.

Bell, G.J. and Wenger, H.A. (1988) The effect of one-legged sprint training on intramuscular pH and nonbicarbonate buffering capacity, *European Journal of Applied Physiology*, **58**, 158–164.

Bergh, U., Thorstensson, A., Sjodin, B., Hulten, B., Piehl, K. and Karlsson, J. (1978) Maximal oxygen uptake and muscle fibre types in trained and untrained humans, *Medicine and Science in Sport*, **10**, 151–154.

Berklund, B. (1992) High-altitude training: aspects of haematological adaptation, *Sports Medicine*, **14**, 289–303.

Bigland-Ritchie, B. and Woods, J.J. (1984) Changes in muscle contractile properties and neural control during human muscular fatigue, *Muscle and Nerve*, **7**, 691–699.

Bigland-Ritchie, B., Dawson, N.J., Johansson, R.S. and Leppold, O.C.J. (1986) Reflex origin for the slowing of motoneurone firing rates in fatigue of human voluntary contractions, *Journal of Physiology*, **379**, 451–459.

Biral, D., Betto, R., Danieli-Betto, D. and Salviati, G. (1988) Myosin heavy chain composition of single fibres from normal human muscle, *Biochemical Journal*, **250**, 307–308.

Birch, R., Noble, D. and Greenhaff, P.L. (1994) The influence of dietary creatine supplementation on performance during repeated bouts of maximal isokinetic cycling in man, *European Journal of Applied Physiology*, **69**, 268–270.

Boobis, L.H. (1987) Metabolic aspects of fatigue during sprinting, in *Exercise. Benefits, limits and adaptations* (Eds. D. Macleod, R. Maughan, M. Nimmo, T. Reilly and C. Williams) pp. 116–143. E. & F.N. Spon, London.

Brodal, P., Ingjer, F. and Hermansen, L. (1976) Capillary supply of skeletal fibres in untrained and endurance trained men, *Acta Physiologica Scandinavica*, Suppl. 440.

Bunc, V. and Leso, J. (1993) Ventilatory threshold and work efficiency during exercise on a cycle and rowing ergometer, *Journal of Sports Sciences*, **11**, 43–48.

Cabri, J., De Witte, B., Clarys, J.P., Reilly, T. and Strass, D. (1988) Circadian variation in blood pressure response to physical exercise, *Ergonomics*, **31**, 1559–1565.

Conconi, R., Ferrari, M., Sigmo, P.G., Droghetti, P. and Codeca, L. (1982) Determination of the anaerobic threshold by a non-invasive field test in runners, *Journal of Applied Physiology*, **52**, 869–873.

Cooper, K.H. (1968) *Aerobics*. Bantam Books, New York.

Costill, D.L., Coyle, E.G., Fink, W.F., Lesmes, G.R. and Sitzmann, F.A. (1979) Adaptations in skeletal muscle following strength training, *Journal of Applied Physiology*, **46**, 96–99.

Dawson, B., Pyke, F.S. and Morton, A.R. (1989) Improvements in heat tolerance induced by interval running training in the heat and in sweat clothing in cool conditions, *Journal of Sports Sciences*, **7**, 189–203.

Dempsey, J.A. (1986) Is the lung built for exercise? *Medicine and Science in Sports and Exercise*, **18**, 143–155.

Derham, S. and Reilly, T. (1993) Ergometric assessment of kayak paddlers, in *Kimnanthropometry IV* (Eds. W. Duquet and J.A.P. Day) pp. 150–156, E. & F.N. Spon, London.

Donaldson, S.B.K. (1990) Fatigue of sarcoplasmic reticulum. Failure of excitation–contraction coupling in skeletal muscle, in *Biochemistry of Exercise* VII (Eds. A.W. Taylor, P.D. Gollnick, H.J. Green, S.D. Ianuzzo, E.G. Nobble, E. Metivier and J.R. Sutton) pp. 49–57, Human Kinetics, Champaign, IL.

Donovan, C.M. and Pagliassotti, M.J. (1990) Enhanced efficiency of lactate removal after endurance training, *Journal of Applied Physiology*, **68**, 1053–1058.

Edman, K.A.P. (1992) The contractile performance of normal and fatigued skeletal muscle, in *Muscle Fatigue Mechanisms in Exercise and Training. Medicine and Sports Science 34* (Eds. P. Marconnet, P.V. Komi, B. Saltin and O.M. Sejersted) **34**, 20–42. Karger, Basel, Munich, Paris, London and Sydney.

Essén, B. (1978) Studies on the regulation of metabolism in human skeletal muscle using intermittent exercise as an experimental model, *Acta Physiologica Scandinavica*, Suppl. 454, 1–32.

Essén, B., Hagenfeldt, L. and Kaijser, L. (1977) Utilisation of blood-borne and intramuscular substrates during continuous and intermittent exercise in man, *Journal of Physiology*, **265**, 489–506.

Firth, M.S. (1981) A sport specific training and testing device for racing cyclists, *Ergonomics*, **24**, 565–571.

Fox, G., Henckel, P., Juel, C., Falk-Rønne, and Saltin, B. (1986) Skeletal muscle buffer capacity changes in standardbred horses; effects of growth and training, in *Equine Exercise Physiology* (Eds. A. Fillespie and S. Robinson) pp. 341–347, ICEEP Publishers, Davis, CA.

Gaitanos, G.C., Williams, C., Boobis, L.H. and Brooks, S. (1993) Human muscle metabolism during intermittent maximal exercise, *Journal of Applied Physiology*, **75**, 712–719.

Garbutt, G., Boocock, M.G., Reilly, T. and Troup, J.D.G. (1994) Physiological and spinal responses to circuit weight-training, *Ergonomics*, **37**, 117–125.

Gollnick, P.D. and Hermansen, L. (1973) Biochemical adaptations to exercise: anaerobic metabolism, in *Exercise and Sport Sciences Reviews* (ed. J.H. Wilmore), Vol. 1, Academic Press, New York.

Gore, C.J., Hahn, A.G., Watson, D.B., Norem, K.I., Campbell, D.V., Scroop, G.S., Emonson, D.L., Wood, R.J., Ly, S.V., Bellenger, S.J. and Lewton, T.W. (1995) $\dot{V}O_2$max and arterial O_2 saturation at sea level and 610 m, *Medicine and Science in Sports and Exercise*, **27**, S7.

Greenhaff, P.L., Casey, A., Short, A.H., Harris, R.C., Soderlund, K. and Hultman, E. (1993) Influence of oral creatine supplementation on muscle torque during repeated bouts of maximal voluntary exercise in man, *Clinical Science*, **84**, 565–571.

Greenhaff, P.L., Bodin, K., Soderlund, K. and Hultman, E. (1994) Effect of oral creatine supplementation on skeletal muscle phosphocreatine resynthesis, *American Journal of Physiology*, **266**, E725–E730.

Harris, R.C., Soderlund, K. and Hultman, E. (1992) Elevation of creatine in resting and exercised muscle of normal subjects by creatine supplementation, *Clinical Science*, **83**, 367–374.

Harris, R.C., Viru, M., Greenhaff, P.L. and Hultman, E. (1993) The effect of oral creatine supplementation on running performance during maximal short term exercise in men, *Journal of Physiology*, 467–474.

Hellsten, Y. (1994) Xanthine dehydrogenase and purine metabolism in man with special reference to exercise, *Acta Physiologica Scandinavica*, **151**, Suppl. 621, 1–73.

Hellsten-Westing, Y., Norman, B., Balsom, P.D. and Sjödin, B. (1993) Decreased resting levels of adenine nucleotides in skeletal muscle following high intensity intermittent exercise in man, *Journal of Applied PhysiologyS*, **74**, 2523–2528.

Hickson, R.C. (1980) Interference of strength development by simultaneously training for strength and endurance. *European Journal of Applied Physiology*, **42**, 372–376.

Holloszy, J.O. and Coyle, E.F. (1984) Adaptations of skeletal muscle to endurance training and their metabolic consequences, *Journal of Applied Physiology*, **56**, 831–838.

Hughes, E.F., Turner, S.C. and Brooks, G.A. (1984) Effect of glycogen depletion and pedalling speed on 'anaerobic threshold', *Journal of Applied Physiology*, **52**, 1598–1604.

Hultman, E. and Sjöholm, H. (1983) Energy metabolism and contraction force of human skeletal muscle in situ during electrical stimulation, *Journal of Physiology*, **345**, 525–532.

Ingjer, F. and Myhere, K. (1992) Physiological effects of altitude training on young elite male cross-country skiers, *Journal of Sports Sciences*, **10**, 49–63.

Jacobs, I. (1981) Lactate, muscle glycogen and exercise performance in man, *Acta Physiologica Scandinavica*, Suppl. 495.

Jacobs, I., Esbjörnsson, M., Sylvén, C., Holm, I. and Jansson, E. (1987) Sprint training effects on muscle myoglobin enzymes, fiber types, and blood lactate, *Medicine and Science in Sports and Exercise*, **19**, 368–374.

Jansson, E. and Sylvén, C. (1985) Creatine kinase MB and citrate synthase in type 1 and type II muscle fibres in trained and untrained men, *European Journal of Applied Physiology*, **54**, 207–209.

Jehue, R., Street, D. and Huizenga, R. (1993) Effect of time-zone and game time changes on team performance: National Football League, *Medicine and Science in Sports and Exercise*, **25**, 127–131.

Johansen, L. and Quistorff, B. (1992) ^{31}P-spectroscopy used for evaluating metabolic response during repeated maximal isometric contractions in different training groups. Abstract. The 11th annual scientific meeting of the *Society of Magnetic Resonance in Medicine*, Berlin, August 1992, 2709.

Juel, C., Bangsbo, J., Graham, T. and Saltin, B. (1990) Lactate and potassium fluxes from skeletal muscle during intense dynamic knee-extensor exercise in man, *Acta Physiologica Scandinavica*, **140**, 147–159.

Karvonen, M.J. (1959) Problems of training of the cardiovascular system, *Ergonomics*, **2**, 207–215.

Klein, J.P., Forster, H.V., Stewart, R.D. and Wu, A. (1980) Haemoglobin affinity for oxygen during short-term exhaustive exercise, *Journal of Applied Physiology*, **48**, 236–242.

Lakomy, H.K.A. (1986) Measurement of work and power output using friction loaded cycle ergometers, *Ergonomics*, **29**, 509–517.

Larsson, B., Larsen, J., Modest, R., Serup, B. and Secher, N.H. (1988) A new kayak ergometer based on wind resistance, *Ergonomics*, **31**, 1701–1707.

Lees, A. and Arthur, S. (1988) An investigation into anaerobic performance of wheelchair athletes, *Ergonomics*, **31**, 1529–1537.

Leger, L. and Lambert, J. (1982) A maximal 20 m shuttle run test to predict VO_2max, *European Journal of Applied Physiology*, **49**, 1–12.

Leger, L.A., Mercier, D., Gadoury, C. and Lambert, J. (1988) The multistage 20 metre shuttle run test for aerobic fitness, *Journal of Sports Sciences*, **6**, 93–101.

McArdle, D. and Reilly, T. (1993) Consequences of altering stroke parameters in front crawl swimming and its simulation, in *Biomechanics and Medicine in Swimming: Swimming Science V1* (Eds. D MacLaren, T. Reilly and A. Lees) pp. 125–130. E. and F.N. Spon, London.

McCartney, N., Spriet, L.L., Heigenhauser, J.F., Kowalchuk, J.M., Sutton, J.R. and Jones, N.L. (1986) Muscle power and metabolism in maximal intermittent exercise, *Journal of Applied Physiology*, **60**, 1164–1169.

McKenna, M.J., Schmidt, T.A., Hargreaves, M., Cameron, L., Skinner, S.L. and Kjeldsen, K. (1993) Sprint training increases human skeletal muscle Na^+-K^+-ATPase concentration and improves K^+ regulation, *Journal of Applied Physiology*, **75**, 173–180.

Mader, A., Madsen, O. and Hollman, W. (1980) Die Ausdanerleustungsfahigkeit bei verschiedenen Sportarten inter besonderer Berucksichtigung des Metabolismus: Zur Ermittling der optimalen Belastungsintensität in Training; *Leistungssport*, **7**, Suppl. 63–79.

Margaria, R., Edwards, H.T. and Dill, D.B. (1933) The possible mechanisms of contracting and paying the oxygen debt and the role of lactic acid in muscular contraction, *American Journal of Physiology*, **106**, 689–715.

Margaria, R., Cerretelli, P., Di Prampero, P.E., Massari, C. and Torelli, G. (1963) Kinetics and mechanism of oxygen debt contraction in man, *Journal of Applied Physiology*, **18**, 371–377.

Margaria, R., Aghemo, P. and Rovelli, E. (1966) Measurement of muscular power (anaerobic) in man, *Journal of Applied Physiology*, **21**, 1661–1664.

Margaria, R., Olivia, R.D., Di Prampero, P.E. and Cerretelli, P. (1969) Energy utilization in intermittent exercise of supramaximal intensity, *Journal of Applied Physiology*, **26**, 752–756.

Maughan, R.J. (1991) Fluid and electrolyte loss and replacement in exercise, *Journal of Sports Sciences*, **9**, S117–142.

Medbø, J.I. and Tabata, I. (1989) Relative importance of aerobic and anaerobic energy release during short-lasting exhausting bicycle exercise, *Journal of Applied Physiology*, **67**, 1881–1886.

Medbø, J.I., Mohn, A., Tabata, I., Bahr, R. and Sejersted, O. (1988) Anaerobic capacity determined by the maximal accumulated oxygen deficit, *Journal of Applied Physiology*, **64**, 50–60.

Metzer, J.M. and Fitts, R.H. (1987) Role of intracellular pH in muscle fatigue, *Journal of Applied Physiology*, **62**, 1392–1397.

Mizuno, M., Juel, C., Bro-Rasmussen, T., Mygind, E., Schibye, B., Rasmussen, B. and Saltin, B. (1990) Limb skeletal muscle adaptation in athletes after training in altitude, *Journal of Applied Physiology*, **68**, 496–502.

Monod, H. and Scherrer, J. (1965) Work capacity of a synergic muscular group, *Ergonomics*, **8**, 329–338.

Nevill, M.E., Boobis, L.H., Brooks, S. and Williams, C. (1989) Effect of training on muscle metabolism during treadmill sprinting, *Journal of Applied Physiology*, **67**, 2376–2382.

Noakes, T.D., Myburgh, K.H. and Schall, H. (1990) Mean treadmill velocity during the $\dot{V}O_2$max test predicts running performance, *Journal of Sports Sciences*, **8**, 35–45.

Oja, P., Laukkanen, R., Pasanen, M. and Vuori, I. (1989) A new fitness test for cardiovascular epidemiology and exercise promotion, *Annals of Medicine*, **21**, 249–250.

Pate, R.R., Barnes, C. and Hiller, W. (1985) A physiological comparison of performance-matched female and male distance runners, *Research Quarterly for Exercise and Sport*, **56**, 245–250.

Pilegaard, H., Juel, C. and Wibrand, F. (1993) Lactate transport studied in sarcolemmal giant vesicles from rats: the effect of training, *American Journal of Physiology*, **264**, E156–160.

Pilegaard, H., Bangsbo, J., Richter, E.A. and Juel, C. (1994) Lactate transport studied in sarcolemmal giant vesicles from human muscle biopsies: relation to training status, *Journal of Applied Physiology*, **77**, 1858–1862.

Pollock, M.L. and Wilmore, J.H. (1990) *Exercise in Health and Disease: Evaluation and Prescription for Prevention and Rehabilitation*, 2nd edn, W.B. Saunders, Philadelphia.

Porcari, J.D., Ebbeling, C.B., Ward, A., Freedson, P.S. and Rippe, J.M. (1989) Walking for exercise testing and training, *Sports Medicine*, **8**, 189–200.

Rasmusson, R., Klausen, B., Clausen, J.P. and Trap-Jensen, J. (1975) Pulmonary ventilation, blood gases and blood pH after training of the arms and the legs, *Journal of Applied Physiology*, **38**, 250–256.

Reilly, T. (1992) Physical fitness: for whom and for what? In: *Sport for All* (Eds. P. Oja and R. Telama), pp. 81–88, Elsevier, Amsterdam.

Reilly, T. and Secher, N. (1990) Physiology of sports: an overview, in *Physiology of Sports* (Eds. T. Reilly, N. Secher, P. Snell and C. Williams), pp. 465–485. E. and F.N. Spon, London.

Reilly, T. and Thomas, V. (1978) Multi-station equipment for physical training: design and validation of a prototype, *Applied Ergonomics*, **9**, 201–206.

Reilly, T., Hopkins, J. and Howlett, N. (1979) Fitness test profiles and training intensity in skilled race-walkers, *British Journal of Sports Medicine*, **13**, 70–76.

Reilly, T., Secher, N., Snell, P. and Williams, C. (1990) *Physiology of Sports*, E. and F.N. Spon, London.

Reilly, T., Kirton, E., McGrath, E. and Coulthard, S. (1993) Ergonomic evaluation of ski-simulators, in *Contemporary Ergonomics*, **93** (ed. E.D. Megaw), pp. 315–320, Taylor and Francis, London.

Rusko, H. (1987) The effect of training on aerobic power characteristics of young cross-country skiers, *Journal of Sports Sciences*, **5**, 273–286.

Sahlin, K. (1986) Muscle fatigue and lactic acid accumulation, *Acta Physiologica Scandinavica*, **128**, 83–91.

Sahlin, K. and Henriksson, J. (1984) Buffer capacity and lactate accumulation in skeletal muscle of trained and untrained men, *Acta Physiologica Scandinavica*, **122**, 331–339.

Sahlin, K. and Ren, J.M. (1989) Relationship of contraction capacity changes during recovery from a fatiguing contraction, *Journal of Applied Physiology*, **67**, 648–654.

Saltin, B. (1973) Metabolic fundamentals in exercise, *Medicine and Science in Sports*, **5**, 137–146.

Saltin, B. and Essén, B. (1971) Muscle glycogen, lactate, ATP and CP in intermittent exercise, in *Muscle Metabolism During Exercise: Advances in Experimental Medicine and Biology* (Eds. B. Saltin and B. Pernow) Vol. II pp. 419–424, Plenum Press, New York.

Saltin, B. and Gollnick, P.D. (1983) Skeletal muscle adaptability. Significance for metabolism and performance, in *Handbook of Physiology: Skeletal muscle* (Eds. L.D. Peachey, R.H. Adrian and S.R. Geiger) pp. 555–631, Bethesda, American Physiological Society.

Sargent, L.W. (1924) Some observations on the Sargent test of neuromuscular efficiency, *American Physical Education Review*, **29**, 47–56.

Saubert, C.W., Armstrong, R.B., Shepherd, R.E. and Gollnick, P.D. (1973) Anaerobic enzyme adaptations to sprint training in rats, *Pflügers Archive*, **340**, 305–312.

Sharp, R.L., Costill, D.L., Fink, W.J. and King, D.S. (1986) Effect of eight weeks of bicycle ergometer sprint training on human muscle buffer capacity, *International Journal of Sports Medicine*, **7**, 13–17.

Sinnerton, S. and Reilly, T. (1993) Effects of sleep loss and time of day in swimmers, in Biomechanics and Medicine in *Swimming IV* (Eds. D. MacLaren, T. Reilly and A. Lees) pp. 399–404, E. and F.N. Spon, London.

Söderlund, K. (1991) Energy metabolism in human skeletal muscle during intense contraction and recovery with reference to metabolic differences between type I and type II fibres (thesis). Huddinge University Hospital, Karolinska Institute, Stockholm, Sweden.

Spriet, L.L., Lindinger, M.I., McKelvie, S., Heigenhauser, G.J.F. and Jones, N.L. (1989) Muscle glycogenolysis and H^+ concentration during maximal intermittent cycling, *Journal of Applied Physiology*, **66**, 8–13.

Stathis, C.G., Febbraio, M.A., Carey, M.F. and Snow, R.J. (1994) Influence of sprint training on human skeletal muscle purine nucleotide metabolism, *Journal of Applied Physiology*, **76**, 1802–1809.

Tegtbur, U., Busse, N. and Braumann, K.M. (1993) Estimation of an individual equilibrium between lactate production and catabolism during exercise, *Medicine and Science in Sports and Exercise*, **25**, 620–627.

Tesch, P.A., Thorsson, A. and Fujitsuka, N. (1989) Creatine phosphate in fibre types of skeletal muscle before and after exhaustive exercise, *Journal of Applied Physiology*, **66**, 1756–1759.

Thorstensson, A., Sjödin, B. and Karlsson, J. (1975) Enzyme activities and muscle strength after 'sprint training' in man, *Acta Physiologica Scandinavica*, **94**, 313–318.

Tzankoff, S.P., Robinson, S., Pyke, F.S. and Brawn, C.A. (1972) Physiological adjustments to work in older men as affected by physical training, *Journal of Applied Physiology*, **33**, 346–350.

Vandenborne, K., McCully, K., Kakihira, H., Prammer, M., Bolinger, L., Detre, J.A., De Meirleir, K., Walter, G., Chance, B. and Leigh, J.S. (1991) Metabolic heterogeneity in human calf muscle during maximal exercise, *Biochemistry*, **88**, 5714–5718.

Van der Woude, L.H.V., Veeger, H.E.J. and Dallmeijer, A.J. (1995) The ergonomics of wheelchair sports, in *Sport, Leisure and Ergonomics* (Eds. G. Atkinson and T. Reilly) pp. 3–12. E. and F.N. Spon, London.

Voy, R.O. (1986) The U.S. Olympic committee experience with exercise-induced bronchospasm 1984, *Medicine and Science in Sports and Exercise*, **18**, 328–330.

Ward-Smith, A.T. (1986) Altitude and wind effects on long jump performance with particular reference to the world record established by Bob Beamon, *Journal of Sports Sciences*, **4**, 89–99.

Wasserman, K. (1986) The anaerobic threshold: definition, physiological significance and identification, *Advances in Cardiology*, **35**, 1–23.

Williams, A., Reilly, T., Campbell, I. and Sutherst, J. (1988) Investigation of changes in responses to exercise and in mood during pregnancy, *Ergonomics*, **31**, 1539–1549.

INDEX

Note. Page numbers in *italic* refer to tables.

abdomen, protruding 152
abducted scapulae 152, 154, 157
accommodation (visual) 9
action speed training 289, 310–11
active speed training 289, 292, 305–6, 308–9, 322
acuity (kinesthetic) 31
acuity (visual) 7–8, 14, 16–17
adenosine triphosphate (ATP) 353
  aerobic energy production 356
  anaerobic energy production 353–5, 367
  anaerobic training 371–3
  debt theory 195
  intermittent exercise 360
  muscle fatigue 367
  speed training 290
  supramaximal exercise 357–8
adolescents *see* juniors
aerobic energy production 356
  altitude effects 400–1
  oxygen transport 360–3, 400–1
  supramaximal exercise 358
aerobic exercise 351–2
  components of training 351
  indirect assessment 383–5
  intensity 351
  and speed 339
aerobic performance
  altitude effects 400–1
  ergometers 383, 384
  lactate responses 381–2
  running economy 382
  specificity 382–3
  ventilation threshold 381
  $\dot{V}O_{2max}$ test 378–81, 383
aerobic training
  aerobics 388, 390
  circuit weight 387–8
  endurance 385–6
  interval 386–7

  timing 391
aerobics 388, 390
age factors
  flexibility 247–8, 256–8
  speed training 295, 307, 308, 314
altitude training 362, 398–402
American football
  body proportionality 178
  flexibility 243, 244, 280–1
  mental training 94
  posture 162–3, 165
  visual skills 19–20, 24
anaerobic energy production 353–5
  altitude effects 399–400
  anaerobic capacity 364, 365–6
  anaerobic power 364–5
  creatine ingestion 368–70
  intermittent exercise 360
  measurement 364–6
  supramaximal exercise 358
anaerobic exercise 351–2
  components of training 351
  intensity 351
  speed training 290, 310, 337–8, 339
anaerobic training 370
  cellular effects 371–6, *372*
  components 370
  and performance 370–1
  principles 376–8
  speed endurance training 376–8
  see also speed training; strength training
analysis of technique *see* technique analysis
antagonist reflexes 296
anterior pelvic tilt (APT) 157, 160
anthropometry 168, 169
anticipatory skills
  speed training 295
  visual 20–1, 22, 23, 24–6

archery 8, 50, 51, 52, 120
arousal regulation 78, *79*, 85–9, *104*
asthma 362
attention
    mental training 78, 93–7
    movement and control 52–5
    and speed training 295–6
Australian football
    body proportionality 178
    flexibility 243, 244, 280–1
    posture 162–3, 165
autogenic inhibition 251–2
automaticity, movement skills 52–5
avulsion fractures 256

back, postural defects 152, 155, 156, 157, 160
back pain 257
badminton 22, 120, 156, 171, 272–3
balance, vestibular system 29–30, 296
ballistic stretching 259–62, 263, 268
baseball
    body proportionality 169, 178, 186
    flexibility 240, 281
    mental training 95
    posture 164
    visual skills 8, 25
basketball
    body proportionality 178
    decision-making skills 35–6
    energy production 353
    flexibility 281–2
    mental training 74
    posture 164
    strength training 216
    technique analysis 120, 121
    visual skills 10, 19–20
Bassin timer 12–13
biofeedback training 52, 87–8
biological clocks 391–2
biomechanical assessment 117–18
    biomechanical feedback 140–2
    objective methods 118, 121–2
        dynamometry 128–34, 324–5
        electromyography 134–8
        image analysis 122–8, 141, 142, 259, 324
    predictive methods 118, 138–40
    sources of error 120–1
    speed performance 324–5
    subjective methods 118–21
biomechanical feedback 140–2
2, 3-bisphosphoglycerate 363, 400, 401

blood
    heat loss mechanisms 393–4, 397
    muscle fatigue 367
    oxygen transport 361–2, 363, 399, 400–1
blood doping 400–1
blood tests
    aerobic performance 381–2
    speed diagnostics 325
bobsledding simulation 27, 139–40
body posture *see* posture
body proportionality *see* proportionality
body temperature
    circadian rhythms 391
    training in heat 392–3, 396
body type, and posture 149–50, 156
body water 393, 394, 395
bodybuilding 195, 199, 203
Bohr effect 363
bow legs 153, 154
boxing
    body proportionality 181
    flexibility exercises 282–3
    kinematics 46
    posture 154, 164
    strength training 201, 203, 210
brachial index 168, 171
brain waves, EEGs 49, 50, 51, 52

calcium, muscle fatigue 367
cameras
    movie photography 123–4
    videography 127
canoeing
    aerobic performance 383
    body proportionality 169, 172
    flexibility 273, 274
    kinesthetic judgements 33–4
    posture 157
carbohydrates, energy production 356
cardiac output 363–4
central nervous system 224, 251–2, 295, 317–19
children *see* juniors
choice reaction time (CRT) 36–9, 40
chondromalacia 257
cigarette smoking 363
cinematographic analysis 122–7, 259, 324
circadian rhythms 391–2
circuit training 200, 387–8
climatic factors 392–8
closed circuit TV image analysis 127
clothing 395, 396, 397, 398

cognitive evaluation theory 97–8
cognitive factors
    mental training 74–5
        goal setting 82
        imagery 90, 91
        motivation 97–8
        stress management 86, 88–9
    movement control 53–5
    speed training 295–6, 311–12
coincidence-timing skills 12–13, 14
cold weather training 396–8
colour vision 10, 14
communications, athlete–coach 78, 87
competition-goal-setting model 82–3
complex action speed training 310–11
complex speed capability 307–10
complex speed forms 293, 303, 307–10
complex speed tests 322–3
computers
    biomechanical feedback 141–2
    simulation 26–9, 138–40, 142
    virtual reality 26–9, 139–40
concentration
    mental training 78, 93–7
    speed training 295–6
confidence building 79, 80–1
connective tissue 249
contact field sports see American
    football; Australian football; rugby
contract–relax–contract stretching 263
control skills 3–4, 5
    attentional demands 52–5
    biofeedback training 52
    electrophysiology 49–52, 134–8
    gross performance tests 44–5
    kinematics 45–7, 48, 125, 133, 134
    kinetics 48–9, 125
    processes 43–4
    see also kinesthesis; technique analysis
coordination of partial impulses 298
coping strategies 76, 77, 85–9
core body temperature 391, 392–3
court sports see basketball; netball;
    volleyball
creatine 353
    anaerobic training 371–3, 374
    ingested 368–70
    intermittent exercise 360, 368–70
    speed training 290, 310, 325
    supramaximal exercise 357–8
cricket
    body proportionality 178
    flexibility 240, 281

kinesthetic judgements 32
    mental training 89
    posture 154, 164
    technique analysis 126, 130, 132
    visual skills 22, 26
cruciate ligament 125–6, 134, 156
crural index 168, 171, 172, 173, 178
cyclic speed 292–3, 299, 303, 308, 313
    diagnostics 322, 323
    sprinting 331–2
    swimming 337
cycling
    aerobic training 390
    biomechanical feedback 141
    body proportionality 175, 178
    heat acclimatization 396
    kinesthetic judgements 33–4
    posture 154, 160
    technique analysis 136–7, 140

deception skills 40, 41–3
decision-making 3–4, 5
    deception skills 40, 41–3
    option selection 36–40
        assessment 36–8
        choice reaction time 36–9, 40
        Hick–Hyman law 37–8, 39–40
        sports performance 38–9
        training 39–40
    processes 35–6
    in rapid succession 40–3
        assessment 40–2
        inter-stimulus interval 41–2
        psychological refractory period 41,
            42
        sports performance 42
        training 42–3
    speed training 295, 303–5
dehydration 393, 394
depth perception 9–10, 14, 17
disabled athletes 383
discus throwing 201, 206, 208
diving
    body proportionality 169, 172–3
    flexibility 240, 243, 266, 274, 275–7
    kinesthetic judgements 33
    movement execution 43
    posture 165
    strength training 229
    technique analysis 139
drinks, hot climates 394, 395, 396
dual-task performance 53–5
duck feet 153, 156

dynamometry 128–9
  applications 128–9
  artefacts 134
  biomechanical feedback 141
  centre of pressure 129, 130, 131–2
  force platforms 129–30, 235, 324–5
  pressure mats 131–2
  speed performance 324–5
  strength testing 132–4, 235
dysplasia 148–9, 245–6

ectomorphs, posture 149
efficacy theory 80–1
effort, perception of 33–4, 35
elasticity of muscle–tendon unit
  injury prevention 254–5
  stretch shorten cycle 217–19, 221–4,
    252–3
    jumping 229
    speed training 297
    sprinting 226–7
  stretching exercises 262, 274, 277–8,
    280, 281, 283
  warm-ups 301
electrocardiography (ECG) 49, 51–2
electroencephalography (EEG) 49, 50,
  51, 52
electrogoniometers 259
electrolytes 393, 394, 396
electromyography (EMG) 49–50, 51, 52,
  90, 134–8, 325
elementary movement programmes
  298–300, 301–3, 308, 323
elgons 259
endomorphs, posture 149–50
endurance, and speed training 309–10,
  327, 337–8, 339
endurance (long-lasting force) training
  190–1
  ATP-debt theory 195
  biological factors 192, 194–6
  bodybuilding 195, 199
  circuit training 200
  concentric contractions 191, 192
  eccentric contractions 193
  general adaptations 194–6
  general methods 198–200
  general structure 191–4
  gymnastics 191, 192, 197–8
  ice skating 191
  impulse maximization 191
  isometric contractions 191, 192, 193,
    205

juniors 200
  and maximum strength 191–6, 198–9
  mechanical factors 193–4
  medium workouts 199–200
  muscle cross-sectional area 192, 194–5,
    199
  muscle hypertrophy 194–6, 197, 198–9
  neuromuscular factors 193
  pyramid workouts 199
  rowing 191, 196–7, 200
  ski-ing 191, 192, 197, 200
  stimulus-tension theory 194–5
  strength optimization 198
  submaximal workouts 195, 197, 199
  swimming 191
endurance speed 289
endurance sports
  aerobic training 390
  heat acclimatization 396
  heat injury 392–3
  $\dot{V}O_{2max}$ 378, 381
endurance training 385–6
  or altitude training 402
  cardiac output 363–4
  oxygen consumption 382
  speed 376–8
  and strength 390
energy production 352–3
  aerobic 356
  anaerobic 353–5, 364–70
  continuous exercise 356–8
  creatine ingestion 368–70
  fatigue 359–60, 365, 366–8
  intermittent exercise 358–60, 368–70
  oxygen transport 358, 360–4
  submaximal exercise 356–7
energy storage
  stretch shorten cycle 252–3
    speed training 297
    strength training 217, 218–19, 222,
      229, 230
  stretching exercises 274, 277–8, 281
engram theory 299, 302
environmental engineering, stress
  management 86–7
environmental factors
  flexibility 248
  training 391–402
enzymes
  aerobic energy 356
  anaerobic energy 353–5, 372, 373–4,
    377
ergometers 34, 365, 383, 384

erythropoeitin (EPO) 400–1
everted feet 153, 156
exertion, perception of 33–4, 35
extra-pyramidal system 296
eyesight *see* visual skills

fake movements 40, 41–3
fartlek 387
fascia 249
fatigue
  anaerobic power 365, 366–8
  intermittent exercise 359–60
  speed training 317–19
fencing 201
field dependence–independence 13, 14
field hockey 21–2, 160–1, 178, 279–80
field sports *see* American football;
  Australian football; baseball; cricket;
  field hockey; football (soccer); golf;
  jumping; lacrosse; rugby; throwing
  sports
figure skating *see* ice skating
film photography 122–7, 259, 324
fitness testing *see* aerobic performance
flat feet 153, 154
flexibility
  age factors 247–8, 256–8
  anatomical limitations 249–50
  definition 239
  environmental factors 248
  exercises
    active stretching 265
    aquatic sports 273–4
    ballistic stretching 259–62, 263, 268
    concentration during 268–9
    court sports 281–2
    cycling 277, 278
    dangers 269
    field sports 277, 278–81
    gymnastic sports 275–7, 283
    intensity 269
    martial arts 282–3
    passive stretching 266
    power sports 275–7
    preparation 268
    proprioceptive neuromuscular
      facilitation 263–5, 271
    racquet sports 272–3
    schedules 268–9, 271
    specificity 268
    static stretching 262–3, 270–1
    track sports 277, 278
  functional testing 258–9

gender factors 248
growth effects 247, 256–8
hypermobility 243–4, 257
hypomobility 244, 257
injury prevention 242, 248, 253–5
injury rehabilitation 255–6
joint specificity 244–6
measurement 244, 245–6, 258–9
muscle elasticity 252–3
  exercises 262, 274, 277–8, 280, 281,
    283
  and injury 254–5
physiological limitations 250–2
psychological benefits 248–9
screening tests 244, 245–6
static testing 258–9
and strength training 244, 253
stretching guidelines 267–9
value of stretching 239–43, 248–9, 272
flexometers 259
fluid intake 394, 395, 396
football (American) *see* American
  football
football (Australian) *see* Australian
  football
football (rugby) *see* rugby
football (soccer)
  body proportionality 178
  flexibility 240, 279–80
  kinematics 46
  posture 160–1
  technique analysis 120, 139
  visual skills 10, 17, 18–19, 21–2
force measurement, dynamometry
  128–34, 235, 324–5
force platforms 129–30, 235, 324–5
force production *see* strength training
force sensitivity 48–9
foreign reflexes 296
forward head 152
frequency speed training 292, 306–7,
  308–9, 310, 322

gender factors
  flexibility 248
  oxygen transport 363
genu recurvartum 152, 156, 160–1, 163
genu valgum 153, 154
genu varum 153, 154
gluconeogenesis 356
glycogen
  aerobic training 390
  anaerobic training 373

glycogenolysis 356, 358, 373, 376–7
glycolysis 354–5, 356
  anaerobic training 373, 374, 376–7
  intermittent exercise 360
  submaximal exercise 356–7
  supramaximal exercise 358
goal setting 79, 81–5, 84, 95–6, 97, 104
golf
  body proportionality 178, 186
  electrocardiography 52
  electroencephalography 50
  flexibility 240, 242, 281
  mental training 90, 94, 95
  posture 164
  technique analysis 120, 124
  visual skills 10
Golgi tendon organs 250, 251, 296
goniometers 258–9
gymnastics
  body proportionality 169, 172, 182, 185
  flexibility 240, 243, 266, 274, 275–7,
    283
  kinesthetic judgements 33
  mental training 83, 92
  movement execution 43
  posture 157, 165
  strength training 191, 192, 197–8, 216,
    219, 229
  technique analysis 120, 121, 129, 139

H^+
  lactate transport 375–6
  muscle buffering 374–5
haemoglobin 362, 363, 400, 401
hammer throwing 141–2
headgear 396, 397
health-related fitness 388, 391
heart rate
  aerobic performance 381, 384
  aerobics 388
  biofeedback 88
  cardiac output 363
  electrocardiography 49, 51–2
  heat exhaustion 393
  interval training 386
heat, training in 392–6
heat acclimatization 394–6
heat exhaustion 393
heat injury 392–3, 394
heat loss 393–4, 396, 397, 398
heat stroke 393
Hick–Hyman law 37–8, 39–40
high jump

body proportionality 170, 173
  mechanical model 119–20
  strength training 216, 219–21, 228–9
hockey (field) 21–2, 160–1, 178, 279–80
hockey (ice) 22, 24, 53
hollow back (lordosis) 152, 157
hot weather training 392–6
Howard–Dolman test 10
hurdling 158, 277, 278
hydration 393, 394, 395
hypermobility 243–4, 257
hypomobility 244, 257
hypothermia 397, 398
hypoxia, altitude effects 398–400, 401–2

ice hockey 22, 24, 53
ice skating 77, 89, 191, 240, 266
image analysis 122–3
  biomechanical feedback 141, 142
  body flexibility 259
  closed circuit TV 127
  equipment 123–5, 127
  landmark data 125
  multi-camera 3D 126–7
  multi-camera planar 126
  sampling rate 122–3
  single camera planar 125–6
  speed training 324
  uses 123
  videography 122–3, 127–8
    biomechanical feedback 141, 142
    body flexibility 259
    decision-making skills 39, 40
    speed performance 324
    visual skill training 25–6, 28
imagery, mental training 78, 79, 87, 90–3,
  96, 104
imagery relaxation 87
inertial force dissipation effect 298
information pick-up, visual 19, 22, 23, 24
information processing
  effort sensitivity 33–4
  rate of visual 11, 14, 19
information-processing theory 91
injury prevention
  circadian rhythms 391
  endurance training 386
  flexibility 242, 256, 257
  stretching 242, 248, 253–5
  warm-ups 301, 397–8
injury rehabilitation 255–6
insertion points, tendons 169–70, 184
interval training 386–7

inverse myotatic reflex 251–2
inverted feet 153, 156, 160, 163, 164, 165
inverted-U hypothesis 85
iron supplements 401, 402
isokinematic dynamometry 133, 134

javelin throwing 140, 142, 201, 206, 208
jogging, endurance training 386
joints, flexibility *see* flexibility
judo 12, 164, 178, 282–3
jumping
    body proportionality 170, 173
    flexibility exercises 278–9
    posture 160
    power training 211–12
    reactive strength 217, 219–21, 223–4,
        228–30, 231, 232–3, *234*
    technique analysis 119–20, 128
juniors
    flexibility 244, 247, 256–7
    speed training 295, 302, 303, 307, 308,
        314
    strength training 200, 215, 232–3, 244
    stress management 87

kayaking *see* canoeing
kinanthropometry 168, 169
kinematics of movement patterns 45–7
    dynamometry 133, 134
    and kinetics 48
    motion analysis 125
    speed performance 324
kinesthesis
    generalised skills 29–30
        assessment 30–2
        development 31
        limb positioning 32
    hierarchy of senses 6–7
    and imagery perspective 92
    sport-specific skills 32
        assessment 33–4
        limb positioning 33, 34
        sensitivity to effort 33–4, 35
        and sports performance 34
        and training 35
    and vision 6–7, 29–30, 32, 35
    visual–vestibular information 29–30
kinetics of movement patterns 48–9
    force sensitivity 48–9
    motion analysis 125
knock knees 153, 154
kypholordosis 152
kyphosis 152

lacrosse 160–1, 178, 279–80
lactate metabolism 355
    aerobic performance 381–2
    aerobic training 387
    altitude effects 400
    anaerobic capacity 366
    anaerobic training 374–6, 377, 378
    fatigue 366–7
    intermittent exercise 359, 360
    interval training 386
    muscle buffer capacity 374–5
    speed diagnostics 325
    speed and endurance 310, 337–8, 339
    speed training 290
    submaximal exercise 356–7
    supramaximal exercise 358
    transport capacity 375–6
lactate minimum concept 382
lateral epicondylitis 257
leg hyperextension 152, 156, 160–1, 163
Leighton flexometer 259
lever lengths 169, 170
ligaments, range of movement 250, 257
limb coordination, kinematics 45–6
limb positioning, kinesthesis 32, 33, 34
limb proportionality *see* proportionality
liquid intake 394, 395, 396
little league elbow 257
locomotor speed 289, 327–8, 331–2
long jump 216, 227–8
lordosis 152, 157
LSD training 385, 386
lungs, oxygen transport 361–2

maintenance training 376, 377–8
martial arts
    flexibility exercises 282–3
    kinematics 46
    mental training 73, 81, 89
    posture 154, 164
    proportionality 178, 181, 186
    strength training 201, 203, 210
    visual skills 12
medial epicondylitis 257
mental skills training 69–70
    applications 70, 71–2
    arousal regulation 78, *79*, 85–9, *104*
    athlete–coach communication *78*, 87
    attention 78, 93–7
    by coaches 99, 100, 101, 103, 110
    by sports psychologists 99
        barriers to entry 108–9
        case study 102–3

mental skills training (*continued*)
    coach support 110
      programme content 110–11
  candidates for 71–2
  case study 101–8
  concentration 78, 93–7
  coping strategies 76, 77, 85–9
  crisis management *79*
  definition 70
  efficacy theory 80–1
  energy management *104*
  evaluation research 74–5, 83
  goal setting *79*, 81–5, *84*, 95–6, 97, *104*
  imagery 78, 79, 87, 90–3, 96, *104*
  importance 73–4
  individual psychology 76, 77
  interpersonal conflicts *79*
  juniors 87
  mental skills ratings 77–9
  motivation 82–3, 97–9
  myths about 71–2
  obstacles 108–11
  peak performance model 75–7
  personality factors 76, 77
  programme content 100, 103–5, *104*,
    110–11
  programme delivery 103
  programme evaluation 101, 105–8
  programme length 100, 105, *106*
  programme schedules 100–1, 105, *106*
  programme timing 100, 105, *106*, 110
  relaxation *78, 79*, 87, 89, 96
  self-confidence 79, 80–1
  self-esteem 78, *79*
  self-talk strategies *78, 79*
  stress management *78, 79*, 85–9
  US ski team 101–8
  visualization 78, 79, 87, 90–3, 96, *104*
mesomorphs, posture 149–50, 156
microcycles, speed training 317–18, 319
motivation, mental training 82–3, 97–9
motor skills *see* perceptual–motor skills;
  technique analysis
movement
  range of
    aquatic sports 273–4
    court sports 281–2
    field sports 279–81
    gymnastic sports 274–7
    hypermobility 243–4, 257
    hypomobility 244, 257
    injury prevention 254
    limitations 249–52

    martial arts 282
    measurement 244, 258–9
    proprioceptive neuromuscular
      facilitation 263–5
    racquet sports 272–3
    stretching guidelines 268–9
    track sports 278
    value of flexibility 240
  stretch shorten cycle 252–3
movement execution skills 3–4, 5
  attentional demands 52–5
  biofeedback training 52
  electrophysiology 49–52, 134–8
  gross performance tests 44–5
  kinematics 45–7
    dynamometry 133, 134
    and kinetics 48
    motion analysis 125
    speed performance 324
  kinetics 48–9, 125
  processes 43–4
  see also technique analysis
movement sense *see* kinesthesis
movement times 10–11
  kinematics of movement patterns 45–
    7
movie photography 122–7, 259, 324
muscle
  aerobic performance 381–2
  anaerobic power 364–5, 366–8
  anaerobic training 371–6
  energy production in 353–64
  and speed *see* neuromuscular factors,
    speed
muscle activity measurement (EMGs)
  49–50, 51, 52, 90, 134–8, 325
muscle buffering capacity 374–5
muscle coordination
  firing rate 297
  recruitment 296–7
  spinal motor reflexes 296
muscle cramps 393
muscle fatigue 359–60
  anaerobic power 365, 366–8
  anaerobic training 375
  speed training 317–19
muscle fibre arrangement 297
muscle fibre recruitment 193, 296–7
muscle fibre types 297
  anaerobic training 373
  endurance sports 364
  fast-twitch 295, 296, 297, 309, 360, 364,
    373

slow-twitch 295, 296, 297, 360, 364, 373
strength training 192, 193
muscle injury
  circadian rhythms 391
  prevention 242, 248, 254–5, 397–8
  rehabilitation 255–6
  warm-ups 301
muscle relaxation, stretching for 243
muscle soreness, prevention 242–3, 255, 263
muscle spindles 250, 251, 296
muscle strength
  endurance training 390
  and speed training 295, 297
  training for see endurance (long-lasting force) training; power training; reactive strength training
muscle stretching
  age factors 256–7
  aquatic sports 273–4
  cycling 277–8
  elastic properties 252–3, 262, 277–8, 280, 281, 283
  exercises 262, 263, 266, 268, 269, 270–1
  field sports 277, 278–81
  gymnastic sports 274–7
  limitations 249, 250–1
  martial arts 282–3
  racquet sports 272–3
  speed training 296
  track sports 277, 278
  value 241–3, 248
  see also stretch shorten cycle
muscular imbalance 298
myoglobin, anaerobic training 374
myotatic (stretch) reflex 251, 296

negative thought stopping 88
netball 53–4, 164, 178, 281–2
neuromuscular factors
  muscle fatigue 367–8
  speed 290–300
    age factors 295, 308, 314
    aptitude 295
    complex 293
    cyclic 292–3, 299
    diagnostics 322, 323
    elementary movement programmes 298–300, 301–3, 308, 323
    engram theory 299, 302
    extra-pyramidal system 296
    fast-twitch fibres 295, 296, 297, 309

firing rate 297
fusiform muscles 297
inertial force dissipation 298
intermuscular coordination 295, 296
intramuscular coordination 296–7, 308
muscle fibre recruitment 296–7
muscle–tendon factors 297–8
muscular imbalance 298
neural factors 296–7, 308, 323
non-cyclic 292, 293, 299
pennate muscles 297
planning guidelines 313, 314
preactivation 297
pure 291–3, 309
pyramidal system 296
sensory–cognitive factors 295–6
slow-twitch fibres 295, 296, 297
speed endurance 293
speed influencers 292, 293–8
speed strength 293, 295, 297, 307–9, 315
speed strength endurance 292, 293, 308
spinal motor reflexes 296
stretch shorten cycle 297, 308, 323
time programmes 299–300, 302–3, 308
vestibular system 296
warm-ups 298
strength training 193, 203, 205–6, 308–9
visualization 90, 91
neuromuscular measures see electromyography

objective skill analysis see technique analysis
observation, skill analysis 119–21
ocular dominance 8, 14
ocular muscle balance 9
optimisation research 138, 140
overuse injuries 257, 386
oxygen deficit, anaerobic capacity 365–6
oxygen transport 358, 360–4
  aerobic exercise 387–8, 390
  altitude effects 362, 399, 400–1, 402
oxygen uptake
  aerobic performance 378–81, 382, 383, 384–5
  aerobic training 385, 386, 387
  altitude training 398, 399, 400

partlauf 387
pattern recognition 19–20, 22, 23, 24
perceptual–motor skills
    comparison sub-process 6
    decision-making 3–4, 5
        assessment 36–8, 40–2
        option selection 36–40
        processes 35–6
        in rapid succession 40–3
        sports performance 38–9, 42
        training 39–40, 42–3
    defining skilled performance 1–4
    detection sub-process 6
    hierarchy of senses 6–7
    kinesthesis
        generalised 29–32
        hierarchy of senses 6–7
        and imagery perspective 92
        sport-specific 32–5
        and vision 6–7, 29–30, 32, 35
    movement execution and control 3–4,
        5
        attentional demands 52–5
        electrophysiology 49–52, 134–8
        gross motor performance 44–5
        kinematics 45–7, 48
        kinetics 48–9
        processes 43–4
        see also technique analysis
    reactive speed training 303, 304
    recognition sub-process 6
    selective attention 6
    sources of perception 6
    vision 6–7
        assessment 7–13, 19–21
        and kinesthesis 6–7, 29–30, 32, 35
        and movement execution 10–11, 46,
            54
        sports performance 13–15, 21–3
        training 15–19, 23–9
        virtual reality 26–9
perceptual style 13, 14
performance massage 266
peripheral vision 11–12, 14, 16–17, 54
pes cavus 154
pes planus 153, 154
pH
    muscle buffering capacity 375
    muscle fatigue 366–7, 375
phoria 9
phosphate metabolism 353–5
    anaerobic training 371–3, 374
    and creatine ingestion 368–9

intermittent exercise 360
    muscle fatigue 367
    speed training 290, 310, 339
    strength training 195
    supramaximal exercise 357–8
photography, image analysis 122–7, 141,
    142
physical stress management 86, 87–8
physical working capacity 384
physiological diagnostics
    aerobic performance 381–2
    speed training 325
pigeon toes (inverted feet) 153, 156, 160,
    163, 164, 165
poked head 152
posture 145–6
    anterioposterior defects 152
    aquatic sports 154, 156–7, 163, 165
    assessment 154–5
    causes of defects 150–1
    court sports 164
    cycling 154, 160
    during growth 147
    dynamic 153, 165
    dysplasia 148–9, 245–6
    evolution 146–7
    field sports 160–4, 165
    good 147–8
    gymnastics 157, 165
    importance 147–8, 155–6
    individual diversity 148–9
    injuries from defects 153–4
    interrelations of defects 151–2
    lateral defects 152–3
    maintenance 147
    martial arts 164
    modification 164–6
    poor 148
    power sports 157
    preventing defects 154
    racquet sports 156
    and somatotype 149–50, 156
    static 153–4, 164–5
    track sports 153–4, 157–60, 165
potassium 367–8, 376
power production, measurement 133,
    233–4, 236, 364–5
power training 189–90
    biological factors 203
    block training 214–15
    bodybuilding 203
    boxing 201, 203, 210
    classification 201

combined training 214–15
components 202, 204
determining factors 203
diagnostics 233–4, 236
explosive 203, 205, 210, 213–14, 236
    and flexibility 240, 241–2, 274,
        277–8, 283
fencing 201
force and velocity 204, 205, 206,
    207–11, 214, 236
free weights 212
general adaptations 204–6
general methods 212–15
general structure 202–4
jumping 211–12
juniors 215
maximal workouts 213–14
maximizing single impulses 201,
    202–3
and maximum strength 203, 204–6,
    207–8, 212, 236
mechanical factors 203
muscle cross-sectional area 203, 204
muscle hypertrophy 204–5, 309
neuromuscular factors 203, 205–6
pre-movement silence 205–6
rate of force development 213–14
and reactive strength 218, 221
running 206
submaximal workouts 204–5, 207,
    209–10
tennis 201, 206, 208–10, 342
throwing sports 201, 203, 206, 207–8
volleyball 201, 211–12
weight lifting 201, 203, 205, 206–7
weight machines 212
wrestling 203
predictive analysis methods 118, 138–40
pregnancy, aerobic fitness 384
pressure mats 131–2
production training 376–7
progressive relaxation training 87, 89
pronated feet 153, 156
proportionality 145–6, 166
    aquatic sports 171–3, 185
    body modification 183–4
    court sports 178, 181
    cycling 175, 178
    extremities indices 170
    field sports 173–8, 181, 186
    general characteristics 170
    and growth 166–7, 184
    gymnastics 169, 172, 182–3, 185

individual comparisons 168–9
    kinanthropometric assessment 168,
        169
    lever lengths 169, 170
    martial arts 178, 181, 186
    power sports 173, 182–3, 184
    racial characteristics 181–3
    racquet sports 171, 185
    significance 166
    somatograms 168
    technique modification 184–6
    tendon insertion points 169–70, 184
    track sports 173, 181–2
    trunk index 170
    unisex phantom 168, 169
proprioceptive neuromuscular
    facilitation (PNF) 263–5, 271
psychological factors
    movement and control 52–5
    speed training 295–6, 310–11
    stretching exercises 248–9
    see also mental skills training
psychological refractory period (PRP)
    41, 42
psychoneuromuscular theory 90, 91
psychophysiological information-
    processing 91
pulmonary ventilation 361–3, 400
pure speed forms 291–3, 309
pyramid model, peak performance 75–7
pyramid training 387
pyramid workouts 199
pyramidal system 296

Q-angle 154

racial characteristics, proportionality
    181–3
racquet sports see badminton; squash;
    tennis
racquetball 171
range of movement see movement, range
    of
rational thinking 88–9
reaction time
    decision-making 36–9, 40
    visual 10–11, 14, 46
reactive speed training 289, 291–2,
    303–5, 311
    diagnostics 321–2
    sprinting 327, 328–30
    swimming 336
    tennis 340–1

reactive strength training 217–21
  block training 231–2
  combined training 231–2
  energy storage 217, 218–19, 222, 229,
    230
  general adaptations 221–6
  general methods 230–3
  jumping 217, 219–21, 223–4, 227–30,
    231, 232–3, *234*
  juniors 232–3
  and maximum strength 219, 233
  planning 231–2
  and power 218, 221
  reflex activation 217, 218, 219, 221–2,
    225, 230
  regulation velocity and precision
    224–5, 230
  skiing 224–5, 230
  and speed 308
  sprinting 223–4, 226–7, 330–1
  stiffness adjustment 218–19, 226,
    229–30
  surfing 224–5
  tendon stretchability 222–3
  volleyball 231
reflex activation, strength training 217,
  218, 219, 221–2, 225, 230
reflexes, stretch 251–2, 296
relaxation
  attention enhancement 96
  imagery training 92–3
  importance *78, 79*
  muscle 243
  training 87, 89
round back 152
round shoulders 152, 154, 157
rowing
  aerobic performance 383
  biomechanical feedback 141
  body proportionality 169, 172
  flexibility 273, 274
  kinesthetic judgements 33–4
  posture 157, 165
  strength training 191, 196–7, 200
  technique analysis 129
rugby
  body proportionality 178
  flexibility 243, 244, 280–1
  posture 162–3, 165
running
  aerobic training 390
  biomechanical feedback 141
  body proportionality 173

endurance training 385, 386
  energy production 353
  flexibility 277, 278
  heat acclimatization 396
  heat injury 393
  kinesthetic judgements 33–4
  mental training 94
  posture 153–4, 157–60, 165
  speed training 297, 316, 319, 322,
    326–32, 341–2
  strength training 206, 216, 223–4,
    226–7, 330–1
  technique analysis 124, 128

salt intake 396
sarcoplasmic reticulum fatigue 367
scientific stretching for sport (3S) 263
scoliosis 152, 156
self-confidence 79, 80–1
self-directed relaxation 87
self-efficacy theory 80–1
sensory factors
  range of movement 250–1
  speed training 295–6
  vision *see* visual skills
Sheuermann's disease 152
shooting 8, 47, 50, 51–2
shot put 201, 203, 206, 207–8
shuttle-run test 384–5
sight *see* visual skills
simulation
  attention enhancement 95
  biomechanical feedback 142
  technique analysis 138–40
  virtual reality 26–9, 139–40
skating 77, 89, 191, 240, 266
ski-ing
  mental training 88, 90, 95–6, 101–8
  strength training 191, 192, 197, 200
    stretch shorten cycle 216, 224–5, 230
  technique analysis 125–6
ski-jumping, strength training 211
ski-simulators 390
skill analysis *see* technique analysis
skilled performance defined 1–4
sleep 391, 395
smoking 363
snooker 8, 22, 47, 48
soccer *see* football
sodium/potassium pumps 376
softball 8, 87, 94
somatograms 168
somatotypes 149–50, 156

speed endurance training 376–8
speed play 387
speed strength 293, 295, 297, 307–9, 315,
  321
speed strength endurance 292, 293, 308
speed training 287–8
  action speed 289, 310–11
  active speed 289, 292, 305–6, 308–9,
    322
  age factors 295, 307, 308, 314
  aptitude 295
  biomechanical diagnostics 324–5
  complex action speed 310–11
  complex speed capability 307–10
  complex speed forms 293, 303, 307–10
  complex speed tests 322–3
  cyclic speed forms 292–3, 299, 303,
    308, 313
    diagnostics 322, 323
    sprinting 331–2
    swimming 337
  diagnostics 320–5
  elementary movement programmes
    298–300, 301–3, 308, 323
  and endurance 309–10, 327, 337–8, 339
  endurance speed 289
  fatigue 317–19
  frequency speed 292, 306–7, 308–9,
    310, 322
  general guidelines 312–14
  juniors 295, 302, 303, 307, 308,
    314
  load concentration method 316–17
  locomotor speed 289, 327–8, 331–2
  long-term 314–17
  microcycles 317–18, 319
  motor test systems 321–3
  muscle-tendon factors 297–8
  neural factors 296–7, 308, 323
  non-cyclic speed forms 292, 293, 299,
    303, 308, 313
    diagnostics 322, 323
    swimming 336–7
  periodization 315–17
  physiological diagnostics 325
  planning 311–20
  psychological factors 295–6
  pure speed forms 291–3, 309
  reactive speed 289, 291–2, 303–5, 311
    diagnostics 321–2
    sprinting 327, 328–30
    swimming 336
    tennis 340–1
  sensory-cognitive factors 295–6
  short-term 317–19
  situation training 310–11
  speed influencers 292, 293–8
  speed strength 293, 295, 297, 307–9,
    315, 321
  speed strength endurance 292, 293,
    308
  sprinting 310, 316, 319, 322, 326–32
  and strength training 308–9, 330–1,
    335–6, 340
  structure of speed 288–300
    ATP release 290
    classification systems 289, 291–3
    controlled fitness 289
    fitness–energetic capability 290
    neuromuscular capability 290–300
  swimming 317, 332–8
  tennis 338–43
  time programmes 299–300, 302–3, 308
  warm-ups 298, 301
spinal postural defects 152, 155, 156, 157,
  160
sports imagery training (SIT) 93
sports psychology see mental skills
  training
sprinting
  body proportionality 173, 182
  energy production 353
  flexibility 277, 278
  motor stereotype 224
  performance limiting factors 326
  phases 327
  posture 153–4, 157–60, 165
  speed training 326–32
    acceleration 327–8, 330–1
    diagnostics 322
    frequency speed endurance 310
    load concentration method 316
    microcycles 319, 332
    reactive speed 327, 328–30
  strength training 216, 223–4, 226–7,
    330–1
squash 22, 120, 156, 171, 272–3
step tests 383–4
stereopsis 10, 14
stiffness adjustment, strength training
  218–19, 226, 229–30
strain-gauge dynamometers 128–9
strength
  endurance training 390
  speed 293, 295, 297, 307–9, 315, 321
strength testing 132–4, 233–6

strength training 189–90
  and flexibility 244, 253
  and hypermobility 244
  importance 190
  for long-lasting force 190–200, 205
  power 189–90, 201–15, 233–4, 236, 309,
    342
  reactive strength 217–33
  and speed training 308–9, 315, 330–1,
    335–6, 340
  stretch shorten cycle 215–33
stress management 78, 79, 85–9
stretch reflexes 251–2, 296
stretch shorten cycle (SSC) 252–3
  speed training 297, 308, 323
  strength training 215–16
    block 231–2
    central nervous system 224
    combined 231–2
    energy storage 217, 218–19, 222, 229,
      230
    force–time curves 219–21, 223–4
    general adaptations 221–6
    general methods 230–3
    jumping 217, 219–21, 223–4, 228–30,
      231, 232–3, 234
    juniors 232–3
    and maximum strength 219, 233
    optimization 226
    planning 231–2
    and power 218, 221
    processes during 216–21
    reflex activation 217, 218, 219, 221–2,
      225, 230
    regulation velocity 224–5, 230
    skiing 216, 224–5, 230
    sprinting 216, 223–4, 226–7
    stiffness adjustment 218–19, 226,
      229–30
    tendon stretchability 222–3
stretching
  active 265
  aquatic sports 243, 244, 266, 273–4
  ballistic 259–62, 263, 268
  concentration during 268–9
  court sports 281–2
  cycling 277, 278
  dangers 269
  field sports 277, 278–81
  general guidelines 267–9
  gymnastic sports 240, 243, 266, 275–7,
    283
  for injury prevention 242, 248, 253–5

for injury rehabilitation 255–6
  injury with 262, 269
  intensity 269
  juniors 256–7
  martial arts 282–3
  movement limitations 249–52
  muscle elasticity 252–3, 262, 274,
    277–8, 280, 281, 283
  in old age 257–8
  passive 266
  power sports 275–7
  preparation for 268
  proprioceptive neuromuscular
    facilitation 263–5, 271
  racquet sports 240, 272–3
  schedules 268–9, 271
  static 262–3, 270–1
  track sports 277, 278
  value of 239–43, 248–9, 272
subjective skill analysis 118–21
submaximal exercise
  energy production 356–7
  strength training 195, 197, 199, 204–5,
    207, 209–10
sun, heat acclimatization 395, 396
surfing, strength training 224–5
sweating 394, 395–6, 397
swimming
  aerobic performance 383
  aerobic training 390
  body proportionality 169, 171, 185
  flexibility 243, 244, 266, 273, 274
  kinesthetic judgements 33
  mental training 83
  posture 154, 156, 163, 165
  speed training 317, 332–8
  strength training 191, 335–6
symbolic learning theory 90, 91

table tennis 8, 47
technique analysis 117–18
  biomechanical feedback 140–2
  objective methods 118, 121–2
    dynamometry 128–34, 324–5
    electromyography 134–8
    image analysis 122–8, 141, 142, 259,
      324
  predictive methods 118, 138–40
  sources of error 120–1
  subjective methods 118–21
technique training 301–2
temperature (ambient) 392–8
temperature (body) 391, 392–3, 396, 397,
  398

temporal occlusion tests 20–1
tendons
  elastic properties 222–3, 252–3, 254–5
  insertion points 169–70, 184
  range of movement 250
  and speed performance 297–8
tennis
  body proportionality 169, 171, 185
  flexibility 240, 272–3
  mental training 88
  posture 156
  reactive speed 340–1
  running speed 341–2
  serving 208–10
  speed training 338–43
  strength training 201, 206, 208–10, 340,
    342
  stroke speed 342–3
  technique analysis 120, 121, 126
  visual skills 12, 17–18, 22, 25–6, 28
tennis elbow 257
thermoregulation 393–4, 396, 397
thought stopping 88, 89
throwing sports
  biomechanical feedback 141–2
  body proportionality 174
  flexibility exercises 279
  optimisation 140
  strength training 201, 203, 206, 207–8
tibial torsion (inverted feet) 153, 156, 160,
  163, 164, 165
time programmes, speed training
  299–300, 302–3
time zones, training schedules 391–2
track sports see hurdling; running
trampolining 35, 229
transfusional polycythemia 400
triatheletes 33–4, 390
triple-code model of imagery 91
triple jump 173, 216, 233

urea, speed diagnostics 325
urine, and heat acclimatization 395, 396
US ski team, mental training 101–8

ventilation, pulmonary 361–3, 400
ventilation threshold 381
vergence eye-movement 9
vestibular system 29–30, 296
videography
  biomechanical feedback 141
  body flexibility 259
  decision-making skills 39, 40

speed performance 324
  technique analysis 122–3, 127–8
  visual skill training 25–6, 28
virtual reality 26–9, 139–40
visceral ptosis 152
visual skills 6–29
  accommodation 9
  acuity 7–8, 14, 16–17
  anticipation 20–1, 22, 23, 24–6
  assessment 7–13, 19–21
  coincidence-timing 12–13, 14
  colour 10, 14
  depth perception 9–10, 14, 17
  eye movement behaviour 21, 22–3
  field dependence–independence 13, 14
  hierarchy of senses 6–7
  information pick-up 19, 22, 23, 24
  information processing rate 11, 14, 19
  and kinesthesis 6–7, 29–30, 32, 35
  and movement execution 54
  object detection 19, 22, 23, 24
  ocular dominance 8, 14
  ocular muscle balance 9
  pattern recognition 19–20, 22, 23, 24
  perceptual style 13, 14
  peripheral 11–12, 14, 16–17, 54
  phoria 9
  reaction time 10–11, 14, 46
  search patterns 21, 22–3
  and sports performance 13–15, 21–3
  stereopsis 10, 14
  training 15–19, 23–9
  vergence 9
  virtual reality 26–9
visualization, mental training 78, 79, 87,
  90–3, 96, 104
$\dot{V}O_2$ 362–3
  aerobic performance 378–81, 383,
    384–5
  aerobic training 385
  endurance sports 364
volleyball
  body proportionality 169, 178
  flexibility 281–2
  mental training 74–5
  posture 164
  strength training 201, 211–12, 231
  visual skills 22, 24

walk tests 384
walking, technique analysis 128, 136, 139
warm-ups
  cold conditions 397–8

warm-ups (*continued*)
   flexibility 248, 269
   speed training 298, 301
water polo 156, 171–2, 240, 273, 274
weight lifting
   body proportionality 169, 173, 182–3,
     184
   flexibility 274–5
   posture 157
   strength training 201, 203, 205, 206–7
weight training, circuit 387–8
wheelchair athletes 383

wind surfing 224–5
Wingate test 365
workload, perception of 33–4, 35
wrestling
   body proportionality 178
   flexibility exercises 282–3
   mental training 73, 81, 89
   posture 154, 164
   strength training 203

'yo-yo' test 385
youths *see* juniors

Index compiled by Liz Granger